AF770058

Technology and Young Children:

Bridging the Communication-Generation Gap

Sally Blake
Flagler College, USA

Denise Winsor
University of Memphis, USA

Lee Allen
University of Memphis, USA

Information Science
REFERENCE

Senior Editorial Director:	Kristin Klinger
Director of Book Publications:	Julia Mosemann
Editorial Director:	Lindsay Johnston
Acquisitions Editor:	Erika Carter
Development Editor:	Michael Killian
Production Editor:	Sean Woznicki
Typesetters:	Adrienne Freeland, Milan Vracarich, Jr.
Print Coordinator:	Jamie Snavely
Cover Design:	Nick Newcomer

Published in the United States of America by
Information Science Reference (an imprint of IGI Global)
701 E. Chocolate Avenue
Hershey PA 17033
Tel: 717-533-8845
Fax: 717-533-8661
E-mail: cust@igi-global.com
Web site: http://www.igi-global.com

Copyright © 2012 by IGI Global. All rights reserved. No part of this publication may be reproduced, stored or distributed in any form or by any means, electronic or mechanical, including photocopying, without written permission from the publisher. Product or company names used in this set are for identification purposes only. Inclusion of the names of the products or companies does not indicate a claim of ownership by IGI Global of the trademark or registered trademark.

Library of Congress Cataloging-in-Publication Data

Technology and young children: bridging the communication-generation gap / Sally Blake, Denise Winsor, and Lee Allen, editors.
p. cm.
Includes bibliographical references and index.
Summary: "This book presents the view that beliefs, history, research, and policy are essential to changing the educational system with technology"--Provided by publisher.
ISBN 978-1-61350-059-0 (hardcover) -- ISBN 978-1-61350-060-6 (ebook) -- ISBN 978-1-61350-061-3 (print & perpetual access) 1. Educational technology. 2. Internet in education. 3. Computers and children. I. Blake, Sally, 1949- II. Winsor, Denise, 1965- III. Allen, Lee, 1955-
LB1028.3.T396643 2012
372.133--dc23

2011026945

British Cataloguing in Publication Data
A Cataloguing in Publication record for this book is available from the British Library.

All work contributed to this book is new, previously-unpublished material. The views expressed in this book are those of the authors, but not necessarily of the publisher.

Practitioner Reviewers

Judy Brown, *Tennessee Pre-K Pilot Program, USA*
Mary Jo Palmer, *Southwest Community College, USA*
Sandra Brown Turner, *Barbara K. Lipman Early Childhood School and Research Institute, USA*
Carol Coudeau Young, *Barbara K. Lipman Early Childhood School and Research Institute, USA*

Faculty Reviewers

Wendy Jacocks, *South Eastern Louisiana University, USA*
L. Antonio Gonzalez, *University of Texas at El Paso, USA*
Trish Ainsa, *University of Texas at El Paso, USA*
Scott Starks, *University of Texas at El Paso, USA*
Jorge Lopez, *University of Texas at El Paso, USA*

Author and Reviewer

Andrew Gibbons, *New Zealand Tertiary College, New Zealand*
Kathleen Spencer Cooter, *Bellarmine University, USA*
Amy Smith, *Pink Sky Education, USA*

Table of Contents

Detailed Table of Contents

Foreword

This book brings together two of the most exciting and important areas of educational research being conducted today. The importance of the first few years of life to the cognitive and social development of a child cannot be overstated. In their book on school reform, *Disrupting Class,* Christensen, Horn, and Johnson, state (2008):

And a rather stunning body of research is emerging that suggests that starting these reforms at kindergarten, let alone in elementary, middle, or high school, is far too late. By some estimates, 98 percent of education spending occurs after the basic intellectual capacities of children have been mostly determined. (p. 148)

Equally intriguing for many researchers is the potential for well designed educational technologies to create customized opportunities that promote rich learning interactions. Christensen et al. argue that the maturity of the computer based learning industry will make "student-centric technology a reality" (p. 123). What this all means is that the ideas presented in this book will have an ever increasing chance at implementation and subsequent impact.

On a personal level, I am intrigued by the book as it provides an opportunity for me to reflect on the upbringing and development of my two young children. As an educational technology researcher, I frequently justify the acquisition of the latest gadgets as a professional expense. I then give them to my boys and watch how they interact with the different programs and devices. Many of them engender initial curiosity but few hold their continued interest. One of the common threads of the popular devices was the capacity to interact in some way with friends. For my generation, the killer app was email. For subsequent generations, it seems to be social networking sites.

The gaps between generations and the use of these contemporary technologies are large. While some of this is to be expected, the degree of the difference can present monumental challenges in supporting the development of our youth. For example, 73% of teens report using social networking sites compared to 40% of adults over 30 (Pew, 2009).

Unfortunately, it is very difficult to find information regarding the use of technology in the very young. When the teen use of social networking sites is further broken down the use of 12-13 year olds is 55% and 14-17 is 82%. Clearly the use decreases with younger students. However, it is just as clear that there is at least some use among the very young. Age restrictions for user accounts on services such as Facebook, Google, and MySpace limit the access to widely used tools. However, many children (my own included) are quickly finding alternatives through companies such as Disney and Nickelodeon. The chapters in this book will help build an understanding of the import (and possible danger) of these sites to the development of young children.

Another technology that will inevitably find its way into the hands of young children is the mobile phone. You do not need to travel far to hear adults lamenting about the widespread use of cell phones among the youth. In particular, the pervasiveness of text messaging seems to rankle many an adult. The picture of a group of teens at table texting away with negligible interaction in the group (at least verbally) can elicit emotions ranging from confusion to anger. Of course many of us have tempered our criticisms as we have begun to appreciate the positive attributes of these new communication technologies. Personally, I appreciate the ability to send short, typically logistical messages to others without the requisite formalities required of a phone call.

These devices are now as powerful as any personal computer built 10 years ago. They also have more intuitive and natural interfaces. With these devices, well designed applications that take advantage of the audio/video capture and interactions with others will lead to an explosion of learning opportunities for young children.

As you will see in the different chapters of this book, the effective use of technology is dependent upon how and why it is being used. As a former high school biology teacher, I was very interested in the potential of virtual dissection software. While the virtual tools had advantages over the real (albeit deceased) it was not clear cut. For example, while the computer diagrams made the organs easily identifiable, the real organism was much less obliged to make the necessary clues obvious.

As the technology advanced, the attributes of the well designed virtual systems helped close the gap between the real and the virtual. This tipped the balance towards the virtual dissection. The important lesson from this is that educators and researchers should be clear about the purpose and goals of any technology use. What is it that this technology provides or what problem does it solve?

This is what makes this book so valuable. General statements about the value of technology to learning are of little value without an understanding of the details of design and implementation. In this book, you will find details about the use of technology with specific goals in mind. This includes discussions of uses in learning mathematics, science, and with students with special needs. These descriptions are framed with more general investigations of the epistemological societal concerns.

Kenneth Hartley
University of Nevada at Las Vegas, USA

REFERENCES

Christensen, C. M., Horn, M. B., & Johnson, C. W. (2008). *Disrupting class*. New York, NY: McGraw-Hill.

Madden, M. (June, 2010). *Four or more: The new demographic*. Pew Internet & American Life Project LITA President's Program ALA – June 27, 2010. Retrieved from http://www.pewinternet.org/Presentations/2010/Jun/Four-or-More--The-New-Demographic.aspx

Preface

In our book, Technology and Young Children: Bridging the Digital Communication –Generation Gap, we write about the socio-cultural gap between educational environments, teachers, and children as influenced by technology. A generation gap implies a vast difference in cultural norms between a younger generation and their elders. A generation gap is a frustrating lack of communication between young and old, a stretch of time that separates cultures within a society, allowing each to develop their own character (Safire, 2008). The popularization of the term generation gap is attributed to the 1960's era in the United States when socio-cultural changes diversified the behavior and values between generations at an unprecedented rate. This, in part has been explained by the size of the young generation during the 1960s, which gave it unprecedented power and willingness to rebel against societal norms. We believe this gap was intensified through the evolving cultural changes influenced by technology communication systems during that time. The current gap, referred to as the digital communication-generation gap is different from others as the rapid development and acceptance of technological tools have changed the interactions and relationships across four generations and is exponential. Technology has shifted the traditional generational power roles from the adult as the expert to children as experts and is an important component of the current generation gap, a change that redefines the role of teachers and education and what learning means to the citizen of this generation. The keepers of knowledge, the schools, have lost their place at the head of the line as researchers have not found the innovations of technology in classrooms. Instead technology innovation is breaking out of the administrative office leaving teachers behind to maintain their traditional classroom practices (Collins & Halverson 2009). The concept of taking courses in schools to learn is becoming antiquated as the goal of life-long learning becomes a reality when learners negotiate their own learning through a variety of experiences not available in schools.

The chapters in this book present the view that beliefs, history, research, and policy are essential to changing the relationships of the social, cultural educational system with technology. The content should help teachers reflect on what is happening as the center of learning power moves outside a classroom. The suggestions for use of technology are designed to help educators ease into the use of technology rather than leap off the cliff of innovation, developing confidence and competence in their teaching. We do not try to push educators into the future world of technology but give them ideas for the here and now. The book is organized into four sections related to the digital generation gap. Our book describes how technology has impacted and can impact the learning of young children through formal and informal environments. This includes ways technology has dramatically changed research of children and their capabilities for academic success, the power structure of schools, the access to information, and social networking interactions.

The new generation of children comes to early childhood programs with many informal experiences in technology and as members of the social communication (millennium) generation. There is much written about this gap between the children and the teachers of children in the comfort levels of technology acceptance and use. Bridging the communication/generation gap has become a concern because with today's technology, that generation gap is getting fairly wide and continues to grow across all levels of education. We hope to help teachers and educators start building the bridges to connect the gap between generations as they read the contents of this book. The future of schools will depend on the acceptance of how this new generation learns, not how we think children should act and learn.

Teachers of young children are the technology gatekeepers in childcare programs. They are vital to the appropriate use of technology, yet little is documented concerning training and understanding of teachers' use in classrooms. Teachers need to understand how to develop learning, what types of learning should be facilitated, and how to serve the needs of diverse populations using technology. Computers are more than tools for bringing efficiency to traditional approaches; they can open new and unforeseen avenues for learning.

Audience

The proposed audience for this book includes university faculty for use in early childhood courses, Head Start and child care center teachers and professional development personnel, and public school teachers and administrators working with young children. The book will assist parents and families to better understand how technology influences the lives of young children. We propose an international market also for similar childhood programs.

College students and college educators are our target audience. This book will be highly suitable as a personal reference for early childhood practitioners, for administrators, and for parents of young children. Early childhood educational organizations such as Head Start programs and the National Association for the Education of Young Children, childcare centers, preschools, kindergartens, and primary schools (1st through 3rd grades) might find this book useful. As a secondary market, both public and university libraries, book stores, book clubs, as well as educators, school personnel, educators, and university libraries may find this writing of interest. There is inclusion of international authors for use in multiple countries. We anticipate this book will be also important for parents of young children to help them better understand how technology will be used and impact their children's development and education and more important their changing roles in learning.

Section 1. Understanding the Digital Communication Generation Gap: Values, Beliefs, Social Cultural Systems that Influence Teaching Practice

Our first section explores how technology and the beliefs about technology influence and change the world view of educational environments, children and teachers. This section includes six chapters that discuss the binary oppositions of adult-child, self-other, and artificial-real, the cultural history of technology, the changing social cultural power structures of education influenced by technological advances, and how the epistemology of teachers guides instructional decisions and classroom environments.

Chapter 1: The Impact on Technology on Early Childhood Education: Where the Child Things are? Adults, Children, Digital Monsters and the Spaces in Between

In our first chapter Andrew Neil Gibbons discusses bridging the communication-generation gap through an analysis of the child's play with hi-tech toys. Through early play experiences with the range of toys, whether digital or not, the child plays with the symbols, themes and values associating real products with their fictional source, and with the other multimedia manifestations that offer children the opportunity to engage with the questions of the nature of real, artificial, conscious, alive, dead, adult, and child. He illustrates the gaps that appear between technological generations through the show *Digimon,* a term that means "Digital Monsters," and is a media franchise encompassing anime, manga, toys, video games, trading card games, and other media. This chapter explores the complexity of the toy and of the toys contemporary troubling of adulthood and has regarded the latest hi-tech shows as productive in supporting such exploration of a set of binary oppositions. These themes highlight challenges to binary oppositions of adult-child, self-other, and artificial-real. Andrew writes about different ways of both understanding and analyzing gaps between child and adult through the symbol of the toy and writes about the importance of preparing an ICT-rich environment.

Chapter 2: Enculturation of Young Children and Technology

The second chapter talks about the enculturation of children through technology. Alex Spatariu, Andrea Peach, and Susan Bell discuss key points about how social institutions and informal experiences shape the world of the young child. They use the term technology to encompass more than just computers but include many experiences that young children bring to the classroom. The chapter is divided into three main discussion sections. The first section discusses various types of technology used by children in non-school settings. Parental issues and developmental considerations are included to give the reader a more comprehensive understanding of how the digital age touches all parts of children's lives. The second section examines the use of technologies with young children from a developmental perspective. The authors also address concerns with the uses of these technologies in relationship to teaching and learning. Authors also hope to dispel some of the technology myths that teachers of young children have about technology and learning in the early childhood classroom. The concept of the digital divide is addressed in this section as well. The last section of this chapter discusses technology evaluation issues and concrete use of technology by educators of young children.

Chapter 3: Children's Power for Learning in the Age of Technology

In chapter 3 Julie McLeod, Lin Lin, and Sheri Vasinda discuss children's power through technology in relation to education and educational environments. Technology has changed the power structures of education, a change many adults may find uncomfortable. Children are now experts in something that is truly important in the adult world, which dramatically changes the interactions and roles in educational environments. The authors believe that current power structure of classrooms inhibits children from exerting their power and motivation for learning. As schools move from an outdated model based on the need for obedient workers during the Industrial Age into the Digital Age, teachers need to reflect on the needs of today's citizenship, life-style, and skills for the future work force. Their view of social power as the capacity for action is especially compelling, particularly because technology has enabled even very young children to take action in society in ways that are important, public, and inconceivable without the technology. The identification of types of power should allow educators to identify beliefs about their changing roles in classrooms and the commitment and liberation for their own and children's learning.

Chapter 4: Technology in Three American Preschools: Technological Influences on Ideology and Social Class

Chapter 4 is an ethnography: *Technological Influences on Ideology and Social Class*. This chapter explores the marriage of popular culture and technology in preschool settings, specifically the manner in which social class and preschool ideology contribute to or detract from children's access to popular culture technology. It stems from a comparative ethnographic study of popular culture in three preschools that differ socio-economically and ideologically. After reading this chapter the reader should develop a better understanding of the connection of ideology and social class in the acceptance or rejection of technology as a pedagogical tool. It attempts to call into question practices that are seen as natural or "appropriate" as specific to a cultural group. By examining this topic from a critical perspective it is the intent to clarify curricular and pedagogical tools as not without class biases and intentions. This chapter discusses class discrimination as well as religious and theoretical beliefs in the appearance of technology in both educational programs and the home lives of preschoolers. Allison writes about the emerging technological age, and in the era of accountability, preschools are dealing with technology in very different manners. This chapter shows that in early childhood sectors, the embracing of technology is not universal, and if it is, depends heavily on the context in which it is used. Media images, viewed in some settings as fancifully benign are the same images that are rejected for their questionable morals or influence from mass marketing. Furthermore, this ethnography demonstrates that within preschool sectors ideology and social class plays a major role for the type of popular culture technology that children in the United States will interact with in various preschools, and this context often contributes to the meaning that they make out of these images.

Section 2. Bridging the Gap between Technology-Based Educational Research Methods and Child Development

The second section, *Bridging the Gap between Technology-based Educational Research Methods and Child Development*, explores how technology has changed research of young children. The two chapters in this section discuss the role of technology in child development research and how technology has enhanced the power of observational data. The new understanding of children's potential due to technological advances has dramatically changed what we once accepted as guides and limitations for child study. This information is important for teachers as they are the key to implementing research implications in classrooms.

Chapter 5: Technology: Changing the Research Base on Young Children

In chapter 5, Shannon Audley-Piotorwksi, Neha Kumar, Yeh Hsueh, and Melanie Sumner discuss how technology has changed the understanding of child development and learning. The writing team for this chapter is unique as it includes a member of the millennium generation who is already engaged in research using technology. Neha is an example of how this generation comes to educational environments with competence and confidence in the tools of technology. Understanding the role of technology and the evidence of children's development has opened new ideas about the capabilities of children. Teachers need to understand how these technologies are being used and how researchers support learning and development based on this new approach to information collection with young children. What we know about young children's development is dependent upon the availability of technology. The discussion informs teachers about common technologies, and how these technologies are used in research on the development of young children. The writing helps teachers understand how technology has helped advance knowledge about older issues, such as literacy development, in research, and how these findings indirectly inform pedagogy. Some major implications for teachers include that children's emotional and behavior regulation is not simply a reflection of the child's will, but is based on individual differences in the child's nervous system, as measured by heart rate and cortisol levels. It can be seen how factors outside of the child's control, such as poverty, can literally reshape a child's memory and change the brain's ability to think critically. Likewise, brain imaging technologies, such as fMRI, have also suggested that emotions can influence what information a child learns, and how that knowledge can be applied.

The availability of new technology allows researchers to continuously refine their understanding of young children's development. It is important for educators and parents to be aware of the current technologies that researchers use, and how these technologies advance knowledge about young children's development. If educators understand the current technology and trends in research on child development, they are one step closer to merging research with classroom pedagogy.

Chapter 6: The Role of Video in the Preschool in Three Cultures Method

The sixth chapter written by Yeh Hsueh and Joseph Tobin illustrates the influence technology is having on approaches to research and study of children and teachers. Yeh and Joseph discuss the use of video as an ethnographic research tool for studying preschool education and offers insight into how video can be used to inform researchers, practitioners, and parents of young children. The approach referred to as video-cued multivocal ethnography is intended to highlight differences across cultures, and to reveal continuity and change in preschool education. The study described in this chapter investigated preschool programs in three countries over the course of a generation. As the researchers worked through their study, they discovered the videos were also valuable for promoting teachers' reflections and development of cross-cultural understandings. The authors discuss this innovative approach to using video in early childhood education research, an approach that uses video not as data, but rather as a stimulus or cue for getting teachers and directors in different cultures to reflect on the thinking behind their practices. While technology may seem to collapse and shorten the ethnography's traditional period of extended fieldwork there have been other benefits. Video produces rich insights not evident through traditional observations. By reviewing the data researchers can see new nuances of interactions on video which open new doors to investigation. This question-generating aspect of the video-cued interviews, especially in the repeated interviews with key informants, is also conducive to capturing features of dynamic reforms in early childhood education. The reflection of the authors on their research gave them new insight into technology and ways to adapt their work for use with pre-service and in-service professional development of teachers.

The Preschool in Three Cultures chapter address the concerns of quality research design as it continues to add to a growing scientific knowledge base of what influences preschool environments from multiple dimensions and diverse perspectives. The community of practitioners and researchers is one of the powerful ideas from this method. The researchers join teachers, administrators and parents in grappling with their own taken-for-granted beliefs and practices in a new light, as well as to widen their horizons of what is possible by being exposed to approaches used in other places in their own culture and in other cultures.

Section 3. Bridging the Gap between Pedagogy and Technology

The third section, Bridging the Gap between Pedagogy and Technology, discusses how technology can support the educational environment through five domains. These are teacher training, second language learners, science, mathematics, and special needs children. The integration of technology must go beyond placing a computer in a classroom. These chapters give specific examples of how to use technology to support instruction and how technology supports domain specific learning for teachers and children. The technology myths associated with early childhood education and learning are challenged in these chapters to help teachers better understand how technology supports instructional practice.

Chapter 7: Early Childhood Teachers: Closing the Digital –Divide

In Chapter 7, Kevin Thomas and Kathleen Spencer Cooter argue that teachers and others working in the world of education at both the practitioner and preservice levels have been slow to respond to the tremendous and irreversible cultural shift, thus creating a second and even more inequitable digital divide, the divide of technological opportunity. They discuss appropriate change for teacher training programs in early childhood education to close the digital divide through both social cultural change and practical classroom applications. This chapter reviews the state of technology training for early childhood educators in teacher preparation institutions across the country. Using NCATE and NAEYC standards as benchmarks of practice, the chapter outlines some current issues and research on technology training at the preservice level - such as course sequence, textbook choice, content infusion, field experiences, et cetera. The chapter also identifies three technologies for use by teachers: Web 2.0, Google Earth, and the Virtual Manipulatives that are accessible, free to users, require little teacher training, and have evidence to support their instructional benefits. These three well-developed technologies can easily be introduced to students and teachers as exemplars of constructivist pedagogical technology in early childhood science and mathematics classrooms. Suggested activities for teachers using these tools and resources are included to help teachers start or increase their use of technology.

Chapter 8: Technology and Second Language Learning: Developmental Recommendations for Early-Childhood Education

The eighth chapter, by Nathan E. Ziegler and Florian C. Feucht, addresses the growing population of second language learners in classrooms and how language and technology can be mutually supportive. Nathan and Florian write about second language classrooms from a developmental and methodological perspective. They establish a theoretical framework that looks at the relationship between cognitive development, second language teaching methods, and technology. More specifically, the framework aligns the different teaching methods and technology with Piaget's four levels of cognitive development. Second language learners at the sensory motor, preoperational, and concrete level of cognitive development should be using technology that presents communication in a second language in real-world contexts. This is even true for the learner at the formal operations; however, if technology is too abstract, the learners will not be able to comprehend meaning behind the sounds and the texts. As the second language learner develops, they are able to understand more abstract aspects of communication and can use technology that facilitates their second language abilities at the formal operations and meta-cognitive level. They provide a rubric to assist second language teachers in an early-childhood classroom in designing developmentally appropriate lesson plans with technology. Nathan and Florian use a lesson as the thread that binds this chapter together so teachers can see how even good planning may not be age appropriate for second language learners. This chapter bridges the fields of technology, second language learning, and cognitive development in childhood. The authors try to help teachers better understand how their teaching methods correspond with the learners' cognitive stage of development and the technology that is chosen to assist in instruction. The authors give suggestions and rationale for different types of technology to support teachers as they work with second language learners in their classrooms. The chapter concludes with educational, conceptual, and methodological implications as they pertain to technology research and development in early second language classrooms.

Chapter 9: Science Technology and Young Children

In Chapter 9, Brian Giza provides a framework for evaluating and applying tools for science in all classrooms. Teachers of young children have access to an ever increasing diversity of technology tools. Brian includes a series of vignettes that illustrate the application of technology in the context of a tools-task-strategy approach. Early childhood and primary level science teachers, especially novice science teachers, are confronted with a number of challenges when they try to integrate technology into the classroom. Sometimes the tools that they have are not appropriate for young children. Sometimes the tools that they have are not appropriate for anyone - they are obsolete hand-me-downs, computers and software passed from upper grades to the earlier ones. Fortunately, partly due to the reduction of costs of computers, school districts are beginning to equip early grades with computers that are of recent vintage. Even when the computers or other technology tools available are modern and grade-level appropriate, teacher may not realize how best to use them in their teaching. Brian writes about ways to develop and assist an engaged and active campus planning team and provides advice and suggestions for the individual teacher who may or may not benefit from the resources that an effective support structure may give. To help users assess and integrate technology in pedagogically sound ways, he frames the use of technology in terms of tools, tasks, and strategies. We recommend that the user is best served when they first consider the task that they want to accomplish before they select the tool - and that they should consider the strategy (pedagogy) that they wish to use before they proceed into the using a particular tool for a task.

Chapter 10: Mathematics Learning through the Use of Technology

The tenth chapter, written by Amy Smith, Amy Gentry, and Sally Blake, provides a description of how some technological tools, when applied with sound inquiry-based pedagogy and driven by ongoing assessment, can facilitate learning in today's increasingly technological world. The authors discuss three broad applications of technology for early childhood teachers to support mathematics learning. These are: technology as a teacher resource, technology as a support tool for teaching, and technology as process support for learning. This chapter examines the nature of children's learning and the associated impacts that technology is making on the young learner. Amy, Amy, and Sally discuss elements of effective technology-based teaching. They include a discussion of some of the issues surrounding technology and mathematics for young children including the use of Mathematics and Technology Talk for teachers. The identification of technology and mathematics in relation to Bloom's taxonomy of higher order thinking can guide teachers away from the traditional, memorization-only approach to teaching. The authors talk about age-appropriate use of technology and mathematics including a sample checklist for assessment and a framework for developing assessment tools. Considerations for future research as well as a list of relevant, practical resources for teachers to experiment within their own classrooms are also included to help teachers move towards a more tech-friendly instructional approach and classroom environment. For the sake of brevity, much of the information shared in this chapter is framed around a kindergarten (ages 4-5 in the United States) level; however, with simple modifications, the information can be applied to a range of learning differences. It is the intent of the authors to give examples that focus on the mathematics and technology rather than specific age levels. There are some ideas that would be appropriate across the age levels 3 to 9.

Chapter 11: Technology for Young Children with Special Needs

In Chapter 11, David and Sara Bicard write about the amazing changes technology has made in the lives of special needs learners. The Bicards explain how technology supports children identified with disabilities that qualify for special education, including physical disabilities such as deafness or blindness, mental disabilities, such as Down's syndrome and autism, medical conditions, such as oxygen dependence or traumatic brain injury, learning deficits, such as dyslexia, and behavioral disorders, such as attention deficit hyperactivity disorder (ADHD) and conduct disorders. These children would have difficulty accessing and participating in the instructional environment in public educational institutions without technology. David and Sara write about how teachers can give special needs children the opportunity to participate and succeed in what is considered the general curriculum for children in schools. The gap in special education is often between curriculum delivery for special needs children and traditional teacher training programs. As inclusion of these children becomes a reality in all classrooms, teachers may feel inadequate to deal with the responsibility of instructional practices to support special needs learning. Too often it is assumed these children are not capable of learning the material required in the high accountability environment of modern schools. This chapter approaches the use of technology in early childhood programs through three types of applications: adaptation of existing computers and other technology (adapt); computer software programs to address particular skill deficits (address); and specialized technology used to assist the functioning of a child with disabilities (assist). The Bicards give specific descriptions of each type of assistive technology devices and how teachers can use these to support learning. They identify possible solutions to financing and finding assistive technology for teachers and suggestions for working with parents. This chapter provides a framework for the use of technology to assist these exceptional children in early childhood and primary level classrooms.

Section 4. Bridging the Gap between Policy and Practice

The fourth section, Bridging the Gap between Policy and Practice, is an abridged case study of what has happened in Mexico, the first country to implement mandatory preschool education for all children. This dramatic mandate brought promise for parents and children as Mexico attempted to provide support for all young children's educational development. This chapter discusses the issues with policy and implementation and how technology has evolved in preschool programs in Mexico, Spain, and the Latin American Countries. The lessons learned from this dramatic reform effort will inform teachers about the gap between policy and implementation and help them rethink their role in change.

Chapter 12: Bridging the Gap between Policy and Implementation: Preschool Education in Mexico, Latin America and Spain

The twelth and final chapter in this book explores an abridged case study of the implementation of reform in early childhood education. The dramatic reform in Mexico during the last decade brought international focus to the educational systems as the Law of Mandatory Pre-schooling made Mexico the only country in the world with mandatory education for 3-year olds. The reform policies were influenced by the changing economic policies as Mexico surged forward in development of technology related industries. As Mexico continued to move toward a more technological state, it was vital that the schools keep up by preparing the children of Mexico for global economy. Jorge Lopez, the author of this chapter, discusses the gap between policy and implementation of reform efforts in an attempt to help teachers better realizes the importance of their role in political decisions. The chapter examines the issues when top down reform (decisions about policy made by politicians or governing agencies) is implemented without the counsel of practitioners and how teachers and educational environments address issues to support children's learning. Jorge also builds a case for the importance of early childhood teachers and programs in the development of thinking and explains the influences that have changed him from a Nuclear Physicist to an advocate for the field of early education. This chapter includes data from Spain, Mexico, and Latin American countries relating to the realities of technology use in these countries. Lessons learned from this chapter can help teachers become stronger advocates for reform, reflect on change and their role, and find solutions to closing the gaps between policy and implementation in their educational institutions.

Summary

The issues discussed in this book are not isolated to early childhood environments but evident across the continuum of education. The university must also rethink their ideas about learning and what students need to succeed in the new digital age.

REFERENCES

Collins, A., & Halverson, R. (2009). *Rethinking education in the age of technology: The digital revolution and schooling in America*. New York, NY: Teachers College Press.

Hofer, B. K. (2001). Personal epistemology research: Implications for learning and teaching. *Journal of Educational Psychology Review*, *13*, 353–383. doi:10.1023/A:1011965830686

Safire, W. (2008). *Safire's political dictionary*. New York, NY: Oxford University Press.

Acknowledgment

Barbara K. Lipman Early Childhood School and Research Institute. The Barbara K. Lipman Early Childhood School and Research Institute under the direction of Sandra Turner-Brown is located on the University of Memphis campus. This school is partially supported through the Lipman Foundation, contributions, tuition, and the College of Education. Without the collaboration of this school and teachers we would never be able to conduct our research. These professionals and the children and parents of Lipman are our lifeline to research, practice, and intellectual stimulation for our work. We want to acknowledge their support, expertise, contributions, and patience with us as we continue to write. These extraordinary professionals are identified below.

Sandra Brown Turner: My history with Lipman School dates back to 1975 when I did my student teaching here and then in 1986-1987 when I was honored to be a graduate assistant. Before becoming the Director of Lipman School in July 2000, I was a tenured Associate Professor of Early Childhood Education at Southwest Tennessee Community College. I have served on numerous local, state, regional, and national boards, task forces, committees, and presented workshops or keynotes all over the United States. I am published in a variety of professional journals with a particular interest in the development of spirituality in young children. It is my joy to come here each day and see the growth and development of the children, their families, and their teachers.

Carol Cordeau Young: I have been a Supervising Teacher at Lipman School since 1995. I received my undergraduate degree in 1982 from Saint Bonaventure University, New York, and I hold a Master's degree in Early Childhood Education Special Education from Saint Joseph College, West Hartford, Connecticut. I have taught in a variety of programs such as Science Museum of Connecticut Nursery School and the Martha O'Bryan Center in Nashville, TN. I present workshops and in-service training for local, state, and national early childhood professional groups. In addition to publishing articles on curriculum and parenting, my interests include reflective practice and science.

Jan Kidder: I am a native Texan and received my undergraduate degree from the University of Dallas in 1976. After receiving my Master's degree from Vanderbilt University in 1979, I adopted Tennessee as home and I have been teaching in Memphis ever since. I hold an American Montessori Society Pre-Primary certificate from Memphis Montessori Institute, and have taught in Montessori schools, Memphis City Schools, and adjunct for Southwest Tennessee Community College. I have been the Supervising Teacher in the Montessori I classroom at Lipman School since 2000.

Harmony Swenson: I am a native Memphian and my husband and I have a two-year-old daughter. I received my B.S. Ed. in early childhood education in 1999 here at the University of Memphis. After teaching with Memphis City Schools and Shelby County Schools I was pleased to come in 2001 as the kindergarten teacher and become a part of the unique and magical environment of Lipman School. I am currently pursuing my Master's degree in Instruction and Curriculum Leadership.

Jodie Friedman: I have been a Supervising Teacher at Lipman School since January, 2006, just after completing my student teaching assignment and finishing my M.A.T. at the University of Memphis (May, 2006). I received my B.S. in Business Administration from Boston University in May, 2003. It was then that I knew that I wanted to be a teacher of young children. I believe that children learn best while actively engaged in a comfortable learning environment; I work daily to achieve this in my classroom.

Erin King: I have a long history with Lipman School. My journey began many when I attended Lipman as a kindergartner. I believe my early experiences in this caring and creative environment set the stage for my later academic and artistic pursuits. I returned to the University of Memphis as a young adult and earned a B.F.A. After pursuing different venues for a career, I decided to return to the University to earn a Master's Degree in Early Childhood Education. While working on my M.A.T., I was fortunate to be a Graduate Assistant at Lipman School. In the 2007-08 school year I became Lipman's first atelierista/ art teacher. I found that I could combine my art background and my knowledge of developmentally appropriate practice. I became the Preschool II Supervising Teacher the next year which I thoroughly enjoy. I continue to develop my own artistic yens and am an active artist in the Memphis community.

Odette Patrikios: I was born in Zimbabwe, Africa, and attended business school and later immigrated to the United States with my husband and children. I joined the university several years ago and have been at Lipman School since 2003. Since becoming a staff member at the U of M I have received the university's Outstanding Customer Service Award and was a nominee for the College of Education's Dean's Excellence Award for Support Staff.

Thank you Lipman.

We would also like to acknowledge Candice Burkett, Harley McGee, and Dulcenia Franklin Blake for their support and patience during the development and writing of this book.

Sally Blake
Flagler College, USA

Denise Winsor
University of Memphis, USA

Lee Allen
University of Memphis, USA

Section 1
Understanding the Digital Communication Generation Gap:
Values, Beliefs, Social Cultural Systems that Influence Teaching Practice

Chapter 1
The Impact of Technology on Early Childhood Education:
Where the Child Things Are? Adults, Children, Digital Monsters and the Spaces in Between

Andrew Neil Gibbons
Auckland University of Technology, New Zealand

ABSTRACT

This chapter explores the bridging of the communication-generation gap through an analysis of the child's play with hi-tech toys. The analysis of the young child's play with these toys employs narrative from the show Digimon in order to critique predominant themes in relation to learning and development. These themes highlight challenges to binary oppositions of adult-child, self-other, and artificial-real. In troubling these oppositions, the very idea of the gap becomes of interest in that in the gap are potential alternatives for adults who seek a critical understanding of the complex terrains in which they engage the young child.

INTRODUCTION

Takuya is sprinting down the road, his cellular phone beeps, he looks at it...

Takuya: 5.40!?

He continues his dash down the middle of the street, past a small child kicking a football to his Dad. The Dad's phone makes a strange noise as he runs by, and he looks at it...

Dad: Huh?

Small child: Dad the ball!

DOI: 10.4018/978-1-61350-059-0.ch001

Copyright © 2012, IGI Global. Copying or distributing in print or electronic forms without written permission of IGI Global is prohibited.

Takuya: Sorry.

Dad: The phone? That noise?

Takuya: I'll get it.

Dad: Kids these days

Takuya runs into a T junction after the ball, puts his foot on the ball, and stops. He kicks the ball back up the street. A truck approaches; the driver is staring at his cellular phone, which is making the same strange noise. The driver looks back to the road to see Takuya. He slams the brakes on, the truck skids sideways towards Takuya....

Takuya: Oh perfect... aaarrrrggg... this... is my destiny?

The scene above opens season four of *Digimon* – a Toei Animation animated television and movie series. Digimon, short for "Digital Monsters" is a media franchise encompassing anime, manga, toys, video games, trading card games and other media. The franchise's eponymous creatures are monsters of various forms living in a "Digital World", a parallel universe that originated from Earth's various communication networks. Takuya is about to embark on a fantastic adventure in which he, a digitally destined child, will discover certain, familiar, life boundaries are no longer intact. He is rushing headlong into a new technological future.

Throughout this chapter similar excerpts from *Digimon* provide themes for an exploration of gaps that appear between technological generations. Technological generations can be thought of as a more or less loosely defined classification of people, often chronologically constructed. Takuya, the character in the above excerpt, is a boy of about 12 years old, is a considered a member of a particular generation as a result of his age. Alternatively technological generations can be understood as the outcomes, or products, of technologies. Takuya is an active user of certain technologies and is hence a member of the *Digimon* generation; a child able to communicate with the digital world.

Any gaps between generations might also be understood as constructed. Exploring toys in this chapter provides a context for exploring gaps not to suggest that such gaps are not real, but to examine the ways in which 'we' construct and respond to them. This chapter explores the terrain of the communication-generation gap from the context of the toy. Toys are considered one instance of technology generating human generations. The concepts of 'adulthood' and 'childhood' can be thought of as intimately connected to toys. However technological gaps are generated around more than the dichotomy of the adult-child. Notably, the gap between real and artificial is a technologically determined gap, as are gaps between rich and poor.

From the seemingly most simple and natural stick, to the most complex multimedia pocket monster, toys reveal thoughts about the nature of child and adult, and of the gaps between them. This chapter begins with a brief family history of the toy, providing context for an analysis of the current 'generation' of toys, and in particular of the ways in which these toys are celebrated as powerful and educational or feared as unnatural and corrupting.

This kind of analysis of technology has its perils. If a writer is seen to be promoting the use of new technologies for young children, he or she may attract criticism from advocates for a less cluttered and electronic child. Similarly, if he or she is problematising the child's play with new media he or she is likely to attract the interests of advocates for hi-tech learning. From either position the research will be pulled apart for its scientific weaknesses and the values will be hauled across someone else's normative coals.

While this chapter cannot avoid these perils, it does attempt to look at the ways in which we respond to the phenomena as much as the phenomena itself. In other words, the focus is upon relationships. Relationships stress to the researcher not what is known as much as what is done with what is known. The generational digital gap is very much about relationships between children and technology and how each new generation comes to our schools with experiences and development influenced by available technology.

In this sense, toys are a means with which we can understand lived experience. Our relationships to toys determine collective and individual horizons. For instance generational identity is a product of toys (think for instance of the children of the 'playstation' generation), and each collective group's experiences and perceptions are different due to toys. In a sense experiences and accepted toys establish a common thread or identifier of one's age. In this chapter the ways in which toys make sense of, and to, our relationships are explored with the hope that reader will be interested in other ways of thinking about and questioning toys, and about the broader themes of education and technology. A vast amount of information about human values, styles of thinking, and behavior patterns is gained from the extensive modeling in the symbolic environment of the mass media" (Cooper, 2005, pp. 270-271).

The chapter is built around the *Digimon* narratives. These narratives reveal particular kinds of technological relationships, drawing out an idea that in the child's connection with the toy there is a world that is in some way disconnected to the world of adults. After briefly exploring histories of toys and associated human thought, the chapter engages contemporary hi-tech instances of children's technologies. Themes of learning and development are related to these technologies in order to analyse the ways in which an adult world makes sense of the child's play. These themes reveal interesting gaps between adulthood and childhood that the chapter explores in order to consider some educational implications.

Given the widespread interest in the gaps between adulthood and childhood, the notion that children are in some way more confident navigators of a 21st century terrain is explored with the purpose of challenging the very ideas of child and adult, and hence the 'problem' of communication-generation gaps. This position is in essence one of questioning taken-for-granted boundaries and oppositions that have predominated in making sense of our lives. As such the purpose of the chapter is to explore the idea and experience of child and adult in order to consider how the ideas and experiences might be understood as a result of technology. We continually call upon ourselves to act in relation to these terms guided by observations that both making sense of the world (Luke, 1999) and making the right decisions in the world (Turkle, 1996) are seen to be increasingly complex cultural, social, and political tasks.

Objectives

This chapter explores the nature of communication-generation gaps through analysis of the evolution of the digital toy. The purpose of the chapter is to present different ways of both understanding and analyzing gaps between child and adult through the symbol of the toy. Readers will be introduced to a range of historical and theoretical positions in order to promote a critical understanding of human-technology relationships and inform reflective pedagogies. The reader will:

- Develop a better understanding of the role of toys and generation identity
- Reflect on how digital toys influence children's development and interactions
- Analyse the relationship between technology and generations

BACKGROUND: THE NEW WORLD OF DIGITAL REALITY

Until recently, the surge in young children's digital-media-based learning has drawn scant attention.

That situation is rapidly changing (Weigel, James, & Gardner, 2009). Digital toys have become big business in the economic community. In today's digital-intensive world, young children represent a key target demographic for digital consumer electronic (CE) devices. Technology has become a part of what is called the edutainment industry. The edutainment segment of the toy industry is distinguished by innovative uses of existing technology typically found in mainstream consumer electronics. Over the past three years, there has been a sharp escalation in the development and marketing of edutainment toys aimed at toddlers, grade-school children, and more recently, at infants. (In-Stat, 2008)

Recent research by In-Stat (2008) found the following:

- One of the fastest growing segments in the overall toy industry is the edutainment market.
- The worldwide market for edutainment toys will reach $9 billion by 2012.
- The worldwide market for edutainment toys will grow to 146 million units by 2012

This increasing availability and interaction with the digital world further increases the generational gap in many ways. Bandura (2001) observed that "learning occurs either directly or unintentionally from models in one's immediate environment. The digital environment our children experience in their formative years will clearly impact their world views. Exploring these relationships through analysis of the evolution of digital toys can help us better understand the new world of this generation.

Exploring the Historic Relationships Among Toys, Philosophy and Education

It's the summer holidays. Six children meet each other for the first time at a summer camp. They're unaware that the world is experiencing an environmental meltdown until it begins snowing. As they wonder about this impossible scenario the sky opens and six bright objects crash into the ground around them, then rise into the air in some kind of selection ritual.
Sora: What... are these?

Matt: My guess is some sort of miniature remote digital apparatus.

The devices seem purposeful; the children grab the devices and are transported into a digital dimension. As Tai wakes up he is frightened by a pink bouncing head with fangs that introduces itself:

Tai: That's the last time I eat camp food.

Koromon: Hey, you don't need to be afraid of me, I'm your friend, I'm your friend, I'm your friend.

Tai: Just what are you? Have you had your rabies shots?

Koromon: Everthing's going to be alright now Tai, I've been waiting for you...

Tai:... waiting for me?

Koromon: My name's Koromon, and we're... partners!

Tai: Koromon? That mean's... talking head?

Koromon: It means brave little warrior, and don't forget it Tai.

Tai: What did you mean you've been waiting for me, and how did you know my name?

While Koromon declares itself a brave warrior partner, it is also known to us as a digital pet, an evolution of the toy: a toy-pet animal hybridisation whose genealogy is complex. Koromon may not accept its designation as mere toy. Yet perhaps toys are anything *but* mere given their interest for psychological, media and educational studies. To trace Koromon's family tree, this first section explores toy histories with a particular interest in the human subjectivities and relationships that are evident around the toy.

One such subjectivity is the child itself. Childhood has appeared within certain contexts (see Aries, 1962), and disappeared in other contexts (see Postman, 1994). In this state of flux, the image of childhood, and of the child, reveals and conceals terrain between the adult and the child. This perpetual morphing of the terrain, or gaps, in between adult-child is evident in the technologies with which the child plays. In other words, toys provide one measure of the changing generational boundaries.

Like childhood as a distinct object of study, toys provide historians with evidence of the ways in which the world has been, and is, perceived and experienced across time, and across cultural settings (Marsh 2002; Sutton-Smith, 1986, 1997). Archaeological evidence suggests toys including spinning (or twirler) tops, marbles, hoops, knucklebones, toy animals, dolls and rattles have been 'around' since early human civilisation, and across many cultures; made with a wide range of material, design, and intended use (Cross, 1997; McClary, 1997).

Evidence of the toys of the past additionally appears to us in images that require considerable interpretation and intuition. For instance in Andrew McClary's *Toys With Nine Lives:A Social History of American Toys* (1997) images from Antiquity, through the Middle Ages and on to Modernity present opportunity to make sense of the history of toys:

It's interesting to try and guess why the lady of classical Greece is whipping her top. Perhaps she was participating in some kind of sport, or simply engaging in a nervous habit like smoking (McClary, 1997, p. 95-96).

What appears to McClary in this archaeology of the toy is an acknowledgement of the status and purpose of objects that had playful, ceremonial, leisurely, palliative, and perhaps even work-related purposes. It is less apparent whether objects such as hoops and tops were regarded as educational in the sense that any activity might have been linked to learning. In part this is perhaps because, in McClary's investigation, ancient toys are generally illustrated as the objects of players who appear to be adults – this of interest to the historian. Why is the adult playing with the child's toy? Is this evidence that an ancient illustrator did not differentiate between child and adult in their work? Is this evidence that the object was not one of child's play, or not solely an object in the domain of the child? Were there no such gaps between child and adult?

Here history, as an adult practice, presents through observation an interpretation of technologies, ascribed as toys. The toys and their associated roles in social activity and experience are characterised as having significant influence, evident in their longevity as recognisable artefacts; and in many instances their influence in complex toy family histories. Toys then are the object of an adult world in the sense that meanings ascribed to toys are established for children within thoughts that span centuries. However the unobserved toys of childhood are obscured in the secret, untold, world of childhood (van Manen & Levering, 1996). They do not exist; at least, not as toys, and they do not contribute to the ancient construction of childhood. In the period of Antiquity, when philosophers were intrigued by form, universal qualities of beauty and truth, did a hoop, or a spinning top, give presence to an ideal? Did the toy have an essential role in establishing the nature and qualities of civilisation?

The modernisation of the toy from the 17th century constructs the child as free to discover the world through the innocence of play. Play is seen as a rational component of the child's life path and worldly contributions. Play with toys is a stage in progression towards adulthood. So while we can only speculate about gaps between ancient parents and their children, in Modernity boundaries were staked such that gaps might be more visible. The context for the modern toy can be in part understood through again turning to philosophers and educationalists whose questions concerning children and childhood produced technological answers.

In answering the question, "What is the purpose of education?" I relied at that time upon the following observations: Man lives in a world of objects, which influence him, and which he desires to influence; therefore he ought to know these objects in their nature, in their conditions, and in their relation with each other and with man kind (Froebel, 1886, p. 69).

In Frobel's text an essence of 'man' emerges that demands attention to the ways in which the child plays. Educational relationships are oriented around objects and exploration of them for the purpose of first truth of their nature, and then their capacity to make human life in some way better. An essence of being understood in this way draws together philosophers and educationalists including John Locke, Jean-Jacques Rousseau and of course Frobel himself. While each attends to different children in different times, the thread that connects them is the importance of the things the child plays with.

...Locke said that a mother should teach the child human vaues, such as love and discipline, and needed skills, such as reading. These missions could be carried out with the help of toys. Earlier, toys had been dismissed as mere baubles or even as sinful, but now they became important teaching aids (McClary, 1997, p. 217).

Essential to Locke was a freedom to learn promoted by both Plato and Aristotle. Freedom and play were connected around the object of the toy; however, it is also clear that this freedom is only a semblance, in that the purpose of the play is to become virtuous. The central difference to earlier lessons in virtue is perhaps most simply the belief that play is likely to be more effective than a whipping or recital of verse. In other words, play worked.

Another quality of these toys is their apparent openness to the child's desires. The toy and the child resonated, at least when compared to the toy and the adult, whose interests were turned towards the outside world of industry and growth.

...mechanical figures, miniatures, and even ball games that had once edified or amused adults became the playthings of young people. Even the often violent and sensual rituals of carnival and mumming were tamed and then passed down to children. When adults abandoned these toys and games, their daily lives became more "serious." Still, on special occasions they could escape the world of rationality, competition, and achievement by joining their children in a world of play that had been transformed into innocent delight. Wonder was saved from rationality and progress when it was given to children (Cross, 2004, pp. 26-27).

Both Locke and Froebel develop the importance of an adult interest in child's play – for wider social aspirations – and of the increasing rationalisation of children's toys, a rationalisation that led to the economic, political and social role of the toy through its influence on the child's informal and formal education. Regulation of play was both managing risk and opportunity (Cross, 2004) in the emerging social world of a city dwelling child. Opportunity was a central ideal that was applied to the manufacturing of the toy in an industrialising paradigm, while fears for the innocence of the child led to the importance of the toy in protecting the child from the adult world of the city. Again, gaps appear.

In the late 19th and 20th centuries toys became things to manufacture rather than things to tinker with, to make more complex, more collectible, to provide rationalisations for, and also to provide some sense of order and governance such that children's play was leading somewhere. Spinning tops and hoops began to appear static in relation to construction sets. Where, the adults began to ask, is the educational value in a hooped stick when compared to the construction set and its potential for complex play that would contribute to both the child's imagination and their preparation for the real industrial world?

Modernity and industrialisation brought new toys, new places to play, and it brought new attitudes towards the toy, attitudes that delimit emerging generational gaps. The desires of the child are measured against those of the adult world; children are seen to desire the latest toy. Adults who create and profit from these toys are often seen to be endangering the innocence of childhood in enjoining the child in the will to progress.

Innovations in manufacturing, transport, and information and communication technologies provide the possibilities that progress of the toy might reach expanding audiences through, for instance, the television show, the advertisement, and in the late 20th century the Internet. The increasing visibility of the toy, and the toy industry, led to changing toy behaviours:

... the very fact that modern versions of tops and marbles have been re-designed to be used by small children with little skills has hurt their popularity. Once, they belonged to the world of sports and games, but today, they have been replaced by newer, and more exciting... items such as in-line skates, mountain bikes, and Frisbees (McClary, 1997, p. 114-115).

Multiple identities of the child are distinguished in relation to the toy. Gaps appear within generations of childhood. However the generations, and their gaps, are not static. For example, in *James May's Toy Stories* toys that epitomise a 20th century British play are recreated in 'adult' scales (May, 2010). Modern toys such as the construction set, or model train, are revived in the worlds of those adults who hold to the significance of toys from their childhood. These toys then do not provide a reliable measure of adulthood and childhood. Toys such as electric trains and construction sets and kitset models bridged generation gaps and, at least in the 50s, were targeted by manufacturers at the father son dyad (Cross, 2004). Many toys were complex to assemble and required significant time spent on them. They provided a bridge for adults back to a time of fantasy and fun that was, Cross (2004) argues, consigned to childhood with the rise of Science and reason. In a sense the Enlightenment, Science, Rationalism all conspired to tear a rent between child and adult – adulthood and childhood appeared as banks of a swiftly flowing river.

Cross (2004) argues that the giving of toys to children was intended to keep children happy in their childhood, and hence purposefully not educational. Educational was seen to prepare children for the adult world. While in Cross' analysis it appears that the toy established a connection between generations in order to protect a certain human essence, toys and play are also technologies for the control of childhood. That wonder and delight of the secret world of childhood is also a world of risk. In this sense an adult-child binary opposition is constructed around the unknown of childhood, in order to discover, monitor and organise the unknown child.

Toys concomitantly provided adults with evidence that their children were developing as educated and economic beings. Think for instance of the ways in which children are observed to manage their collections of toys. Cross argues that the "the underlying assumption was that children had natural and autonomous desires that parents could not know or challenge" (Cross, 2004, p.

15) but to which they had a moral responsibility to foster. Cross (2004, p. 20) notes:

... battles between consumerism and education have been with us for generations. Novelty toymaker Louis Marx said in 1955, "I don't go along with psychologists who want to sneak up on [children] and jam education into them through toys ... [Only] spinster aunts and spinster uncles and hermetically sealed parents who wash their children 1,000 times a day give educational toys." Marx was voicing the bias of a lifelong manufacturer of windup boxing Popeye figures and "Fort Apache" play sets.

Yet fears of an unruly childhood meant that any rationalisation of how to promote the child's security and future were becoming attractive to parents who were increasingly aware of their accountability to new social and political institutions whose concerns included the management of a generation of children that were out of the matrix of Modern control.

The questions of generations, of childhood and adult, and of gaps between them are questions that concern people in different ways. The very nature of this questioning establishes a sense of who we are. In the analysis above a particular context is revealed, one in which knowledge and experience are thrust into logical relationships, positioned within the hula hoops of a Venn diagram. However these categories, classifications are unstable measurements and, in a world valorised as multicultural and postmodern, they are revealed as inadequate.

Robot Invasion of the Toy World

Malomyotismon: And the worlds shall unite in darkness, ha ha ha ha, then they shall both be mine.

In *Digimon* season two Malomyotismon's project of world domination revolves around synthesising the worlds of digital and human beings. In the culmination of the season this grotesque figure of cyborg fantasy has enveloped planet earth in darkness, engendering despair in the human race. Here *Digimon* engages a human fear of technology in the form of a sentient robot.

The robot is an enduring metaphor for science fiction writers that has played its part in establishing gaps between worlds, both earthbound gaps of humans and their tinkering with artificial life, and interstellar gaps of human and robot 'races'. The robot also symbolises a 20th century invasion of the child's play, observed by ever expanding modes of adulthood. In other words, it is not the robot but the professional that is observed milling around the child as she plays with her new toys. The robot may have initially entered the world of a child's play as a fun toy, at least for those children whose economic contexts allowed for such play. However the technological essence of the robot, when associated with the psychological and cybernetic sciences, revealed a particular mission for the robot as a pre-programmed and serious educational toy.

There are a number of interesting sources for this programming, particularly within the sphere of cybernetics. Alan Turing, for instance, articulated artificial intelligence in terms of developing infant cognition, connecting "the question of what makes people think machines can think... [with] a question about what makes us think other people can think" (Croissant, 1998, p. 292). An interest in what makes people think, and in the child's play with her toys, provided Jean Piaget's genetic epistemology with a focus in his search for a stable structure and regulation of systems (Gibbons, 2007). Piaget provided many adults, and particularly those interested in science and technology, with evidence that children were naturally inclined to be scientific and technological (Turkle, 1998).

One of Piaget's young colleagues, Seymour Papert, advocated for new educational computational technologies, in reinforcing the constructivist epistemology around the concept of the 'knowledge machine' (Papert, 1993). This machine provided for Papert the possibility that education might become a practice and experience responsive to progress. Of particular interest was the development of new generations of electronic toys expected to transform a child's thinking in some way.

Briefly, Papert regarded a bridge built between building blocks, construction sets, and the computer chip as encouraging a child's learning, and in particular learning of mathematics, that might be more concrete and personal than the pedagogical methods of the time. Children using computers experience a synthesis between aesthetics and science in a manner more meaningful than is possible in tradition educational, classroom, environments (Papert, 1991a).

Building and playing with castles of sand, families of dolls, houses of Lego, and collections of cards provides images of activities which are well rooted in contemporary cultures and which plausibly enter into learning processes that go beyond specific narrow skills. I do not believe that anyone fully understands what gives these activities their quality of "learning-richness." But this does not prevent one from taking them as models in benefiting from the presence of new technologies to expand the scope of activities with that quality (Papert, 1991b, p 6).

The 'upgrading' of dolls, building block, card games, through the incorporation of computer technologies altered the nature of the toy in some complex and often uneasy ways, uneasy at least for adults who were not willing to accept the hybridisation of their traditions. Children playing with these technologies are seen to be engaged in complex theory construction.

Papert, and others, regard new computer technologies as engendering a valued kind of learning, termed bricolage. Being a bricoleur, the child's learning is regarded as having the quality of knowledge-tinkering. Within this context the activity of making sense of and acting out one's play is not a nice whole and self-contained experience (see for instance Gibbons, 2007). The bricoleur may not be a new phenomenon for the child, but it is a new phenomenon for explaining the child's behaviour in educational contexts, and thereafter for designing the curricula in such ways as to be bricoleurian.

In part the intention here is to reach out, across a perceived generational gap, to the child in order to solve the problem of education's lack of appeal to younger generations. Gee (2005, p. 5) reflects that "we all know from school, young people are not always eager to do difficult things." Yet that eagerness seems to appear when the difficult thing is a computer game. Gee (2005, p. 5) asks: "How do good game designers manage to get new players to learn their long, complex, and difficult games and not only learn them but pay to do so?"

I believe it is something about how games are designed to trigger learning that makes them so deeply motivating ... the designers of many good games have hit on profoundly good methods of getting people to learn and to enjoy learning (Gee, 2005, p. 5).

Yet a turn to toys and games generally elicits scepticism for those who are yet to throw out their pedagogical babies with their educational bath water. Hence in pedagogical circles it is important to highlight that gaming "learning methods are similar in many respects to cutting-edge principles being discovered in research on human learning" (Gee, 2005, p. 5). For some, the idea that the computer game is a carrier of meaningful learning might be less of interest than their viral qualities; computer games occupy central concerns in relation to child consumption of violence, antisocial tendencies, obesity through inactivity, and a general subservience to the market forces of high technology.

The advocates for learning with new technologies are quick to adapt and respond to concerns as they are given voice. Amidst concerns, in the early

80s, that computers were too artificial, pedagogies were promoted that focused on a child's natural inclination to explore the world. New technologies then are coupled to the educational toy world in accepting that learning through play is an essential component of the child's education particularly in relation to the domains of mathematics, science and technology. Children playing with the right toys are being scientists and mathematicians, developing concepts and behaviours that reveal them to be more than a becoming scientist; they are being scientists (Lind, 2005). Put simply, where an educational gap is proclaimed, the technology is reprogrammed to bridge the gap.

A key inference here is that the young children will accept a computer as a natural part of the environment in a way that adults either will not, or cannot. For example, Gebhardt-Seele (1985, p. 5) observed "children approach the miracle computer with the same unprejudiced sense of wonder as a germinating pea". Despite the admission that the pea's germination is as complex, if not more, as the computer's digital systems, advocacy turned to the essential role of the computer in education, and not that of the pea.

We as educators do not have the choice of whether or not to establish the computer as part of the child's environment. All we can do is decide on the consequences that the fact of computers, as part of the child's environment, will have in our prepared environment in the school and the home (Gebhardt-Seele, 1985, p. 7).

The poor old pea that we left under the child's mattress (to prove to ourselves that she is real) has been genetically modified into a virtual pea, just as the animal has transformed in the virtual pet. The virtual pet, of which a *Digimon* toy is one instance, is an object of pedagogical interest on account of its capacity to encourage a range of pro-social behaviours. In part this may reveal that pets have been treated like educational toys.

Animals have long been an important part of children's lives, offering comfort and companionship, and promoting the development of moral reciprocity and responsibility. Yet in recent years there has a movement to create technological substitutes for pets, such as the Tamagotchi, i-Cybie, Tekno, and Poo-Chi (Kahn, Friedman, Perez-Granados, & Freier, 2004, p. 1449)

Psychological interest in "children's reasoning about and behavioural interactions with one of the most advanced robotic pets" (Kahn, Friedman, Perez-Granados, & Freier, 2004, p. 1449) has provided the adult world with evidence that children are thinking differently about life. In a sense "robotic pets, as representative of an emerging technological genre in HCI, may be (a) blurring foundational ontological categories, and (b) impacting children's social and moral development" (Kahn, Friedman, Perez-Granados, & Freier, 2004, p. 1449).

Kahn, Friedman, Perez-Granados, and Freier (2004), researching robotic pets, believe that a new generation of technology is evident in the child's robotic toys in that relative to previous generations the toy exhibits particular autonomy, adaptation, and personification in a moving, interacting toy. One of their concerns is that such a toy shifts the boundaries of how we can talk about technology, and hence new language is required.

...it may not be the best approach to keep asking people if this emerging technological genre is, for example, "alive" or "not alive" if from the person's experience of the subject-object interaction, the object is alive in some respects and not alive in other respects, and is experienced not simply as a combination of such qualities... but as a novel entity (Kahn, Friedman, Perez-Granados, & Freier, 2004, p. 1450).

The expectation here is that the adult world of rationalising human behaviour may need to respond to the child's world of rationalising life

(Kahn, Friedman, Perez-Granados, & Freier, 2004). In other words, new social and cultural phenomena require new psychological branches and new academic questions.

First, what does it mean to morally care about an entity that (as the majority of the children recognized) is not alive? In this sense, a person can "care" very deeply about a car they have owned for decades, and cry when it is finally towed to the junkyard; but that would seem to us a derivative form of caring, supported only by the person's projection of animacy and personality onto the artifact, concepts which may first have to be developed in the company of sentient others (Kahn, Friedman, Perez-Granados, & Freier, 2004, p. 1452).

The digital pet, or a digital doll, is perceived to have an interactive and developmental capacity that engenders the toy as more complex than previous toys. For instance, the child can purchase new data to add to the features of the toy. However, while there is some attention to the complexity of the artefact, there is some debate about this, and the debate generally orients around the complexity of the child's interactions. In other words, if the child is seen to be merely responding to directions of a toy, the child is regarded as a passive player, whereas if the child is seen to be developing new ways of thinking about the world then the toy is encouraging valued complex play.

This complexity debate orients around the aspirations of the adult world in relation to the nature and purpose of education. Is there 'real' or 'deep' learning going on when a child is engaged with a toy? A central connection for Papert's theory of learning is that real and deep are related to the ideas of fun and happiness through, in particular, the expectation that his toys encourage fantasy play, a kind of play not unfamiliar to the likes of Lewis Carroll or A.A. Milne, both of whom regarded the child's toy as a gateway to deep learning, however more on that later.

In the age of the digital monster, Koromon is evidence of the will to either make sense of, or make a problem of, new technologies and their 'real-life' pedagogical manifestations in the play of the child. This play is evident in the fantasy worlds that are both presented to the child as narratives to mediate/consume, and in addition present to the child certain narratives about being a child, whether that child be Christopher Robins, or Takato.

Playing with the Boundaries of the Real

An urban playground, out of sight in the belly of a dinosaur statue, Takato and Kazu are hunched over a gaming board, holding card reading digivices, selecting creatures from their playing cards strewn across the ground, competing in card battles.

In this scene, beginning season three of *Digimon*, the show becomes real within the show. Takato and Kazu have been watching and playing *Digimon* seasons one and two. They represent real children. As children who really play the *Digimon* game, they have digivices, character cards and a game board. However Takato is soon to find out that the *Digimon* are real, and that to defeat their enemies they have to become one with their digitally destined friend. For Takato the gaps between real and artificial have become indistinct.

Here the show popularizes what Papert (1993) argued as important connections between concrete and abstract life experiences. He regarded the knowledge machine as a bridge between concrete (real) and abstract (artificial). In his theory of constructionism the concrete nature of an object must involve the "person who constructs the object" (Wilensky, 1991, p. 197) and hence constructionism looks not at the object's concrete nature but the "person's construction of the object, at the relationship between the person and the object" (Wilensky, 1991, p. 198).

The object was made concrete in the soft and hard machinery of Logo and the interconnection between Logo and the building blocks of LEGO, hence connecting the world of microchip networks to that of the mass produced building block. Hi-tech toys such as LEGO/Logo products are articulated as educational toys in which the child can embody herself (Papert, 1991a), connecting with and instructing the robotic creation (Resnick & Ocko, 1991) in much the same way as Tai and Koromon or, as seen below, Takato and Guilmon. In altering herself she alters reality:

One characteristic of children's play is the ability to experiment with and transform reality. Through this process, children can assume control over given situations and select the important issues they want to deal with (Kafai & Harel, 1991, p. 136).

However, if this is a characteristic of play, is the computer a necessity? Might a stick or a teddy bear provide a medium for reality transformation? Perhaps this very question led to an interest in the technology of the child's brain as the fantasy-producing medium. Yet in order to understand the brain, computational technologies re-emerge. Turkle (1996, p. 25), for instance, suggests "the development of genetics as a computational biology [reflects] the extent to which we assume ourselves to be like machines whose inner workings we can understand."

The micro-isation of the computer made it possible for toys to become more 'human' and more child-friendly. While a computer was the size of a small room, or a desktop, it was fairly safe from being the object of a child's affections. When it was inserted into the body of an action figure, teddy bear, and so on, the computer chip synthesized with the toy and assimilated its qualities as efficiently as an intergalactic Borg cube.

In a new mode of discovery, Turkle (1996, p. 10) argues the child playing with a robot is 'led' to "speculate about whether computers are smart and what it is to be alive." Children are engaged, in this sense, in the kind of philosophical inquiry that most adults are not, with the exception of philosophers and science fiction writers.

The movement towards explaining how a computer thinks, as children are observed to do (Turkle, 1996), and of designing computers that are more human, has led to problematising notions of thought and of the natural/artificial dichotomy. Children have developed a human-like relationship; interpreting their relationships with technology in terms supposedly reserved as criteria for human relations (Turkle, 1996).

Turkle (1996, 1998, & 2005) has gathered extensive data on the ways in which children engage with computer technologies. She observed that these technologies make psychological sense to children. More than this, the 'opaque' quality of such technologies encourages children to, Turkle (1996) argues, actively interpret the nature of the technologies they use. Her observations of explanations of the nature of new technologies show that the children often explain the operation of the technology in terms of psychological presence – thinking, knowing, remembering.

According computers a psychological life once reserved for people led to some important changes in how children thought about the boundaries between people, machines, and animals (Turkle, 1996, p. 81).

Where a plastic doll might have physical presence, a robotic baby doll has psychological presence, in that the child's explanation of the doll draws upon a discourse of emotion and thought. "For today's children, the boundary between people and machines is intact. But what they see across the boundary has changed dramatically" (Turkle, 1996, p. 83). What they saw, past tense, was movement as evidence of life, although this did not apparently raise a question regarding whether an immobile human is alive. What children have seen, since the late 70s, is thought. Perhaps ironically Turkle (2005, p. 320) notes:

Our culture will develop ways of thinking about the computer that, in a sense, require no thought. As these reach the ears and minds of children, they may change the child's discourse about these objects.

One such example of thought-less engagement with new technologies may be the simulated life game. Programmers developed simulated life games during the 80s in which the player could set in motion a life or lives that had a seeming disconnect with the player (Turkle, 1998) but that necessarily draw upon the programmer's assumptions about life and evolution. Of interest to Turkle is however not the programme's demarking of what counts as real life, but the child's developing understanding as a result of engagement with artificial life. The 'cyborg child' (Turkle, 1998) does not distinguish between "online and offline, or virtual and real; the digital is so much intertwined into their lives and psyche that the one is entirely enmeshed with the other" (Thomas, 2006, p. 126). Children's lived experiences in their virtual worlds are regarded as real experiences. Children exploring the world with their new digital devices are building bridges between the once distinct human and artificial world.

Through early play experiences with the range of toys, whether digital or not, the child plays with the symbols, themes and values associating 'real' products with their fictional source, and with the other multimedia manifestations that offer children opportunity to engage with the questions of the nature of real, artificial, conscious, alive, dead, adult, and child. The child engaged in play with the gaps that make sense to the adult world is in a particular space that is of interest to the adult world in terms of the nature of children's developing identities.

Today's adults grew up in a culture that equated the idea of a unitary self with psychological health and in a scientific culture that taught that when a discipline achieves maturity, it has a unifying theory. When adults find themselves cycling through varying perspectives on themselves... they usually become uncomfortable... But such alternations may strike the generation of cyborg children who are growing up today as "just the way things are" (Turkle, 1998, p. 327).

Turkle has observed that the child in some way is predetermined to be open to the new technology in a way that differentiates child from adult. Citing Walt Whitman she notes: "A child went forth every day. And the first object he look'd upon, that object he became" (1998, p. 328) and wonders whether, in the terrain of the Internet and computer game, and in the hi-tech playroom, the child's experiences of life and self are substantively different. For Turkle (1996, p. 22) an interest in "what we are becoming if the first objects we look upon each day are the simulations into which we deploy our virtual selves" suggests an interest in engaging with a self that is emerging from the gaps present around humanity. Gee similarly notes that "when a person is manipulating a robot at a distance or watering a garden via a webcam on the Internet - [it] causes humans to feel as if their bodies and minds have stretched into a new space" (2005, p. 8). The condition for Turkle that engenders the experience as different for the user is their nature as child, in that such new spaces are not distinct from 'old' spaces and hence the child is not disturbed by a multiplicity of selves – a problem for adults who are worried about the impact of a loss of self in the cyber world and hence their disconnect with real life (Thomas, 2006).

The instability sensed here has taken the discursive form of the cyborg and the process of "cyborgification" (Croissant, 1998, p. 285). Gaps appear in the fixed identities of childhoods and adulthoods. Parents peer into unfamiliar worlds, whether they be new worlds of leisure, or of employment (Croissant, 1998), or of 'their' children. The child is an alien nation. That 'they', the children, play with life in their play with the digital world suggests that there is some alliance, or perhaps even some kind of symbiosis: the child becomes the cybernetic creature.

Yet for children, and for commentators who align themselves with a fluid and dynamic self, there is no problem, just a wonder at what the fuss is all about: "For children who are immersed in media from their earliest memories, life on the screen is an everyday, natural practice; they know no other way of being" (Thomas, 2006, p. 128). The technology then becomes a new measure of a child's potential, free from static, fixed, linear identities and life pathways (Dreyfus & Spinosa, 2002).

It would be naive to suggest that previous lives were singular. But singularity was, within some horizons, that which was what would be looked for in the self. Hence the 'reformation' of childhood around us is as much about the way in which childhood has emerged as an ontological challenge to adults. In particular, transformations of the child and adult self provide empirical evidence of the instability of these selves and hence of the educational and technological realities that have been sewn into their shadows. Children, as navigators of the cyber world, able to engage multiple spaces of on- and off- the line, flowing between relations and behaviours, are capable and critical beings. Children of *Digimon* are in this sense engaged in critical pedagogy.

The child's new toys are enticing not just for technological 'advance' in education and the supposed benefits these advances bring for children, but also for those interested in the capacity of new electronic technologies to shake up educational power and knowledge relationships. The toy's critical pedagogical qualities encourage "investigating institutional and societal practice with a view to resisting the imposition of dominant social norms and structures" (Keesing-Styles, 2002, p. 109).

... critical pedagogy ... has the task of engaging students and teachers in transformative social practices which, by their very nature, challenge unequal and antidemocratic structures and processes, and seek to establish more egalitarian and "humanizing" alternatives in their place (Lankshear, Peters & Knobel, 1996, p. 151).

A kind of cyber or virtual critical pedagogy 'opens' up the space between child and adult as a terrain in which traditions of rationalism and positivism might be disrupted. More than this, the child and adult subjects are replaced by a critical pedagogue, a self that has transformed with and through technology, and is evidence of the newness of technological relationships, but also of the limitations of our ability to express these relationships. In some ways grotesque figures appear to us, such as the techno-tot (Davis-Floyd & Dumit, 1998) – a hybrid animated futuristic cyborg child.

For this future child meaning and structure are constantly negotiated; the authority of interpretation and meaning is dispersed (Lankshear, Peters & Knobel, 1996) in the gap. This dispersal of self is no surprise given the attack on knowledge as stable, predictable, definable, meaningful, and knowable. The critical pedagogue no longer wishes to know what to teach, or be taught, and neither does she know the teacher or student, adult or child. New life-metaphors emerge in the digital matrix and challenge traditional assumptions about life and learning, and reflect a flux capacity inherent in, for instance, the Internet, a capacity structurally conducive to critical and decentralised thinking (Lankshear et al 1996; Luke & Luke 2001). The new life-metaphor, the cyborg, is a negotiated subject – networked, rhizomatic, narrative, fluid and dynamic (Gough, 2004). However this new identity is not simply a fun project, it is a necessary response to a similarly unstable world. Luke (1999, p. 623), for instance, argues that the pervasiveness of media symbols and experiences in a young child's life necessitates the development of skills to disseminate information – to develop media literacy, which "aims to make students (a) critical and selective viewers and consumers of popular culture; (b) able to reflect critically on media messages, their own selections, and pleasures form media and texts; and (c) able to use those critical skills in the production of their own multimedia or audiovisual texts."

The Evolution of the Child-Machine

Takato (to Guilmon):... we're together, we can do anything.

Beelzemon: We're not going to do this again are we?

Takato: I wish I could fight him with you Guilmon, Beelzemon wouldn't stand a chance against the two of us together.

Guilmon: I'm sure there's a way Takato, maybe you just have to wish for it really hard, it worked when you needed the blue card.

Takato: Alright then... I really want to fight with Guilmon...

Lights stream around Takato and Guilmon, a DNA pattern envelops them. The bodies of Takato and Guilmon merge together...

Guilmon: Guilmon biomerge to........ Gallantmon.

Turkle (1996, p. 21) claims that as "human beings become increasingly intertwined with the technology and with each other via the technology, old distinctions between what is specifically human and specifically technological become more complex." This complexity is evident in the digivolution of child and digimon into a hybrid digidestined. The digivolved being has augmented power, heightened awareness and enhanced empathy. This cybernetic synthesis of child and machine has strong evolutionary tones (Croissant, 1998), however for some the question is not when humans will be synthesised with machines but rather what makes us think we are not (Ellul, 1964).

The child's cyborgness is evident in the "widening gap between the children who embody the ideals of flexibility and robust motor programming and are capable of moving gracefully, who are effective information managers in the cognitive domain, who will be the adults who manage and move with and for transnational capital flows, and those for whom such movement is a struggle, a luxury, or a dream" (Croissant, 1998, p. 292). The possibility that the child is a compatible evolutionary mate with a digital monster reflects the design of each in the mould of the other. In other words, the child is explained as the machine that is designed with the child in mind.

The evolutionary theme in *Digimon* introduces children to a range of cybernetic and AI issues. In particular from one *Digimon* series to the next the link between the child and the digimon is seemingly more complex. As fantastic as this biomerge might seem, the plot emphasises that both the child and the machine might benefit from their increasing complex real world relationships. This evolution to human-machine links back to the multiplicity of selves explored above, in which the child is not simply multiple, because it is not simply human (Croissant, 1998). However the thought that technology interwoven with the child leads to a new level of evolution raises some concerns for the connections between adult and child. A 'narrative of evolution' pushes further apart the generations of child and adult (Croissant, 1998). The incessant messages regarding rearing better children through technologies of ergonomic childhood establishes the child's machination as known only to the technicist. Adults no longer assume they understand children. And Rousseau, lamenting the precocious child's opulent technological fetishism, is not a happy philosopher.

In *Digimon*, the artificially-intelligent digimon, were created by adult human programmers who were unaware their creations existed autonomously in the digital dimension. This secret digiworld is populated by evolving digital characters that collaborate with children to save the world. The digimon and the digidestined children build increasingly complex relationships in which the child "owns and controls, mediates and remediates the new modes of representation... in homes and classrooms" (Luke & Luke, 2001, p. 104).

...the future has already arrived, given that there now exists an entire generation of young people who do not know any other way of being than living with technology and the Internet. For children, there exists a seamlessness of life in, out and around technological spaces (Thomas, 2006, p. 126).

The irony here is that product of adult invention authors the distancing of adult from child. The gap between child and adult appears around the toy and the machine, and in particular around the different relationships seen to be had with the machine. While "children were obliged to work, helping parents with baby siblings and doing the housework that mothers had no time for" (Cross, 1997, p. 13) the gaps between child and adult were quite different to those when in the 90s the child's time was not taken with chores, but with engaging with technologies that children would then teach adults about (Turkle, 1996). Here "adults have become outsiders to kids' insider know-how, their exclusive community anti-languages, symbol systems, and frames of reference" (Luke & Luke, 2001, p. 103).

An interesting rhetorical inversion has been put in place. With the emergence of new youth competence and practice, the key educational question has shifted from incompetence, malpractice and disengagement with communications technologies viewed as a sign of educational deficit, to its photo negative: technological competence, practice and engagement as a sign of deficit (Luke & Luke, 2001, p. 103).

Parents are in a position where they must buy and maintain and update these technologies because of their own sense of obligation to the rhetoric of progress. It is unsettling perhaps to think of certain phenomena turned on their head, the ideas that children might be more experienced than adults, that artificial technologies can elicit emotional and meaningful relationships, that virtual social networks can satisfy needs for intimacy and interconnectedness, or the idea that toys and games might be more educationally educational than textbooks and teacher instruction. These unsettlements are only unsettling if we need the world to be the right way up and the gaps to be in the right place.

The idea that there is a divide between child and adult does not fit with the paradigm of seamlessness, whether thought of educationally (be educatable throughout life) or technologically (be able to apply certain technological behaviours to all spheres of life). In a seamless world gaps should not be appearing. However the secret lives of children continue to be important to both children and adults (Cross, 2004; van Manen & Levering, 1996). They are important to adults because some spheres of the adult world are not considered appropriate for children. It is better for a child to be engaged in fantasy play, it follows, than in consumer activity. So when fantasy play and economic behaviour synthesise further problems occur in delimiting the gaps between the child and the adult. In other words, children are now occupying a consumer status considered appropriate only to adults in certain communities (Cross, 1997). Shows like *Digimon* continue to push these boundaries. The show's connections of television, toy, card game, personal computer, and the Internet present to the child a consumable multiple media package. Hence the genealogy for a 21st century multi-media corporate toy paradigm is evident in *Digimon*.

Meanwhile adults who have a passion for the in-between are marginal adults; adults who are still children. Think for instance of the many TV characters who exist in this in-between terrain: the Comic Store guy in *The Simpsons*, the geeky geniuses in *The Big Bang Theory*, and the inept dad from *Modern Family*. Adults who attempt to be children resist "giving up their toys" (Cross, 2004, p. 160); such resistances go on in the gap between adult and child. In order to become an adult one must give up the capacity to navigate the gap between adult and child. Reminiscent of C.S. Lewis' *Narnia* chronicles, it appears that entering adulthood disables the capacity to participate in alternate dimensions.

Cross (2004) identifies a romantic and traditional image of the child as being, and requiring, a simple world, and that the complexity of the adult world should be kept at bay. However, it is now adult worlds that seem simple as they peer into what appears to be the complex world of children in order to make some sense of it. From opposite sides of the gap, the other appears alien (Luke & Luke, 2001). However the occupation of bridge building may not be necessary.

In a techno paradigm some adults see a critical response to the simplicity and destructiveness of modernity, an "emergence of different life pathways, different forms of identity and skills" (Luke & Luke, 2001, p. 95). Is such life experience accessible and/or understandable to an old world order? Can the adult resist perpetuation of a fear of youth:

The spectre of unruly, uncivil youth has a long and undistinguished history, one that enables us to anticipate the uses and abuses of 'crisis' that accompany changes in communications media (Luke & Luke, 2001, p. 99).

Fear of the generation gap is amusing, in that the gap is a construction. Generating generations fits well with technologies of the social sciences through which social groups are constructed and used as labels to govern individuals and groups, whether that governing be in the form of state surveillance, or economic exploitation. In terms of the former, generation X was a suggestion that computer kids were alienated generation, while in the latter, the MTV generation were victims of popular culture (Luke & Luke, 2001).

This is not to suggest that there is nothing new to the digikid, but to suggest that the kind of evolutionary addiction that we have, to think that the kids of cyberspace are more complex, is a product not of their complexity but of our forgetfulness, a forgetfulness which established itself in the toys of years gone. For instance, if we believe that we had more control over children watching television, or playing monopoly than we do with the child on the Internet, then we forget a time of initial fear.

Surveilling and securing the parameters of childhood and adolescence is an ongoing historical battle. Each generational wave of adult anxieties and protest about the next generation's declining moral, cultural, or literacy 'standards' is based on adult experience and romanticized reminiscences of their own youth and schooling in a previous and often mythologicized golden age (Luke & Luke, 2001, p. 105).

Perhaps the most optimistic response to this apparent syndrome (one which might in itself define adulthood) is to resist the communication-technology gap as evidence of a Modern narrative crisis. Jean-Francois Lyotard (1999) observed in certain new configurations of information the conditions of postmodernity. One aspect of his analysis was the development of a crisis in predominating narratives. These narratives secure margins between adults and children – in the safety of knowing that adults are defined by their knowing, whereas children are defined by their ignorance. As the information age has taken hold of our consciousness, we can no longer have such security. This is not to suggest that things were ever more secure, but that they were known by some as more secure, while others were seen to be judged by their failure to know. Inspired by Nietzsche, Lyotard and others have ventured that this security was merely imagined, no less important in its imaginariness, but imagined all the same.

Children of the information age are then not children as adults know them, and adults by extensions cannot be adults in a familiar oppositional relationship. However, while in postmodernity new organisations of life pathways might exist (Luke & Luke, 2001), this should not be read to mean that old life pathways were stable, but rather that they were interpreted as stable within certain traditions.

When considering the history of the toy the role of adults in narrating the story evidences these traditions and the binaries that helped make them meaningful. Education and play, artificial and real, natural and technological, adult and child: all productive binaries that have helped to make sense of the world, yet at the same time they have served to limit this making sense, and to marginalise some senses.

IMPLICATIONS AND FUTURE TRENDS

Takato is late for school, he stands in the empty corridor outside his class and sighs...

Mrs Sagi: I heard that, you know the rules, if you show up late, you'll have to wait.

Takato: Who me? (the class laughs)... I'm sorry I'm late Mrs Sagi.

Takato grabs some paper and a pencil and sits down in the corridor. Sometime later he is allowed in class.

Mrs Sagi: Now I want you all to pay close attention, this is going to be on your test.

Takato begins to draw a digimon character, talking to himself...

Takato: Yeah that works, red is definitely a power color. I'll give him the strongest attack ever; no-one will ever expect that, especially from a rookie. I'm going to make him even better than Agumon. I'll call it Pyrosphere.

Mrs Sagi: Are you designing a Halloween costume?

Takato:Huh? No, it's a digimon, don't you know anything?

Mrs Sagi: Well Takato, despite your apology you certainly don't seem very sorry about being late do you.

Takato: Ahhh, yes, I mean no, ma'am, actually I do mean yes, I mean I'm sorry, I'm really sorry (the children laugh again).

The bell goes and Takato is left in the class alone while the other children play outside, Takato is still designing and naming the digimon that will later become Guilmon.

In the *Digimon* show school is generally (not exclusively) a place where otherwise brilliant and capable children dwell in a confused and unhappy state. Learning at school cannot compete with its digital world variant. Luke and Luke (2001) highlight this embarrassing educational phenomenon: schools are ill-prepared for an ICT-rich curriculum in terms of resources, teacher knowledge, pedagogy, and arguably in the eyes of the student. Even more embarrassing for adults is the evidence that children don't seem to need schools in order to succeed technologically. Visions of a future in which children download their education in their own time are not too distant as visions.

Freed from the adult constraints of school, children of the *Digimon* era see communication and generation differently. For these children the communication and generation gaps refers to a kind of epoch, in or part of a more-or-less particular time, or in a particular context, that is familiar, yet alien. The technological complexity of the child's cyber learning world troubles the meaning of being a learner and/or a teacher. Should the child be freed from school?

The concern for some commentators is the possibility that school is necessary to ensure that a critical attitude towards particular, generally new, technologies is promoted. A critical attitude is a 'healthy' attitude (Falbel, 1991) rather than a negative one. In other words, it is not healthy to dismiss new technologies simply because they appear to disturb certain generational truths.

One critical position, discussed in the previous section, is to think differently about adulthood and childhood. Taking this idea further, critique might productively engage with the very gap that artificially separates the child from the adult. To think differently about the gap is to consider that generations do not generate; it is the gap that generates. A gap draws together and pushes apart. In other words, where the gap is drawn, we find difference. The gap reveals ways of thinking and being in the sense that technological phenomena and technology in general, are related to human conditions and purposes. For instance, a will to exploit the world through technology is one such condition and purpose (Heidegger, 1977).

A third critical position involves the connection of culture to the study of new technological life worlds. For instance, observing variances in the way children perceive aliveness locates the child and the observer in a cultural and historical context. Cultures define and respond to technology differently. One difference is the valorisation of technological success, and the great lengths individuals will go to in order to be identified and immortalised in relation to technological innovation. This tendency exhibits itself in societal terms through the regard that nations have for their own technological development as compared to that of other nations. Is it possible that some cultures do not a) regard invention as the mother of all good, and b) the result of individual enterprise? Fleer (1999) traces recent critique of Eurocentric thinking about technology and progress such that international power relations are explained and legitimated in narrow technological terms.

As educators we need to foster respect for the multiple ways people have developed solutions to problems. The focus must be on cultural similarities and shared needs. As educators we must move away from using examples from the poor majority ... to the over consumption of the rich minority (Fleer, 1999, p, 11).

The potential of this current analysis is to destabilise certain predominant ways of thinking about education, technology, humanity so as to be open to, and welcoming of, other constructions. In this sense technology in a postmodern world opens up a valuing of difference. Adults, teachers in particular, might experience some sense of freeing if they dive into the gap in which there is no adult or child.

Freeing us from having a total fixed identity so that we may experience ourselves as multiple identities disclosing multiple worlds is what Heidegger calls technology's saving power (Dreyfus & Spinosa 2002, p. 189).

A prediction for the future then (one that might prepare us for the arrival of the alien other): the ways in which children perceive the communication-generation gaps around them will in some way be determined by the way in which childhood continues to exist as a metaphor for a generation. Will that generation assist the robot in a quest to become real? Or would Tai, or Takato, or Takuya say to the Koromons and Guilmons, the Pinocchios of the future: 'the boundaries between real and artificial are themselves artificial, you are no more or less a real boy than I' (Ghiraldelli, 2002).

CONCLUSION

Fifty years ago, when Piaget was formulating his theories, a child's world was full of things that could be understood in simply, mechanical ways (Turkle, 1998, p. 317).

To suggest that in previous generations the world was 'more simple' is particularly narrow in scope and context. This chapter has explored the complexity of the toy, and of the toys contemporary troubling of adulthood and adulthood and has regarded the latest hi-tech shows as productive in supporting such exploration of a set of binary oppositions. However, while the text above has played around with the 21st century narratives of *Digimon*, the endgame is one of questioning not just adulthood and childhood, but also simplicity and complexity. The predominant themes could have been equally as evocative supported by A.A. Milne (2007, pp. 104-105):

Christopher Robin came down from the Forest to the bridge, feeling all sunny and careless, and just as if twice nineteen didn't matter a bit, as it didn't on such a happy afternoon, and he thought that if he stood on the bottom rail of the bridge, and leant over, and watched the river slipping slowly beneath him, then he would suddenly know everything that there was to be known, and he would be able to tell Pooh, who wasn't quite sure about some of it. But when he got to the bridge and saw all the animals there, then he knew that it wasn't that kind of afternoon, but the other kind, when you wanted to do something.

'It's like this, Christopher Robin,' began Rabbit. 'Tigger – '

In Digimon the partners in the game should not be regarded as complex on the basis that we conveniently interpret Pooh, Christopher Robins and the game of Poohsticks as engaged in simplistic relationships. This would be a reinterpretation on the basis that technology and the child's world has somehow got more complex. But the criterion that determines one thing as more complex than another has been predetermined. The winner might always be the digital monster if measured in a digital paradigm. Winnie the Pooh won't fight at any rate, as he is far more interested in a contemplative existence. But wait, in Winnie's contemplation, the unitary wholeness of the self is revealed as myth. So too then is the cyborg alternation a myth, and Winnie the Pooh is just as complex a player as Koromon.

Reflecting on Bridging the Communication-Generation Gap Through an Analysis of the Child's Play with Hi-Tech Toys

This section gives you some questions and activities to help you think about how you can use some of the ideas from this chapter in your work.

Research

1. Conduct a chronological stock take of the resources that your early childhood education centre provides for children.
2. Consider the use of the 'old' and the 'new' resources and, in particular, the ways in which the children engage with resources.
3. Observe the interests of children and extend upon these interests through questions about 'intention' and 'design'.
4. Listen to the languages that children use to describe and relate to toys.

Reflect

1. Create your own 'toy story' – a genealogy of your toys – and reflect on how this story has shaped your values and beliefs regarding play and education.
2. Gather information on the television shows that children are interested in and take the time to watch these shows and the ways in which technology is presented to the viewer.
3. Have a discussion with your colleagues about what it means to be an adult and/or a child, considering for instance how our beliefs regarding adulthood and childhood shape our aspirations for children.
4. Examine your feelings about technology and the factors/people that have shaped the way you perceive yourself in relation to technology.

Practice

1. Research in your community for individuals and groups that collect, restore and recycle technologies and invite them to your centre and/or organize a trip. Ask them to talk about why they collect, restore and recycle.
2. Draw upon your knowledge of the individual and collective interests of the children and families to prepare an activity centre that promotes concepts of real, natural, artificial, alive, mechanic, and more (perhaps start with a germinating pea and a virtual pet).

REFERENCES

Ariès, P. (1962). *Centuries of childhood* (Baldick, R., Trans.). London, UK: Jonathan Cape.

Bandura, A. (2001). Social cognitive theory and mass communication. *Media Psychology*, *3*, 265–299. doi:10.1207/S1532785XMEP0303_03

Croissant, J. (1998). Growing up cyborg: Development stories for postmodern children. In Davis-Floyd, R., & Dumit, J. (Eds.), *Cyborg babies: From techno-sex to techno-tots* (pp. 285–298). New York, NY: Routledge.

Cross, G. (1997). *Kids' stuff: Toys and the changing world of American childhood*. Cambridge, MA: Harvard University Press.

Cross, G. (2004). *The cute and cool: Wondrous innocence and modern American children's culture*. New York, NY: Oxford University Press.

Davis-Floyd, R., & Dumit, J. (1998). *Cyborg babies: From techno-sex to techno-tots*. New York, NY: Routledge.

Dreyfus, H. L., & Spinosa, C. (2002). Highway bridges and feasts: Heidegger and Borgmann on how to affirm technology. In Dreyfus, H., & Wrathall, M. (Eds.), *Heidegger re-examined: Art, poetry and technology* (*Vol. III*, pp. 175–193). New York, NY: Routledge.

Ellul, J. (1964). *The technological society* (Wilkinson, J., Trans.). New York, NY: Vintage Books.

Falbel, A. (1991). The computer as a convivial tool. In Harel, I., & Papert, S. (Eds.), *Constructionism* (pp. 29–37). New Jersey: Ablex Publishing.

Fleer, M. (1999). *Technology for children: Developing your own approach*. Sydney, Australia: Prentice Hall.

Fleer, M. (2001). *Science for children: Developing a personal approach to teaching*. Frenchs Forest, New South Wales, Australia: Pearson.

Froebel, F. (1886). *Autobiography of Friedrich Froebel* (Michaelis, E., & Moore, H. K., Trans.). London, England: Swan, Sonneschein and Co.

Gebhardt-Seele, P. G. (1985). *The computer and the child: A Montessori approach*. Rockville, MD: Computer Science Press.

Gee, J. P. (2005). Learning by design: Good video games as learning machines. *E-learning*, *2*(1), 5–16. doi:10.2304/elea.2005.2.1.5

Ghiraldelli, P. Jr. (2000). The fundamentals of Gepeto's philosophy of education: Neopragmatism and infancy in the postmodern world. *Educational Philosophy and Theory*, *32*(2), 201–207. doi:10.1111/j.1469-5812.2000.tb00444.x

Gibbons, A. N. (2007). *The matrix ate my baby*. Amsterdam, The Netherlands: Sense Publishers.

Gough, N. (2004). RhizomANTically becoming-cyborg: Performing posthuman pedagogies. *Educational Philosophy and Theory*, *46*(3), 253–265. doi:10.1111/j.1469-5812.2004.00066.x

Heidegger, M. (1977). The question concerning technology. In Heidegger, M. (Ed.), *The question concerning technology and other essays* (pp. 1–49). (Lovitt, W., Trans.). New York, NY: Harper & Row.

In-Stat. (2008). *Continued growth in the worldwide market for portable, electronic based edutainment toys* (Report No. IN0804073ID) Retrieved from http://instat.com/ newmk.asp

Kafai, Y., & Harel, I. (1991). Children learning through consulting: When mathematical ideas, knowledge of programming and design, and playful discourse are intertwined. In Harel, I., & Papert, S. (Eds.), *Constructionism* (pp. 111–140). New Jersey: Ablex Publishing.

Kahn, P. H., Jr., Friedman, B., Perez-Granados, D. R., & Freier, N. G. (2004). *Robotic pets in the lives of preschool children*. CHI, 24-29 April, Vienna, Austria, (pp. 1449-1452).

Keesing-Styles, L. (2002). A critical pedagogy of early childhood education: The Aotearoa/New Zealand context. *New Zealand Research in Early Childhood Education*, *5*, 109–121.

Lankshear, C., Peters, M. A., & Knobel, M. (1996). Critical pedagogy and cyberspace. In Giroux, H., Lankshear, C., McLaren, P., & Peters, M. A. (Eds.), *Counternarratives: Cultural studies and critical pedagogies in postmodern spaces* (pp. 149–188). New York, NY: Routledge.

Lind, K. K. (2005). *Exploring science in early childhood* (4th ed.). Clifton Park, NY: Thomson Delmar Learning.

Luke, A., & Luke, C. (2001). Adolescence lost/childhood regained: On early intervention and the emergence of the techno-subject. *Journal of Early Childhood Literacy*, *1*(1), 91–120. doi:10.1177/14687984010011005

Luke, C. (1999). What next? Toddler netizens, Playstation thumb, techno-literacies. *Contemporary Issues in Early Childhood*, *1*(1), 95–100. doi:10.2304/ciec.2000.1.1.10

Lyotard, J.-F. (1999). *The postmodern condition: A report on knowledge* (Bennington, G., & Massumi, B., Trans.). Minneapolis, MN: University of Minnesota Press.

Marsh, J. (2002). Electronic toys: Why should we be concerned? A response to Levin & Rosenquest (2001). *Contemporary Issues in Early Childhood*, *3*(1), 132–138. doi:10.2304/ciec.2002.3.1.3

May, J. (2010). *James May's toy stories*. London, England: Conway Publishing.

Milne, A. A. (2007). *The house at Pooh Corner*. London, England: Egmont.

Papert, S. (1991a). Perestroika and epistemological politics. In Harel, I., & Papert, S. (Eds.), *Constructionism* (pp. 13–28). New Jersey: Ablex Publishing.

Papert, S. (1991b). Situating constructionism. In Harel, I., & Papert, S. (Eds.), *Constructionism* (pp. 1–12). New Jersey: Ablex Publishing.

Papert, S. (1993). *The children's machine: Rethinking school in the age of the computer*. New York, NY: BasicBooks.

Postman, N. (1994). *Disappearance of childhood*. New York, NY: Vintage Books.

Resnick, M., & Ocko, S. (1991). LEGO/Logo: Learning through and about design. In Harel, I., & Papert, S. (Eds.), *Constructionism* (pp. 141–150). New Jersey: Ablex Publishing.

Sutton-Smith, B. (1986). *Toys as culture*. New York, NY: Gardener Press.

Sutton-Smith, B. (1997). *The ambiguity of play*. Cambridge, MA: Harvard University Press.

Thomas, A. (2006). MSN was the next big thing after Beanie Babies: Children's virtual experiences as an interface to their identities and their everyday lives. *E-learning*, *3*(2), 126–142. doi:10.2304/elea.2006.3.2.126

Turkle, S. (1996). *Life on the screen: Identity in the age of the Internet*. London, England: Weidenfeld & Nicolson.

Turkle, S. (1998). Cyborg babies and cy-dough-plasm: Ideas about self and life in the culture of simulation. In Davis-Floyd, R., & Dumit, J. (Eds.), *Cyborg babies: From techno-sex to techno-tots* (pp. 317–329). New York, NY: Routledge.

Turkle, S. (2005). *The second self: Computers and the human spirit*. Cambridge, MA: MIT Press.

Van Manen, M., & Levering, B. (1996). *Childhood's secrets: Intimacy, privacy, and the self reconsidered*. New York, NY: Teachers College Press.

Weigel, M., James, C., & Gardner, H. (2009). Learning: Peering backward and looking forward in the digital era. *International Journal of Learning and Media*, *1*(1), 1–18. doi:10.1162/ijlm.2009.0005

Wilensky, U. (1991). Abstract meditations on the concrete and concrete implications for mathematics education. In Harel, I., & Papert, S. (Eds.), *Constructionism* (pp. 193–203). New Jersey: Ablex Publishing.

Chapter 2
Enculturation of Young Children and Technology

Alexandru Spatariu
Georgetown College, USA

Andrea Peach
Georgetown College, USA

Susan Bell
Georgetown College, USA

ABSTRACT

Children are exposed to technology in many ways. As technology use in informal settings like the home, the community, the library, the zoos, and museums increases, children are exposed to a variety of applications and technology availability. Each generation of children come to early childhood programs with increasingly different experiences and exposure to technology. Technology has become a strong cultural influence in the lives of children, and we need to explore and think about how this will impact development and learning.

INTRODUCTION: ENCULTURATION ENVIRONMENTS IN TECHNOLOGY

Enculturation is "the process by which an individual learns the traditional content of a culture and assimilates its practices and values" (Meriam-Webster, 2010). But, in this technological world, the content and tools used by the traditional culture are changing at a staggering rate. Just think about it. We live in a world where we now use our phones to send texts instead of talking on them, where we 'TiVo' instead of watching live television shows (or, we watch the shows on our computers), where we can instantly access and read books and newspapers on portable e-book readers and 'tablets', and where young children

DOI: 10.4018/978-1-61350-059-0.ch002

Copyright © 2012, IGI Global. Copying or distributing in print or electronic forms without written permission of IGI Global is prohibited.

play with robotic pets and toys. By the time the 'traditional' culture adopts one of these new technology tools, the tools change.

Although teachers and parents may only think of computers when hearing the word 'technology', most young children today are growing up in an environment abundant with technology of all kinds. So, for this chapter, we will broaden the definition of technology to encompass more than just computers. Plowman & Stephen (2003), for example, discussed information and communications technologies (ICT) that not only covered computers, but also computer-related devices (e.g., musical keyboards, recorders, electronic toys, and even remote controls). Because of the convergence of computers and media, we have also included in this definition of technology computer-based portable devices, such as video game consoles (both hand-held and larger), mobile media devices (such as the Apple iPod and other MP3 players and PDAs, both with and without video capabilities), and e-book devices (such as the Apple iPad, Amazon Kindle, and other e-readers). Non-interactive television will not be discussed in terms of the use of technology, however it should be mentioned that young children may be influenced in their use of technology through what they view on television and other screen-based media (Rideout, Vandewater, & Wartella, 2003). Computers, cell phones, video games, music players, computer-based animation, 3d movies and other mobile or fixed technologies are available everywhere from people's homes to stores, restaurants, and school classrooms; therefore we will discuss enculturation of young children and technology as it relates to these types of devices.

The National Center for Education Statistics (2003) conducted an early childhood longitudinal study on computer access at home and at school. Results indicate that in only one year, from 1999 to 2000, Internet access increased from 49% to 60% for home access and from 75% to 92% for school and classroom access. Considering the rapid development and decrease in cost of technology we can foresee that, within the 10 years that have passed since this survey was conducted, virtually every home and classroom in the United States has computer and other types of technology access for regular use.

As the availability of computers, Internet connections, and various types of software has increased tremendously inside and outside the classroom setting, parents and teachers in all grade levels seek to use and integrate these new technologies to improve students' learning. Thus, since this media / technology use increases with the age of the child (Lee, Bartolic & Vandewater, 2009; Roberts & Foehr, 2008), the main issue with existing technology becomes the developmental appropriateness of how it is used by children of different age and grade levels (Haugland, 2000).

The chapter is divided into three main discussion sections. The first section discusses various types of technology used by children in non-school settings. Parental issues and developmental considerations are included to give the reader a more comprehensive understanding of how the digital age touches all parts of children's lives. The second section examines the use of technologies with young children from a developmental perspective. We also address concerns with the uses of these technologies in relationship to teaching and learning. We hope to dispel some of the technology myths that teachers of young children have about technology and learning in the early childhood classroom. The concept of the digital divide is addressed in this section as well. The last section of this chapter discusses technology evaluation issues and concrete use of technology by educators of young children.

Objectives

While technology is experienced by all age groups in different ways, the goal of this chapter is to address young children from birth to 8 years of age. After reading this chapter the reader should develop a better understanding of:

- What types of exposure to technology do young children experience in the early home setting
- What the implications for early development and learning are through exposure to technology
- What the best practices for teachers and parents are for technology and with young children
- How children are enculturated through technology in formal and informal settings

BACKGROUND: YOUNG CHILDREN'S EXPOSURE TO TECHNOLOGY IN THE HOME AND OTHER NON-SCHOOL SETTINGS

Children are exposed to technology in many ways. As technology use in informal settings like the home, the community, the library, the zoos and museums increases children are exposed to a variety of applications and technology availability. Each generation of children come to early childhood programs with increasingly different experiences and exposure to technology. Technology has become a strong cultural influence in the lives of children and this enculturation process changes the images of childhood.

Home and Non-School Related Computing

Children are exposed to technology in the home from the time they are born. In a study reported by Vandewater and others (2007), 78% of homes with young children had computers and 69% had Internet access. In addition, one half of the surveyed households had a video game console and between one-fifth (0-2 year olds) and one-third (5-6 year olds) had access to a hand-held video game (Vandewater et al., 2007). Not surprisingly, children spend more uninterrupted time on computers at home rather than at school (Plowman & Stephen, 2003).

Children under the age of 2 do not use computers as much as children from the age of 3 to 6. Only five percent of children under 2 years of age have used a computer and only three percent have played video games. When you expand this to include 3-year- olds, 10% of boys and 5% of girls use computers in a typical day, and, when examining the computer use of 4 to 6-year-olds, these numbers increase to 28% of boys and 23% of girls (Rideout & Hamel, 2006). According to Vandewater and others (2007), 27% of 5 to 6- year-olds used computers 50 minutes on average per week. When you include other electronic devices, like cell phones, MP3 / iPods, monitoring devices such as baby monitors and 'Nanny cams', video, image, and audio recording devices (cameras), and other portable media devices (including those found in many cars and other transportation options), an even greater exposure to technology by very young children is evident.

Ubiquitous and Pervasive Computing

"The most profound technologies are those that disappear. They weave themselves into the fabric of everyday life until they are indistinguishable from it" (Weiser, 1991, p.2). First introduced by Mark Weiser, ubiquitous computing refers to the occurrence of computer-like functionality that exists in the absence of traditional computer hardware (Ubiquitous computing, 2010). Essentially, these are computers that exist in everyday objects, "from coffee cups to raincoats to the paint on the walls" (Greenfield, 2006, p. 11). Ubiquitous and pervasive computing is already having an impact on everyday life. For example, think about driving a car. From the built-in computer that optimizes the engine and notifies you if the oil is low, to the stop lights that change depending on how many cars are stopped on the sensor block, computers, while basically invisible to the user, are everywhere and pervasive (Stringer, Halloran, Hornecker, and Fitzpatrick, 2005). Another example includes the fairly recent proliferation of portable hand-held network-enabled computing devices, such as smart phones, personal digital assistants (PDAs), e-book readers, and even some portable music (MP3) players. The educational uses of these devices are of great interest to many researchers. For example, augmented reality instructional environments and games, which utilize the Global Positioning System (GPS) capabilities built into cell phones and other portable devices, have been developed to immerse students in simulated environments which allow them to investigate real-world problems in an artificial world. An example of this use of augmented reality is the Handheld Augmented Reality Project (HARP), which has designed a 'game' that involves the students in an educational simulation, incorporating math and science skills, discovering why 'aliens' have landed on Earth (Hough, 2007). Vint Cerf, one of the early architects of the Internet and now at Google, recently theorized that even socks may someday be connected to the Internet, so that, if one fell behind the washer, it would notify the other sock where it was (Bilton, 2010).

Technology-Based Toys

Another form of ubiquitous computing is found in toys. In recent years, the availability of technology-based toys has exploded. Frazel (2007) mentions some of these toys, including toy cell phones, computer-like devices by Oregon Scientific, Vtech, and Fisher Price, toy calculators, walkie talkies, and PDAs. Since 2007, however, even more sophisticated toys have emerged. The toys listed on the Parent's Choice Awards for 2009 included many toys with electronic / computer components, including digital cameras, a night-vision camcorder, PDA/laptop-type devices that teach spelling, counting, and handwriting, remote-controlled devices, board games with electronic features, and even a robotic 'bug'. Even traditional toys like Legos had kits that were based on a technology / science fiction theme (Parent's Choice Awards, 2009). Other popular toys are paired with websites and computer games. In the near future, toys with 3-D or virtual-reality based interfaces should be available. A promising prototype of these 'future' toys are "Siftables", which are like electronic building blocks. Users can move these small devices around (e.g., "piling, sorting, stacking") in order to interact with computer-based content and media (Sifteo, 2010). Early examples of applications may include games in which the Siftables work with each other or with a computer and even include new ways of writing music (Technology Review, 2010).

Media Convergence

As mentioned earlier, computers are merging traditional media (e.g., books, magazines) with CD-ROMS, websites, smart books, toys, and interactive TV. This is causing distinctions between media to blur. For example, instead of containing text-based stories and photographs, many electronic newspapers, magazines, and books now contain digital video and/or audio content, interactive elements such as games, forms and surveys, and social networking tools like blogs, discussion forums, and links to sites like Facebook and Twitter. Savvy Internet users can even create their own 'mashups' of a variety of electronic resources from different sources to create their own electronic 'newspapers' or 'magazines' (see Feedly.com for an example of a tool to create a mashup of various Internet-based resources).

Children seem to move between these media seamlessly. For example, children's introduction to computer software is often related to TV shows, animated films, or games (Marsh & Thompson 2001). Young children (infancy to age 3 or so) may be exposed to wonderful educational television shows like Sesame Street or Dora the Explorer and then may have the opportunity to play with spin-off toys like the Elmo Live Encore by Fisher

Price, an electronic plush toy that tells stories, sings songs, and has very life-like motions, or a Dora The Explorer 'LeapPad' book by the LeapFrog company that not only reads the story, but also includes interactive activities and games. Older preschoolers and children (ages 3-8) have even more sophisticated choices, including computer-based, console (such as the Nintendo Wii), or handheld (such as the Nintendo DS or Leap-frog systems) educational or non-educational video games based on movie or television characters (for example, Disney characters like Winnie the Pooh, Tinkerbell, and the 'Cars' movie characters), or even video games and videos based on popular toys (such as Barbie and GI Joe). By using educational image and animation software like KidPix (http://www.mackiev.com/kid_pix.html) or Scratch (http://scratch.mit.edu/), children can write and animate their own digital stories based on their favorite media characters. Children can even download pictures from the Internet and use them as the 'wallpaper' for cell phones and download cartoon theme music as ringtones. This phenomenon is similar to what Kinder (1991) refers to as 'trans-media intertextuality', which refers to television, film or videogame spin-offs such as clothing, confectionery, lunch boxes, toys, and magazines.

New Media Technologies

It is also important to understand that new media technologies such as online gaming, texting, and social networking are a central part of young children and young adults' life. Although they could be somewhat viewed by parents as a waste of time, these activities can promote motivation, self-directed learning, socialization and independence (Ito et al., 2008).

Young children with older siblings at home may even be exposed to technology at a higher rate as the older children are already heavily engaged in media use. According to the recent *Generation M2: Media in the Lives of 8- to 18- Year Olds* (Rideout, Foehr, & Roberts, 2010) report by the Kaiser Family Foundation, children from ages 8 to 18 years spend, on average, 1 hour and 13 minutes a day playing video games, 1 hour and 29 minutes using computers, and 2 hours and 31 minutes listening to music or audio, in addition to 4 hours and 29 minutes watching TV. This accounts for almost 7 hours and 38 minutes a day. Many times, these older children are multi-tasking (i.e., watching TV while playing video games and texting friends).

Likewise, young parents are influencing young children with their use of media and technology. For example, the Video Consumer Mapping Study (2009) found that young adults ages 18 to 34 (a group typically represented by today's parents of young children) spend an average of 163.0 minutes using computers, 19.9 minutes per day playing video games, and using mobile technologies an average of 33.4 minutes *(Video Consumer Mapping Study*, 2009).

As was found within the M2 study, media multitasking was equivalent for all age groups under 55. Additionally, a study conducted by Mandese (2008), reported that more than half of adults rely on at least one web 2.0 platform (a participatory Internet application for information sharing, such as Facebook or Twitter) for regularly communicating with friends, family or colleagues. When you focus on adults ages 18 – 34, the number soars to 85% (Mandese, 2008). While there is a fair amount of research on the influence of parent involvement on the achievement levels of their children (Desimone, 1999; Roberts, Jurgen, & Burchinal, 2005), very little is still known about the parental use of technology and what role that plays in young children's appropriation and engagement with new media.

Home-Based Assistive Technology

Children who have special physical and behavior/learning needs may be exposed to early home-based specific assistive technology. Studies have shown that children under the age of 3 can benefit from assistive technology, ranging from prosthetic hands, to switches for operating toys, power mobility devices, and communications tools. However, even though organizations such as The National Association for the Education of Young Children and The Division for Early Childhood (a division of the Council for Exceptional Children) have set guidelines for using assistive technology with young children, the actual implementation is seemingly low (Galyon-Keramidas & Collins, 2009). The low implementation could be due to a series of factors ranging from lack of funds for equipment to insufficient training.

Educational Uses of Technology by Young Children at Home

Buckingham & Scanlon (2001) refer to the growing 'curricularisation' of learning in the home, as exemplified by the proliferation of broadly educational magazines aimed at the pre-school market. The *Young Children's Access to Computers in the Home and at School in 1999 and 2000* survey (Rathbun, West, & Hausken, 2003) reported that over 85% of children who used computers at home used them for educational purposes. In the study by Rideout & Hamel (2006), 69% of parents reported that using computers helps children's learning. Plowman and Stephen (2003) reported that parents want to buy computer technology that has educational purposes.

The fast advancement of educational-related technology tools and the increase in access to it at home and public places have led to a discrepancy between in and out of school use (Buckingham, 2007; Purcell, 2010). This situation has led to two main education-related issues. First, schools have to deal with a whole new type of student who is technologically skilled and has contact with education beyond the classroom walls (Ito, et al., 2010; Oblinger & Oblinger, 2005; Reingold, 2006). So, educators need to learn new technologies and how to incorporate what students use from home into classroom settings so they can continue the effective and conducive venues that technology brings to learning.

Second, when children are at home, parents have a stronger perception that their children are protected and free from harm. Advancement of technologies has opened up house walls as children can chat with the wrong peers or predators, look up inappropriate or disturbing information, and become very physically inactive or lethargic (Plowman & Stephen, 2003). To combat this potential issue, parents and educators should strive to increase their students' ability to locate pertinent and useful information. It is evident that simply using social networking sites and other Internet-based applications does not guarantee the proper and optimal use of these resources (Campbell, 2010). In addition to making sure Internet savvy children develop proper computer literacy so they can discern valuable from bad information (Barlow, 2010), researchers propose that students need to develop good word processing and presentation skills in order to properly create, format, edit, organize and deliver content (Heinrichs & Lim, 2010). The development of these skills could, and perhaps should, start at home.

Educational Computing Outside Home but not in School Setting

As mentioned previously, children are exposed to technology in many areas outside of the home environment. From riding in a car, shopping in a store, eating at a restaurant, or going to the doctor's office, technology is prevalent throughout everyday life. Other quasi-educational experiences allow the young child to have a more interactive role with the technology. Children's museums, for example, have interactive exhibits that allow young children to play with different aspects of technology. According to Mayfield, (2005), children's museums are "user friendly, interactive, hands-on, attractive, non-threatening and stimulating places designed and developed for children"

(p. 181). These museums, many times, use various forms of technology, including computer kiosks, electronic toys, PDA's, and technology-based simulated environments, to allow children to interact with the exhibits (Mayfield, 2005; Wang et al, 2009). Other education-based activities, like zoos, aquariums, smaller theme-based exhibitions, camps, libraries, and even theme parks, have similar types of technology-based activities designed for preschool children.

Although most current research does not report on the technology access for children outside both the classroom and the home, it may be surmised that some children who do not have such access still may encounter technology either through friends, public spaces such as libraries, exhibits or stores, or through other everyday life settings, and, as such, these children are functioning in a rapidly technologically advancing environment.

Early Child-Care Technology Access

Many young children spend time in non-school related daycare situations, either in a private home, religious- or facility -based child care situation (i.e., church nursery, fitness center childcare, Mother's Day Out program) or a licensed day care facility. According to the U.S. Department of Health and Human Services (2006) 55% of children were cared for in a licensed day care facility, and another 2% in unlicensed facilities (excluding group homes). Many (if not most) of licensed daycare facilities have and use technology-based resources. For example, according to a study by Lynch and Warner (2004), the majority of licensed day care centers in the state of Texas had computers and allowed the children to use them in different ways. Besides computers, the children would, most certainly, be exposed to other technology similar to what they would see at home (i.e., electronic toys and games, media devices). In religious institutions, children will often experience the use of technology in ways not experienced in the home, such as singing to music projected by data projectors, seeing musicians play on electronic musical instruments, and singing with the use of microphones. Going on a 'play date' at a friend's home or visiting with relatives further exposes young children to technology in everyday life.

Parental Guidance of Young Children Using Computers

Parents are many times active participants with their children while using computers. For example, Rideout & Hamel (2006) found that over two-thirds of parents of children from infancy to pre-school age either always or, at least partially, monitor or help their children use the computer. However, 27% of parents reported allowing their young children to use the computer without direct supervision. In addition, while 18% of these young children have been on the Internet looking for child-friendly websites with parental assistance, 10% of young children are not directly supervised while browsing the Internet and parents report that these children have gone to websites by themselves. Setting rules on computer use was reported by 75% of parents whose children use computers (Rideout & Hamel, 2006).

Not surprisingly, computer games are the most popular use of computers by children. Some parents allow their children to play computer games as ways to help them become more familiar with computers and, thus, to be ready for computer use in schools. (Plowman & Stephen, 2003). Cuban (2001) argues that this belief is not based on research but it does drive parental investment of computer use for their children (Sutherland, Facer, Furlong, & Furlong, (2000).

Many researchers caution parents against allowing young children under the age of 3 to use screen-based technology, primarily because the learning styles of young children seemingly do not match the experiences of using computers. (Haugland, 2000). Parents are also concerned about increased levels of computer use (Sutherland et al., 2000). Most concerns of technology use by young children revolve around protecting children online. For example, the National School Boards Foundation (NSBF, 2000) surveyed 1735 households (with children between ages 2-17). Children and parents both view the Internet as a positive influence on their children's lives; however the parents reported concerns about content (i.e., pornography, adult content, hate speech). The Annenberg Public Policy Centre (Turow & Nir, 2000) also found that parents are concerned about privacy issues and Internet use. A study by Gilutz & Nielsen (2002) found that children click on website ads because they misperceive them as web content. This study calls for adults to help teach children about Internet advertising. Other concerns about technology use include vision issues (American Optometric Association, 2010), repetitive strain injuries (Subrahmanyam, Kraut, Greenfield, & Gross, 2000), addiction, increased aggression, or other behavior problems (Hastings, Karas, Winsler, Way, Madigan & Tyler, 2009), and sedentary lifestyles / obesity (Subrahmanyam et al., 2000), but many of these studies tend to focus on older children. Concerns about exposure to violence while using computer software, even software designed for educational computer use, is mentioned as well. Haugland (2000) even specifies the KidPix software program and how the interface allows children to 'blow up' objects that the children want to erase.

Others fear that use of technology will result in less human (parent / teacher) – child interaction, less chance for playing in the 'real world', and more of an emphasis on academics rather than on social development. (Cordes & Miller, 2000). However, Clements & Sarama (2003) refute these claims and discuss research that shows the positive effects of using computers with children, even young children. While much of this research was published prior to 1999, the evidence shows not only academic, but also socio-emotional, effects of using technology. Later studies have shown that media use (including computer-based media) had no relation to time spent playing outside or reading (Vandewater et al., 2007). Studies reflecting the broad-based developmental benefits of children's use of technology will be specifically addressed later in this section.

Parents can take some steps to ensure proper use of technology. While at home, parents can ask the children questions about the software they are using and games they are playing. The parents can also make sure that their children get plenty of physical activity in place of computer, game, or television time. Also, by introducing their children to rich educational technologies and allowing opportunities for other siblings and friends to use these technologies, parents can have a great impact on future educational experiences (PBS Parents, 2010).

A potential issue of parents interacting with children when it comes to new media is the inability of the parent to relate to the media and understand their children's social, communication, and gaming needs and actions. Simply instituting restrictions and barriers will not solve the problem. It is more advisable to keep in touch with the technology, the ways of communication, and the Internet culture as a whole. Knowing this type of information allows for a better understanding of children's electronic whereabouts and permits parents to protect their children from harm in a very informed manner (Ito et al., 2010).

Technology and Unstructured Play

Unstructured, exploratory play has been deemed critical for the development of school readiness skills such as self-regulation, representational or symbolic thought, memory (Li & Atkins, 2004; Ritchie, Maxwell, & Bredekamp, 2009) and creativity (Howard-Jones, Taylor, & Sutton, 2002). Research has shown that game playing is also characteristic of young adults where motivation and participation was connected to gender, engagement, and hours of time spent playing. Gaming was reported to be relaxing, cognitively challenging, and socially engaging (Hoffman & Nadelson, 2009; Schrader, & McCreery, 2007). It appears that young people use online media as an excellent means to connect and make friends, explore personal interests, join social groups, advertise personal music and art, and build projects as well as engage in learning activities based on their own interests that are not common within mainstream educational institutions (Ito et al., 2008).

Only 3% of children under the age of 2 have played a video game. However, by age 3, the percent of video game use increases to 15% of boys and 10% of girls. Not surprisingly, these figures increase to 64% of boys and 48% of girls when looking at children from 4 to 6-years-old (Rideout & Hamel, 2006). It may be that this increase is connected with advanced development which takes place at this age, and allows for higher levels of engagement, motivation, challenge, and social interaction that games usually provide.

As seen above, boys are nearly twice more likely to play video games than are girls (Bickham et al., 2003; Rideout & Hamel, 2006). Play during early childhood is remarkably gender-segregated (Fabes, Martin, & Hanish, 2004). Decades of research studies have defined gender differences in friendship group composition and play style, with girls preferring small, intimate, cooperative play activities, and boys engaging in competitive, active play in larger same-gender groupings (Weinberger & Stein, 2008). Gender preferences for on-line and other technology-based activities follow predictable patterns. Girls communicate to connect while boys compete to dominate. Thus, boys would be expected to exhibit a preference for the primarily competitive activity of video game playing.

It has been observed frequently that one of the most powerful aspects of technology is the level of sustained engagement it compels. In a review of video gaming in particular, Miller and Robertson (2010) identify several motivational factors including: a) the experience of being "in the zone" or having one's attention totally absorbed in the activity, b) the improvements in confidence or increased self-esteem that accompany mastery of learning or performance goals, and c) the sense of participating in a culturally valued activity (i.e., gaining expertise in computer games).

EARLY CHILDHOOD EDUCATIONAL DEVELOPMENT AND TECHNOLOGY

In this next section, we will delve more into these developmental milestones and how they can help both parents and educators use technology more effectively with young children. We will also discuss how other factors, such as the digital divide and cultural factors can influence the optimal use of technology with young children.

Technology Impact on Development and Learning

Early childhood curricula and instruction is rooted in the theoretical models of Piaget (1952) and Vygotsky (1978). Piaget's cognitive developmental model proposes that children's thinking and reasoning gradually matures through a series of stages from infancy to adulthood. As part of this maturation process, children take an active role in constructing their own knowledge from interactions with people and objects in the classroom environment. Children construct schemas or mental representations of their experiences. As they come into contact with information relevant to a particular concept (e.g., fish), they assimilate it, enriching their knowledge base (e.g., different colors or sizes of fish; fish that live in salt or freshwater environments). Another Piagetian cognitive process, accommodation, occurs when the child encounters an experience that doesn't quite fit an existing schema. (For example, when the child views information about dolphins, a new schema must be constructed; a category must be created for mammals that live in the water but are not fish.) Technology-based activities can expand the breadth and depth of experiences, prompting both assimilation and accommodation on a variety of topics.

As children progress through successive cognitive developmental stages, Piaget hypothesizes that thought processes become increasingly rule-governed and complex. During the sensorimotor stage, infants struggle to orient toward sensory input (i.e., sights, sounds, smells, tastes. or tactile sensations) and eventually to coordinate motor responses to control their occurrence. Many of the computerized toys marketed to parents of infants provide multi-sensory stimulation from the slightest of movements. The intent is to capture the baby's interest and facilitate mastery of cause-effect linkages. Object permanence is a major accomplishment of this stage. As the child understands that objects continue to exist out of sensory awareness, the infant begins to enjoy toys that incorporate "seek and find" or "peek-a boo" elements.

Toward the end of the sensorimotor stage and the beginning of the preoperational stage, toddlers use words, pictures or play to symbolize or represent objects or events. It is usually at this age that children first benefit from interaction with computerized books or games. The preoperational child's strong interest in fantasy and egocentric point of view are apparent and influence preferences for technology-based activities that are highly engaging. Rules must be simple and provide obvious and immediate consequences.

Moving into the next stage, concrete operations, the child becomes increasingly capable of logical, rule-governed play. Activities that require classifying, ordering, or otherwise arranging objects are of interest. Children become increasingly proficient at computer games that involve cooperation, perspective taking, and/or competition.

The constructivist model emphasizes the critical role of teacher collaboration in children's learning (Hong & Trepanier-Street, 2004). Vygotskian theory (1978) discusses the importance of identifying the zone of proximal development (ZPD) for each individual child. The ZPD is the point at which a child can accomplish a task with cues and/or guidance, but is incapable of independent functioning. A closely related concept, scaffolding, involves the role of the skilled peer or teacher who gradually supports the inexperienced child in his or her efforts at understanding and mastery of some concept or task. In many early childhood classrooms, technology use is changing the nature of child-directed learning activities and the role of teacher scaffolding of that process. In the next section, we discuss the importance of adult scaffolding of technology-related activities in early childhood.

From another theoretical perspective, cognitive psychologists examine the maturation of children's cognitive skills over time. As one example, memory capacity (i.e., the number of separate items or events that the child can hold in memory simultaneously or the ability to follow multi-step directions), speed and space for processing (i.e., how much information the child can process in a given period of time), strategy use (i.e., for young children, the internalization of rules and routines), knowledge base (i.e., factual and procedural information), and metamemory (i.e., monitoring and improving the memory system) gradually improve with chronological age (Barry, 2006). Choices for child technology use should reflect an understanding of this cognitive maturation process, ensuring a match between cognitive capability and task demand.

A special issue of the journal *Developmental Psychology* focused on the developmental impact of technology and Internet use on young children and adolescents. In an introduction to the series, Greenfield and Yan (2006) described the Internet as a toolkit with a myriad of applications, each of which could be used for good or ill. As mentioned earlier, despite early concerns over potential academic, social, or physical harm, evidence is mounting for skill enhancement in such areas as planning, resource location, critical evaluation of information, and visual memory (Subrahmanyam, et al., 2000; Tarpley, 2001). In a recent study, Johnson (2010) assessed the cognitive skills of children from first through fifth grade and questioned parents about their children's Internet use. Time spent in Internet activities such as online learning, communication, and playing contributed more to variance in cognitive development than family socioeconomic status.

It is recommended that early computer use should be based on the developmental level of the child, and the young child should not be pushed into using computers too soon as technology can damage or hinder the development process (Healy, 1998). In general video-based activities are not seen as effective and instrumental in child development as manipulative objects. However, early exposure may make children more prepared to use computers in subsequent school settings (Haugland, 2000). Technology has advanced so fast that currently there are three- dimensional applications and also manipulative games that can develop visual, motor, and intellectual skills at the same time.

Does this Early Use of Technology in the Home Truly Have a Positive Effect on Learning?

Research supporting early use of computers at home is promising. The use of computers by these children have positive effects on their ability to operate technology, with between 66 and 71% of five- to six-year-olds having the ability to use a mouse (Rideout & Hamel, 2006; Vandewater et al, 2007), 37% being able to load a CD-ROM, and 33% being able to actually to turn on the computer (Rideout & Hamel, 2006).

In addition, Xiaoming, Atkins, and Stanton (2006) indicated that children who used computers with developmentally-appropriate software 15-20 minutes a day outperformed control students in a standard Head Start curriculum on school readiness tests. The students who performed the best were those who used computers both at home and at school. Li and Atkins (2004) found that computer access at home was reported to have a significant positive effect on preschool concepts and cognitive skills (Clements & Sarama, 2003; Li & Atkins, 2004). The positive effects encompassed increased performance on school readiness (Boehm 3 Preschool) and cognitive tests (WPPSI-R) but did not indicate a strong connection to visual motor or gross motor skills.

Plowman (1998) proposed that early computer use could help young children with beginning literacy skills, including being familiar with screen conventions, exhibiting electronic text understanding, researching information, creating electronic text, and evaluating media text sources. For example Lewin (2000) researched the effects of electronic books talking to 5- to 6-year-old children. It appeared that the electronic books can have positive cognitive and affective outcomes. Even younger children can develop word recognition and vocabulary skills with this type of software. However, particular attention needs to be paid to the developmental stage of the child when using new media as it may not be effective unless it adapts or corresponds to particular levels of development. Shilling (1997) researched the use of electronic speech feedback and found out that children with metalinguistic awareness benefited from it and improved word identification and construction while those who were not aware could not perceive the nature of the speech-synthesized feedback.

Facilitation of Knowledge and Skill Development Through Computer Use

Access to developmentally appropriate computer-based activities in the early childhood classroom has resulted in broad developmental gains in study after study. Research has documented differential gains in emergent literacy, fine motor skills, pre-math skills, concept learning, language and vocabulary skills, motor skills, creativity, social and emotional competence, and self-esteem with computer-based learning (Ainsa, 1989; Li & Atkins, 2004; Nikolopoulou 2007; Parette, Hourcade, and Heiple, 2000). In an early study of the impact of technology on developmental progress, Haugland (1992) found that 3- and 4-year-old children who used computers in a Head Start classroom demonstrated significantly greater gains in such diverse domains as problem-solving and memory, language, and motor skills when compared with children in comparable classrooms without such access to technology. Teacher support was an important aspect of this success.

Classroom technology is not limited to computer software. In a later study, Hong and Trepanier-Street (2004) demonstrated the effectiveness of the use of a wide range of technological devices (e.g., digital and video cameras, scanners, and Internet access) to help children represent and organize their individual ideas, communicate with classmates, collaborate on projects, and share their learning with the broader community outside the classroom. A particularly unique aspect of this use of technology was the degree to which parents felt empowered to actively participate in their children's learning. As parents viewed pictures and videos of the process, they increasingly responded with suggestions and hands-on assistance.

Social Skills

An initial concern was that increased use of technology would come at the expense of the child's opportunities for social interaction with adults and peers. However, the number of computers available to children within a given classroom is limited. According to the findings of the Early Childhood Longitudinal Study, the student-to-computer ratio was 8.4 to 1 in Kindergarten and 7. 4 to 1 in first grade classrooms, far from the recommended access of 1 to 4 (Judge, Puckett, & Cabuk, 2004). In many classrooms, then, this means that computer time still presents opportunities for cooperation, turn-taking, sharing, negotiating, and conflict resolution. Yelland's (2005) review of a decade of research on technology use in early childhood classrooms revealed that computers increase children's interest in collaboration on learning tasks and facilitates collaboration with peers.

In a Swedish study of the roles that children take vis-à-vis computer use in the early childhood classroom, Ljung-Djarf (2008) found that children occupy circumscribed positions or roles with regard to group play at the computer. Children were observed and videotaped for 10-12 days over a period of three to four weeks. Researchers identified three specific roles: the owner (i.e., the one in charge of the mouse and/or keyboard and the person in power), the participant (i.e., the one who sits nearby, offering suggestions and support to the owner), and the spectator (i.e., the interested audience with no real influence on the activity, but who occasionally comments or intrudes).

Far from solitary, children's interactions in computer activities, then, are much like play found in any of the less technologically-based centers in the classroom. This approach to computer play may explain why access to technology has been found to support language development, facilitate prosocial behavior (i.e., more skilled children help less experienced peers negotiate the software or children cooperate together to accomplish the goals of the program), and encourage social interaction (Ljung-Djarf, 2008).

Emergent Literacy

Exposure to print, particularly in the form of children's literature, has long been the gold standard for encouraging emergent literacy in young children. Reading during the preschool years, however, now includes interpretations of on-screen symbols in a variety of technologies (Glister, 1997). Making meaning from digital text, including these on-screen symbols and icons, precedes, and later facilitates, children's ability to make sense of print (Levy, 2009). Parette, Boeckmann, & Hourcade (2008) described the promise of a specific software program (Writing with Symbols 2000) in developing such emergent literacy concepts as phonemic awareness, vocabulary, comprehension, and general knowledge about the meaning and use of print. In a follow-up article, Parette, Hourcade, Boeckmann, & Blum (2008), recommended the use of Microsoft PowerPoint software for similar purposes.

Physical Activity

A continuing concern is that increased use of technology inevitably will result in decreased time spent in active, vigorous, and healthful exercise. Recently software developers have addressed this concern with games and activities that are highly interactive and encourage whole body movement (e.g., much of the software associated with games for the Nintendo Wii). Ueoka and Hirose (2008) recently tested a technology to encourage children to learn while sustaining high levels of physical activity. Their play tool, Sound Tag, requires children to wear a device that emits sound feedback to direct children in a game that incorporates elements of traditional tag along with mastery of the sounds of musical instruments. Their research found that preschoolers sustained high levels of voluntary physical activity while operating the radio frequency identification system associated with the Sound Tag game.

Child-Directed Activity

In keeping with constructivist theory, children learn best when they are "in charge" of the learning activity, and engaged in active exploration of a topic. Technology allows children to experiment and express their individual creativity, keeping the focus on the process of learning, not the final product (Nikolopoulou, 2007). This has implications for the types of technology selected for inclusion in the early childhood classroom. Haugland (1992, 1995) cautions against the use of software that has a limited focus on drill and skill practice. She suggests, instead, that software that is designed to be open-ended, allowing a high degree of child creativity and direction, is more beneficial in facilitating developmental gains.

Digital Divide

Digital divide understanding has evolved from its incipient phase of socioeconomic and physical access to technologies to a more complex phase of a) estimating the ratio of available technology per student, b) considering gender, cultural and ethnic barriers, and c) evaluating accessibility by type of technology (Barron, Walter, Martin, &Schatz, 2010; Hargittai, 2010; Judge, Puckett, & Bell, 2006; Robinson & Crenshaw, 2010). A number of studies have examined aspects of economic status and technology access as main contributors to the digital divide. Results of an early childhood longitudinal study (Rathbun, West, & Hausken, 2003) indicated that almost all young kindergarten children had computer access at school. Even though children's access to private or public in-school technologies did not significantly differ, socioeconomic status was still a predictor of technology use, particularly computer use, in the home environment. As children move to first grade and beyond, the digital divide was found to widen, even within the school setting. High poverty schools had less computer and software programs available, creating a major technology access issue (Sharon, Kathleen, & Burcu, 2004). Students with more access to technology at home know how to utilize a broader range of learning resources, and manifest more self-confidence in their technology skills (Barron, Walter, Martin, &Schatz, 2010). Measures have been taken to improve the level of technology access at school for all children (Puma, Chaplin, & Pape, 2003) and although many accomplishments have been made, the digital divide has taken new turns (i.e. gender, culture, generational, and special needs differences) that are currently being explored (Barron, Walter, Martin, &Schatz, 2010; Hutlinder & Johanson, 2000; Robinson & Crenshaw, 2010). It is possible that these new issues emerged as the availability of technology is less of a concern than how people use it. For instance, some games may be more appealing to certain age or social groups than others, or computer software may be more suitable for certain cultural groups, all depending on who creates them, for what purpose and what audience.

A current issue in digital divide at the global level deals not only with socioeconomic status, but also with other demographic characteristics and with conflict processes. Existing research points out differences even among individuals within generations with similar exposure to computer technology. Results of an empirical study of young adults and Internet use show that subjects with comparable access and experiences differ based on higher levels of parental education, being male, and being white or Asian American, characteristics which are, in general, associated with more advanced skills (Hargittai, 2010).

Both internal and external national factors play an important role in the digital divide. These societal aspects have a big impact on Internet access and use in developed as compared with developing countries (Robinson & Crenshaw, 2010). Conflicts and political issues impact the divide and the divide, in turn, contributes to political participation (Sylvester & McGlynn, 2010).

Efforts continue to attempt to diminish the digital divide. One major initiative in technology infusion at the national level has been major governmental grant funding to prepare teachers to use technology (Intime, 2001; Project Thread, 2004; Plowman & Stephen; 2003; PT3, 2002). Many technology projects towards closing the divide also have been developed in special education (Hutlinder & Johanson, 2000) and towards closing generational divide gaps between adults and children (Cruz & Snider, 2009). One can surmise, based on existing empirical research, that the current generations of young children will manifest digital divide differences based on ethnicity, and bias in type of technology use (i.e. software centered towards a certain population or promoting violence). The technology gap can be reduced by educators as well as the game producing companies. Software companies need to pay more attention to research findings and incorporate them in technology applications development. The government, different foundations (i.e. National Science Foundation), charities (i.e. Bill and Melinda Gates foundation) and other organizations have taken important steps in equipping many schools with the latest technologies and training educators in the use of new technologies as well.

Selecting and Incorporating Developmentally Appropriate Software

The last section of the chapter presents educators with guidelines for selecting and incorporating developmentally appropriate software within the early learning environment. Previous technology experiences can be identified by teachers on a case-by-case basis by talking with the student and parents and by observing the student in the school setting. Students with special technology needs can be identified through specific assessments, and recommendations for appropriate technology can be made by special education teachers and related services personnel (e.g., speech or occupational therapists).

As new generations are growing up surrounded by fast evolving tools requiring technology fluency, many educators are expressing a greater need to investigate the use of technology tools and young children (Baker & O'Neil, 2003). The normalcy of technology in children's home lives makes the divide between teachers and students grow, therefore the use of technology in the classroom needs to be expanded to include tools such as Web 2.0, cell phone applications, social networking sites, and other new digital media (Digiovanni, Schwartz & Greer, 2009; Lee & Spires, 2009). Current research on generational differences makes it even more important for us to research and construct developmentally appropriate technology for young children. Currently, our schools have surpassed the millennial generation consisting of people born in between 1982 and 2000 and have moved into the generation z consisting of people born after the year 2001. This new generation is characterized among other things by being protected as children, needing meaningful work, intruding, receiving instant feedback, and craving community (Reeves & Eunjunh Oh, 2008). One can foresee how fast growing technology can both satisfy and exacerbate some of these characteristics that we as educators need to understand and capitalize on. We can use social media as a learning tool by infusing learning tasks and goals, understand the new directions in culture sharing and literacy, and capitalize on peer-based learning by becoming more involved in interest based Internet sites (Ito et al. 2008).

ISSUES, CONTROVERSIES, PROBLEMS

As mentioned earlier, the impression of the role of technology as a tool for early childhood learning and development has not always been positive. The early report, Fool's gold: A critical look at computers in childhood (Cordes & Miller, 2000), expressed fears that an increasing reliance on learning activities involving computers would somehow provide an inferior educational experience. Developmental progress would suffer from decreased interactions with real world objects, and children's social skills would be impacted by participation in increasingly solitary play. This ominous warning of potential harm to cognitive and social development led early childhood educators to proceed with caution in the use of classroom technology until research demonstrated otherwise.

The National Association for the Education for Young Children (NAEYC) developed a position statement on the use of technology in early childhood classrooms (1996). These guidelines described the importance of choosing technology that is a) developmentally, individually and culturally appropriate, b) integrated easily into the classroom curriculum, thereby extending traditional learning activities and materials, c) designed with maximal opportunities for child choice, creativity, and problem-solving, and d) created with no depictions of violence. In addition, the position statement recommends the use of computers and related technology in ways that facilitate cooperation and collaboration between children and their teachers and peers.

Early Childhood Curriculum

There is a general consensus that applications of technology within the early childhood curriculum should: a) be developmentally appropriate, b) foster classroom learning goals and objectives, and c) be integrated as a part of the daily routine across a wide range of classroom activities and ongoing projects (Haugland, 1992; Judge, Puckett, & Cabuk, 2004; Mitchell, 2007; NAEYC, 1996; Nikolopoulou, 2007). In elementary school settings, computer software also should dovetail nicely with the state and district standards for specific curricular areas (Haugland, 1995). Rather than primarily choosing the software for interest and accessibility, and, secondarily assessing the goals and objectives it could address, Haugland recommends the reverse – to first delineate curricular objectives, and then select software specifically designed to meet them.

Most early childhood researchers also emphasize the importance of identifying the curricular themes (e.g., emergent literacy, art, music, science) and preferred child outcomes (e.g., improved language development or mastery of basic concepts) prior to selecting a technological tool directed toward that purpose (Hutinger & Johanson, 2000). Hong and Trepanier-Street (2004) describe the use of a broad range of technology in a Reggio Emilia-inspired early childhood classroom. Well beyond an exclusive focus on the classroom computer time, this program uses a range of technologies to enhance, extend and document learning (e.g., video cameras, scanners, and digital cameras).

Importance of Teacher Scaffolding

In the developmentally appropriate early childhood classroom, technology should never replace opportunities for children to have face-to-face interaction with other children and adults (Mitchell, 2007). As mentioned in the previous section, children typically engage with technology in groups, taking more or less active roles, and negotiating choices. At times, however, teachers must step in to provide assistance for a novel or challenging activity.

Children learn best when teachers provide appropriate levels of assistance in navigating the essential elements of the software, and give feedback on individual child choices. Teachers can play a variety of roles when extending children's learning through technology. These may include guidance (i.e., what to do and how to do it), motivation (i.e., when, how long, and to what end?), scaffolding (i.e., what to do now/ instead), and problem-solving (i.e., whose turn is it? who chooses?) (Haugland, 1999; Schmid, Miodrag, & Di Francesco, 2008). Far from one-way instruction, Hong and Trepanier-Street (2004) found that children frequently identified aspects of classroom software with which the teachers were unfamiliar. In effect, these children were teaching their teachers.

Hutinger and Johanson (2000) summarize the major components of a comprehensive technology system for early childhood. Their Early Childhood Comprehensive Technology System focuses on four discrete areas: teacher training, technology assessment of the individual child (i.e., assessment of how to tailor technology use to the child's skills and needs), curricular integration, and Kindergarten transition activities. While this model focuses primarily on the needs of children with disabilities, it is instructive for the broader early childhood community. It is imperative that teachers receive training in the selection and curricular integration of developmentally appropriate software, and the links between the use of technology tools and children's developmental gains (Haugland, 1999).

Technology Evaluation

A very important consideration in successfully using existing technology with young children is evaluation. The widespread use of computers makes software, website, mobile and other technology evaluation very important for improving student learning. For example, software needs to a) be developmentally appropriate, learner-centered, and capable of adjusting to individual needs, b) support exploration, imagination, interactivity, and problem solving, c) build on prior knowledge, and d) activate visual, auditory, vocal, and kinesthetic senses (Buckleitner, 1999; Geissinger, 1997; NCREL, 2004; NETC, 2005; Schrock, 2010). In addition, educators and parents also must have a clear purpose in mind before deciding on using a particular software (i.e. skill development, content understanding).

Other educators, evaluation websites or organizations, and educational conferences are some of the venues that can provide trustworthy software evaluation. Web sites can be valuable resources for teaching and learning as well. In selecting resources for technology evaluation, the authorship, purpose, recency of information, and appropriateness for the students need to be considered (Schrock, 2010). In order to make informed decisions for technology adoption with children, educational conferences featuring technology papers, posters, or demonstrations can be attended in person or accessed through relevant databases (i.e. Association for the Advancement of Computing in Education). There are also numerous organizations that provide technology evaluations (i.e. software, games) if schools do not have a system in place for it.

FUTURE TRENDS

The Cognition and Technology Group at Vanderbilt (2003) identifies and discusses three main principles about learning and teaching. The first principle is that students bring to class preconceptions about the world and knowledge. Some of this background knowledge involves misinterpretations or inaccurate understandings. Educators need to engage the students' existing knowledge when introducing new information in class, especially if this knowledge is inaccurate, in order to build more complex and solid new meanings (Ormrod, 2009). The second principle is that students need solid factual and conceptual knowledge in order to be able to arrange knowledge for retrieval and application purposes. Good knowledge organization is necessary, not just mere memorization of facts, in order to be able to make meaning and connections. The third principle is that students need to develop and engage metacognitive processes in order to define and achieve learning goals. Processes contributing to meaningful learning include, but are not limited to, domain knowledge, self-efficacy, and knowledge of strategies (Bandura, 1997; Horn, Bruning, Schraw, and Curry, 1993; Hoffman & Spatariu, 2007). Technology can be instrumental in assisting students with these three important principles of learning by creating an environment that could be knowledge-centered, learner-centered, and assessment-centered, while promoting community engagement and independent learning at the same time (The Cognition and Technology Group at Vanderbilt, 2003). Intelligent technology-based learning environments can provide the necessary scaffolding, information, feedback, social connection, and strategy prompting for students to have a successful and meaningful learning experience and accomplish learning goals (Azeavedo, 2005; Moos & Azevedo, 2008).

CONCLUSION

Young children are immersed in a technological culture from birth, both through informal home and community exposure and through quasi-educational situations. We have also mentioned the importance of recognizing the developmental stages that should encompass optional technology use by young children. Given the new insights of digital divide discussed in this chapter, we as educators have to be aware of ways in which the gaps can be narrowed. Ways to reduce the gap include technology selection without gender or ethnic bias, getting to know the children and their previous technology experience including exposure in the home, and identifying special needs and selecting adequate technology for these needs.

Educators need to pay particular attention to the appropriateness of technology young children get access to, how it is integrated in the school curriculum, and how it addresses established cognitive principles of teaching and learning. We have also indicated the importance for parents to educate themselves about choosing appropriate technology for children.

The increasing presence of technology in all aspects of the digital-age child has changed the socio-culture environment. Enculturation of young children will vary depending on family, school and community experiences. Children coming into early childhood programs bring a variety of experiences with technology from formal and informal settings. Schools and teachers will face the challenge of closing this gap through teacher training and providing appropriate materials.

Reflecting on the Enculturation of Young Children and Technology

This section gives you some questions and activities to help you think about how you can use some of the ideas from this chapter in your work.

Research

1. Organize a focus group of parents, teachers, and young adults from the digital generation to discuss different indicators of technology enculturation in your community.
2. Interview the children in your classroom to learn about their technology experiences. Give each child a disposable camera to take home and take 10 pictures of what they think is technology in their homes. Code the pictures into categories to determine how your children understand technology.

Reflect

1. The statement "The most profound technologies are those that disappear. They weave themselves into the fabric of everyday life until they are indistinguishable from it" may help you think about how technology becomes a part of culture. What types of technology have become parts of modern community in your lifetime?
2. How does early use of technology in the home influence learning? Think about your personal use of technology and experiences you and your family have had with technology use. How have these impacted your family?
3. This chapter provides research on several "area of concern" associated with early learning and technology. How does this information support or conflict with your thinking about technology prior to reading this chapter?
4. Does technology support your thinking about child development and learning? Why or why not?

Practice

1. One particularly unique aspect of technology was the degree to which parents felt empowered to actively participate in their children's learning. How can you use this information to develop parent engagement in your classroom? Make a list of activities that will strengthen your parent involvement through technology.
2. This chapter presents educators with guidelines for selecting and incorporating developmentally appropriate software within the early learning environment. Work with your colleagues to identify how you can implement these guidelines in your school.
3. How can you, as a professional, integrate the informal experiences of children with technology into your learning environment to support learning?
4. What the implications for early development and learning are through exposure to technology? How could these implications inform your practice?

REFERENCES

Ainsa, T. (1989). Effects of computers and training in Head Start curriculum. *Journal of Instructional Psychology*, *16*, 72–78.

American Optometric Association. (2010). *Impact of computer use on children's vision.* Retrieved from http://www.aoa.org/ x5379.xml

Azevedo, R. (2005). Using hypermedia as a metacognitive tool for enhancing student learning? The role of self-regulated learning. *Educational Psychologist*, *40*(4), 199–209. doi:10.1207/s15326985ep4004_2

Baker, E. L., & O'Neil, F. (2003). Evaluation and research for technology: Not just playing around. *Evaluation and Program Planning*, *26*(2), 169–176. doi:10.1016/S0149-7189(03)00008-9

Bandura, A. (1986). *Social foundations of thought and action: A social cognitive theory*. Englewood Cliffs, NJ: Prentice Hall.

Barlow, D. (2010). The teachers' lounge. *Education Digest*, *75*(6), 65–68.

Barron, B., Walter, S. E., Martin, C. K., & Schatz, C. (2010). Predictors of creative computing participation and profiles of experience in two Silicon Valley middle schools. *Computers & Education*, *54*(1), 178–189. doi:10.1016/j.compedu.2009.07.017

Barry, E. S. (2006). Children's memory: A primer for understanding behavior. *Early Childhood Education Journal*, *33*(6), 405–411. doi:10.1007/s10643-006-0073-3

Bickham, D. S., Vandewater, E. A., Huston, A. C., Lee, J. H., Caplovitz, A. G., & Wright, J. C. (2003). Predictors of children's electronic media use: An examination of three ethnic groups. *Media Psychology*, *5*, 107–137. doi:10.1207/S1532785XMEP0502_1

Bilton, N. (2010, March 1). Connecting your car, socks and body to the Internet. *Bits Blog, NYTimes.com*. Retrieved from http://bits.blogs.nytimes.com/ 2010/03/01/ connecting-your- car-socks-and- body-to-the-Internet /

Buckingham, D. (2007). *Beyond technology: Children's learning in the age of digital culture*. Malden, MA: Polity.

Buckingham, D., & Scanlon, M. (2001). Parental pedagogies: An analysis of British edutainment magazines for young children. *Journal of Early Childhood Literacy*, *1*(3), 281–299. doi:10.1177/14687984010013003

Buckleitner, W. (1999). The state of children's software evaluation, yesterday, today and in the 21st century. *Information Technology in Childhood Education Annual*, 211–220.

Campbell, M. (2010). Collaborations between librarians and faculty in a digital age. *Education Digest*, *75*(6), 30–33.

Clements, D. H., & Sarama, J. (2003). Young children and technology: What does the research say? *Young Children*, *58*(6), 34–40.

Cognition and Technology Group at Vanderbilt. (2003). Connecting learning theory and instructional practice: Leveraging some powerful affordances of technology. In O'Neil, H., & Perez, R. (Eds.), *Technology applications in education: A learning view*. Mahwah, NJ: Lawrence Erlbaum Associates.

Cordes, C., & Miller, E. (2000). *Fool's gold: A critical look at computers in childhood*. College Park, MD: Alliance for Childhood.

Council for Research Excellence. (2009). *Video consumer mapping study*. Retrieved from http://www.researchexcellence.com/ VCMFINALREPORT_4_28_ 09.pdf

Cruz, F. M. F., & Snider, S. L. (2009, November). Storying with technology: Using the multiple literacies of the new technology and media landscape to connect with young learners. *Contemporary Issues in Early Childhood*, *10*(4).

Cuban, L. (2001). *Oversold and underused: Reforming schools through technology, 1980-2000*. Cambridge, MA: Harvard University Press.

Desimone, L. (1999). Linking parent involvement with student achievement: Do race and income matter? *The Journal of Educational Research*, *93*, 11–30. doi:10.1080/00220679909597625

Digiovanni, L., Schwartz, S., & Greer, C. (2009). I think, iPod(cast), I learn: Using digital media and podcasting in teacher education. In I. Gibson, et al. (Eds.), *Proceedings of Society for Information Technology & Teacher Education International Conference 2009* (pp. 1812-1819). Chesapeake, VA: AACE.

Fabes, R. A., Martin, C. L., & Hanish, L. D. (2004). The next 50 years: Considering gender as a context for understanding young children's peer relationships. *Merrill-Palmer Quarterly*, *50*(3), 260–273. doi:10.1353/mpq.2004.0017

Frazel, M. (2007). K12 online conference. *Beyond the Horizon: The Online Journal of Adventures in Genealogy, Technology, and Research*. Retrieved from http://midgefrazel.net/blog/ 2007_09_01_midgefrazel_archive.html

Galyon-Keramidas, C., & Collins, B. C. (2009). Assistive technology use with the birth to three population: A rural perspective. *Rural Special Education Quarterly*, *28*(1), 38–48.

Geissinger, H. (1997). *Educational software: Criteria for evaluation*. Retrieved from http://www.ascilite.org.au/ conferences/perth97/ papers/ Geissinger/ Geissinger.html

Gilutz, S., & Nielsen, J. (2002). *How children use the Web. 70 design guidelines from usability studies with kids using websites*. Fremont, CA: Nielsen Norman Group.

Glister, P. (1997). *Digital literacy*. New York, NY: John Wiley and Sons.

Greenfield, A. (2006). *Everyware: The dawning age of ubiquitous computing*. CA: New Riders.

Greenfield, P., & Yan, Z. (2006). Children, adolescents, and the Internet: A new field of inquiry in developmental psychology. *Developmental Psychology*, *42*, 391–394. doi:10.1037/0012-1649.42.3.391

Hargittai, E. (2010). Digital na(t)ives? Variation in Internet skills and uses among members of the net generation. *Sociological Inquiry*, *80*(1), 92–113. doi:10.1111/j.1475-682X.2009.00317.x

Hastings, E., Karas, T., Winsler, A., Way, E., Madigan, A., & Tyler, S. (2009). Young children's video/computer game use: Relations with school performance and behavior. *Issues in Mental Health Nursing*, *30*(10), 638–649.. doi:10.1080/01612840903050414

Haugland, S. (1992). The effect of computer software on preschool children's developmental gains. *Journal of Computing in Childhood Education*, *3*(1), 15–30.

Haugland, S. (1995). Selecting or upgrading software and websites in the classroom. *Early Childhood Education Journal*, *32*(5), 329–340. doi:10.1007/s10643-005-4401-9

Haugland, S. (1999). What role should technology play in young children's learning? Part 2. *Young Children*, *54*(6), 26–31.

Haugland, S. (2000). Computers and young children. Champaign, IL: ERIC Clearinghouse on Elementary and Early Childhood Education. Retrieved from http://ceep.crc.uiuc.edu/ eecearchive/ digests/ 2000/haugland00.pdf

Healey, J. (1998). *Failure to connect: How computers affect our children's minds – For better or worse*. New York, NY: Simon and Schuster.

Heinrichs, J. H., & Lim, J. (2010). Information literacy and office tool competencies: A benchmark study. *Journal of Education for Business*, *85*(3), 153–164. doi:10.1080/08832320903252371

Hoffman, B., & Nadelson, L. (in press). Motivational engagement in video gaming: A mixed methods study. *Educational Technology Research & Development,* 57(6).

Hoffman, B., & Spatariu, A. (2008). The influence of self-efficacy and metacognitive prompting on math problem-solving. *Contemporary Educational Psychology*, *33*(4), 875–893. doi:10.1016/j.cedpsych.2007.07.002

Hong, S. B., & Trepanier-Street, M. (2004). Technology: A tool for knowledge construction in a Reggio Emilia inspired teacher education program. *Early Childhood Education Journal*, *32*(2), 87–94. doi:10.1007/s10643-004-7971-z

Horn, C., Bruning, R., Schraw, G., & Curry, E. (1993). Paths to success in the college classroom. *Contemporary Educational Psychology*, *18*, 464–478. doi:10.1006/ceps.1993.1035

Hough, L. (2007) Handhelds, avatars, and virtual aliens. *Retrieved from*http://www.gse.harvard.edu/ news_events/ed/2007/ fall/features/ handhelds.html

Howard-Jones, P. A., Taylor, J. R., & Sutton, L. (2002). The effect of play on the creativity of young children during subsequent activity. *Early Child Development and Care*, *172*(4), 323–328. doi:10.1080/03004430212722

Hutinger, P., & Johanson, J. (2000). Implementing and maintaining and effective early childhood comprehensive technology system. *Topics in Early Childhood Special Education*, *20*(3), 159–173. doi:10.1177/027112140002000305

InTime. (2001). *Integrating new technologies into the methods of education.* Retrieved from http://www.intime.uni.edu/

Ito, M., Horst, H., Bittanti, M., Boyd, D., Herr-Stephenson, B., & Lange, P. G. … Robinson, L. (2008). Leaving and learning with new media: Summary of findings from the digital youth project. *MacArthur Foundation. Retrieved from*http://digitalyouth.ischool.berkeley.edu/ iles/report/ digitalyouth-WhitePaper. pdf

Johnson, G. M. (2010). Internet use and child development: Validation of the ecological techno-subsystem. *Journal of Educational Technology & Society*, *13*(1), 176–185.

Judge, S., Puckett, K., & Bell, S. M. (2006). Closing the digital divide: Update from the early childhood longitudinal study. *The Journal of Educational Research*, *100*(1), 52–60. doi:10.3200/JOER.100.1.52-60

Judge, S., Puckett, K., & Cabuk, B. (2004). Digital equity: New findings from the Early Childhood Longitudinal Study. *Journal of Research on Technology in Education*, *36*(4), 383–396.

Kinder, M. (1991). *Playing with power in movies, TV and video games*. Los Angeles, CA: University of California Press.

Lee, S. J., Bartolic, S., & Vandewater, E. A. (2009). Predicting children's media use in the USA: Differences in cross-sectional and longitudinal analysis. *The British Journal of Developmental Psychology*, *27*, 123–143. doi:10.1348/026151008X401336

Lee, S. J., & Spires, H. (2009). What students think about technology and academic engagement in school: Implications for middle grades teaching and learning. *AACE Journal*, *17*(2), 61–81.

Levy, R. (2009). You have to understand words… but not read them: Young children becoming readers in a digital age. *Journal of Research in Reading*, *32*(1), 75–91. doi:10.1111/j.1467-9817.2008.01382.x

Lewin, C. (2000). Exploring the effects of talking books software in UK primary classrooms. *Journal of Research in Reading*, *23*(2), 149–157. doi:10.1111/1467-9817.00111

Li, X., & Atkins, M. S. (2004). Early childhood computer experience and cognitive and motor development. *Pediatrics*, *113*(6), 1715–1722. doi:10.1542/peds.113.6.1715

Ljung-Djarf, A. (2008). The owner, the participant and the spectator: Positions and positioning in peer activity around the computer in pre-school. *Early Years*, *28*(1), 61–72. doi:10.1080/09575140701846487

Lynch, S. A., & Warner, L. (2004). Computer use in preschools: Directors' reports of the state of the practice. *Early Childhood Research and Practice, 6*(2). Retrieved from http://ecrp.uiuc.edu/ v6n2/ lynch.html

Mandese, J. (2008). MediaPost Publications OMG! UM finds Web 2.0 breeding consumers 2.0, social media attains critical mass. *Online Media Daily*. Retrieved from http://www.mediapost.com/ publications/?fa=Articles.showArticle&art_aid=85025

Mayfield, M. I. (2005). Children's museums: Purposes, practices and play? *Early Child Development and Care, 175*(2), 179–192.. doi:10.1080/0300443042000230348

Miller, D. J., & Robertson, D. P. (2010). Using a games console in the primary classroom: Effects of Brain Training programme on computation and self-esteem. *British Journal of Educational Technology, 41*(2), 242–255. doi:10.1111/j.1467-8535.2008.00918.x

Miriam-Webster Dictionary. (2010). *Enculturation*. Retrieved from http://www.merriam-webster.com /dictionary/ enculturation

Mitchell, L. M. (2007). Using technology in Reggio Emilia-inspired programs. *Theory into Practice, 46*(1), 32–39. doi:10.1080/00405840709336546

Moos, D. C., & Azevedo, R. (2009). Self-efficacy and prior domain knowledge: To what extent does monitoring mediate their relationship with hypermedia learning? *Metacognition and Learning, 4*(3), 197–216..doi:10.1007/s11409-009-9045-5

NAEYC. (1996). *Technology and young children – Ages 3 through 8*. Washington, DC: National Association for the Education of Young Children.

NCES. (2003). *Young children's access to computers in the home and at school in 1999 and 2000.* Washington, DC: NCES. Retrieved from http://nces.ed.gov/ pubs2003/2003036. pdf

NCREL. (2004). *An educator's guide to evaluating claims about educational software*. Retrieved from http://www.ncrel.org/ tech/claims/ index.html

NETC. (2005). *Northwest educational technology consortium*. Retrieved from http://www.netc.org/

Nikolopoulou, K. (2007). Early childhood educational software: Specific features and issues of localization. *Early Childhood Education Journal, 35*(2), 173–179. doi:10.1007/s10643-007-0168-5

NSBF. (2000). *Safe and smart. Research and guidelines for children's use of the Internet*. Alexandria, VA: National Schools Boards Foundation.

Oblinger, D., & Oblinger, J. (2005). Is it age or IT: First steps towards understanding the net generation. In D. Oblinger & J. Oblinger (Eds.). *Educating the Net Generation* (pp. 2.1-2.20). Boulder, CO: EDUCAUSE. Retrieved from http://www.educause.edu/ educatingthenetgen

Ormrod, J. E. (2009). *Essentials of educational psychology* (2nd ed.). New Jersey: Merill, Pearson.

PT3. (2002). *Preparing tomorrow's teachers to use technology*. Retrieved from http://www.pt3.org/

Parent's Choice Awards. (2009). *Parents' choice award winners: Toys*. Retrieved from http://www.parents-choice.org

Parents, P. B. S. (2010). *Computers: Grade schoolers*. Retrieved from http://www.pbs.org/ parents/ childrenandmedia/ computers-grade.html

Parette, H. P., Boeckmann, N. M., & Hourcade, J. J. (2008). Use of Writing with Symbols 2000 software to facilitate emergent literacy development. *Early Childhood Education Journal, 36*, 161–170. doi:10.1007/s10643-008-0270-3

Parette, H. P., Hourcade, J. J., Boeckmann, N. M., & Blum, C. (2008). Using Microsoft PowerPoint to support emergent literacy skill development for young children at-risk or who have disabilities. *Early Childhood Education Journal, 36*, 233–239. doi:10.1007/s10643-008-0275-y

Parette, H. P., Hourcade, J. J., & Heiple, G. S. (2000). The importance of structured computer experiences for young children with and without disabilities. *Early Childhood Education Journal*, *27*(4), 243–250. doi:10.1023/B:ECEJ.0000003361.21759.48

Piaget, J. (1952). *The origins of intelligence in children* (Cook, M., Trans.). New York, NY: New American Library. doi:10.1037/11494-000

Plowman, L. (1998). Reading multimedia texts. *Language Matters, Spring,* 19-22.

Plowman, L., & Stephen, C. (2003). A benign addition? Research on ICT and pre-school children. *Journal of Computer Assisted Learning*, *19*(2), 149–164. doi:10.1046/j.0266-4909.2003.00016.x

Project, T. H. R. E. A. D. (2004). *Technology helping restructure educational access and delivery*. Retrieved from http://www.unlv.edu/ projects/ THREAD /index.html

Puma, M., Ghapin, D., & Pape, A. (2003). *E-Rate and the digital divide: A preliminary analysis from the integrated studies of educational technology*. Washington, DC: The Urban Institute.

Purcell, K. (2010). *Teens and the Internet: The future of digital diversity*. Presented at Fred Forward Conference. Pew Research Center's Internet & American Life Project.

Rathbun, A. H., West, J., & Hausken, E. G. (2003). *Young children's access to computers in the home and at school in 1999 and 2000*. (NCES-2003-036). Washington, DC: National Center for Education Statistics. Retrieved from http://nces.ed.gov/pubs2003/ 2003036.pdf

Reeves, T. C., & Oh, E. (2008). Generational differences. In Jonnasen, D. H. (Ed.), *Handbook of research on educational communications and technology* (pp. 295–305). New York, NY: Macmillan.

Reingold, H. (2006). *The pedagogy of civic participation*. In New Media Consortium Second Life Symposium on Impact of Digital Learning. Symposium conducted at the meeting of New Media Consortium, NMC Campus in Second Life. NMC (Producer). [Audio Podcast]. Retrieved from www.nmc.org/ podcast/ pedagogy-civic-participation

Rideout, V. J., Foehr, U. G., & Roberts, D. F. (2010). *Generation M2: Media in the Lives of 8- to 18- year olds* (pp. 1–82). Kaiser Family Foundation.

Rideout, V. J., & Hamel, E. (2006). The media family: Electronic media in the lives of infants, toddlers, preschoolers, and their parent*s. Kaiser Family Foundation. Retrieved from*http://www.kff.org/ entmedia/upload/ 7500.pdf

Rideout, V. J., Vandewater, E. A., & Wartella, E. A. (2003). Zero to six: Electronic media in the lives of infants, toddlers and preschoolers. *Kaiser Family Foundation. Retrieved from*http://www.kff.org/ entmedia/upload/ Zero-to-Six-Electronic-Media-in-the-Lives-of- Infants-Toddlers-and-Preschoolers-PDF.pdf

Ritchie, S., Maxwell, K. L., & Bredekamp, S. (2009). Rethinking early schooling: Using developmental science to transform children's early school experiences. In Barbarin, O. A., & Wasik, B. H. (Eds.), *Handbook of child development and early education: Research to practice* (pp. 14–37). New York, NY: Guilford.

Roberts, D. F., & Foehr, U. G. (2008). Trends in media use. *The Future of Children*, *18*(1), 11–37. doi:10.1353/foc.0.0000

Roberts, J., Jurgens, J., & Burchinal, M. (2005). The role of home literacy practices in preschool children's language and emergent literacy skills. *Journal of Speech, Language, and Hearing Research: JSLHR*, *48*, 345–359. doi:10.1044/1092-4388(2005/024)

Robinson, K. K., & Crenshaw, E. M. (2010). Reevaluating the global digital divide: Socio-demographic and conflict barriers to Internet revolution. *Sociological Inquiry*, *80*(1), 34–62. doi:10.1111/j.1475-682X.2009.00315.x

Schmid, R. F., Miodrag, N., & Di Francesco, N. (2008). A human-computer partnership: The tutor/child/computer triangle promoting the acquisition of early literacy skills. *Journal of Research on Technology in Education*, *41*(1), 63–84.

Schrader, P. G., & McCreery, M. (2007). The acquisition of skill and expertise in massively multiplayer online games. *Educational Technology Research and Development*, *56*(5-6), 557–574. Retrieved from http://www.springerlink.com/ content/ n2496u376825u512/. doi:10.1007/s11423-007-9055-4

Schrock, K. (2010). *Kathy's Schrock guide for educators*. Retrieved from http://school.discoveryeducation.com/ schrockguide/

Sharon, J., Puckett, K., & Burcu, C. (2004). Digital equity: New findings from the early childhood longitudinal study. *Journal of Research on Technology in Education*, *36*(4), 383–396.

Shilling, W. A. (1997). Young children using computers to make discoveries about written language. *Early Childhood Education Journal*, *24*(4), 253–259. doi:10.1007/BF02354842

Sifteo. (2010). *Siftables*. Retrieved from http://sifteo.com

Stringer, M., Halloran, J., Hornecker, E., & Fitzpatrick, G. (2005). Situating ubiquitous computing in everyday life: Some useful strategies. Retrieved from http://www.informatics.sussex.ac.uk/ research/ groups/ interact/papers/pdfs/stringer_ ubicomp05. pdf

Subrahmanyam, K., Kraut, R., Greenfield, P., & Gross, E. (2000). The impact of home computer use on children's activities and development. *The Future of Children*, *10*, 123–1444. doi:10.2307/1602692

Sutherland, R., Facer, K., Furlong, R., & Furlong, J. (2000). A new environment for education? The computer in the home. *Computers & Education*, *34*, 195–212. doi:10.1016/S0360-1315(99)00045-7

Sylvester, D. E., & McGlynn, A. J. (2010). The digital divide, political participation, and place. *Social Science Computer Review*, *28*(1), 64–74. doi:10.1177/0894439309335148

Tarpley, T. (2001). Children, the Internet, and other new technologies. In Singer, D. G., & Singer, J. L. (Eds.), *Handbook of children and the media* (pp. 547–566). Thousand Oaks, CA: Sage.

Technology Review. (2010). *Building blocks of a new interface*. Retrieved from http://www.technologyreview.com/ article/22801/

Turow, J., & Nir, L. (2000). *The Internet and the family 2000: The view from parents, the view from kids. APPC Reports, 33*. Philadelphia: University of Pennsylvania.

Ueoka, R., & Hirose, M. (2008). Soundtag: Children's interactive play based upon RFID employed wearable computer. *Digital Creativity*, *19*(3), 162–173. doi:10.1080/14626260802312699

United States Department of Health and Human Services. (2006). *Administration for Children and Families: FFY 2006 CCDF data tables: 6-Percent of children served in all types of care*. Retrieved from http://www.acf.hhs.gov/ programs/ccb/ data/ccdf_data/ 06acf800/ table6.htm

Vandewater, E. A., Rideout, V. J., Wartella, E. A., Xuan, H., Lee, J., & Shim, M. (2007). Digital childhood: Electronic media and technology use among infants, toddlers, and preschoolers. *Pediatrics*, *119*, e1006–e1015..doi:10.1542/peds.2006-1804

Vygotsky, L. S. (1978). *Mind and society: The development of higher psychological processes* (Cole, M., John-Steiner, V., Scribner, S., & Souberman, E., Eds.). Cambridge, MA: Harvard University Press.

Wang, Y., Stash, N., Sambeek, R., Schuurmans, Y., Aroyo, L., & Schreiber, G. (2009). Cultivating personalized museum tours online and on-site. *Interdisciplinary Science Reviews*, *34*(2/3), 139–153..doi:10.1179/174327909X441072

Weinberger, N., & Stein, K. (2008). Early competitive game playing in same- and mixed-gender peer groups. *Merrill-Palmer Quarterly*, *54*(4), 499–514. doi:10.1353/mpq.0.0006

Weiser, M. (1991). *The computer for the 21st century.* Pervasive Computing. Retrieved from http:// www.media.mit.edu/ resenv/classes/ MAS961/ readings/ weiser_reprint.pdf

Wikipedia. (2010). *Ubiquitous computing*. In Wikipedia, the free encyclopedia. Retrieved from http://en.wikipedia.org/ wiki/ Ubiquitous_computing

Yelland, N. (2005). The future is now: A review of the literature on the use of computers in early childhood education (1994-2004). *AACE Journal*, *13*(3), 201–232.

Chapter 3
Children's Power for Learning in the Age of Technology

Julie McLeod
University of North Texas, USA

Lin Lin
University of North Texas, USA

Sheri Vasinda
Texas A&M University – Commerce, USA

ABSTRACT

This chapter situates discussions of children's power for learning in the context of new media and technology. We assert that for learning to take place, children must exert their own power and take initiatives in their learning; yet, the current power structure of classrooms inhibits children from exerting their power and motivation for learning. Tracing the seminal works on power, we provide examples of children's power in learning and argue for a power structure transformation necessary in a technology-rich classroom of the twenty-first century.

INTRODUCTION

A class of third and fourth graders engages in a lively discussion on food chains, what eats what, and how decomposers break down dead matter, when the discussion turns to composting plant waste. "Oh yeah, we compost in RuneScape so our veggies will grow better!" Faran chimes in. Several other boys enthusiastically discuss plant matter they have virtually composted as well as other quest related tasks they encounter in this popular online game. The depth of discussion on this ecological process is amazing. There is a hefty amount of text these third and fourth graders willingly read to improve their play of this game. Along the way they are determining their own purpose for reading, encountering content specific vocabulary such as: vegetation, produce, organic, and rotting; academic vocabulary such as: treated,

DOI: 10.4018/978-1-61350-059-0.ch003

Copyright © 2012, IGI Global. Copying or distributing in print or electronic forms without written permission of IGI Global is prohibited.

yield, increase, and interacting with one another online in a cooperative manner.

What motivates these young children to engage in the traditional literacy demands required by school on their own time? What motivates them to master a video game, engage in online play, or seek information on a topic that sparks their interest or curiosity?

In synthesizing an abundance of research on motivation, Daniel Pink (2009) attributes this kind of motivation as the boys' desire to direct their own life, to improve their skill at the game, and to be a part of a large game playing group. According Pink (2009), motivation comes not from the old behaviorist carrot and stick model of rewards and punishments; instead, motivation comes from three factors: autonomy (the ability to direct our own lives), mastery (the urge to get increasingly better at something that matters), and purpose (the desire for what we do to be in the service of a larger purpose). Clearly, within these descriptors of motivation lies a sense of power. One achieves a sense of power when one is confident and capable of achieving his or her goal autonomously and meaningfully.

Our schools are on the cusp of change. As the Industrial Age gives way to the Digital Age, schools find themselves clinging to an outdated system that no longer reflects the needs of today's citizenship, life-style or work force. The societal landscape of the Industrial Age produced the factory model of schooling. Businesses needed workers, schools provided them. Those who did not go on to college were trained to respond to bells, be on time, and do boring repetitive work. In the factory model of schooling, students are viewed as products; teachers, in turn, take on the role of factory technicians making the additions and adjustments to their products required during their year (Schlechty, 1990). There is little power in being a product - or a factory technician.

The factory jobs of the past have been automated. Even jobs that require a certain knowledge skill set, such as tax preparation, customer service, or information systems support can be outsourced to less expensive labor forces in any place on the globe with Internet access. As we struggle through this transition period of letting go of old models without yet knowing how the new model should look (McLeod & Vasinda, 2009b), educators sense the power structures of old begin to blur and the change as our students have knowledge and skills that many times surpass our own in areas of technology usage. Children remind us how to use our Interactive White boards, how to animate a Power Point, or how to join a social networking group. They are eager to teach us how to navigate digital worlds. They are in a technology world, a context that makes the discussions of the focus of this chapter, children's power for their own learning important, even urgent.

Objectives

After reading this chapter the reader will develop an awareness of how the perception of power structures in early childhood classrooms is shifting due to the influence of technology. The reader will be able to reflect on the instructional environment and interactions in their classrooms as influenced by the power roles of children and teachers. The reader will be able to better understand:

- Context of learning
- Power structures in schools
- Power of technology
- Information power

BACKGROUND: THE IMPORTANCE OF NEW MEDIA AND TECHNOLOGY BEING THE CONTEXT

The importance of a context has been highlighted in many historical events. History is replete with great ideas that, because of lack of the right technology, could not come to fruition. The thinking was in place long before another, in a different time, could see the idea to its successful intent. Da Vinci, for instance, designed machines capable of flight but could not build them because the technology and societal infrastructure of the day was not available (Papert, 1993). The Wright brothers succeeded where Da Vinci fell short, not because they were so much smarter, but because of their context. They had the technology and the societal infrastructure to build the first airplane.

In a similar way, because of their context, the preprimary schools of Reggio Emilia in Italy have succeeded in embracing the educational philosophies of John Dewey when we in America are still under the influence of Thorndike's mechanistic view of quantifying the educational experience and outcomes (Gibboney, 2006). In the aftermath of the devastation and rubble of World War II, a group of parents who understood the social change in which their community had undergone wanted something better for their children (Gandini, 2002; Palestis, 1994). The landscape of war and resistance to fascist leadership was the context and catalyst for change and the desire to create a more just world that was free from oppression (Barazzoni, 2000). This Italian region's history of solidarity and cooperation made it possible for these parents, and later a group of teachers with the guidance of Loris Malaguzzi, to create what have been referred to as the best and most innovative preschools in the world (Newsweek, 1991). Their foundational focus is the image of the child as a protagonist of their own learning. Children are seen as full of potential and capable of constructing their own learning, not in isolation, but in relationship with the family, other children, the school and the wider society. Teachers and children work together as partners in the process of learning and document their work together. The practices of Reggio Emilia provide a landscape for continuous research, analysis, reflection and action that results in the formulation of new theories, hypotheses, ideas and strategies about learning and teaching (Gandini, 2002).

Cognitive scientists and educational researchers have long noted that the context in which learning takes place is critical (Godden & Baddeley, 1975). John Dewey (1997) advocated that children's educational experience needs to be connected to their daily experiences. Lave and Wenger (1991) suggested that all learning is contextual and situated in a social and physical environment. Situated learning emphasizes that the ongoing processes in which one is involved, for instance, the surroundings and social network of others doing the same thing, change the capacity for learning. Brown, Collins and Duguid (1989) stated that "the ways schools use dictionaries or math formulae, or historical analyses, are very different from the ways practitioners use them." Consequently, students often do not see connections between learning in school and their real life situations, and lose interest in what they study in school.

The context today includes the ubiquitous nature of technology in our postmodern or knowledge-based society, and the continuing ease of use have opened many possibilities for learning and collaboration as well as new challenges. One facet of postmodern society and thinking is characterized by multiple voices or alternative perspectives emerging with the rapid development of new media and social networks. Technological platforms such as Facebook, Twitter, Blogs, and Wikis have made it easy for the general public (not just authorities or celebrities) to make their voices heard and to impact public opinions and policy changes. Many of these voices are from those of underrepresented cultures, ethnicities and genders (Slattery, 1995), to which we will add the culture of youth, more specifically young children.

Living in a world of technology, new media and technology are children's social and physical environments and are their daily experiences. Because of new media, the learning environments designed for children by educational theorists including Dewey, Piaget, and Vygotsky are now able to take flight. However, standing in the way are archaic classroom power structures that do not fit into our twenty-first century context. Therefore, in this chapter, we will begin our discussions with the current power structures in school settings, followed by understanding power through the historical and philosophical lens. Then, we will look to the power structures necessary in a technology-rich classroom of the twenty-first century.

Power and Power Structure in School Settings

When power is considered in a school setting, it is typically with phrases such as "empowering children." But the term "empower" entails giving power. In other words, just using the word empower connotes that all power resides in the adults and that it is at the adults' discretion whether or not the power is shared with the children. It further implies that power is something that can be given away. In this chapter, we will challenge these held beliefs.

Currently, educators are grappling with how to use the technology their students value, are comfortable, adept and unafraid to experiment with and use as well as keeping current with technology's continuous invention and evolution. Phil Schlechty (2009) describes what he calls the "digital imperative" as follows:

The revolution created by the application of digital technologies to the organization, management, processing, and presentation of information, images, data, and all manner of human expression cannot be appreciated as long as these technologies are viewed as tools for instructors. What is most powerful about them is that they place instruction under the direct control of the person being instructed: the learner. In the digital world, the learner, not the instructor, is in charge of what will be learned, as well as how and when that learning will occur.

In his work with teachers, Schlechty (2009) found that teachers recognize that technology provides a platform for students to take a more active role in the classroom and it becomes, as one teacher quoted, "a shared space where teachers and students learn together and from each other" (Schlechty, 2009). He also found that more commonly, teachers undervalue the potential of technology as a learning tool and that it is often regarded as something to which needs to be controlled.

Clearly, power structures are deeply ingrained in schools. Therefore, it is important to begin this chapter with an understanding of power: what it is, what is embedded in the power, what are outcomes derived from power, and why it is relevant and urgent to discuss power issues in the context of technology.

The Definition and Nature of Power in the Context of New Media and Technology

Cartwright (1959) noted years ago that a consistent definition of power eluded the field and the ensuing fifty years has not substantially changed that fact. Cartwright himself used a mathematical formula to depict power as the force an agent can use to influence and the resistance of that influence by a target. Yukl (2006, p. 146) similarly defines power as the "capacity of one party (the agent) to influence another party (the target)." These definitions seem to equate power with a type of domination of one person over another person. Foucault (1980), however, moves beyond these domination-themed definitions and views power as a productive network in society. He identifies power in relations of any kind, such as family, work or school. This is a view of power as socially negotiated rather than dictated. Barnes (1988) identifies power as socially negotiated as well. For Barnes, social power is akin to mechanical power in that it is a capacity. While mechanical power is a capacity for work, social power is the capacity for action in society.

It is this view of social power as the capacity for action which is especially compelling, particularly because technology has enabled even very young children to take action in society in ways that are important, public and inconceivable without the technology. Tapscott and Williams (2006) posit that for the first time in history, children are experts in something that is truly important in the adult world. Because children have these life experiences as a valued, contributing and important member of a society, they taste social power in a way that we did not know at their age. It has also expanded the number and types of societies available to children. For example, even young children can join societies such as Webkinz World or Club Penguin, the virtual worlds for kids. In virtual worlds, societies evolve in which children have the capacity to act online, and with some worlds, the societies are not limited online so the capacity to act in the virtual society extends to the physical world as well. This experience leaves an aftertaste that children find hard to set aside in other parts of their lives. Thus, for this chapter, our definition of power will be closely akin to both Foucault's and Barnes', that is, *power is productive, sometimes consensual, capacity for action in society*.

To dig more deeply into the concept of power, Parsons (1963) used an economic metaphor, money, to describe the nature of power and how it is created by society. Just as money is a circulating medium, power circulates through society. Further, like money, power is a symbolic abstraction. Parsons (1963) explained that while in earlier times, coins were made of a metal with an independent value of its own; convenience brought about paper money which then symbolized the metal that represented the money's value. Of course now, the representational metal is not used and paper money has become fully abstract and separate from the metal that once gave it its value. It has value in its own right. Members of society may use a symbolic instrument to make obligations to others and to fulfill those obligations. Similarly, in society powerful people have the capacity to call upon obligations and secure satisfaction of that obligation. It is this capacity to act in society that is at the heart of our definition of power.

Interestingly, Freire (1970) wrote extensively about power structures and education after his experience helping people in Brazil to become literate. He also used an economic metaphor to describe the traditional power structures specific to education. In Freire's view, teachers make "deposits" of knowledge to students. The students' role is limited to receiving the deposits, memorizing the information and repeating it to the teacher when asked. Indeed, Freire argued that this education system limits the "scope of *action* (the authors' emphasis) allowed to the students" (Freire, 1970, p. 72). Since the capacity to act is the definition of power, Freire's banking metaphor for education in which students' action is limited highlights a fundamental contradiction for twenty-first century educators - how do students' new conceptualization of their own capacities for action (i.e., power) in their technological worlds synchronize with an educational system that attempts to limit their actions?

An important consideration in answering this question can come from extending Parsons' (1963) economic metaphor for power. Banks hold deposits for customers. While these customers retain the right to access their funds at any time, the bank also has the right to use a portion of the funds to lend to other customers for a fee. Thus, at any time, two people can have access to the same funds, essentially doubling the economic value of those funds. Power is similar in that leaders may take action and make obligations in support of a particular group's goals without draining any resources. In other words, power is not a zero-sum. An individual's increased power does not have to come at the expense of another person's power. Indeed, society regularly produces power to satisfy needs, desires and goals.

With this concept of power as something that can be expandable and generated, educators can begin to conceive of a classroom with the necessary power structures for twenty-first century teaching and learning: celebrating and encouraging children's power in their learning does not reduce the teacher's or school's power to help children learn. Because of the twenty-first century children's push to move their capacity to act into the classroom, it is important for educators to understand power. By doing so, it becomes possible to envision a style of teaching that honors childrens' power while still accomplishing the established learning goals.

The Elements and Outcomes of Power and its Importance for Children's Learning in the Age of New Media and Technology

McLeod and Lin (2010) traced the discussions of power by seminal and contemporary thinkers including French and Raven (1959), Weber (1968), Freire (1970) and Yukl (2006), and summarized eight separate types of power: legitimate power, reward power, coercive power, referent power, expert power, information power, ecological power, and power over oneself, as shown in the Figure 1.

Legitimate power occurs when an agent has formal or cultural authority over a target. Adult-child relationships in schools are governed by cultural norms that allow teachers to have legitimate power. *Referent power* occurs when the target seeks the approval of the agent or has strong feelings of loyalty or admiration. The agent can influence the target because the target seeks to please the agent. For example, when students struggle to be accepted by their teachers or peers, referent power is at work. *Reward power* is an agent's ability to use rewards to influence the target and gain compliance. Compliance is not guaranteed with reward power as the target will continuously evaluate the probability of receiving the reward and whether the reward is worth the

Figure 1. Typology of power

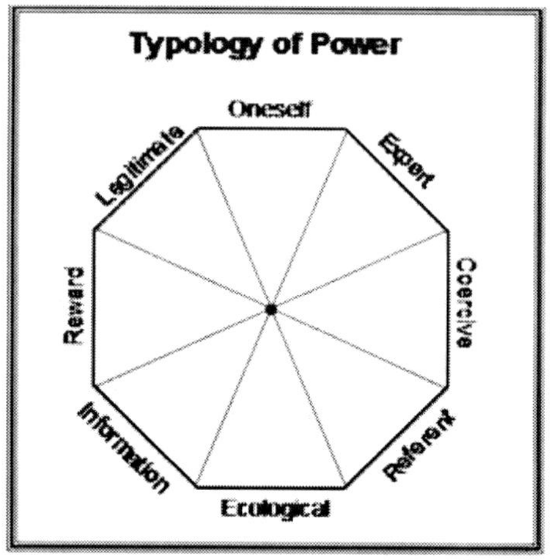

agent's compliance. Many teachers use reward power in the classroom for students who follow the classroom rules. *Coercive power* uses threats or punishments for noncompliance and is typically considered an opposite to reward power. Traditional teachers use coercive power when they take away a privilege or threaten a failing grade.

Expert power occurs when an agent has specific knowledge or skills, particularly unique knowledge and skills. Many times, a target wants advice from another and thus can be influenced via expert power. Teachers traditionally are viewed as having expert power. In twenty-first century classrooms, expert power can also come from students. *Information power* is the control over information. In schools, administrators hold information power. Teachers can also hold information power over students. *Ecological power* is control over the physical environment or technology. Teachers have power over the physical layout of a classroom. Technology lab managers in a school might control teachers' and students' access to the computer lab. *Power over oneself* is that which one exerts over oneself. It is that internal locus of control. In a classroom, ultimately it is students who choose whether they learn a particular lesson. Schlechty (2002) believes students should be viewed as volunteers in the classroom even when their attendance is compulsory. By doing so, teachers recognize that even when students are present, they must choose to engage and learn.

As shown in Figure 1, McLeod and Lin (2010) attempted to juxtapose the elements of the typology so that these elements opposite each other presented themselves as opposite ends of a spectrum or continuum. For instance, *power over oneself* which can be considered a microcosm of power is juxtaposed against *ecological power* which can be exerted at a much broader scale. *Reward power* which typically entails something that is given to another is juxtaposed against *coercive power* which typically entails something that is taken away from someone.

The typologies offered above focus on the source of the power that stems from the agent. This is of course useful in furthering our definition of power, but equally as useful is a discussion of the outcome of the attempts at power, which focuses more on the target than on the agent of power. While Barnes (1988) warns that power should not be measured or conceptualized at the outcome of the action, certainly any study of power should include an evaluation of the result of the power attempt, or the outcome. Figure 2 depicts the outcomes of power, once again derived from seminal and contemporary thinkers such as Yukl (2006) and Freire (1970) and discussed in detail in McLeod and Lin (2010):

In Figure 2, *Commitment* involves the target accepting the power attempt and internalizing a change in behavior, which can be long lasting. Commitment typically results from referent or expert power. *Compliance* describes a situation in which the target performs as requested but with minimal effort and no internalized change. *Resistance* occurs when the target actively avoids and sometimes even sabotages the power attempt. On the contrary, *liberation* occurs as oppressed people liberate themselves through education.

Figure 2. Outcome of power

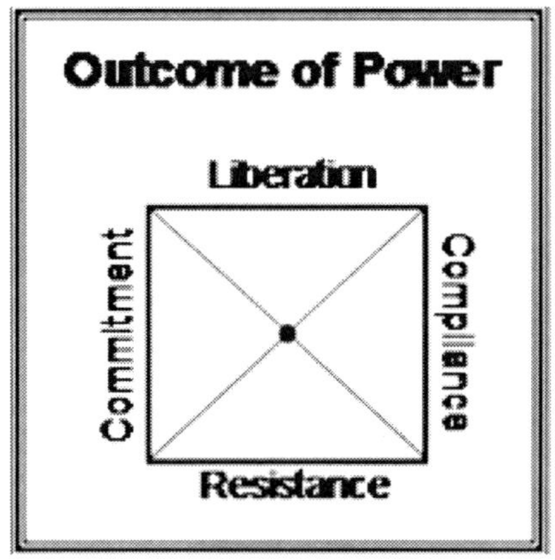

Liberation is viewed as a jointly negotiated reality between the agent and the target. Ideally in school settings, teachers hope to see commitment and liberation in their student's learning and try their best to prevent students from resisting or reluctantly complying to what's been taught at schools.

Referring back to the source of the power that stems from the agent, we can see that the first two pairs of powers, legitimate and referent, reward and coercive powers, are prevalent and dominant in our old and current classroom structures. They present a top-down structure of an educational system that uses external forces or incentives to push students to learn. These powers may work sometimes, but often they do not. It is the second two pairs of powers, namely, expert and information, ecological and power over oneself that are changing in the context of technology. These four powers reside in children's daily experiences and are particularly relevant in our twenty-first century classrooms. The transformational changes of these four powers in classroom settings, we believe, will bring true power to students' learning and to their motivation for learning. Ultimately, these powers will generate in our children the two ideal outcomes of power: liberation and commitment for their own learning.

Children's Power in the Technological World

The following two scenarios are examples of how the power of children enhances learning in a sixth grade classroom. The technology used has changed the interactions of the class and the ownership of the information in a manner that bases the learning in the context of the digital world.

Scenario 1: Folders of Wisdom and Knowledge

The room was buzzing. Each student had a laptop and was working diligently, but not independently. Many times students leaned over to their neighbors to ask about a problem. When their neighbor could not help, the students looked around for the teacher and called the teacher over to help. "Yes!" called one student after a period of working time had elapsed. He had completed the work and was proud of all he had accomplished. Other students called out to him to come help them, but he played coy with them, telling them that they could do it themselves.

In this classroom, students were working on a math task that had just been digitized for the first time. During the previous year, the students in this math classroom struggled to organize all their mathematical knowledge because mathematics tends to be taught in small chunks without any overarching structure. Understanding that one significant difference in the way experts and novices think is in the organization of their knowledge (Bransford, Brown, & Cocking, 2000), the teacher began helping students organizing their knowledge by creating folders with pockets for the main concepts. These pockets were then stuffed over time with envelopes which represented a lower level concept and then with example questions and scenarios inside the envelopes. Students named these folders their Folders of Wisdom and Knowledge.

In the original way the folders were conceived, the example questions and scenarios were printed on index cards so that students could sort the cards into the appropriate envelope. This had been a group activity so that there was a check for students' thinking. Students would read the card and spend a few minutes discerning in which envelope they felt the card would best fit. Then, the teacher would ask for volunteers to share their thinking. Once the decision was made regarding where the card would best fit, the class stuffed the envelope and moved on together to the next card. This was a long and laborious process, although student feedback and their conceptual and organizational knowledge showed that it truly helped them.

Now that each student had access to a laptop in her class, the teacher decided to try to automate the sorting process. She had found during the course of the year that students responded well to technology-rich work because of its individual pacing and immediate feedback. So, she created a Microsoft Excel spreadsheet and copied and pasted the questions and scenarios into the spreadsheet. She then added a drop-down menu along with some rudimentary logic to inform students if they discerned the proper concept that the scenario was addressing. When students finished the virtual sorting work, she asked for feedback about the new digital method of sorting.

Three themes emerged from this brief reflection time. First, students noted that they actually had to think. One student said, "It makes you actually think." This was certainly a surprise because the work was the same in each case as when the students used the paper folders and index cards. However, in the manual sorting task, this student was likely waiting quietly until others offered their suggestions and then just placed the card in the appropriate envelope. This behavior would likely fit into Schlechty's (2002) ritual compliance category in which students expend only enough energy to avoid negative consequences. These students are not fully engaged in the task and do not learn at deep levels. This comment also reminds educators that students are volunteers in our classroom (Schlechty, 2002), with the power to decide whether or not to engage in the learning. The second theme that emerged was that students liked the work better simply because it was "on the computer." They were very clear and resounding that any work is better when they can complete that work electronically. The third theme that emerged was that they liked the virtual sorting better because each student could choose their own pace and identify when they needed to seek help. One student noted that he liked it better because it "went faster." Several students noted that the speed was much more to their liking, noting that "you get the answer quicker." Interestingly, this was not a digital activity in which students were completely immersed in a virtual world. It did not require a significant amount of programming or technological knowledge. But, this simple activity allowed students to negotiate their own learning, become more literate in their mathematical knowledge and certainly were seeking out experts, first their peers and then the teacher. The results of the feedback are discussed through the lens of children's power throughout the remainder of the chapter.

Scenario 2: Mathcasts

"I don't like having to show my work!" "It's too much writing!" "I think UPS-check is just a way for teachers to torture us!" These were the statements from the students at the beginning of the school year during reflective interviews. The students were reflecting on a mathematical process known as UPS-check, which stands for Understand, Plan, Solve and Check. This process is encouraged via state mathematics standards and is implemented beginning in Kindergarten in the school district. In the process, teachers use mathematical word problems and ask students to divide their paper into four equal parts. In each section, students work one part of the UPS-check process. Clearly, students saw little value in the process and they noted that they had to expend considerable energy to complete it. As adults, we understand that this way of thinking is important in many different realms. Yet, students must come to their own understanding of the value in this thinking process if they are to embrace it and use it.

Fast forward to the middle of the school year when we started using digital pens and special notebooks that would record words and pen strokes for the first time. These recordings could then be played back immediately and/or uploaded online creating a movie that could be embedded into websites or blog posts. These recordings were called Mathcasts (McLeod & Vasinda, 2009b). Students were partnered and given a choice of word problems to solve. One partner was the solver and the other partner was the interviewer. The interviewer used a protocol to ask questions of the solver and assisted as necessary in the problem solving process. The interview protocol followed the same questions that students had used for years to guide their thinking through the UPS-check process. Once a problem was solved and recorded, the partners switched roles. A group reflective interview was conducted after this first Mathcast was completed.

One student noted, "I like showing the work." Another student said, "I like putting the important things before solving the question." A third student expressed that he liked "showing how we know the answer is correct." Interestingly, these students expressed that their favorite aspects of the Mathcast were the same aspects that they disliked about UPS-check in our first reflective interview. While some of the difference might have originated from work we did throughout the first semester which invited students to find their own meaning in the UPS-check process, we found that this means of recording words and writing resonated with students as more authentic than the written word alone (McLeod & Vasinda, 2009a). During this process, students were co-creating knowledge by recording Mathcasts that were posted online for others to view and they clearly identified the difference between this work and the work on paper. Another theme that emerged from the interview data was that students could identify their own mistakes by listening to their thinking or by discussing with their partner. In this way, students were negotiating their own learning while becoming even more literate in the UPS-check process. Indeed, Vygotsky (1986) posits that learners mediate their understanding through discussion and that conversation with others becomes internalized into private speech and then the thought process becomes automated.

In both scenarios, students had different reactions towards their learning process when using digital technologies as compared to using the traditional tools. Obviously, situating their learning in their own context – the technological world, has played a role in their excitement for learning. Yet, something else, namely, students' power, has also played an important role in the process. In the following, we will discuss the ecological, expert, information, and power over oneself that the students exhibited in the two scenarios.

Children's Ecological Power

Ecological power is control over the physical environment or technology. Children today are the most technology savvy of any generation. A recent report by Kaiser Family Foundation found that 8-18 year olds in the U.S. spent 7.38 hours on media daily, and that these young people packed a total of 10 hours and 45 minutes worth of content media into 7.38 hours of media use (Rideout, Foehr, & Roberts, 2010). In fact, children spend more time with media than they do with parents, teachers, physical activities, and homework combined.

During their work on virtual sorting for their Folders of Wisdom and Knowledge, students strongly communicated that any work is better if it is on the computer. In this statement, students were clearly identifying their ecological power within the technological context. When they had control over their environment, they felt more deeply connected with their work. To these students, technology-rich learning was a natural way to feel the control over their environment. Further, students enjoyed the work more because they could work at their own pace, again citing ecological power as an impetus for their deep engagement. The students who created Mathcasts also recognized their ecological power. For these students, the UPS-check process was "torture" when it was completed using a pencil and paper. However, when these same students completed the UPS-check process using the digital pens, they felt drastically different about the process. So different that they noted how much they enjoyed the exact same aspects of the process with which they had expressed disdain earlier in the year.

New technologies have become ubiquitous in the lives of young children. Technology, which can be anything from a pencil to a phone to a computer, is not simply a tool in terms of hardware or software for children who use it. Rather, it is meaningful, both for those who create with it and for those who use it. For children living in the technological world, the boundary between creation and consumption has become blurry. Technology creation and consumption are integrated in their lives, their friendships, and their sense of what is important to them.

Children's Expert Power

Along with children's ecological power over technology comes their expert power. Expert power refers to specific knowledge or skills. Children are at the front of technological knowledge and skills. Technology presents a landscape of possibilities and power in which children can and do willingly participate unlike any landscape of the past. They pretend and play, research and report, consume and create on virtual platforms where they are comfortable, proficient and engaged. They have been called "digital natives" (Prensky, 2001) as they have grown up in a world in which much is possible. Because of their fearless tinkering with technology, they often mentor adults in navigating technological media and applications.

Children's expert power was observed during their virtual sorting work on their Folders of Wisdom and Knowledge. Students were working both independently and collaboratively seamlessly. When they were unsure, they typically sought help from their neighbor. Sometimes they also sought help from their classmate across the room, making for a lively sounding classroom! Finally, they sought help from the teacher. This was not a process directed by the teacher, but was naturally occurring among students. Similarly during Mathcasts, students noted that they appreciated the partner discussion and the interview questions so that they could find their own mistakes. Once again, students naturally asked peers for help. When the pair could not decide how to proceed, the teacher was called over for assistance. These examples demonstrate students' innate ability to identify experts and seek assistance. This is a naturally occurring process for children in their worlds outside of school. For example, children playing a game such as Sonic the Hedgehog first exercise their power to act in the world. When they find difficulty, they then seek assistance. This assistance can come from in game characters or from elaborate societies of cheats and help sites online.

Vygotsky (1978)'s work bears relevance, especially his notion of the zone of proximal development (ZPD), or the difference between one's actual and potential levels of cognitive development. ZPD can be achieved when children are collaborating and achieving the same goals together. In a technological world, a child can find someone who is just a few steps ahead in learning how to deal with the environment, someone who still speaks the same language and makes the same mistakes, but at the same time, someone who has achieved a few of the same things that he or she wants to achieve. Since they can communicate most of it rather easily because of technology, it becomes a naturally occurring process to attempt action, seek assistance and learn. On the other hand, it is equally important to be able to turn around and find someone a little behind, because this time, the child gets an opportunity to articulate the achievement by explaining and re-explaining and making it clear to someone who is asking him or her. In Rogoff's (1990, p. 16)'s words: "Children seek, structure, and even demand the assistance of those around them in learning how to solve problems of all kinds. They actively observe social activities, participating as they can."

Children's Information Power

Information power is control over information. Researchers have known for years that children can use technology to obtain information at their finger tips (Perkins, 1985).

Certainly this access to information is a type of information power. However, this is still information to which others also have access. Children now know that information power is more intense if they are the ones creating the information or content and then deciding how and when to share that information. During virtual sorting work on their folders of wisdom and knowledge students demonstrated their sensitivity to information power in a unique way. If a student was able to figure out a question or scenario before his or her neighbor, he/she would have information power. Because of this, students did not wait idly for others to do the thinking; instead, they actively engaged in the thinking themselves. Further, the students also noted that they appreciated moving at their own pace. This individualized pacing increased some students' information power because they had already worked through a question and could be a more capable other for their neighbor (Vygotsky, 1978). During the Mathcasts, students began finding value in the UPS-check thinking process because they were co-creating knowledge that would be available to others online. Indeed, students were creating information and deciding when and how to share that information, which is the essence of information power.

Gee (2003) makes a strong case for the strength of the learning experiences in video games and identified 36 learning principles found in good video games. Without using the terminology of information power, two of Gee's principles speak to this type of power. One of the principles is the Dispersed Principle, meaning that learners share knowledge outside the game. Another principle is the Insider Principle in which the player is an insider, a teacher and a producer. Both of these principles are seen in our scenarios, particularly in the Mathcast scenario where students were creating a video of their thinking to share online. Gee believes that the learning principles in video games offer educators a glimpse of the types of experiences available to students outside the classroom and his text includes a plea for educators to move children's classroom experiences closer to their game-play experiences.

Children's Power Over Themselves

Sometimes called intrinsic motivation or internal locus of control, the essence of power over oneself is that students are choosing to engage in the hard work of learning. When learning becomes less other directed and more self directed and more self directed, students take more ownership of the process and the content (Knowles, 1975). Students demonstrated their power over themselves in several ways. During their folders of wisdom and knowledge work, students appreciated the fact that the work was completed digitally and that each student had a laptop to complete the work. These two aspects combined demonstrate an internal locus of control that is important for students if they are to take ownership of their learning. When working on Mathcasts, the students liked identifying and correcting their own mistakes, sometimes by listening to their own thinking via the digital pen technology and sometimes in collaboration with their partner. Certainly, rework is a difficult part of the learning in school. From editing a piece of writing to checking the work on a math problem, students resist the rework because they see it as monotonous. In their opinion, they have done the work once, why should they do it again? By using the digital pens and listening to their own thinking, students found their own power over their work and their learning. Equipped with this power, students naturally enjoyed the typically painstaking process of rework.

FUTURE TRENDS: LIBERATION AND COMMITMENT AS OUTCOMES OF CELEBRATING CHILDREN'S POWER

The world is rapidly changing with new media and technology. Children are developing knowledge and expertise in the technological world, but schools continue to operate in a way that fails to leverage the technological changes that increasingly influence children's lives (Squire & Jan, 2007). Classrooms remain dominated by print-based materials produced by teacher-centered pedagogy, where students are positioned as passive and powerless receivers.

Because of the drastic change of our technological landscape, we should consider the transformation of power structures in classrooms: to do something new that has never been done (Schlechty, 2009). When the landscape changed for the people of Reggio Emilia, they transformed their schools to fit their vision of something new they wanted for their children. Recently Diane Ravitch, former assistant secretary of education and long-time supporter of the standards and accountability movement, has changed her position in regard to privatization and charter schools, standardized testing, and punitive accountability. She has now come to believe, the result of over forty years of research, that the bottom line business model put into place by policy makers has grievously harmed our educational system (Ravitch, 2010). Maybe the time is right to turn away from the mechanistic thinking of Thorndike and create the landscape of high quality experiences of Dewey. The landscape of the Digital Age could be the catalyst that can place the children at the center of their own learning experiences.

In Gee's (2003) analysis of good learning in video games, he identified the Probing Principle. This principle situates learning as a cycle of actions, including probing the world, reflecting on the action, and forming hypotheses that are then tested as the cycle begins again. Gee's Probing Principle mirrors Freire's (1970) concept of praxis which is also a process of action and reflection. Freire's concept of praxis, however, predates video games. And, importantly, praxis is the process that Freire contends leads to liberation. Certainly, the teacher and students involved in our scenarios experienced liberation. They discerned a new reality in which mathematics is connected to the world, lived and embodied through action.

When children experience school learning in a way that is congruent with their out-of-school learning, they respond with deep commitment. Further, these new power dynamics allow both the students and the teacher to discern a new reality, demonstrating liberation (Freire, 1970). Importantly, Freire (1970) reminds us that when oppressed people experience liberation, they do so not only for their own benefit, but also for the benefit of the oppressors. Through liberation, both oppressors and the oppressed become fully human. Children can already taste this reality in their worlds outside of school. It is now time to move the feast of liberation into the important realm of school learning.

CONCLUSION

Dewey (2001) and Vygotsky (1978) contend that learning is a social process. Power is a social dynamic. Studying knowledge, cognition and learning is studying social theory (Barnes, 1988). Thus, this evaluation of classroom power dynamics in today's society is a worthy effort. Children nowadays experience ecological power, expert power, information power, and power over oneself in their daily life of new media and technology. These powers afford children the natural motivation for learning. Therefore, these powers should be incorporated into the classroom and become the dominant forms of interactions in the classroom of the twenty-first century. Indeed, Bennis (2003) contends that today's leaders must understand that power now follows ideas rather than position and we believe that this is true for young people as well. Further, it is these types of power that are involved in the zone of proximal development (Vygotsky, 1978) as more capable others assist learners. With such a classroom power transformation, we can expect that our children will present the outcomes of power that we as educators hope to realize: their commitment and liberation for their own learning.

Reflecting on Children's Power for Learning in the Age of Technology

This section gives you some questions and activities to help you think about how you can use some of the ideas from this chapter in your work.

Research

1. In your classroom observe which learning enables children to demonstrate their ecological power, expert power, information power or power over oneself to determine if the ideas in this chapter are supported. Video children as they work in different learning centers including one where an adult dictates the steps of an activity and one where children initiate actions. Keep a tally of how many and how long children participate in each type of activity when given free choice.
2. Place a digital camera, cell phone and PDA in a learning center without specifying what they are or how to use them. Video the

interactions of children with these devices. Analyze how the children interact with these.

Reflect

1. Living in a world of technology, new media and technology are children's social and physical environments and are their daily experiences. What does this statement imply for your classroom environment?
2. Schools continue to operate in a way that fails to leverage the technological changes that increasingly influence children's lives (Squire & Jan 2007). Prepare a concept map of your educational environment which includes technology that children use in their daily lives and in your classroom.
3. Living in a world of technology, new media and technology are children's social and physical environments and are their daily experiences. What actions have you observed your children doing that support this statement?
4. As the industrial age gives way to the digital age think about your beliefs about learning. Are you still approaching teaching like the "banking system" of learning? How do your views of learning inhibit or support technology in your classroom?
5. What aspects of Reggio Emlio are incorporated into your classroom ? Why would you want to use his approach in relation to technology?

Practice

1. Students respond well to technology rich work because of its individual pacing and immediate feedback. How will you use this idea in your classroom to give children the opportunity to expand their learning?
2. In twenty-first century classrooms, expert power can also come from students. How will this idea inform your practice? Develop a list of ways you will allow children to explore their power.

One achieves a sense of power when one is confident and capable of achieving his or her goal autonomously and meaningfully. Identify what activities you use in your classroom that supports autonomy of children. Develop more ways you can provide an environment to support this through technology.

REFERENCES

Barazzoni, R. (2000). Brick by brick [*Aprile" people's nursery school of Villa Cella.* Reggio, Emilia, Italy: Reggio Children.]. *Histoire (Paris)*, XXV.

Barnes, B. (1988). *The nature of power*. Urbana, IL: University of Illinois Press.

Bennis, W. (2003). *On becoming a leader*. New York, NY: Basic Books.

Bransford, J., Brown, A., & Cocking, R. (2000). *How people learn: Brain, mind, experience and school*. Washington, DC: National Academy Press.

Brown, J. S., Collins, A., & Duguid, P. (1989). Situated cognition and the culture of learning. *Educational Research*, *18*, 32–42.

Dewey, J. (1997). *How we think*. Mineola, NY: Dover.

Foucault, M. (1980). *Power/knowledge: Selected interviews and other writings 1972-1977* (Gordon, C., Ed.). London, UK: Harvester.

Freire, P. (1970). *Pedagogy of the oppressed*. New York, NY: Continuum.

French, J., & Raven, B. (1959). The bases of social power. In Cartwright, D. (Ed.), *Studies in social power* (pp. 150–167). Ann Arbor, MI: The University of Michigan.

Gandini, L. (2002). The story and foundation of the Reggio Emilia approach. In V. R. Fu, A. J. Stremmel, & L. T. Hill (Eds.) (2002). *Teaching and learning: Collaborative exploration of the Reggio Emilia approach.* Upper Saddle River, NJ: Merrill Prentice Hall.

Gee, J. P. (2003). *What video games have to teach us about learning and literacy*. New York, NY: Palgrave McMillan.

Gibboney, R. (2006). Intelligence by design: Thorndike versus Dewey. *Phi Delta Kappan*, *88*(2), 170–178.

Godden, D. R., & Baddeley, A. D. (1975). Context-dependent memory in two natural environments: On land and underwater. *The British Journal of Psychology*, *66*(3), 325–331. doi:10.1111/j.2044-8295.1975.tb01468.x

Knowles, M. (1975). *Self-directed learning: A guide for learners and teachers*. New York, NY: Association Press.

Lave, J., & Wenger, E. (1991). *Situated learning: Legitimate peripheral participation*. Cambridge, UK: Cambridge University Press.

McLeod, J., & Lin, L. (2010). A child's power in game-play. *Computers & Education, 54*, 517 527.

McLeod, J., & Vasinda, S. (2009a). Electronic portfolios: Perspectives of students, teachers and parents. *Education and Information Technologies*, *14*, 29–38. doi:10.1007/s10639-008-9077-5

McLeod, J., & Vasinda, S. (2009b). Web 2.0 affordances for literacies: Using technology as pedagogically strong scaffolds for learning. In Kidd, T., & Chen, I. (Eds.), *Wired for learning: An educator's guide to Web 2.0*. Charlotte, NC: Information Age Publishing.

Newsweek. (1991, December 2). *The 10 best schools in the world and what we can learn from them*, (pp. 50-59).

Palestis, E. (1994). Lessons from Reggio Emilia. *Principal*, *73*(5), 16–18.

Papert, S. (1993). *The children's machine: Rethinking school in the age of the computer*. New York, NY: Basic Books.

Parsons, T. (1963). On the concept of political power. *Proceedings of the American Philosophical Society of the American Philosophical Society*, *107*, 232–258.

Perkins, D. N. (1985). The fingertip effect: How information-processing technology shapesthinking. *Educational Researcher*, *14*, 11–17.

Pink, D. (2009). *Drive: The surprising truth about what motivates us*. New York, NY: Riverhead.

Prensky, M. (2001). *Digital game-based learning*. New York, NY: McGraw-Hill.

Ravitch, D. (2010). *The death and life of the great American school system: How testing and choice are undermining education*. New York, NY: Basic Books.

Rideout, V. J., Foehr, U. G., & Roberts, D. F. (2010). *Generation M2: Media in the lives of 8- to 18 year-olds*. Menlo Park, CA: Kaiser Family Foundation.

Schlechty, P. (1990). *Schools for the twenty-first century: Leadership imperatives for educational reform*. San Francisco, CA: Jossey-Bass Publishers.

Schlechty, P. (2002). *Working on the work: An action plan for teacher, principals and superintendents*. San Francisco, CA: Jossey-Bass.

Schlechty, P. (2009). *Leading for learning: How to transform schools into learning organizations*. San Francisco, CA: Jossey-Bass Publishers.

Slattery, P. (1995). *Curriculum development in the postmodern era*. New York, NY: Garland.

Tapscott, D., & Williams, A. D. (2006). *Wikinomics: How mass collaboration changes everything*. Portfolio Hardcover.

Vygotsky, L. S. (1978). *Mind in society*. Cambridge, MA: Harvard University Press.

Vygotsky, L. S. (1986). *Thought and language*. Cambridge, MA: MIT Press.

Weber, M. (1968). *Economy and society: An outline of interpretive sociology*. New York, NY: Bedminster.

Yukl, G. (2006). *Leadership in organizations* (6th ed.). Upper Saddle River, NJ: Pearson.

Chapter 4
Technology in Three American Preschools:
Technological Influences of Ideology and Social Class

Allison S. Henward
Arizona State University & University of Memphis, USA

ABSTRACT

This chapter explores the marriage of popular culture images, media and technology and the manner in which these are implemented in preschool settings. Discussing parents' choices and teacher's opinions, this chapter examines popular culture in children's lives as social symbols. It is specifically concerned with the manner in which social class and preschool ideology contribute to or detract from children's access to popular culture technology.

INTRODUCTION

It is 10:00 a.m., center time for the children in Faith Christian's Pre-K Classroom. The four and five-year-old children in the class are engaged in a myriad of activities: A few children are sprawled out on the carpet perusing picture books, while a couple sit at tables with paper and pencils, tracing their names with the teacher. Not far away three children sit on a rug in front of a Teddy Ruxpin doll, a bear that moves his mouth animatronically when a cassette is placed in the player on his back. They are listening to Teddy "recite" a book on tape. In another corner, two other children are sitting at desks, headphones on their ears and a computer mouse in hand. Staring intently at the monitor

DOI: 10.4018/978-1-61350-059-0.ch004

Copyright © 2012, IGI Global. Copying or distributing in print or electronic forms without written permission of IGI Global is prohibited.

in front of them, they are playing games such as Franklin's Adventures and My Very First Little People Farm. These children are autonomous in their interaction with the computer; although the teacher is near they need very little assistance in navigating the games as they move the mouse, point and click from screen to screen with confidence.

Computer time, books on tape and videos are all common activities for children in this preschool, they are seen as alternate modes of instruction, ways in which children engage with the curriculum. The above vignette illustrates how children in this particular preschool are expected and encouraged to interact with technology, specifically computer software. The rationale or goal according to the school is for the children to cultivate "basic computer skills and to develop eye–hand coordination" (website omitted for confidentiality). This preschool, like many others supports technology and the popular culture characters that pair as components of their instructional curriculum.

This is not the case for all preschools; as I will discuss many see technology, media and popular culture as bothersome or even harmful (Buckingham & Sefton-Greene, 1994, 2004; Hodge & Trip, 1986).

Definitional Problems: Amalgamation of Popular Culture Characters and Technology

Traditionally, when one speaks of "technology" they are concerned with hardware: television, video cassette and DVD players, computers, smartphones, videogame systems and educational learning systems. The images and characters, encoded with preferred meanings in a given society (Hall, 1999) are often left out. This omission is particularly problematic as in early childhood toy markets there is a close marriage of technology and popular culture. When using learning systems such Leap Frog Tag Reader, an interactive reading system, children "read" stories featuring Tinkerbelle from *Peter Pan*, *Cars* and *Madagascar* Penguins. And popular culture images, have in turn "branded" many hardware systems. As rudimentary laptops emblazoned with Hello Kitty and SpongeBob, Disney Princess television sets and Mickey Mouse Wii controllers have taught us, the explication from each other is difficult and boundary lines are often imprecise. Understanding the close ties, for the purpose of this chapter I use the term popular culture technology to include images and ideas but also the hardware systems needed to access the images and ideas.

This chapter explores the marriage of popular culture and technology in preschool settings, specifically the manner in which social class and preschool ideology contribute to or detract from children's access to popular culture technology. It draws on data collected in a study using comparative ethnographic methods in which I examined the uses and meanings ascribed to popular culture in three preschools in the United States that differ socio-economically and ideologically. For the purpose of this study I use the term social class to represent the income of parents in the United States and status of the students in a stratified system. I determine the socioeconomic level of each preschool by analyzing tuition required to attend each school. In addition I examine the economic criteria for tuition being waived for certain preschools.

Preschools that steadfastly reject children's interaction with technology and media figures may do so with the supposition that interaction with these media detract from a more authentic and "natural" learning experience. This critique often times pairs with the theory of Developmentally Appropriate Practice (DAP) to view children's interaction with popular culture through technological means as less than desirable and in many cases detrimental to social and cognitive development, particularly if the children are younger than three (Elkind, 1998; Haugland, 1999; NAEYC, 1996). In addition to criticisms of pedagogical implementations is the pervasive association of popular culture with the common or pedestrian and thus relegated to that of the working class. As Dyson argues, (1997) knowledge of certain symbolic systems, Greek Myths for example, when compared to the knowledge of Saturday morning cartoons, work to position children within stereotypical class relations.

Settings

The three preschools selected for this study vary both in the identified social class, as defined in the United States, of the families they serve, as well as in their underlying program philosophy. I examined tuition or income qualifications for tuition waivers to determine the socioeconomic level of the families in each preschool.

Working class: Hermosa: Hermosa is a public pre-k readiness preschool that serves a working class population, largely comprised of children of Hispanic descent. The preschool program is open to anyone residing within the elementary school district boundaries provided they will enter Kindergarten the following year. The tuition for families varies by income; if the family's income exceeds the identified income qualification they can elect to attend under an optional "paid tuition" slot. However in the four years the program's Early Childhood coordinator has been employed, no child registered for the Hermosa preschool has qualified for a paid tuition slot, in each case the family income has been below the line for the free and reduced lunch qualification and consequently receives a tuition waver from the school district. Noting this factor helps to understand this program only serves children whose family income is less than 185% of the federal poverty line (United States Department of Health and Human Services, www.hhs.org). This means that a family of four in order to attend Hermosa Preschool must report an annual gross income of less than $40,792.50 USD. As it is publically funded, Hermosa is the only preschool in which parents are required to report income in order to qualify for program services. The remaining two preschools' social class was determined by the monthly tuition charged to parents.

Upper-middle class: Biltmore Montessori: I categorize Biltmore Montessori as an upper-middle class preschool serving a population of children, the majority of whom are of European descent. Biltmore Montessori is a privately funded center which serves children infants to eighth grade, albeit on separate campuses. Tuition to attend the mandatory five day a week program for children ages three to six, not including lunch, is nearly $1,000 USD a month. While this cannot guarantee all children attending the school are from an upper middle class background, the post-tax tuition ($12,000 USD annually) makes this a school financially out of reach of the majority of families. The school does offer scholarships and discounts to children of the teachers, diversifying the school population. The Montessori program emphasizes self-expression and creativity. Children are expected to be self-directed learners that are capable of making their own decisions and working independent of other students as well as the teacher.

Lower-middle class: Faith Christian: Faith Christian is an independent, privately funded preschool connected with a Pre K with a religious curriculum's tuition falls somewhere in between the other two schools with a monthly base tuition of around $400 USD. This however does not include additional "aftercare" tuition most children were charged for a full day of attendance. Tuition in this case increased to approximately $600 USD a month (children in aftercare were charged an hourly rate making the exact fee vary by child). It does accept subsidies from the Department of Economic Security to attract children from the surrounding working class neighborhood although the majority of the children attending the preschool do not qualify as their family income is too great Faith Christian emphasizes religious instruction and conservative values. In this setting children often work in large groups to accomplish tasks prescribed by the teacher.

The combination of class, program ideology and the pedagogical approaches associated with each preschool makes each an individual site for study. Each site brings with it assumptions of the best approaches to Early Childhood Education which allows for identification of practice based on social class and ideology. These assumptions can provide a view of perceptions and acceptance of technology.

Objectives

After reading this chapter the reader should develop a better understanding of the connection of ideology and social class in the acceptance or rejection of technology as a pedagogical tool. It attempts to call into question practices that are seen as natural or "appropriate" as specific to a cultural group. By examining this topic from a critical perspective it is my attempt to clarify curricular and pedagogical tools as not without class biases and intentions. This study endeavors to discuss class discriminates as well as religious and theoretical beliefs in the appearance of technology in both educational programs and the home lives of preschoolers. The reader should be able to use this information to analyze their beliefs about technology through the lens of personal and programmatic ideology and how this can influence their decisions about technology use in educational programs.

BACKGROUND: PRESCHOOL SETTINGS IN THE UNITED STATES

In the United States, preschool is non-compulsory and the provision of preschool includes many different kinds of programs. These include federal, state, and municipal funded preschools; private for profit preschools; and private non-profit programs, some of which are religious. These widely varying types of preschools generally serve relatively economical and culturally homogeneous groups of children. This is in part to the largely privatized nature of early childhood education in the United States. In addition to and as a result of the "optional" nature of preschool in the United States, preschool has become a largely privatized sector of education with many different approaches to early childhood education. Some are play based, some constructivist, while others promote early literacy in school readiness programs. There is very little regulation of preschool programs and the funding of preschools come from a variety of sources. This privatization has created what Tobin, Hsueh and Karasawa (2009, p.9) describe as a "highly crazy quilt of early childhood education programs." This leads to many conflicting and contrasting views of the methods in which children should be educated and what content should be taught.

The preschools in this study are located within a seven mile radius of each other in an urban area of a major city located in the Southwestern United States but have widely varying tuition requirements as well as criteria for admission. I identify this, as the homogeneous urban environment helps to highlight the extreme privatization of preschools that can happen within a fairly close proximity. As all three preschools are in urban environments, it allows examination on how parents segregate preschools based on economic and ideological factors and not proximity. It helps to emphasize that the choice of preschools is not arbitrary (although some could be) and not simply based on locality. With widely varying access to preschools, many factors such as tuition, location and school hours affect the choice of preschools for parents. For example a preschool with a high tuition and limited morning hours may not attract parents on fixed incomes that need extended care for children in order to work, Likewise parents of middle and upper middle class will not qualify for school readiness programs or headstart. Parents also choose preschools to reflect individual philosophical needs. A parent that endorses deference to authority would not typically endorse a child centered ideology found in many progressive, constructivist preschool programs.

These philosophical beliefs play an important role in children's access to technology as they are the underpinnings of the curriculum. While many constructivist philosophies such as Reggio Emilia and "school readiness preschools" endorse the idea of technology, (specifically computers) as an added benefit and resource to preschool children, other more holistic philosophies such as Montessori and Waldorf often view technology as developmentally inappropriate and a hindrance to more naturalistic and authentic learning (Montessori 1995; Petrash,2002). The three preschools in this study can be described as serving working class, lower-middle class, and upper-middle class children respectively, but such economic labels describe only a part of their cultural capital and ideological location within American society. As in Joseph Tobin's work *Good Guys Don't Wear Hats* (2000), this study explores the way nationally and increasingly globalized circulating popular culture is used and given meanings in particular local settings, as influenced by class, ethnicity, and local political and social factors. These sites are not "self-contained cultures, but local site(s) in a complex larger society" (Tobin, 2000, 149).

This mixture of economic and ideological factors allows me to explore the interaction or intersectionality of economic and ideological factors, rather than to ascribe differences in how these three programs deal with popular culture technology to the workings of either class or ideology alone. These sites are not simply working class, lower-middle class, or upper-middle class preschools; but instead sites where class, ethnicity, religion, and ideology intersect. This study can help us understand how teachers of a lower- middle class, socially conservative Christian preschool approach popular culture technology, but I take care not to suggest that this finding can be extended to all Christian preschools or all lower- middle class schools. One of my key findings is that ideology influences the opinions and practices as much, or more than, social class. In the upper-middle class Montessori program parents and teachers react in a much different manner than would be found in a study conducted in an upper-middle class socially conservative (e.g., church or temple based) preschool. The intersection of conservative ideology and upper-middle class when studied in the preschool space would most likely present findings that reflected both ideology and class. It cannot be one or the other but it is the space or this crossroad of parents' social class, teachers' social class and ideologies that determine practices in the classroom.

Preschools are rich sites for conducting research on technology and popular culture because they are places where the culture of home encounters the culture of schooling, where the private and public domains meet. Preschools are sites where beliefs of children, parents, and teachers come into contact and sometimes clash. These sites are spaces where there is a constant negotiation of meanings and, like markets and carnivals as discussed by Bakhtin in *Rabelais and His World* (1984), sites for the interaction and interpenetration of discourses and ideologies.

It is in this space that meaning is localized and contextualized. In the tradition of educational anthropology this study's interest lies in the situated use of the products in these spaces. In each setting it is not just the technology in the setting that is of interest but also the meaning that children and adults alike ascribed to these images and media. In each setting I consider the school as a site where the opinions of parents were influenced by many factors.

The Vicissitude of Popular Culture Technology

A succinct definition of what comprises media is problematic when discussing popular culture and technology, for in many cases they blend to possess synonymous definitions and are often considered as such. This in part is attributable to the manner in which children interact with popular culture. Access to and interaction with popular culture images is delivered in technological means, thus blurring the definition. Although it is feasible for a child to access popular culture without technology (such as reading a book about Disney's *The Little Mermaid*) the story of the mermaid and the animated images contained in the pages are reflective of a technology, in this case a movie. As most of the character books are typically written above emergent literacy (they are not heavily populated with sight words and repetitive phrases) the manner in which the children engage with the text is not actually through the written word but either through viewing the images (pictures reflective of the movie) or from prior experience watching the movie.

Tobin's discussion of the evolution of the global phenomenon Pokémon in *Pikachu's Global Adventure*, (2004, p.3) helps to illuminate the amalgamation of popular culture and technology and explains the definitional instability of popular culture media.

Pokémon which began life as a piece of software to be played on Nintendo's game boy (a handheld computer for playing video games) quickly diversified into a comic book, a television show, a movie, trading cards, stickers, small toys and ancillary products such as backpacks and tee shirts.

This description illuminates the dynamic and widespread nature of children's commercial culture. Ideas and images that begin in one technological medium such as television can quickly spread to others. Pokémon, as described by Tobin began as a video game but it is one of the few popular culture characters *stemming* from video games that appear in the lives of preschoolers. In most cases children access popular culture through television, videos and DVDs. But as Tobin points out the images can quickly spread into subsidiary products.

Perhaps there is no better example of popular culture enduring and transcending media boundary lines than Lewis Carroll's *Alice's Adventures in Wonderland.* Originally published in 1856, the story took on many screen adaptations and in 1951 was modified by Walt Disney to an animated feature length film but was not released on home video until October 15, 1981. This had the single greatest effect in opening up the image to a larger audience. (Before the home video release children had to attend one of the three theatre releases to view the movie. Afterwards it was possible for anyone with a VCR to view the movie at any time.) As was the case with most Disney movies the characters from *Alice in Wonderland* have appeared as figurines, tee shirts, and cups (Disneystore.com). *Alice in Wonderland* game was released for Nintendo's Game boy in 2000. Even more recently the story was retold as a non-animated film by Director Tim Burton. New appropriations on the classic characters have been developed as figurines; clothing and plush animals as well as digital merchandize and technology, (specifically video games) which have been released for Nintendo DS and computer platforms.

A.A.Milne's Winnie the Pooh (1926) is another excellent example of the fluidity of popular culture images. The image of Pooh bear and the other inhabitants of the hundred acre wood were introduced through children's literature. It was reimagined and redrawn in the 1930's to include the modern day Pooh Bear's trademark red shirt. It was then was licensed to Disney in 1961; they in turn created the animated series, movies, and the merchandizing that exists today. The characters from Pooh Corner now appear on merchandize such as baby bassinets, baby mobiles, strollers, clothing, shoes, movies, pencils and pens, as well as Leap Frog Tag Junior stories, videos, televisions and telephones in the shape of pooh bear and Nintendo DS games and covers (Target, 2010).

I reference this not to critique the extensive distribution of these images but to emphasize the method in which popular culture and technology have largely become synonymous as well as the ability of these images to transcend media and time. These images, partially due to the roots in classic children's literature are for the most part seen as innocent, fanciful and benign. This is certainly not the case for all popular culture images.

Media and the Effects Paradigms

Media studies are often fraught with binaries of good and evil, in many cases children's popular culture technology is seen as either extremely harmful or fancifully benign. As a result the issues and debates surrounding popular culture are often polarized in assumptions of the effects of popular culture technology on children,

It is no surprise that subjects of commercialism, consumption and pop culture elicit responses that resemble a political debate. The literature on children and pop culture falls into two camps that differ on the relative powers of media messages and the agency of children. This is sometimes referred to as the debate of structure versus agency (Buckingham, 1998; Buckingham and Sefton Green, 2004). The roots of the debate are located in understandings of childhood, of child development, popular culture, and consumption.

The first school of thought centers on the notion of interpellation. Interpellation, as theorized by Althusser (1970), describe a mechanism whereby the human subject is constituted by pre-given structures and ideologies. Interpellation assumes that media effects can be traced to the accrual over time of repeated experiences of being hailed by the same ideological messages (Tobin, 2000). The concern is that if children are repeatedly exposed to adverse messages embedded in popular culture, that they will internalize the messages Sammond (2005) identifies this as a profoundly durable idea, the idea that people in general and children in particular can and do absorb values directly from the media they consume. It posits villains (children's media and toy producers) and implies the need for programs of social correction and control.

This is largely because media studies discourses often construct children as innocents, as victims of current commercial media and potential threats to the future social order (Molnar, 2005, Thorne, 1987, Zelziner, 1985). Lemish (2007, pp.102) names this ideology as "dominant force theory," characterizing it as a strong effects theory of mass communication that focuses on studies of public opinion and political campaigns. Pervasive in mid-twentieth century North American research, the basic premise is viewing television changes behavior and that the alteration is detrimental to the well being of the child. There is an assumption that television violence instigates violent behavior, commercials lead to the purchase of consumer products, and sex on television leads to permissive sexual behavior. Reminiscent of classical social psychological studies such as Alfred Bandura's Bobo Doll study, this viewpoint leaves little room for agency. Sammond (2005) elaborates that the critique of popular culture undervalues the potential agency of the members of this culture who are seen as defenseless

Curiously enough, this "media effects" camp has united liberals and conservative in common cause in support of protectionism. Both conservative proponents of Victorian family values and left wing critics of manipulative consumerism embrace parents' and children's rights to be freed from the pressures of consumerism (Cross, 2004, pp.180). The political right attacks the notion of popular culture for its lack of morality. Conservative parents have sought to isolate their young from threats to their religious, moral and even political values (Cross, 2004. 164). In *Babes in Tomorrowland*Sammond (2005) identifies right wing critiques of Disney movies (and images) as focused on delivering encoded pro-homosexual, pedophiliac and antichristian messages to American children.

In leftist political arenas, "television is often regarded as an extremely powerful agent of dominant ideology, a kind of propaganda machine which is responsible for brainwashing children into consumerism and other forms of false consciousness" (Buckingham, 1993, pp.7). With roots in the Frankfurt school and theorists including Horkheimer and Adorno, this viewpoint critiques mass or consumer culture as enfeebling non-commercial culture and thwarting the possibilities for revolutionary social change. In the words of Curren (2003, pp.166):

They scrutinize the pedagogical and sociological functions of the cultural industries in the reproduction of contemporary societies and held that mass culture and communication stand at the center of leisure activity are important agents of socialization and education, are mediators of political reality and thus should be seen as major institutions of contemporary societies within a variety of economic political cultural and social effects.

The primary concern here is the message of commercialism rather than threats to morality. This theorizing from the left fears the influence of commercialism; that it may weaken youths' later ability to be creative, to make rational judgments or to defer gratification. Therefore there is a need to shield children from this exposure (Cross, 2004). Rooted in a Marxist and neo-Marxist ideology, this viewpoint is critical of mass culture as it is seen to control manipulate, segment and debase society, and to contribute to the breakdown of local communities and to produce harmful forms of individualism and materialism (Kenway and Bullen, 2003).

In addition to critiques stemming from inappropriate content, popular culture and particularly technology are often perceived as cutting children off from the social atmosphere and peer culture in which they need to function. Vygotskian in nature, the assumption commonly associated with Developmentally Appropriate Practice conveys the expectation that children learn best when engaged with peers or adults in a social setting. Aside from judgments on the effects of content of popular, this helps to explain why video games, popular culture movies and sometimes computers are largely viewed pedagogically as a detrimental agent in preschool children's lives. As Ellen Seiter succinctly describes:

Child experts, television critics and protectionists are convinced that television deters children from achieving normative agendas of child development: direct interaction with peers and parents, "large motor" skills, socialization, cognitive and physical development. Television is excluded from the list of activities that can "stimulate" growth-and stimulation is something that parents are supposed to provide in endless supply from infancy onward. (Seiter, 1998, p.312)

Kenway and Bullen parallel Seiter's representation of the media effects theory: "The media is blamed for kids short attention spans; it is seen to render them passive, to undermine their capacity to play independently, to entertain themselves and also to threaten their creativity" (2001 p.3). This critique, content specific in nature also addresses the pedagogical implications of the popular culture/technological product.

The secondary viewpoint credits consumers (sometimes children) with a greater degree of agency in interpretation and mediation of these messages. Scholars that adopt this viewpoint view the construal of these images to be largely dependent on the consumer's context and prior knowledge of the subject. Twitchell demonstrates a rather critical perspective of the effects paradigm when calling into question the assumption that it makes about consumers as easily duped. "Why has the hypodermic metaphor (false needs injected into a docile populace) become the unchallenged explanation of consumerism?" (2000, p.272).

I locate my work in this more optimistic tradition (one similar to Buckingham's (1984) which considers context and prior knowledge in determining what children make of technology in preschool settings. In rejecting the practice of binary opposition of structure and agency, I acknowledging that popular culture technology and the subjects that it delivers is neither wholly beneficial, benign, nor malevolent. It is the interpretation and the context or situated meaning that can inform. I am not as concerned with the originated content as the focus but rather how parents, teachers and children interpret these messages and what they do with the images.

Stuart Hall's articulation of preferred meanings helps to illuminate this point (1999). Mass commercial culture artifacts carry meanings that are "intended" by marketing and advertizing, ascribed with particular characteristics and ideas for consumption. But children, much like adults may take this subject matter and use it to suit their own tastes and desires. As Erica Rand (1995) shows, consumers understand these images but use them for their own purposes. In recalling childhood play with Barbie women discuss from an adult's perspective the manners that they used Barbie to suit their own desires. Rand reveals "while the actual products and advertisements/explanations produced by Mattel clearly had an effect on what consumers wanted, saw and did, Barbie consumption still looks quite different than the Barbie Play on commercials. (1995, p.126). One of the reasons she states was limited means of the children to attain all of the parts represented by merchandise but then opened her explanation to include perspectives grounded in queer theory.

Elizabeth Chin in *Purchasing Power, (2001)* a study of consumption with working class African American youth echoes this sentiment as she shows girls reconfiguring images of Barbie to reflect ideas that are more indicative of African American working class culture. The girls in study had very little access to "ethnically correct dolls, they were only able to access the stereotypically blonde haired, white skinned middle class Barbies. Chin reveals that "Girls in Newhallville worked on their dolls materially and symbolically, blurring racial ab-solutes by putting their hair into distinctively African American styles using beads, braids, and foil in ways racially marked as black" (1999, 306). She notes, drawing on Bourdieu (1984) that consumption under capitalism is inherently mediated by culture. It is in this manner children can negotiate meanings and display agency. Objects and ideas that are brought into a space with one meaning particularly a shared space such as a classroom can have new meanings ascribed to them. The meaning of an object is not fixed but can be reappropriated based on the ideas and cultural knowledge that adults and children brings to the table (Hall, 1999). As Hall suggests, "The same photo or image can carry several quite different sometimes diametrically opposite meaning... There is no one 'true' meaning, meaning floats."(1997, p.228)

These scholars are more confident in the ability of children to construct their own meaning of these messages. This more libratory viewpoint does not suggest that children never internalize messages set forth from multinational billion dollar corporations, but it assigns greater agency to the viewer in deconstructing and reappropriating messages based on context and prior experiences. James Jenks and Prout (1998, 6) explain that this is a "piece of a new paradigm in which children are understood to be actors shaping as well as shaped by their circumstances." This trajectory does not reject the Birmingham Cultural Studies approach of identifying multinational corporations and marketing giants in assigning preferred meanings to objects, it simply opens a space for considering the way particular consumers in particular contexts use and makes sense of media texts and other popular cultural products. In other words children do interesting and novel things with these popular culture characters particularly in their interaction with popular culture technology. Activity is present in consumption and the meaning of a product or text is negotiated between producers and consumers. De Certeau (1984) outlines that the intent of appropriation made by the producers (marketing giants and advertisers) is not always the usage of the consumers:

The presence and circulation of a representation (taught by preachers, educators and populizers as the key to socioeconomic advancement) tells us nothing about what it is for the users. We must first analyze it's manipulation by users who are not its makers. Only then can we gage the difference or similarity between the production of the image and the secondary production hidden in the process of its utilization. (de Certeau, 1984, pp. xii).

Thus it rejects a structure and agency paradigm. Children are not bound by the storylines presented in popular culture media but may use these storylines in ways considered libratory when compared with the traditions of the Frankfurt School. In discussing children and technological media I am less concerned with the effect that media technology has on children then the manner in which children interact with it.

ISSUES, CONTROVERSIES, PROBLEMS: THE CONFLICT OF DIGITAL MEDIA AND "AUTHENTIC" LEARNING

In preschool settings digital media particularly that concerned with popular culture is often seen as a poor substitute for the materials children should be interacting with. The preferred objects are typically viewed as more concrete terms; examples are manipulatives such as sand and water tables, blocks and puzzles. The preference for these materials is often unquestionable as they are seen as classic, simple and pro-educational. The underlying discourse of these often conjures up a somewhat nostalgic and utopian view of "appropriate" children's activities. As Cross (2004) and others discuss, the carefully chosen materials are typically seen as markers of good middle class taste (Cook, 2004; Cross, 2004). I present this not to critique the pedagogical applications of such materials in the classroom but to suggest that these are often held as a benchmark of appropriate instructional practices. The implicit binary, following Derrida (1998) is that technological media when compared to these authentic and quality goods is somehow lacking. This is typically caught in a nostalgic discourse of simpler times and simpler toys void of popular culture and technology.

Many scholars have written of the privileging of the written word and traditional literary discourse over more popular culture texts such as Pokémon (Gee, 2004, 2007; Tobin, 2004). As mainstream literacy criticism and the educational establishment "in practice have tended to be elitist, they are generally opposed to popular texts that are enjoyed by children and hostile to any cultural form that seems to threaten the written word" (Hodge and Trip, 1986, pp.4). As historically popular culture media is seen as having a low value when compared to the knowledge economy of the school (Bourdieu, 1984), it has resulted in the outlawing of popular culture representations by some school administrations in official policy as well as practice. The knowledge economy or legitimate culture has been described as the official knowledge of school (Gee, 2004), but why? It rests on the supposition of class distinctions (and biases), that one type of knowledge is indicative of a more genteel class. Children, in order to adequately function within the promise of middle class society, must adopt an official school knowledge that is often rooted in higher cultural knowledge. Bourdieu (1984, pp.23) writes, "The educational system defines non-curricular general culture (La Culture Libre) negatively at least by delimiting within the dominant culture the area of what it puts into its syllabus and controls by its examinations."

At the root of the debate is the preference middle class parents may display for activities and materials that align more closely with school. Bourdieu's notion of cultural capital in the embodied state (1984) helps to illuminate the privileging of the written word as a marker of middle and upper middle class taste. This explains the preference for traditional literary discourse over more popular culture texts such as Pokémon (Gee, 2004; Tobin, 2004). As popular culture technology typically takes on an informal method of instruction, it can be attained by a person of any class. Save the entrance fee of technology, it by its very definition is relegated to be of the masses. As de Certeau (1984, pp.xv) writes, "Popular culture, as well as a whole literature called popular take on a different aspect as they present themselves essentially as arts of the making." When compared to official knowledge of school curriculum (which typically requires formal schooling) popular culture almost always plays second fiddle in importance. Apple recognizes additional implications, that behind the rejection of a lower or non legitimate culture (such as popular culture) is a class specific motivation, noting "the ways in which such class conversion strategies privilege particular class actors in education and de power others and an analysis of these strategies are crucial if we are to more fully comprehend the ways in which the struggle counts as legitimate culture versus popular culture" (2006, pp.ix).

Popular Culture Technology as Social Symbols

Stephen Kline in *Out of the Garden* (1993) argues that goods used in preschools (and preschools themselves) are social symbols that articulate social aspirations and convey complex social relations. The interpretations of these objects depend on a shared understanding of meaning and vary from setting to setting. Within sites the meanings of objects of popular culture can vary greatly between children and their parents and teachers. In other words, children are in a sense like a class or interest group with their own beliefs and forms of cultural capital. These beliefs and forms reflect without reproducing those of the adults, peers and media around them.

A central concern of this study is how the rejection or acceptance in school of certain types of popular culture technology reflects the workings of social class, especially of parents' and teachers' cultural capital. Cultural studies scholars (Bourdieu, Barthes, Baudrillard, and Hall among others) analyze the way objects, including popular cultural objects and texts, carry meaning. As Bourdieu writes, "Taste classifies and classifies the classifiers" (1984, pp. 6). The assumption of this study, following Bourdieu, is that by consuming (or rejecting) particular forms of popular culture and technology people attempt to locate themselves and the children they educate and care for in a desired class identity.

Annette Lareau's (2003) middle class concept of "concerted cultivation" helps to inform class biases of indulging in popular culture as a deficient or less than desirable behavior. She outlines that parents of middle and upper middle class see that the choices that they make in children's activities as preparation or skill building. Children are exposed to carefully chosen educational environments, lessons and activities in the hopes of preparing children to be successful middle class adults. They are also learning behaviors of these activities that mimic school behaviors and carry a high degree of cultural capital. For example, Cross (2004) suggests that the habitus or cultural practice of upper middle class American parents leads them to discourage many forms of children's popular culture as unrefined or common. As middle class and upper-middle class parents begin this cultivation early, toys and activities are seen as part of this preparation. Judgment of working class families are often caught in this effort. As concerted cultivation is habitus, any deviation is seen as unacceptable. As Bourdieu (1984) discusses, class specific behaviors become so normalized and ingrained that behaviors outside the class become distasteful or disgusting. The sexualized plastic toys that working class children are given and the violent or mature movies that children are allowed to watch become more than arbitrary choices. Framed in this middle class discourse they are not just unacceptable, they are seen as an unrefined form of indulgence that inadequately prepare children for life.

While these ideas may reflects an upper-middle class bias and are not accepted across all social classes in the United States they provide a better understanding of how class systems perceive and accept technology and pop culture. It also explains why some forms of popular culture are held in a lower regard across class systems.

Upper Middle Class: Technology as a Gateway

Biltmore Montessori, a private Montessori preschool draws students from affluent upper middle class households. It has the most expensive tuition; it nears 1,000 dollars a month for the preschool program. It also held the most rejectionary views of popular culture. In this preschool popular culture technology was overwhelmingly viewed as a distraction and a harmful influence. The director, Ms.Millie steadfastly attempted to block what she saw as an intrusion into their mission of peace. In comparison to other sites where popular culture technology was viewed as largely a whimsical interest of children, at Biltmore Montessori popular culture technology is interpreted as consumeristic and devious. The director, adopting a viewpoint consistent with the effects paradigm felt that media targeted children and "taught them to be consumers." As a result of the perceived influence of popular culture, the school even had rules banning popular culture clothing and images. Consistent with AMI Montessori schools Technology such as videos, movies, computers and popular culture images were also not a component of the primary (age 3-6) classroom. This is not to suggest that children in this setting were void of technological interaction. To the contrary, children in this setting interacted with popular culture technology to a greater degree that children in other settings did, in this case the images came exclusively from the children's time spent at home.

Among the upper-middle class the conflict over toys and television was not based on affordability (as was the case in other preschools) but on ideological and aesthetic objections. Parents often saw popular culture media as representative of corporate influence. Parents were much more interested in the message that the toys and media conveyed; their primary concern was the educational implications of the interaction. Popular culture media was endorsed when it promoted values that aligned with types of knowledge typically found in formal education (Gee, 2004). Expressing admiration for children's play that displayed a more scientific or analytical theme, the parents of this setting would seek out technological products that claim to offer "edutainment "and that prepare and educate children to "get ahead" and separate their children from the masses. As represented in the transcript from a focus group, one mother explains:

I have three daughters, ages 4, 5 and 7 they (their interest in popular culture characters) used to fluxuate… now, and their kind of unusual favorite is criminal minds. They identify with Dr. Reid. Dr. Reid is a very intellectual character, has 187 IQ and can read 20,000 words a minute so they all want to be in the FBI and be just like Dr. Reid.

The mother explained that although it was a more "mature" show she really liked the positive influence. The detail given of Dr. Reed's character in terms of intellectual capacity and capability helps to uncover the rationale for support. In this case the mother sees this as an intellectual role model with an advanced degree. Following Bourdieu (1986)the framing of popular culture in terms of intellectual capacity speaks to support of cultural capital of the embodied state. It becomes a way for parents to support endeavors that further trajectories closest to formal education.

Observations of children in the preschool reflected a likeminded opinion from other parents. The children through play indicated an exposure to technology that had a scientific and educational undercurrent. In my observation of work time at Biltmore I observed one preschooler display this practice:

Toby: I'm making a rocket out of this. These are the astronauts, they have a Moon Lander. They are about to land and go back to Earth, roger that, I have a rocket. There's an exploration kit inside the other part...It's moving back to command module, commencing to redock bshhhhsbbbbshhhhh (making a noise as he lowers the block to the ground.) (He switches into a deeper and much more serious voice.) Houston says Apollo 11 commencing to redock... roger that....this part....they are about to leave Moon Lander. These shoes (points to his sneakers) these are moonboots. There isn't any gravity when I walk with them.

I suspected based on the vocabulary and tone that he "switched into" that he had experience with some form of technology that emitted such phrases as "Houston says Apollo commencing to redock." Reminiscent of Bahktin's heteroglossia (where speakers bring traces of other discourses within their speech,) Toby's utterances indicated an alternate source (Bahktin, 1986). Indeed when asked "how do you know about Houston and shuttles", Toby references his movie "*Journey to the Moon.*" The assistant teacher added that Toby's "thing" was space; his parents had been to visit the NASA station and had brought the movie back as a souvenir.

In addition to emphasis on a scientific knowledge parents supported popular culture technology when it promoted values that parents saw as more refined.

Parent: "The Barbie movie that I was talking about it is called Swan Lake- I mean it has Barbie but it has the music from Swan Lake and it's not bad at all it exposes them to something positive, and they have no idea what they are being exposed to but they recognize the songs and love them and the Nutcracker and I kind of like that

Another parent: I am gonna go get these movies

This "something positive" is the professed knowledge of classical music. Explaining "I mean it has Barbie but it is music from *Swan Lake*", she clarifies that the value of the video is not Barbie but the inclusion of Tchaikovsky's composition. Bourdieu (1984) specifically outlines professed knowledge of composers to be a marker of upper class taste, indicative of a higher degree of cultural capital.

Consistent with Bourdieu's findings, parents of children in the upper-middle class school at Biltmore Montessori had a much greater knowledge of how specific toys and TV programs could prepare their children for academic success. They did not see their choices as arbitrary or happenstance. They were calculated based on their ability to contribute to the trajectory of educational success (Lareau, 2003).

Computers, while rejected by the school as an AMI Montessori were universally endorsed by parents, seen as a mode of preparation. Parents while endorsing computer games overall specifically spoke with approval of games that they felt had pro-educational attributes. This caused parents to seek out computer games that would further their educational goals. Criteria for games included an educational trajectory however parents shied away from choices that they saw as overly didactic, as a recurring theme in this setting was an emphasis on the activity and creativity in the interaction. As represented by a focus group discussion a father discussed the frustration he felt for educational games that held children's interest, supplying: "they market these as fun games that are to be learning games and you get into them and it's like what's 2+2 and it's like... How long is this gonna keep and they really don't... compared to the regular games, I mean we let them on PBS Kids, and they are just kinda looking around, goofing around." The critique while initially concerned with the rudimentary nature also speaks to the concern that upper middle class parents have regarding procedural and overly didactic curriculum.

Alternative suggestions that met parental approval included games that promoted financial literacy. One parent expressed that the recent Christmas holiday had supplied her family with a computer game by Robert Kiyosaki, the author of the book *Rich Dad Poor Dad*: "it's a really cool game. It teaches them about managing money and obtaining financial security and I love that. They don't know what they are doing but they are getting a dose of something pretty useful."

In addition to their support of computers, parents endorsed learning systems and media that were overtly educational. Leap frog laptops were substituted for Nintendo DS on supposition that they better supported cognitive growth. Tag reader systems, while not discussed in this setting are another "learning system" produced by Leapfrog and marketed as proeducational. Both of these products pair extensively with characters from television and movies, increasing the draw for children and parents alike to consume media. Many parents saw it as a good compromise. While the parents did express concern with messages of popular culture as antifeminist and commercial when it was applied in an educational manner they acquiesced.

Parents conceded that while they attempted to engage their children with computers, video games had the most intensive pull for the children. Incidentally this is also where most of the more common or mainstream popular culture characters entered. Nintendo DS, a handheld computer game system was an area of great tension between parent and adult. Marketed to children and adults, it has games deemed educational as promoted and advertized to pair with games such as *Brain Age*. The system, coveted by children was viewed as marginally acceptable by parents. Parents did not endorse the interaction nearly to the backing they gave computers but "gave in" to purchasing the system which has many features similar to a traditional video game system. Much like a computer the games available on the system can vary from those traditionally considered educational to more mainstream popular culture titles. Incidentally the children reported consuming titles that were more concerned with mainstream popular culture than educational titles.

Pokémon, available on the Nintendo DS was a favored game that was a topic of much contention at Biltmore Montessori. Administration saw Pokémon as possessing harmful influences on the students' behavior. The director Ms. Millie explained that while videogames have never been allowed, cards and dramatic play revolving around Pokémon was permitted in the past, but were later banned for their "violent influence." She felt the children "totally assumed the role of Pokémon" and that they were "taken over" and it was "challenging to stop that." "They would come to school and pretend to be the Pokémon characters." Ms. Millie explained that the rule was that no cards were to be brought to school and if they were, they were confiscated. I asked for further explanation of the rules governing Pokémon:

Allison: Are they allowed to make up scenarios or games about Pokémon as long as they don't bring the cards? You know, can they talk about them, play the game outside?

Ms. Millie: No, we would stop anything to do with Pokémon. It was combative you know, the aggressive kicking and hitting.

Part of the reason Ms. Millie was supportive of a ban on Pokémon was because of her own feelings on the subject. She explained that she went to a Pokémon movie with her own son and was very displeased with how she felt the characters acted towards each other. She said they were "nasty" to each other. The strong feelings of the administration did little to quell the students' interest in this media, as represented by a discussion that I has with one student:

Alan directs his question toward me, "Do magnets fall off?

Allison: Do magnets fall off? (Pause) I don't know what you mean.

Alan: (Ignoring my question) these are slicing things (pointing to two blocks.) People. Charion comes out of here (moves one of the pieces aside). He's one of the hardest people and when you beat this you meet another slicer.

Allison: How do you beat them?

Alan: You beat them by Pokémon. You see, the boat appears and a secret platform comes out of here and they can (pause), the green part and the yellow part, they block you from getting into the red part. You have to, you have to (pause), it teleports you on a secret platform. This part looks like guns because it is broken off of the ground. And this part teleports you to a secret island called (pause), Genora. Then a piece of ground comes up and bshhhhhh, I play Pokémon. You send out Pokémon until health gets knocked out and when you, when you capture the master ball. I have Pokémon Mystery Dungeon Explorers of Sky. I beat Pokea but Diego is harder. I like this and this other magnets work better than other things.

Allison: Why?

Alan: The other ones you have to build a certain thing. This way (motions to the magnet blocks) you can build whatever you want.

Allison: And you can play Pokémon. Are you allowed to play Pokémon here?

Alan: Well, yes, no, no video games here. We have work, lunch, playground and art.

While the administration steadfastly attempted to block what they saw as a harmful intrusion parents in this setting were more willing to have the children engage with the characters that held their attention. The emphasis in this setting, on the intellectual capacity of popular culture was seen as something that could mediate perceived ill or less than desirable effects of media.

Working Class: A Child's World

In sharp contrast to the upper middle class setting of Biltmore Montessori is the working class community of Hermosa. Hermosa falls into the category of a Title I school, under the 1965 Elementary and Secondary Education Act (ESEA). This division affords "Financial Assistance to Local Educational Agencies for the Education of Children of Low-Income Families" (United States Department of Education, 2009). In order to qualify for this designation more than 40 percent of the families that the school serves must be considered low income, according to the United States Census. Title I, the largest elementary and secondary education program, supplements state and local funding for low-achieving children, in high-poverty schools.

The preschool program as part of a school readiness platform endorsed early literacy skills, dramatic play and social development. Facilitated by large amounts of time in child-directed centers, there were also commonly whole group instruction of stories, finger plays and songs. The teacher Ms. Lena used this time to enhance literacy and self expression.

When discussing popular culture in the classroom and the meanings ascribed it is also important to consider not only what the presence of popular culture suggests but what the absence of popular culture reveals. In Biltmore Montessori it reflected a belief that children were best educated with traditional Montessori materials and that popular culture was believed to infringe on a "natural peaceful education". Hermosa preschool also displayed very few examples of popular culture technology in the classroom but for diverse reasons. True to its mission of a school readiness preschool, the primary objective in this setting was to advance children in manners of literacy, numeracy and social skills. Ms. Lena focused on activities that were literacy based such as read alouds. In addition to structured whole group activities children were afforded a large degree of autonomy in individual play. Ms Lena saw this as promoting language and social skills through interaction. The school did provide one computer for student use but in two months of observation no child interacted with it. As my field work for this preschool occurred in the first two months of the school year it is possible that observations later in the year would yield a much different result.

Language development was arguably the primary focus of this preschool. As the majority of the students spoke Spanish as their home language, there was urgency for cultivation of English. Arizona, where this study took place has legislatively outlawed instruction of students in any other language than English beginning in Kindergarten. Factoring this in allows for a greater understanding of the rationale behind Ms. Lena's choice of activities; those including passive viewing of videos/ computers for curricular content did not further the mission of extending and practicing language. nearly to the extent of child directed play and teacher led activities (such as circle time) This was another albeit hidden objective in the name of school readiness. Ms. Lena did not actively introduce any form of popular culture technology (as was the case at Faith Christian) in the classroom although the classroom library did include books with Clifford and Sesame Street. She while not keenly endorsing characters did not dismiss them provided that they were what she considered "preschool appropriate."

In addition to concerns of language development Ms. Lena focused on social skills and preschool behaviors. Many of the children's in preschool had little experience in a school like setting. In contrast to as the other two schools where the children began preschool at age three or before (Biltmore Phoenix has an infant/toddler program), the Early Childhood Block Grant funds preschools for children for one year before kindergarten. All of the children in the setting entered preschool for the first time at age four.

Although serving a working class population, the Hermosa Preschool program reflects many middle-class beliefs about early childhood education. While the two teachers in the classroom at Hermosa come from working class, immigrant backgrounds, their attitudes about popular culture reflect a middle class viewpoint. One explanation is that Hermosa is accredited by NAEYC. Another is that in the course of taking classes in Early Childhood Education and getting a teacher certification in Early Childhood Education, the teachers at Hermosa have been exposed to and taken on the ideological beliefs of their university instructors and textbooks. For these reasons, it is no surprise that the rules about popular culture at Hermosa reflect the middle class belief that children are vulnerable innocents who need to be shielded from commercialized, morally offensive, vulgar forms of popular culture (Cross, 2004).

For middle class parents, as in mainstream early childhood educational ideology, children's popular culture falls into two categories, one of which is embraced, the other reviled. The first is a category that includes toys and television programs that present themselves as educational, such as Legos, Fisher Price toys, Sesame Street, Bob the Builder, Dora, Blue's Clues and Thomas the Train. In interviews at all three settings parents as well as teachers expressed approval of these forms of popular culture, which were assumed to promote pro-social and educational values and therefore to be beneficial to children's development. In fact, the purported educational value of these programs and toys kept them from being classified as forms of popular culture or as commercial products.

Ideas that hint at "mature" subject matter (interpreted as teenage or adult sexuality) also fall into the, second, despised category of products and programs for children. Popular culture products such as Hannah Montana, Cheetah Girls and Bratz, which are aimed at the tween population and at younger children's aspirational viewing and consumption fall into this category. In alluding to teenage sexuality, they violate middle class norms which emphasize a Victorian innocence of children (Cross, 2004). Upper-middle class parents of Biltmore Montessori were vehemently opposed to Bratz, based mostly on a feminist critique. They saw these dolls as promoting a bad image for girls, with their short skirts and heavy makeup. One parent even went so far as to suggest that that the Bratz dolls were "trashy" and reminiscent of prostitutes. Bourdieu points out that such expressions of disgust are performances of cultural capital, that distastes proceeds tastes, and that: "Different tastes are thus seen as unnatural and rejected, resulting in disgust provoked by horror or visceral intolerance ('feeling sick') of the tastes of others" (1984,p.56).

Toys and programs that fall into this "edgy" category, while not necessarily endorsed by Hermosa parents were not rejected. Instead both categories of popular culture were all seen as toys that their children like to play with and programs they like to watch. Whereas parents mentioned a preference for popular cultural products such as Maya and Miguel, that seem to fall into the first category, they did not reject Bratz, Barbie, Spider-man, and Hulk, who were discussed in much the same way as was Sesame Street.

Consider the following scene I observed at Hermosa where a small group of children were playing with Barbie dolls:

Michelle: I got Bratz dolls.

Allison: You have Bratz Dolls?

Alana: Me too, I got Bratz dolls too, and Barbies. I got lots of them. They pretty.

Allison: What do you play with your Bratz and Barbie dolls?

Alana: They're my sister's, not mine, but they're my favorites.

Matthew: (Chiming in): I got a Hulk doll, but not a real one

Allison: What is a real one?

Matthew: A big one, you know, like the guy on TV, you know I got one at home.

The dolls the children discuss here are clearly common play objects in the home. These types of dolls were somewhat tolerated by the middle-class parents at Faith Christian, rejected at Biltmore Montessori. For the working class the first and second category merged into a larger category of things of interest to children. I mention this not to suggest that the Hermosa parents saw no difference in the categories, some Hermosa parents expressed concern for the content. One father was very concerned with his daughter being exposed to adverse messages, namely violence. His justifications were much in line with the parents of Faith Christian. In his opinion Boz the Bear and Veggie Tales, both Christian program were preferable subject matters to others. He even supplied that he did not like his daughter playing with her cousins as they were allowed to watch content that was not appropriate.

For immigrant families income transcends cultures, but cultural capital often does not. As many of the children that participated in this study are immigrant children from Mexico, this is especially crucial to address in their understanding of popular culture as specific to the dominant (and arguably more powerful) Anglo American culture. In the quest for assimilation and globalization also known as "learning English" the parents are forced to abandon the cultural capital from their own home culture. This helps to highlight that in many cases working class families are not without cultural capital, they possess a separate cultural capital that is not valued in the United States. This facilitates our understanding why working class immigrant parents may endorse products that are seen as non-desirable by upper-middle class parents. With an attempt of assimilation into the dominant white culture combined with the forced abandonment of their own culture, meaning making and class discriminates evolve and change.

Lower Middle Class: Media as a Pedagogical Tool

As demonstrated in the introduction to this chapter, mainstream children's popular culture characters were prolifically scattered throughout Faith Christian. A Winnie-the-Pooh mural was painted on one wall of the entrance area of the preschool (presumably without having paid rights to Disney). This theme continued on the hallways to the classrooms which were lined with a Pooh wallpaper border. The teachers saw this as a friendly way to welcome children and parents to the preschool center. These decorations were seen by the staff at Faith Christian as positive and as possessing a fanciful innocence. We can also read in the presence of these images an expression of the school's view that such commercialized forms of children's popular culture is benign.

Aligning with this belief of popular culture, in contrast to the other two settings, media was an integral component of the pre-kindergarten program of Faith Christian. As described in the introduction media technology was seen as a way to facilitate learning of curriculum. Games and puzzles used as instructional materials often depicted popular culture themes and characters. Activity games such as a Dora the Explorer's bean bag toss and board games such as a SpongeBob version of a Milton Bradley's *Memory* game were also played to support instructional goal such as "number sense" and "identifying similarities and differences." In my field notes I captured the following scenario:

Five children and Ms. Sophia were seated around one of the small tables in the center of the carpeted area of the room, playing a SpongeBob version of the Milton Bradley Game Memory. Each child was allowed two turns to match cards. Ms. Sophia asked the children to identify similarities and differences of pictures, each of which featured a character from SpongeBob Square Pants.

Ms. Sophia mediated this game, reminding the children of turns and scaffolding their ability to match pictures of SpongeBob. She also joined in the conversation about SpongeBob, commenting about the subtle differences of the pictures of Sponge Bob and Patrick the Starfish. The children's knowledge of the characters was detailed, but it was not clear to me if they knew the characters from first-hand television watching, discussions with friends in the classroom, or simply from practice playing this game.

Brittany: Pineapple, I found the pineapple (the house that SpongeBob lives in).

Ms. Sophia: Can you find the other one; do you remember where it might be?

Brittany: Uh, here, oh (picks up a card that does not match the pineapple) it's, it's Sandy the Squirrel.

Ms. Sophia: Put it back then and we can try next turn.

Ms. Sophia engages with the children as a like minded comrade, trading comments and knowledge of the characters to such a convincing degree that I am not sure if she is familiar with the TV show or has simply played the game before.

The inclusion of popular culture technology was overall supportive of the goals and means of the curriculum and preschool as a whole. As the preschool describes itself as "faith-based" teachers in this preschool regularly relied on videos as a way to translate difficult, abstract, biblical concepts into a manner that preschool children could easily understand. Video afforded them this opportunity. Observations of whole activities group reveal the extent to which popular culture technology was integrated in the curriculum through technology:

The children return to the carpet in front of the calendar. It is time for Bible Scriptures. The preschool website describes this as a goal for the children to display "knowledge of age-appropriate Christian songs, prayer and stories."

Ms. Sophia (the teacher) asks," What is the Scripture for today?" She point to the small plastic easel that displays a card. The large laminated card has the letter "B" and the corresponding scripture for the day. (There are scriptures that correlate with each letter of the alphabet). She reads the scripture and then rereads it with the children's accompaniment. She next wheels the media cart in front of the children and places a tape in the VCR. Today they are going to watch a video lesson, *Jay, Jay the Jet Plane: Friends Forever.*

Ms. Sophia tells the kids, "We are going to watch Thomas the Train." She looks at the tape: "Oops I mean Jay Jay."

Evan: Can we watch Pocahontas?

Evan: (turning to ask me) Do you like Pocahontas?

I respond to Evan in a quiet voice: Do you like Pocahontas?

Ms. Sophia: (overhearing our conversation) I didn't show you Pocahontas.

Evan: Uh huh.

Ms. Sophia: No, I think that Ms. Monique showed you that before mom picked you up, not me.

When I later asked Evan where he saw the movie Pocahontas he answered "here".

As Evan in his dialogue with Ms. Sophia demonstrated, videos were commonly shown to children at the preschool. Although both featured characters that could be considered mainstream popular culture it is evident that they were divided into two distinct categories; educational and fun. The conflict arose as Ms. Sophia preferred to show popular culture that she felt reflected values that more closely aligned with the biblical and educational focus of the preschool within the "official" school day. Disney movies such as *Pocahontas* and *Bambi* were shown in the "aftercare" hours between two and six P.M.

The lower- middle class setting had the greatest number of computers, and the children interacted with them in a greater frequency when compared to other preschools. Computer games in the classroom displayed popular culture characters such as Franklin, Little People and Winnie the Pooh. Children were able to access the games during center time and after school.

The inclusion of Teddy Ruxpin, a popular culture character from the 1980's played a crutial pedagogical role in heightening children's access to literacy. As mentioned in the introduction he is an animatronic bear who moves his lips and eyes as if he is the storyteller. Children were able to place tape in his back and listen to stories. This "reader" enabled children to access books to a greater degree as in this preschool books were not typically read aloud, they were considered something for the children to "read" during quiet and center time. The classroom library presented limited options for the children to engage with the text. In comparison to the other two sites, at Faith Christian merchandized books made up a large percentage of the classroom library. They featured characters such as Dora, Disney Princesses, and the characters from Disney's *Toy Story*. Ms. Sonya included these texts in the library as she felt that the inclusion of popular culture would enhance children engagement with books. Although the children were interested in the characters, their engagement with the text was limited. The popular culture texts were above the emergent reading level of preschoolers; these texts did not include a high frequency of site words or repetition; and the language was far too complex for the children to access without assistance. Consequently the children did not engage with the text but rather only with the pictures. While I am not suggesting there is anything wrong with children engaging in text through pictures, the children could have engaged with the text to a greater degree with scaffolding provided by the teacher. The children's interaction with the books was an independent activity; at no time did I witness Ms. Sophia reading the books to the children. The expectation of independent reading meant the children had no way (other than pictures) to interpret plot, prediction, sequencing and comprehension.

Demonstrated by the prolific use of popular culture technology in this setting it is safe to assume that parents and teachers expressed very little concern for the presence of popular culture technology. In this religious setting content that teachers and parents felt was anti-Christian was of much greater concern.

Reflecting on Bridging the Communication-Generation Gap through Technological Influences on Ideology and Social Class

In this emerging technological age, preschools are dealing with technology and images from media in very different manners. This chapter shows that in early childhood sectors, embracing technology is far from universal and if it is brought into the classroom, depends heavily on the context in which it is used. As I have argued here, "understandings" and judgments regarding the appropriateness of popular culture are simply that: understandings. The rejection or inclusion of popular culture technology in pedagogical and curricular matters are culturally based, influenced by the habitus of the individuals and preschools in local communities. Their everyday practices, the choices and judgments made regarding popular culture technology, following Bourdieu (1984), are informed by factors such as social class but also the ideology of the program and parents. This chapter attempts to move towards new understandings of children and how popular culture in early childhood classrooms can be seen not as arbitrary choices (although they could certainly be) but as messages or using Kline's (1994) understanding, as social symbols that are used by different people for different purposes. Noting this fact also points to the importance of interpretation, particularly in local communities. As acknowledged in this chapter, images such as Bratz Dolls were interpreted as glamorous for some children and parents but were considered hyper sexualized and "trashy" for others. Likewise, Disney Princesses might be seen as nostalgic, fanciful and innocent for some parents while commercialized and overtly sexual for others.

Additional issues arise when considering the pedagogical implications of such choices. As shown in this chapter, parents in upper middle class preschool setting had a well honed knowledge of how certain ideas and interactions with certain materials would work to position them in more favorable class relations. Despite objections to content, parents actively endorsed ideas and images that promoted social mobility, particularly when concerned with cultural capital in the embodied state. By actively choosing certain popular culture materials, the parents recognized their role as social symbols and more often than not chose materials for educational advancement. These materials not coincidently had close alignment with school type knowledge.

This section gives you some questions and activities to help you think about how you can use some of the ideas from this chapter in your work.

Research

1. Identify pop culture icons that are evident in your classroom based on the children's interest and parent support. Trace the origin of these icons to determine the role of technology in origin, exposure and availability.
2. Interview your parents to determine their perceptions of pop culture icons as to which are accepted and which are considered inappropriate. Is there a different in these perceptions based on income level?
3. Select a book and a technology based version of the characters or story. Place these in two separate areas of your room and collect frequency of use by children when given free choice of activities. Which venue do children most often use?

Reflect

1. What forms of technology portray pop culture icons in your classroom?
2. What pop culture icons do you consider appropriate in a preschool setting and which do you consider inappropriate? Identify what may influence your decision.(i.e. your religious beliefs, your social status, your peer group influence)
3. Types of preschools generally serve relatively economical and culturally homogeneous groups of children. How might this impact the future social and economic structure of this country?
4. How does the connection of ideology and social class influence your acceptance or rejection of technology as a pedagogical tool?

Practice

1. Identify core learning standards in your classroom. Plan how technology icons can support the outcomes.
2. Within preschool sectors ideology and social class plays a major role for the type of popular culture technology that children in the United States will interact with in various preschools. How will this influence your classroom environment? What can you do to insure children are not labeled by their preference and interaction with technology in your classroom?
3. Work with parents in your classroom to remove social stigma from technology pop culture perceptions.

REFERENCES

Althusser, L. (1970). *Lenin and philosophy and other essays (B. Brewster translation)*. NewYork, NY: Monthly Review Press.

Apple, M. W. (2007). Foreword in J. A. Van Galen & G. W. Noblit (Eds.), *Late to class: Social class and schooling in the new economy*. Albany, NY: State University of New York Press.

Bakhtin, M. (1984). *Rabelais and his world.* Bloomington, IN: Indiana University Press.

Bakhtin, M. (2009). *The Bakhtin reader: Selected writings of Bakhtin, Medvedev, Voloshinov*. London, UK: Bloomsbury.

Barthes, R. (1967). *Elements of Semiology. (A. Lavers & C. Smith translation)*. London, UK: Jonathan Cape.

Bourdieu, P. (1984). *Distinction: A social critique of the judgment of taste*. Cambridge, MA: Harvard University Press.

Bourdieu, P. (1986). The forms of capital . In Richardson, J. (Ed.), *Handbook of theory and research for the sociology of education*. New York, NY: Greenwood.

Buckingham, D. (1998). *Teaching popular culture*. London, UK: UCL Press.

Buckingham, D., & Sefton-Green, J. (1994). *Cultural studies goes to school: Reading and teaching popular media*. London, UK: Taylor and Francis.

Buckingham, D., & Sefton Green, J. (2004). Structure, Agency and pedagogy in children's media culture . In Tobin, J. (Ed.), *Pikachu's global adventure: The rise and fall of Pokémon*. Durham, NC: Duke University Press.

Cashell, B. (2007). *Report for Congress: "Who are the Middle Class?"* Retrieved from http://www.policyarchive.org/ handle/ 10207/bitstreams /4472.pdf

Chin, E. (1999). Ethnically correct dolls: Toying with the race industry. *American Anthropologist*, *101*(2). doi:10.1525/aa.1999.101.2.305

Chin, E. (2001). *Purchasing power: Black kids and American consumer culture*. Minneapolis, MN: University of Minnesota Press.

Cook, D. (2004). *The commodification of childhood: The children's clothing industry and the rise of the child consumer*. Durham, NC: Duke University Press.

Cross, G. (2004). *The cute and the cool: Wondrous innocence and modern American children's culture*. New York, NY: Oxford University Press.

Curren, R. (2003). *A companion to the philosophy of education: Blackwell companions to philosophy*. Hoboken, NJ: Wiley-Blackwell.

De Certeau, M. (1994). *The practice of everyday life*. Los Angeles, CA: University of California Press.

Du Gay, P., Hall, S., Janes, L., & Negus, K. (1997). *Doing cultural studies: The story of the Sony Walkman*. Thousand Oaks, CA: Sage Publications.

Elkind, D. (1998). *All grown up and no place to go: Teenagers in crisis*. Cambridge, MA: Da Capo Press.

Gee, J. P. (2004). *Situated language and learning: A critique of traditional schooling*. New York, NY: Routledge.

Gee, J. P. (2007). *What video games have to teach us about learning and literacy* (2nd ed.). Palgrave Macmillan.

Haas Dyson, A. (1997). *Writing superheroes: Contemporary childhood, popular culture, and classroom literacy*. New York, NY: Teacher's College Press.

Hall, S. (1999). Encoding, decoding . In During, S. (Ed.), *The cultural studies reader*. London, UK: Routledge.

Haugland, S. W. (1999). The newest software that meets the developmental needs of young children. *Early Childhood Journal*, *26*(4), 73–82.

Hodge, R., & Trip, D. (1986). *Children and television: A semiotic approach*. Palo Alto, CA: Stanford University Press.

James, A., Jenks, C., & Prout, A. (1998). *Theorizing childhood*. New York, NY: Teachers College Press.

Kenway, J., & Bullen, E. (2001). *Consuming children: Education entertainment advertizing*. Philadelphia, PA: Open University Press.

Kinder, M. (1999). *Kids media culture*. Durham, NC: Duke University Press.

Kline, S. (1993). *Out of the garden: Toys, TV, and children's culture in the age of marketing*. London, UK: Verso.

Kyiosaki, R., & Lechter, S. (2000). *Rich dad poor dad: What the rich teach their kids that the poor and middle class do not*. New York, NY: Business Plus.

Lareau, A. (2003). *Unequal childhoods: Class, race, and family life*. Berkeley, CA: University of California Press.

Lemish, D. (2007). *Children and television: A global perspective*. Malden, MA: Blackwell Publishing.

Marcus, G. (1995). Ethnography in/of the world system: The emergence of multisite ethnography. *Annual Review of Anthropology, 24*, 95–117. doi:10.1146/annurev.an.24.100195.000523

Molnar, A. (2005). *School commercialism: From democratic ideal to market commodity*. New York, NY: Taylor and Francis Group.

Montessori, M. (1995). *The absorbent mind*. New York, NY: Holt Paperbacks.

NAEYC. (1996 b). NAEYC position statement: Technology and young children-Ages three through eight. *Young Children, 51*(6), 11–16.

Petrash, J. (2002). *Understanding Waldorf education: Teaching from the inside out*. New York, NY: Gryphon House.

Rand, E. (1995). *Barbie's queer accessories*. Durham, NC: Duke University Press.

Sammond, N. (2005). *Babes in tomorrowland: Walt Disney and the making of the American child 1930-1960*. Durham, NC: Duke University Press.

Seiter, E. (1991). *Remote control: Television, audiences, and cultural power*. New York, NY: Routledge.

Seiter, E. (1995). *Sold separately: Children and parents in consumer culture*. New Brunswick, NJ: Rutgers University Press.

Seiter, E. (1998). Children's desires/mother's dilemmas: The social contexts of consumption . In Jenkins, H. (Ed.), *The children's culture reader* (pp. 297–317). New York, NY: New York University.

Seiter, E. (1999). Power Rangers at preschool negotiating media in child care settings . In Kinder, M. (Ed.), *Kids media culture*. Durham, NC: Duke University Press.

Thorne, B. (1993). *Gender play: Girls and boys at school*. New York, NY: Open University Press.

Tobin, J. (2000). *Good guys don't wear hats: Children's talk about the media*. New York, NY: Teacher's College Press.

Tobin, J. (2004). *Pikachu's global adventure: The rise and fall of Pokémon*. Durham, NC: Duke University Press.

Tobin, J., Hsueh, Y., & Karasawa, M. (2009). *Preschool in three cultures revisited: China, Japan, and the United States*. Chicago, IL: University of Chicago Press.

Twitchell, J. B. (2000). *Lead us into temptation: The triumph of American materialism*. New York, NY: Columbia University Press.

United States Department of Education. (2009). *Elementary and Secondary Education Act*. Retrieved from http://www2.ed.gov/ policy/elsec/ leg/ esea02/index.html

United States Department of Health and Human Services. (2009). *2009 Federal poverty guidelines*. Retrieved from http://aspe.hhs.gov/ poverty/ 09extension.shtml

Zelizer, V. (1985). *Pricing the priceless child: The changing social value of children*. Princeton, NJ: Princeton University Press.

Chapter 5
Technology:
Changing the Research Base on Young Children

Shannon Audley-Piotorwksi
University of Memphis, USA

Neha Kumar
University of Memphis, USA

Yeh Hsueh
University of Memphis, USA

Melanie Sumner
University of Memphis, USA

ABSTRACT

Technology has changed the potential for research of young children dramatically. Technology has allowed researchers to capture nuances of children's interactions such as eye movement in infants, heart rate, and physiological reactions that researcher's could never accurately track without the new technologies. Understanding the role of technology and the evidence of children's development has opened new ideas about the capabilities of children. Teachers need to understand how these technologies are being used and how researchers support learning and development based on this new approach to information collection with young children.

DOI: 10.4018/978-1-61350-059-0.ch005

Copyright © 2012, IGI Global. Copying or distributing in print or electronic forms without written permission of IGI Global is prohibited.

INTRODUCTION: TECHNOLOGY AND CHILD DEVELOPMENT

What we know about young children's development is dependent upon the availability of technology. For example, prominent philosophers Aristotle (Chambliss, 1982) and Rousseau (1762/1979) used the technology of their respective times, behavioral observations and logic, to argue that young children were incapable of reason. Several centuries later, and with similar technology, William James (1890/1981), the first American psychologist, also asserted that young children were incapable of reason. He described the infant's world as, "one great blooming, buzzing confusion" (James, 1890/1981, p. 462). In the twentieth century, however, Jean Piaget introduced new technology for examining children's reasoning capabilities– the clinical method (or the *méthode clinque*, see Mayer, 2005). Using the clinical method, Piaget (1926/1960) found evidence to support his argument that young children were, in fact, capable of reason (albeit, it was not the same as adult reason). By using different, and more nuanced technology, Piaget (1926/1960) was able to challenge previous beliefs about a young child's capability to reason. Recently, newer technologies, such as eye-tracking and brain scanning, have allowed researchers to examine more nuanced questions about children's ability to reason, including what does the brain look like when reasoning occurs? And when does the ability to reason first occur? With the aid of this new technology, researchers are now identifying the complex ways that infants and young children reason about their environments.

It is important to note that the technology Piaget utilized was not as electronically advanced as what is available today; the clinical method consisted of interviewing children, asking them to explain their thinking, and writing down their responses. However, technology is not limited to fancy gadgets or electronic devices; it also refers to simple tools, such as making observations or writing down a child's response. The etymology of technology– the craft of a branch of knowledge ("Merriam Webster's Dictionary", 2007)—reveals the simplicity of what technology can be. Technology, especially in relation to the social sciences, refers to the tools and methods that scientists use to study development. While some research technology is relatively simplistic, such as taking a child's resting heart rate, technology can be complex as well, such as brain scanning using fMRI. As technology continues to advance, so will our knowledge of young children's development. Because technology, and thus our knowledge of child development, has rapidly changed over the past ten years, it is important for educators and parents to know what current technologies are used in research with young children, and how these technologies have advanced our knowledge of young children's development.

To present a more comprehensive understanding of this work the team of authors were selected based on educational backgrounds and experiences that span the digital generational gap. The authors of this chapter approach these issues from different perspectives and technology generational lives; the first two authors have backgrounds in science, while the last two authors have backgrounds in early childhood education. The first author of this chapter is a former high school science teacher and biologist who is now a doctoral student in educational psychology. The second author is a high-school student who has research experience in genetics and child development and has grown up in the digital age. The third author is a Professor of early childhood education at the University of Memphis from China and a student of Eleanor Duckworth, one of the close associates of Piaget. He has a deep understanding of the work of Piaget and provides a perspective of what this work can mean to traditional thinking about development. The fourth author has experience as a preschool teacher. She has grounded us in the realities of how teachers think. Our combined experiences have allowed us to consider the importance of technology in child development from both a research and applied perspective. This is important, as research findings do not always clearly translate into educational pedagogy. We feel that it is very important for practitioners to understand *what* types of technology researchers utilize to study child development, *how* these findings extend or challenge current knowledge in the field, and the *applied* practicality of the research to the field of education.

In this chapter, we will describe the current technologies that are used in research with young children and then discuss how these new technologies help fine-tune our understanding of infant and early childhood development. This chapter will be divided into five sections. The first three sections will look at specific technology and the research findings that directly apply to young children's development. First, we will focus on eye-tracking technology, and discuss how eye-tracking technology has shaped our understanding of literacy development in young children. Second, we will explore the technology associated with psychophysiological responses, including heart rate and stress responses, and discuss how these findings have shaped our view of early social, emotional, and cognitive development. Third, we will investigate brain imaging technology - Positron Emission Tomography (PET), Functional Magnetic Resonance Imagining (fMRI), Electroencephalography (EEG), and Near –Infrared Spectroscopy (NIRS)- and then discuss how this technology has shaped our knowledge about the interplay of emotion and cognition. The next section will discuss possible issues and limitations of the new research and application to teaching including issues with practically in application of these research findings. We will end this chapter with future trends of this type of research and the possible influence on teacher training.

Objectives

There are two major objectives of this chapter. First, we want the reader to be informed about common technologies, and how the technologies are used in research on the development of young children. Secondly, we want the reader to be able to specifically understand how technology has helped advance knowledge about older issues, such as literacy development, in research, and how these findings indirectly inform pedagogy. The readers should be able to:

- Identify new forms of technology that have changed ideas about child development
- Relate new ideas from research to classroom instruction
- Identify how technology has changed the field of early childhood development

BACKGROUND

Technology has and is changing the potential for and understanding of children's' learning and development even as you read this chapter. As more and more new technologies evolve in the medical and psychology fields new insights into thinking and learning are also evolving. It is very important for practitioners to understand *what* types of technology researchers utilize to study child development, *how* these findings extend or challenge current knowledge in the field, and the *applied* practicality of the research to the field of education. There is often a gap between research and practice and when there is no communication between the groups it can slow or harm a child's development. Research findings that stay within a narrow group of scientists and are not used to inform practice of teachers does not meet the full potential of the work. Teachers who ignore research because they believe there is no "real world" connection and rely on their instinct and personal experiences can miss many opportunities to improve the lives of young children. As you read the following sections of this chapter we hope you will keep in mind the implications for teachers and trainers of teachers.

Eye Tracking and Cognition

Experimental psychologists have been using eye-tracking for over 175 years to make inferences about adult perceptions and cognition, including decision making, language comprehension, memory, and mental imagery (Boring, 1942; Richardson & Spivey, 2004). Using eye-tracking to make inferences about infant perceptions and cognition, however, is a more recent development (e.g., Fanz, 1958, 1963). Currently, eye-tracking is the most common technique used to study infant perception, cognition, and social development (Aslin, 2007).What can eye-tracking tell us about an infant's perceptions and cognition? Although one can easily see why eye-tracking is used to study perception, as eye movements are fundamental to understanding the human visual system (Hayhoe, 2004; Richardson & Spivey, 2004), it is more difficult to see the connection between eye movement and cognition. This connection exists due to the relation among eye movements and attention mechanisms in the brain (e.g., Amso & Johnson, 2005). Attention mechanisms allow infants, children, and adults to attend to relevant information in the environment. Attending to information simply refers to paying attention to some features of the environment while simultaneously ignoring others. For example, right now you are paying attention to this chapter, while ignoring the table or the chairs that are also in your environment. Like the example above suggested, one way to attend to information is to look at it. Consider for a moment what you are looking at right now; you are looking at this page. Now what are you thinking about? (Hopefully the information we are presenting to you!) Often, a person looks at and thinks about what he or she is attending to (Aslin & McMurry, 2004; Haith, 1966). The same goes for infants and young children.

Efficient visual attention is critical to learning in infancy, as infants can only process the information they pay attention to (Hunnius, 2007). Since eye movements are one of the first voluntary movements that infants are able to control (as early as two months of age; Bronson, 1974, 1982), infants can visually select (choose) what they want to pay attention to. Infants develop this ability around four months (Colombo, 2001). Determining what infants are looking at, and for how long, gives researchers indirect insight into what infants are thinking, what they know about the world, and their future predictions about it (Haith, 1994; Johnson, 1994; Wentworth, 2008). For example, an infant who looks reliably longer at one stimuli than another is said to be able to discriminate between the two stimuli (e.g., Fantz, 1961). That is, the infant 'knows' that the two objects differ. Also, infants look longer at novel, rather than familiar stimuli (Bornstein, 1985) or when something impossible has occurred (e.g., Baillargeon, 1994). Because infants are able to discriminate between objects, identify objects that are were not previously there, and identify when something impossible has occurred, there is reason to believe that infants have expectations about how the world is supposed to work, and are 'surprised' (e.g., look longer) when their experience violates their expectations.

There are limitations with using eye-tracking as a way of studying infant cognition, however. It is common for researchers to use imprecise methods, such as global observation, which cannot detect nuances in infant eye-movement (Alsin & McMurry, 2004; Aslin & Salapatek, 1975). Also, videotaping infant eye-movements and then coding the movements can be time consuming. Advancements in eye-tracking technology, however, have eliminated the above mentioned limitations and helps further our understanding about what infants know about their world and their expectations of the future. We will briefly discuss two technologies, corneal reflection photography and portable eye-tracking devise, before specifically addressing what eye-tracking technology tells us about young children's literacy development.

Corneal Reflection Photography

Corneal-reflection photography emerged in the 1960s (see Haith, 1969; 1980), but the technique has improved with the advent of more sophisticated computer technology (Haith, 2004; Hunnius & Geuze, 2004). The technique itself is relatively simple. A light is positioned so that it is directly reflected off the front surface (cornea) of the eyeball. When the eye is looking directly at the light, the reflection of the light will appear to be in the center of the pupil. As the eye moves with respect to the light, the corneal reflection will move as well. Computers calculate the distance between the pupil and the cornea, which gives a more precise estimate (than global observations) of where an eye is looking. Computers also record how long an eye is looking; eye trackers can take a measurement every 20 milliseconds (Aslin & McMurry, 2004). Thus, researchers can more precisely measure where an infant is looking, and for how long.

Mobile Eye-Tracking Technology

As previously discussed researchers can precisely measure an infant's looking behavior to indirectly assess cognition. However, these interactions are primarily limited to a lab procedure, as the equipment that is used in corneal reflection photography studies infants relatively still in one place and directs their gaze toward a screen. While this technology allows researchers to examine how infants think, it cannot contribute to our understanding of how infants interact and learn from their everyday environment. Mobile eye tracking technology, however, can provide this insight, although the technology is relatively new (see Franchak, Fretch, Soska, Babcock, & Adolph, 2010). New technology uses a lightweight cap with two small cameras placed on an infant's head. One camera records the infant's eye, while the other records the infant's view of the world, thereby allowing researchers to examine how perception influences an infant's interaction with his actual environment. Although this technology is so new that is has not yet contributed to the literature, an early experiment using this technology has found that infants fixate on objects before they interact with them (Franchak et al., 2010). That is, infants deliberately look, and then play with objects. In the future, this and similar technology will shed light on the development of infant's perception and cognition *in vivo*, rather than in contrived lab experiments. This will allow researchers (and us) to more accurately understand how infants come to understand the rules and expectations about the world from 'watching' them interacting with their actual environments.

Eye-Tracking: Connection to Pre-Literacy Development

How can parents and educators promote the development of print-literacy, a crucial pre-reading skill? Parents and educators know that reading aloud to children during the preschool years helps children develop positive attitudes towards reading, including motivation to learn how to read (e.g., Epstein, 1987; Grimmet & McCoy, 1980). However, one common reason that parents and caregivers often give for reading aloud to young children is that it helps with the development of print literacy. That is, the child learns to associate verbal words with printed words. Shared reading, or an adult reading with a child, is only slightly related to later reading skills (Bus, van IJzendoorn, & Pellegrini, 1985; Scarborough & Dobrich, 1994). Before the advent of eye-tracking technology, researchers assumed that shared reading related to later reading skills because the child associated the spoken and printed word. However, recent research with eye-tracking technology has dispelled that association (e.g., Evans & Saint-Aubin, 2005; Evans, Saint-Aubin, & Landry, 2009). For example, Evans et al. (2009) used eye-tracking technology to gauge where pre-school aged children looked when they were read a story. They found that most children looked at the pictures, not the printed words. This finding suggests that for pre-readers, 'reading' a story is a listening activity, not an activity in identifying letters. In fact, children spend more time looking at the pictures (more than 1000 times longer) than at the printed word, even when the pictures are simple, or match the story (Evans, Saint-Aubin, & Roy-Charland, 2006; Justice, Skibbe, Canning, & Lankford, 2005; Roy-Charland, Saint-Aubin, & Evans, 2007). This is even true for children who have some knowledge of the alphabet (e.g., McCann & Miller, 2008). Taken together, these findings suggest that children frequently focus on the pictures, rather than the printed word, when engaging in shared reading. This means that in most cases, shared reading is not an effective way to promote print literacy in young children. However this might indicate that there is an interpretive relationship developing between pictures and words.

There are exceptions, however. The *type* of book being read, in conjunction with a child's letter knowledge, may influence the development of print literacy (Evans et al., 2009). Alphabet books (books highlighting a specific letter, and the words associated with the letter per page) are one such example. When adults read to children from Alphabet books, children who could already identify letters in the alphabet were more likely to look at a letter on a page and look longer at a letter than children who did not have letter knowledge (Evans et al., 2009). This research suggests that shared reading can influence the development of print literacy, if certain conditions are met. Evans & Saint-Evans (2010) offer three suggestions to help parents and educators decide whether or not to use shared reading as a means to promote the development of print literacy. First, a child must already have a critical amount of letter knowledge to even be able to attend to the printed word, let alone help facilitate word recognition. Secondly, reading material should be adapted to children's reading skills. For example, alphabet books can be used to encourage print specific skills with older children who already have letter knowledge. Finally, comments that parents or educators make should focus on the printed word, not on the pictures (e.g., Justice & Ezell, 2002). Taken together, research on children's literacy development, with the aid of eye-tracking technology, suggests that for shared reading to help facilitate print literacy, parents and educators need to make sure that children have previous experience with letter forms and names. Otherwise, shared reading may offer many benefits for the child, but the development of print literacy is not one of them.

Psychophysiological Reactions

How children behave and regulate their behavior is influenced, in part, by their environment. Researchers have long known that a child's environment can positively (or negatively) influence development (e.g., Scarr, 1992). For example, John Watson (1930), an early behaviorist, once claimed that if given twelve healthy infants and the environment of his choice, he could, " train him to become any type of specialist I might select- doctor, lawyer, artist, merchant-chief, and yes, even beggar-man and thief, regardless of his talents, penchants, tendencies [and] abilities..." (p. 82). Researchers now, however, consider Watson's (1930) view extreme; child development is viewed as an interaction of *both* genetics and environment. This suggests that how children behave is not only a function of their environment, but also has a *biological* basis.

Anyone who has worked with young children knows that environment cannot completely explain a child's behavior; the exact same classroom environment, including materials and daily routines, can lead to different behavioral responses in children. For example, in many classrooms, there is a child that is known as the 'biter', or 'spitter', or the one whom cannot follow directions. And yet, is easy for educators to suggest that a child's home life may be pre-empting the antisocial behavior, or that a child is not 'trying hard enough' to be good. However, like Watson's (1930) view, this explanation is over-simplified. Observed behaviors, like hitting or spitting, do not necessarily capture a child's efforts at self regulation (Calkins & Keane, 2004). This means that a child may be putting in an exorbitant amount of effort to follow the directions, but his behavior is not reflecting his desires. As suggested earlier, it is only partly environment that influences a child's ability to self- regulate; biology, especially physiology, is influential as well.

Recent research in the area of psychophysiology, the "measurement of physiological responses as they relate to behavior" (Andreassi, 2007, p. 1), points us in an interesting direction. Psychophysiologists suggest that body functions, like heart rate, influence behavior. With the advent of new technology, there is increasing evidence that biological processes play a role in children's social, emotional, and cognitive development as well, especially as it relates to aggressive and antisocial behaviors (e.g., Kindlon, Mezzacappa, & Earls, 1995; Raine, Venables, & Mednick, 1997; Raine, Reynolds, Venables, & Mednick, 1997). We will first describe the biological basis of a child's emotion and behavior regulation before describing the technologies that aid in this research.

A young child's ability to self regulate (monitor emotional and behavior responses) is biological in basis (Calkins & Keane, 2004). That is, a child's emotional and behavioral correlates are influenced by the maturation of different body systems (Calkins & Dedmon, 2000; Porges, 1996; Porges, Doussard-Roosevelt, & Maitia, 1994). This is no different from saying that a child cannot pick up a cup until his muscles are strong enough to do so, no matter how much he wills himself to do it! The body system that is most associated with the regulation of motor activity and emotion is the parasynthetic nervous system (PNS; Porges, 1996). The parasynthetic nervous system (PNS) is in charge of 'resting and digesting'. Its 'job' is to help relax the body after the sympathetic nervous system (SNS), the 'fight or flight' response, is activated. These two systems work together to create equilibrium for the body (Scott & Fong, 2004). For example, if a child gets scared, the SNS is activated, and stress hormones (such as adrenaline) that increase breathing and energy, are released. After the danger has passed, the PNS sends hormones (like cortisol) through the body to counter these effects and calm the body down. However, the PNS does not automatically activate in young children. The PNS is secondary to the SNS, which means that activation of the PNS requires conscious effort, which young children have not yet acquired (Scott & Fong, 2004). Taken together, this provides a *physiological* explanation for why young children may have difficulty regulating their emotions and behaviors. It can even account for individual differences in children.

Each child is *physiologically* different. This includes lung capacity, resting heart rate, and nervous system functioning. Researchers believe that individual differences in how the nervous system functions might influence the expression and regulation of emotion and behavior in children. Children who are better able to activate their PNS system may also be better at regulating their behaviors and emotions. How can parasympathetic nervous system functioning (PNS) be measured? Research suggests that PNS functioning can be reflected in resting heart rate and the variability in heart rate that occurs at the frequency of breathing (otherwise known as respiratory sinus arrthythmia, or RSA; Porges & Byrne, 1992). Stress responses, such as cortisol level, also gives an indication in the equilibrium of the PNS and SNS. The next two parts of this section will focus on the specific technologies associated with heart-rate, and briefly describe how heart rate is reflective of social and emotional regulation in children, followed by a more detailed examination of how stress responses are measured in children, and how stress responses can (hinder) or help a child's cognitive development.

Heart Rate

Physiological regulation (which can shed insight into a child's self regulation) is determined by measuring resting heart rate and respiratory sinus arrhythmia (RSA). First, we will briefly discuss how to measure resting heart rate, and describe its associations with aggressive and antisocial behavior. Then, we will discuss how researchers use technology to measure RSA and what it can tell us about supporting the development of emotion regulation in children.

Measuring *resting heart rate*, or the number of heart beats per minute when a person is not active, is very simple to do. Place two fingers on the carotid artery located on the left (or right) side of the neck, underneath the jaw bone. Now, count that number of pulses that occur in a one minute period. That is how one measures resting heart rate. While this method seems less technologically advanced, especially compared to the other technologies we have discussed thus far, the correlates that researchers have found with resting heart rate and aggressive and anti-social behavior are staggering. For example, in a meta analysis of 40 studies containing over 5, 868 children, Orwitz & Raine (2004) found that a lower, rather than higher, resting heart rate was associated with *higher* levels of aggressive and antisocial behaviors. This was true for both boys and girls. In fact, another study suggested that low resting heart-rates at age 3 predicted aggressive and antisocial behavior at age 11 (Raine et al., 1997). Higher resting heart rate appears to protect against future adult crime (e.g., Raine, Venables, & Williams, 1995).

Researchers believe that a low-resting heart rate is a partly heritable trait that reflects fearlessness and stimulation seeking behavior (e.g., Raine et al., 1997). This suggests that some stimulation seeking behaviors (which might be interpreted in a young child as aggressive or anti-social) may be physiological in basis. However, this does not mean that all children with lower resting heart rates will develop stimulation seeking behaviors; children with non-low resting heart rates may be aggressive as well. This research does suggest, however, is that due to the relationship between the PNS and a child's behavior, some aggressive behaviors may not be able to be easily modified with punishments and behavioral modification plans- other intervention strategies may be necessary. Although resting heart-rate is a correlate of a child's behavior, it is not the only one that researchers use to predict a child's regulation of emotions and behavior. Heart rate variability must be considered as well (Calkins & Dedmon, 2000; Porges, Doussard-Roosevelt, Portables, & Greenspan, 1996).

Heart rate variability (or respiratory sinus arrhythmia, RSA) is a measure of the amplitude and period of oscillations associated with inhalation and exhalation. While resting heart rate is the number of beats per minute during a resting state, RSA captures how much the heart rate increases when a person inhales, and how much it decreases when a person exhales (Porges, 1991, 1996). This heart rate cycle is connected to the PNS via the vagus nerve. To be able to capture this cycle, pediatric electrodes are placed on a child's chest, and the output is transmitted to a vagal tone monitor for R-wave detection. The monitor then displays the heart rate and computes the RSA for the child.

A body of research has concluded that a high resting RSA is associated with positive developmental outcomes, including appropriate emotional responses (Stifler & Fox, 1990), and the ability to pay attention in early childhood (e.g., Suess, Porges, & Plude, 1994). Another variant of RSA is the vagal regulation of the heart, which is indexed by a decrease (suppression) in RSA where coping or emotional behaviors are required. RSA suppression is a physiological strategy that supports sustained attention and active coping. Suppression of the RSA is associated with self-soothing ability in infants (Huffman et al., 1998), and fewer behavioral problems and more appropriate emotion-regulation responses in early childhood (Calkins & Dedmon, 2000; Porges et al., 1996). A deficiency in the ability to suppress RSA, however, is related to behavior problems in early childhood (e.g., Calkins & Dedmon, 2004; Porges, 1996). This is not to say that RSA rhythms are only a function of physiology. More recent research suggests that RSA rhythms are influenced by culture and family ecology (DeCaro & Worthman, 2007, 2008). Taken together, the information supports researchers notion that the environment and biology interact and influence a child's development. Although a child's physiological response, such as RSA, influences his ability to regulate his emotions and behavior, his physiological response is influenced by the world around him as well.

Measuring Stress Response

Imagine, for a moment, a typical 'first-day' at preschool. Two children are dropped off and cry when their respective mothers leave. The teacher consoles both children. From the teacher's perspective, both children experienced a similar level of stress, and the teacher felt she responded to both children appropriately. However, later on in the day, one of the children seems to have problems adjusting to her classmates and the classroom schedule. The teacher again soothes the one child in the same manner, and the child calms down. This pattern is repeated for several days. The teacher begins to wonder if her strategy to console the child is working. Perhaps the child was never really soothed in the first place? As we have suggested previously, observable behaviors are not necessarily accurate reflections of what a child is experiencing or knows. In this case, a child's behavioral response is not reflective of a child's physiological stress level (e.g., Essex, Klein, Cho, & Kalin, 2002). More importantly, actions that reduce behavioral correlates of stress, such as crying, do not necessarily reduce a child's physiological level of stress (Adam, Klimes-Dougan, & Gunnar, 2007). In order to understand how to appropriately respond to children in duress, we first must know how children physiologically respond to stressors.

In the following paragraphs, we will discuss the current technology and research findings associated with physiological stress responses. First, we will discuss what 'stress' means from a physiological perspective. Then we will discuss how stress is measured. Finally, we will provide a brief overview of chronic stress and its influence on cognitive, social, and emotional development.

Researchers and educators alike understand that high levels of stress will negatively impact a child's development (e.g., Garmezy, Masten, & Tellegen, 1984). However, it is difficult to accurately assess the level of stress a child is experiencing from a child's behaviors, as observed behaviors, such as crying, do not always reflect a child's *physiological* level of stress accurately (Essex et al., 2002; Gunnar, 2001; Perez-Edgar, Schmidt, Henderson, Schulkin, & Fox, 2009). *Physiological* level of stress refers to the body's release of hormones, such as cortisol, and can be triggered by stressful events. There are two types of stressful events, internal and external, that facilitate the release of cortisol (Granger, Weitz, & Kauneckis, 1994; Tout, de Haan, Campbell, & Gunnar, 1998). Examples of stressful eternal events include separating from a parent and entering in a new classroom or peer group (Granger et al., 1994; Tout et al., 1998), while stressful internal events include anxieties, such as fear of peer exclusion (Gunnar & Donzella, 2002; Gunner, Sebanc, out, Donzella, & van Dulman, 2003). However, it is not the amount of stress that one experiences that is harmful, as everyone experiences stress from time to time. Rather, it is the duration of stressors, or its chronicity, that negatively influences development (Gunnar & Donzella, 2002).

Because experiencing stress is part of everyday life, it is difficult to discriminate between acute stress (when a child is momentarily upset) and chronic stress (repeated stressors) by behavioral observation at a specific moment in time. This is especially true as a child's behavioral response to stress is highly individualized, and may differ according to gender (Hatzinger et al., 2007; Shirtcliff, Granger, Booth, & Johnson., 2005; Smider et al., 2002; Tout et al., 1998) and temperament (Perez-Edgar et al., 2009). However by measuring the amount of cortisol that is in a child's body over a period of time, a child's stress level can be accurately assessed.

All humans produce the hormone cortisol, even when they are not experiencing stress. This is known as a base-line cortisol level. Cortisol is also produced following a circadian rhythm, meaning that cortisol is highest in the mornings (after a child awakes), and gradually decreases until the evening, before a child goes to bed. When a child experiences stress, the cortisol level will increase above baseline level (De Kloet, 1991). This is known as a stress response.

Although measuring cortisol may seem like a difficult task, especially when dealing with young children, it is as simple as spitting in a cup. Cortisol is usually measured through analysis in human salvia, and this has proven to be a reliable, valid, and non-obtrusive method (Kirschbaum & Hellammer, 1994. Saliva is collected in a cup, and then is processed using a commercially available radio-immunoassay (RIA) kit. The kit isolates the cortisol from the salvia so it can be measured (Schwartz, Granger, Susman, Gunnar, & Laird, 1998).

It is important for educators to understand the link between increased (chronic) cortisol levels and brain functioning. The HPA axis, which is connected to the hippocampus (the part of the brain that is linked to emotions, learning, and memory), is activated when coritsol levels increase above base-line. This suggests that chronic exposure to stress in early childhood may put a child at risk for later affective and cognitive functioning (Gunnar & Donzella, 2002; Luecken & Lemery, 2004; Vermer & van IJzendoorn, 2006), including memory difficulties in adulthood (Evans & Schamberg, 2009). In other words, constant exposure to stress may hinder a child's ability to learn his ABC's and have positive healthy interactions with his peers.

What factors cause chronic stress? Poverty is one of the top causes of chronic stress (Chen, Cohen, & Miller, 2010; Evans & English, 2003; Evans & Schamberg, 2009), and thus one of the reasons that poverty is a risk factor for lower cognitive development (Duncan & Brooks-Gunn, 2000). There are other steps, besides ending childhood poverty that an educator can take to help alleviate the damaging effects of chronic stress in a classroom. Research suggests that a sensitive, responding adult can dampen the level of stress a child experiences due to parental separation (Gunnar, Larson, Hertsgaard, Harris, and Broderson, 1992). Children who play with peers exhibit lower levels of cortisol that children who do not (Watamura, Donzella, Alwin, & Gunnar, 2003). Finally, large group sizes and small playing space is associated with an increase in cortisol levels for children (Legendre, 2003), thus large play spaces can help reduce cortisol levels in children.

Brain Imaging Technology

In 1997, then President Bill Clinton called a White House Conference on *Early Childhood Development and Learning: What New Brain Research Tells Us About Our Youngest Children.* The focus of the conference was to disseminate knowledge about the neuroscience behind child development to researchers, educators, and policy analysts. Since then, researchers interested in early childhood development have been utilizing technologies that highlight how a child's brain develops, and in the process changing what we know about a child's cognitive, emotional, and social development.

Today we know that the brain is highly malleable; that is, it constantly re-organizes itself depending on the contextual features within the environment (Immordino-Yang, 2007). That means that certain factors, such as socioeconomic status, exposure to books, violence, and even culture shapes the way the brain (and thus the child) thinks (Hackman & Farah, 2009). However, we are just beginning to understand *how* and *when* the brain reorganizes itself. For example, while the brain is highly malleable and able to re-wire itself with regards to language and cognitive abilities, researchers are now finding this is not the case with social- emotional development (Anderson, Bechara, Damasion, Tranel, & Damasio, 1999; Damasio, 2005). As suggested in the introduction, technology allows us to study early child development in ways that were never previously possible. In this section, we will briefly highlight four technologies- positron emission tomography (PET), functional magnetic resonance imaging (fMRI), electroencephalography (EEG) and near-infrared spectroscopy (NIRS) - that that assist researchers in understanding the connection between brain and child development. Then we will discuss how the use of these technologies has the interplay of emotion and cognition.

Position Emission Tomography (PET)

Positron emission tomography, more commonly known as PET, is a nuclear medicine imaging technique that produces 3-D images of body processes. In a typical session a natural substance (like oxygen or glucose) that has been made radioactive (known as a radio tracer) is injected in the body. The brain then metabolizes the radiotracer. As the radioactive substance decays, it releases positrons. A positron detector (otherwise known as a PET scanner) can compute where in the brain these positrons are being emitted, and with the aid of a computer, a three dimensional picture is created (Shonkoff & Phillips, 2000).

PET scans are not normally used to study child development as it is cost prohibitive, but it has made notable impacts in a few studies, including the investigation of synaptogenesis, or the formation of neural networks (Chugani, 1994; Chugani & Phelps, 1986), and in aiding in the identification of autistic children (Brasic, Wong, & Eroglu, 2007). Thus, this technology has allowed researchers to discover that new brain connections form, and that autistic children function differently.

Functional Magnetic Resonance Imaging

Functional magnetic resonance imaging, or fMRI, is a specialized MRI scan that measures the change in blood flow (specifically oxygen) in the brain. For example, when a particular part of the brain needs to perform a task, blood flow (and thus oxygen) is increased in that region. fMRI monitors the changes in blood flow and then 'reconstructs' where in the brain these changes were occurring (Shonkoff & Phillips, 2000).

Since the early 1990s, fMRI has been used in brain mapping due to its wide availability, low invasiveness, and lack of radiation exposure (Racine, Bar-Ilan, & Illes, 2005). fMRI technology has allowed researchers to understand how children remember (e.g., Nelson et al., 2000) and make decisions (Rajah & McIntosh, 2008), and provided brain-based evidence for both interventions that work for children with reading disorders (e.g., Shaywitz et al., 1998, 2004), and for children's theory of mind (e.g., Kobayashi, Glover, & Temple, 2007).

Electroencephalography (EEG)

Electroencephalography, more commonly known as EEG, refers to the recording of the brain's electrical activity along the scalp. The electrical activity in the brain is produced when neurons (brain cells) fire information to other neurons over a short period of time. An EEG can measure how fast (in milliseconds) the brain can respond to stimuli. This electrical activity is measured by multiple electrodes, which are strategically placed on the scalp (Clarkea, Barry, McCarthy, & Selikowitzb, 1998).

An EEG is comparable to an fMRI in that they both study brain functions, and are used in a variety of fields, including research and medicine. The EEG has several benefits over the fMRI; these benefits include that the EEG sensors are more easily accessible as compared to the bulky fMRI machine, the EEG enables higher temporal resolution on the order of milliseconds, lower cost, and the EEG is relatively tolerant of subject movement versus the fMRI. Yet, the EEG does have some limitations compared to the fMRI. These limitations include that it has significantly lower spatial resolution, and most importantly, it is limited to the functioning of the cortex (the outer brain layer).

EEG has been used to identify interventions in children who have ADHD (Hughes, DeLeo, & Melyn, 2000; Lubar, Swartwood, Swartwood, & O'Donnell, 1995), and has shed light on emotional development across the life-span (Greenberg & Snell, 1997). More recently, studies using EEG technology has suggested that socioeconomic status influences have pre-frontal (reasoning) function (e.g., Kishiyama, Boyce, Jimenez, Perry, & Knight, 2009). That is, socioeconomic status influences how the brain functions, and thus how a child thinks.

Near–Infrared Spectroscopy (NIRS)

Technology that applies to brain analysis is constantly changing and becoming more refined. In the past ten years, a brain imaging method called Near-Infrared Spectroscopy (NIRS) has emerged. This technology has three major advantages as compared to the other brain scanning technologies previous discussed: it allows researchers to run psychological experiments (instead of just brain mapping), it is suitable for young children, and it is robust against movement (Chakravarti, Srivastava, & Mittnacht, 2008).

NIRS is a non-invasive, validated technique that measures the near-infrared region of the electromagnetic spectrum (think night vision). The human body absorbs NIR light in a way that reflects blood (oxygen) concentration changes in the brain. That is, like, fMRI, it measures the blood (oxygen) volume change in an area of the brain once that area has been activated.

Although this technology has not been yet be utilized in many developmental studies, it is very promising. This technology has just been recently used to determine how infants process human faces (as compared to adults; Honda et al., 2010; Nakato, Otsuka, Kanazawa, & Yamagichi, 2009), and how children remember their environment (Tsujii, Yamamoto, Masuda, & Watanabe, 2009).

Linking Brain Imaging to Emotion and Cognition

How children feel and interact within their social setting is just as important to educational outcomes as is the more traditional focus on cognitive development. As we previously mentioned, recent research in brain neuroscience has suggested that children who experience pre-frontal damage appear to have never learned the rules that govern social and moral behavior, even though they have normal IQs. (Anderson et al., 1999; Damasio, 2005).The pre-frontal cortex in the brain is associated with emotion regulation, which suggests that brain's emotion and social processing centers do not compensate for damage like the linguistic and cognitive aspects. Meaning, that while a child's brain can re-wire itself to learn languages or overcome reading deficits, this is not the case with social, moral, and emotional development.

Why do educators need to know this, as very few educators will have children with pre-frontal cortex damage in their classes? A growing body of literature suggests that emotion related processes are necessary for skills and knowledge to be transferred from a school environment to real world decision making (e.g., Immordino-Yang, 2009; Immordino-Yang & Damasio, 2007). How? Immordino-Yang & Damasio (2007) suggest that emotions may play a vital role in helping children decide *when* and *how* to apply what they have learned in school to their lives. This also suggests, from a neuroscience perspective, that teaching children logical reasoning skills and factual knowledge may not transfer to real-world situations without emotional motivation. It is essential, then, from a neuroscience perspective, that educators *continue* to consider the vital role that emotions and social interactions play in cognitive development when planning lessons and assessing student knowledge.

ISSUES, CONTROVERSIES, PROBLEMS

Technology, combined with research on child development, provides new insights for both researchers and educators about how children learn. One important issue in the application of research to educational environments is the practical interpretation of research findings, especially in how these findings can inform classroom pedagogy. Technology has greatly aided researchers in understanding child development and creating interventions for at- risk children. These interventions, however, must be applied more cautiously in actual instructional environments due to the complexity of factors (e.g., diverse student backgrounds, gender, cognitive level, etc.) that are present in schools but are often absent in laboratory tests.

At this point in time, we are on the verge of connecting technological research on child development to pedagogical planning and action. A new field, known as NeuroEducation (see Battro, Fisher, & Léna, 2008), has recently emerged which attempts to marry technological research on child development and educational practice. This field is in its infancy, however; researchers and educators are now just starting to connect the research findings to pedagogical practice. As there are no practical guidelines for educators at the present time, it is important to keep the following advice in mind. First, remember that each of these studies was designed to determine how a child develops. These studies were not designed with the purpose of being used as an approach to teaching. For example, as mentioned earlier, research suggests that a child's environment can influence his physiological response. Although this has indirect implications for educators (e.g., that the classroom environment should be carefully planned), it cannot tell us what the *optimal* classroom environment should look like. Secondly, although it is easy for individual teachers to interpret these studies based on their own personal experiences, falling back on personal experiences often reinforces stereotypes. For example, while children from low socio-economic statuses often have more self- regulation and cognitive difficulties due to the environment than children from middle or upper socio-economic statuses, this *does not mean* that all children from low socio-economic backgrounds have these difficulties, or that children with the difficulties must come from these backgrounds, even when personal experience supports these findings. In these cases, one must remember that the research also suggests that the brain is malleable, and exposure to positive supportive environments can re-wire a child's brain and alter perceptions. The challenge for educators, then, is determining how and when to apply what the research suggests to environmental and instructional planning.

We realize that teachers often have intuitive insights into children's learning, but teachers must also be careful not to use their *personal* interpretation of research in environmental and instructional planning. Teachers often work in isolation, validating their beliefs about learning through opinions and subjective interpretation of research findings. This problem can be alleviated if teacher training programs were to work closely with interdisciplinary researchers to better understand the application of research to educational environments and instructional planning. Both practitioners and researchers bring knowledge and insights to the understanding of child development. The practitioner brings rich experiences from everyday interactions with children. Researchers study the influence of physiological responses and environment on children's behavior. However, as it currently stands, each group is isolated, and thus the knowledge base for each group is contained *within* each group. In order for research to inform pedagogy, and for practitioners to inform research, there needs to be a free flow of information between both groups. This means that these two groups must rely on each other to inform each others' practices. Researchers need to understand children's daily activities, and practitioners need to understand how and why research is conducted. It is only then that these groups will be able to work together to use technological research to practically inform teacher training and education.

FUTURE TRENDS

Technology allows us to study early child development in ways that were never previously possible. As technology continues to evolve, a deeper, and more complex, understanding of how the child develops will emerge. The applications of this research will be infused into teacher training and education. Teachers will use a research-based approach when working with young children in order to develop educational environments that support learning. Researchers will use teacher's practical knowledge in order to ask research questions that are more relevant to educational settings, and that will verify teacher's best educational practices.

CONCLUSION

Technology has changed the ability to research young children dramatically. We no longer think of the infant's world, to revisit William James (1890/1981), as "a buzzing, blooming confusion" (p. 462). We now realize, thanks to eye tracking technology that infants process and form their own systematic expectations about how the world should work. We also understand that children's emotional and behavior regulation is not simply a reflection of the child's will, but is based on individual differences in the child's nervous system, as measured by heart rate and cortisol levels. We can see how factors outside of the child's control, such as poverty, can literally reshape a child's memory and change the brain's ability to think critically. Likewise, brain imaging technologies, such as fMRI, have also suggested that emotions can influence what information a child learns, and how that knowledge can be applied.

The technologies reviewed in this chapter- corneal reflection photography, mobile eye-tracking technology, resting heart-rate, RSA, cortisol levels, PET, fMRI, EEG, and NIRS- reflect only a fraction of the technologies researchers have available at their finger tips. And yet, in the next ten to twenty years, these same technologies may be obsolete. The availability of new technology allows researchers to continuously refine their (and our) understanding of young children's development. It is important for educators and parents to be aware of the current technologies that researchers use, and how these technologies advance knowledge about young children's development. If educators understand the current technology and trends in research on child development, then we are one step closer to merging research with classroom pedagogy.

Reflecting on Young Children and Technology Research

This section gives you some questions and activities to help you think about how you can use some of the ideas from this chapter in your work.

Research

1. In your reading you learned that brain is highly malleable. Search sites to better understand what is meant by this and how it could inform your teaching.
2. If we are really going to provide the support young children need to learn and develop we must work with researchers. How can you and your peers develop a respectful working relationship with researchers? How could you use technology resources to inform your work?

Reflect

1. Often when we see repeated misbehavior in young children we assume they are not trying to behave. In this chapter we have learned that a child may be putting in an exorbitant amount of effort to follow the directions, but his behavior is not reflecting his desires. What does this idea mean to you and how you approach interactions with misbehaving children in your class?
2. The implications from new research about children through the use of technology have altered some of the ideas teachers have about learning. List some of the ideas from this chapter that are different from what you thought about development.
3. The issue of the influence of poverty is a reoccurring theme in this chapter. Why do you think children living in poverty have a higher chronic stress level than other children?
4. This chapter clearly indicates that the affective and cognitive domains interact and influence learning and development. What changes will you make concerning your interactions and classroom environment to support this connection for the children in your class?
5. The statement "shared reading is not an effective way to promote print literacy in young children." has some serious implications for what many teachers believe about reading. What steps do you need to take in your classroom to insure shared reading supports early reading?

Practice

1. Now that you are aware of how chronic stress levels influence development and interactions what can you, as a professional, do in your classroom to support child development?
2. Some aggressive behaviors may not be able to be easily modified with punishments and behavioral modification plans- other intervention strategies may be necessary. What kinds of intervention strategies might help a child better self-regulate? Work with your peers to develop alternative approaches to behavior management for your classrooms.
3. New insights into behavior and learning will help you grow as a professional and provide better service to children. Much of the information in this chapter needs to be shared with other practitioners in your school. Develop a presentation for your peers and administrators highlighting the key points from this chapter and share it with others.

REFERENCES

Adam, E., Klimes-Dougan, B., & Gunnar, M. R. (2007). Emotional and social regulation of the adrenocortical response to stress. In Coch, D., Dawson, G., & Fischer, K. W. (Eds.), *Human behavior and the developing brain: Atypical development* (2nd ed., pp. 264–304). New York, NY: Guilford Press.

Amso, D., & Johnson, S. P. (2005). Selection and inhibition in infancy: Evidence from the spatial negative priming paradigm. *Cognition*, *95*, B27–B36. doi:10.1016/j.cognition.2004.08.006

Anderson, S. W., Bechara, A., Damasio, H., Tranel, D., & Damasio, A. R. (1999). Impairment of social and moral behavior related to early damage in human prefrontal cortex. *Nature Neuroscience*, *2*, 1032–1037. doi:10.1038/12194

Andreassi, J. L. (2007). *Psychophysiology: Human behavior and physiological response* (5th ed.). Mahwah, NJ: Lawrence Erlbaum Associates.

Aslin, R. N. (2007). What's in a look? *Developmental Science*, *10*(1), 48–53. doi:10.1111/j.1467-7687.2007.00563.x

Aslin, R. N., & McMurry, B. (2004). Automated corneal-reflection eye-tracking in infancy: Methodological developments and applications to cognition. *Infancy*, *6*, 155–163. doi:10.1207/s15327078in0602_1

Aslin, R. N., & Salapatek, P. (1975). Saccadic localization of visual targets by the very young human infant. *Perception & Psychophysics*, *17*, 293–392. doi:10.3758/BF03203214

Baillargeon, R. (1994). How do infants learn about the physical world? *Current Directions in Psychological Science*, *3*(5), 133–140. doi:10.1111/1467-8721.ep10770614

Battro, A. M., Fisher, K., & Léna, P. J. (2008). *The educated brain: Essays in neuroeducation*. New York, NY: Cambridge University Press. doi:10.1017/CBO9780511489907

Boring, E. G. (1942). *Sensation and perception in the history of experimental psychology*. New York, NY: Appleton-Century.

Bornstein, M. (1985). Habituation as a measure of visual information processing in human infants: Summary, systematization, and synthesis. In Gottleib, G., & Krasnegor, N. (Eds.), *Development of audition and vision during the first year of postnatal life: A methodological overview* (pp. 253–295). Norwood, NJ: Ablex.

Brasic, J. R., Wong, D., & Eroglu, A. (2007). PET scanning in autism spectrum disorders. *E-Medicine Journal*. Retrieved from http://www.emedicine.com/ neuro/ topic440.htm

Bronson, G. W. (1974). The postnatal growth of visual capacity. *Child Development*, *4*(5), 873–890. doi:10.2307/1128073

Bronson, G. W. (1982). Structure, status, and characteristics of the nervous system at birth. In Stratton, P. (Ed.), *Psychobiology of the human newborn* (pp. 99–118). Chichester, UK: Wiley.

Bus, A. G., Van, I., Jzendoorn, M. H., & Pellegrini, A. D. (1995). Storybook reading makes for success in learning to read. A meta-analysis on intergenerational transmission of literacy. *Review of Educational Research*, *65*, 1–21.

Calkins, S. D., & Dedmon, S. E. (2000). Physiological and behavorial regulation in ten-year-old children with aggressive/destructive behavior problems. *Journal of Abnormal Child Psychology*, *28*(2), 103–118. doi:10.1023/A:1005112912906

Calkins, S. D., & Keane, S. P. (2004). Cardiac vagal regulation across the preschool period: Stability, continuity, and implications for childhood adjustment. *Developmental Psychobiology, 45*(3), 101–112. doi:10.1002/dev.20020

Chakravarti, S., Srivastava, S., & Mittnacht, A. J. C. (2008). Near infrared spectroscopy (NIRS) in children. *Seminars in Cardiothoracic and Vascular Anesthesia, 12*(1), 70–79. doi:10.1177/1089253208316444

Chambliss, J. J. (1982). Aristotle's conception of childhood and the poliscraft. *Educational Studies, 13*, 33–43.

Chen, E., Cohen, S., & Miller, G. E. (2010). How low socioeconomic status affects 2-year hormonal trajectories in children. *Psychological Science, 21*(1), 31–37. doi:10.1177/0956797609355566

Chugani, H. T. (1994). Development of regional brain glucose metabolism in relation to behavior and plasticity. In Dawson, G., & Fisher, K. W. (Eds.), *Human behavior and the developing brain* (pp. 153–175). New York, NY: Guliford Press.

Chugani, H. T., & Phelps, M. E. (1986). Maturational changes in cerebral functions in infants determined by 18FDG positron emission tomography. *Science, 231*, 840–843. doi:10.1126/science.3945811

Clarkea, A. R., Barrya, R. J., McCarthyb, R., & Selikowitzb, M. (1998). EEG analysis in attention-deficit/hyperactivity disorder: A comparative study of two subtypes. *Psychiatry Research, 81*(1), 19–29. doi:10.1016/S0165-1781(98)00072-9

Clinton, B. (1997, February 4). *What new brain research tells us about our youngest children.* Conference presented at White House Conference on Early Childhood Development and Learning, Washington D.C. Colombo, J. (2001). The development of visual attention. *Annual Review of Psychology, 52*, 337–367.

Damasio, A. R. (2005). The neurobiological grounding of human values. In Changeux, J. P., Damasio, A. R., Singer, W., & Christen, Y. (Eds.), *Neurobiology of human values* (pp. 47–56). London, UK: Springer Verlag. doi:10.1007/3-540-29803-7_5

De Kloet, E. R. (1991). Brain corticosteroid receptor balance and homeostatic control. *Frontiers in Neuroendocrinology, 12*, 95–164.

DeCaro, J. A., & Worthman, C. M. (2007). Cultural models, parent behavior, and young child experience in working American families. *Parenting, Science and Practice, 7*(2), 17203. doi:10.1080/15295190701306953

DeCaro, J. A., & Worthman, C. M. (2008). Culture and the socialization of child cardiovascular regulation at school entry in the US. *American Journal of Human Biology, 20*(5), 572–583. doi:10.1002/ajhb.20782

Duncan, G. J., & Brooks-Gunn, J. (2000). Family poverty, welfare reform, and child development. *Child Development, 71*(1), 188–196. doi:10.1111/1467-8624.00133

Epstein, J. L. (1987). Parent involvement: What research says to administrators. *Education and Urban Society, 79*, 119–136. doi:10.1177/0013124587019002002

Essex, M. J., Klein, M. H., Cho, E., & Kalin, N. H. (2002). Maternal stress beginning in infancy may sensitize children to later stress exposure: Effects of cortisol and behavior. *Society of Biological Psychiatry, 52*, 776–784. doi:10.1016/S0006-3223(02)01553-6

Evans, G. W., & English, K. (2003). The environment of poverty: Multiple stressor exposure, psychophysiological stress, and socioemotional adjustment. *Child Development, 74*(4), 1238–1248.

Evans, G. W., & Schamberg, M. A. (2009). Childhood poverty, chronic stress, and adult working memory. *Proceedings of the National Academy of Sciences of the United States of America.*. doi:10.1073/pnas.0811910106

Evans, M. A., & Saint-Aubin, J. (2005). What children are looking at during shared storybook reading? *Psychological Science*, *16*(11), 913–920. doi:10.1111/j.1467-9280.2005.01636.x

Evans, M. A., & Saint-Aubin, J. (2010). An eye for print: Child and adult attention to print during shared book reading. In Aram, D., & Korat, O. (Eds.), *Literacy development and enhancement across orthographies and cultures* (pp. 43–53). London, UK: Springer. doi:10.1007/978-1-4419-0834-6_4

Evans, M. A., Saint-Aubin, J., & Landry, N. (2009). Letter names and alphabet book reading by senior kindergartners: An eye movement study. *Child Development*, *80*(6), 1824–1841. doi:10.1111/j.1467-8624.2009.01370.x

Evans, M. A., Saint-Aubin, J., & Roy-Charland, A. (2006, June). *Reading pictures: Preschoolers eye fixations on illustrations during shared book reading*. Colloquiam presented at Royal Netherlands Academy of Arts and Sciences, Amsterdam.

Fantz, R. L. (1958). Pattern vision in young infants. *The Psychological Record*, *8*, 43–47.

Fantz, R. L. (1961). The origin of form perception. *Scientific American*, *204*, 66–72. doi:10.1038/scientificamerican0561-66

Fantz, R. L. (1963). Pattern vision in newborn infants. *Science*, *140*, 296–297. doi:10.1126/science.140.3564.296

Franchak, J. M., Kretch, K. S., Soska, K. C., Babcock, J. S., & Adolph, K. E. (2010). Head-mounted eye-tracking of infants' natural interactions: A new method. *Proceedings of the 2010 Symposium on Eye Tracking Research & Applications*, Austin, Texas.

Garmezy, N., Masten, A. S., & Tellegen, A. (1984). The study of stress and competence in children: A building block for developmental psychopathology. *Child Development*, *55*, 97–111. doi:10.2307/1129837

Granger, D. A., Weisz, J. R., & Kauneckis, D. (1994). Neuroendocrine reactivity, internalizing behavior problems, and control-related cognitions in clinic-referred children and adolescents. *Journal of Abnormal Child Psychology*, *103*, 267–276.

Greenberg, M. T., & Snell, J. L. (1997). Brain development and emotional development: The role of teaching in organizing the frontal lobe. In P. Salovey & D. J. Sluyter (Eds.), *Emotional development and emotional intelligence: Educational implications* (pp. 93 119). New York, NY: BasicBooks.

Grimmett, S., & McCoy, M. (1980). Effects of parental communication on reading performance of third grade children. *The Reading Teacher*, *33*, 303–308.

Gunnar, M. R. (2001). The role of glococorticoids in anxiety disorders: A critical analysis. In Vasey, M. W., & Dadds, M. R. (Eds.), *The developmental psychopathology of anxiety* (pp. 143–159). New York, NY: Oxford University Press.

Gunnar, M. R., & Donzella, B. (2002). Social regulation of the cortisol levels in early human development. *Psychoneuroendocrinology*, *27*, 199–220. doi:10.1016/S0306-4530(01)00045-2

Gunnar, M. R., Larson, M. C., Hertsgaard, L., Harris, M. L., & Brodersen, L. (1992). The stressfulness of separation among nine-month-old infants: Effects of social context variables and infant temperament. *Child Development*, *63*, 290–303. doi:10.2307/1131479

Gunnar, M. R., Sebanc, A. M., Tout, K., Donzella, B., & Van Dulmen, M. M. H. (2003). Peer rejection, temperament, and cortisol activity in preschoolers. *Developmental Psychobiology*, *43*, 346–358. doi:10.1002/dev.10144

Hackman, D. A., & Farah, M. J. (2009). Socioeconomic status and the developing brain. *Trends in Cognitive Sciences*, *13*(2), 65–73. doi:10.1016/j.tics.2008.11.003

Haith, M. M. (1966). The response of the human newborn to visual movement. *Journal of Experimental Child Psychology*, *3*, 235–243. doi:10.1016/0022-0965(66)90067-1

Haith, M. M. (1969). Infrared television recording and measurement of ocular behavior in the human infant. *The American Psychologist*, *24*, 279–283. doi:10.1037/h0028419

Haith, M. M. (1980). *Rules that babies look by: The organization of newborn visual activity*. Hillsdale, NJ: Lawrence Erlbaum Associates, Inc.

Haith, M. M. (1994). Visual expectations as the first step toward the development of future-oriented processes. In Haith, M. M., Benson, J. B., Roberts, R. J. Jr, & Pennington, B. F. (Eds.), *The development of future-oriented processes* (pp. 11–38). Chicago, IL: The University of Chicago Press.

Haith, M. M. (2004). Progress and standardization in eye movement work with human infants. *Infancy*, *6*, 257–265. doi:10.1207/s15327078in0602_6

Hatzinger, M., Brand, S., Perren, S., von Wyl, A., von Klitzing, K., & Holsboer-Traschler, E. (2007). Hypothalamic-pituitary-adrenal (HPA) activity in kindergarten children: Importance of gender and associations with behavioral/emotional difficulties. *Journal of Psychiatric Research*, *41*, 861–870. doi:10.1016/j.jpsychires.2006.07.012

Hayhoe, M. M. (2004). Advances in relating eye movements and cognition. *Infancy*, *6*(2), 267–274. doi:10.1207/s15327078in0602_7

Honda, Y., Nakato, E., Otsuka, Y., Kanazawa, S., Kojima, S., Yamaguchi, M. K., & Kakgi, R. (2010). How do infants perceive scrambled face? A near-infrared spectroscopic study. *Brain Research*, *1308*, 137–146. doi:10.1016/j.brainres.2009.10.046

Huffman, L. C., Bryan, Y., del Carmen, R., Pederson, F., Doussard-Roosevelt, J., & Porges, S. (1998). Infant temperament and cardiac vagal tone: Assessments at twelve weeks of age. *Child Development*, *69*, 624–635.

Hughes, J. R., DeLeo, A. J., & Melyn, M. A. (2000). The electroencephalogram in attention deficit-hyperactivity disorder: Emphasis on epileptiform discharges. *Epilepsy & Behavior*, *1*, 271–277. doi:10.1006/ebeh.2000.0073

Hunnius, S. (2007). The early development of visual attention and its implications for social and cognitive development. *Progress in Brain Research*, *164*, 187–209. doi:10.1016/S0079-6123(07)64010-2

Hunnius, S., & Geuze, R. H. (2004). Developmental changes in visual scanning of dynamic faces and abstract stimuli in infants: A longitudinal study. *Infancy*, *6*, 231–255. doi:10.1207/s15327078in0602_5

Immordino-Yang, M. H. (2007). A tale of two cases: Lessons for education from the study of two boys living with half their brains. *Mind. Brain and Education*, *1*(2), 66–83. doi:10.1111/j.1751-228X.2007.00008.x

Immordino-Yang, M. H. (2009in press). Our bodies, our minds, our selves: Social neuroscience and its application to education. In Feifer, S., & Rattan, G. (Eds.), *The neuropsychology of emotional disorders*. Middletown, MD: School Neuropsychology Press.

Immordino-Yang, M. H., & Damasio, A. R. (2007). We feel, therefore we learn: The relevance of affective and social neuroscience to education. *Mind. Brain and Education*, *1*(1), 3–10. doi:10.1111/j.1751-228X.2007.00004.x

James, W. (1981). *The principles of psychology*. Cambridge, MA: Harvard University Press. (Original work published 1890)

Johnson, M. H. (1994). Covert visual attention and the control of eye movements in early infancy. In Umilta, C., & Moscovitch, M. (Eds.), *Attention and performance XV* (pp. 291–310). Cambridge, MA: MIT Press.

Justice, L. M., & Ezell, H. K. (2002). *The syntax handbook*. Eau Claire, WI: Thinking Publications.

Justice, L. M., Skibbe, L., Canning, A., & Lankford, C. (2005). Pre-schoolers, print and storybooks: An observational study using eye movement analysis. *Journal of Research in Reading*, *28*(3), 229–243. doi:10.1111/j.1467-9817.2005.00267.x

Kindlon, D., Mezzacappa, E., & Earls, F. (1995). Psychometric properties of impulsivity measures: Temporal stability, validity and factor structure. *Journal of Child Psychology and Psychiatry, and Allied Disciplines*, *36*, 645–661.

Kirschbaum, C., & Hellhammer, D. H. (1994). Salivary cortisol in psychoneuroendocrine research: Recent developments and applications. *Psychoneuroendocrinology*, *19*, 313–333. doi:10.1016/0306-4530(94)90013-2

Kishiyama, M. M., Boyce, W. T., Jimenez, A. M., Perry, L. M., & Knight, R. T. (2009). Socioeconomicdisparities affect prefrontal function in children. *Journal of Cognitive Neuroscience*, *21*(6), 1106–1115. doi:10.1162/jocn.2009.21101

Kobayashi, C., Glover, G. H., & Temple, E. (2007). Children's and adults neural bases of verbal and nonverbal theory of mind. *Neuropsychologia*, *45*(7), 1522–1532. doi:10.1016/j.neuropsychologia.2006.11.017

Legendre, A. (2003). Environmental features influencing toddlers' bioemotional reactions in day care centers. *Environment and Behavior*, *35*, 523–549. doi:10.1177/0013916503035004005

Lubar, J. F., Swartwood, M. O., Swartwood, J., & O'Donnell, P. H. (1995). Evaluation of the effectiveness of EEG neurofeedback training for ADHD in a clinical setting as measured by changes in T.O.V.A. scores, behavioral ratings, and WISC-R performance. *Applied Psychophysiology and Biofeedback*, *20*(1), 83–99.

Luecken, L. J., & Lemery, K. S. (2004). Early caregiving and physiological stress responses. *Clinical Psychology Review*, *24*, 171–191. doi:10.1016/j.cpr.2004.01.003

Mayer, S. (2005). The early evolution of Jean Piaget's clinical method. *History of Psychology*, *8*(4), 362–382. doi:10.1037/1093-4510.8.4.362

McCann, H. S., & Miller, K. F. (2008, July). *Word learning and shared book reading: An analysis of eye movements*. Poster presented at the Annual Meeting of the Society for the Scientific Study of Reading, Asheville, NC.

Nakato, E., Otsuka, Y., Kanazawa, S., Yamaguchi, M. K., & Kakigi, R. (2009). When do infants differentiate profile face from frontal face? A near-infrared spectroscopic study. *Human Brain Mapping*, *30*(2), 462–472. doi:10.1002/hbm.20516

Nelson, C. A., Monk, C. S., Lin, J., Carver, L. J., Thomas, K. M., & Truwit, C. L. (2000). Functional neuroanatomy of spatial working memory. *Developmental Psychology*, *36*(1), 109–116. doi:10.1037/0012-1649.36.1.109

Oritz, J., & Raine, A. (2004). Heart rate level and antisocial behavior in children and adolescents: A meta-analysis. *Journal of the American Academy of Child and Adolescent Psychiatry*, *43*(2), 154–162. doi:10.1097/00004583-200402000-00010

Perez-Edgar, K., Schmidt, L. A., Henderson, H. A., Schulkin, J., & Fox, N. A. (2009). Salivary cortisol levels and infant temperament shape developmental trajectories in boys at risk for behavioral maladjustment. *Psychoneuroendocrinology*, *33*(7), 916–925. doi:10.1016/j.psyneuen.2008.03.018

Piaget, J. (1960). *The child conception of the world*. Totowa, NJ: Littlefield, Adams & Co. (Original published in 1926).

Porges, S. W. (1991). Vagal tone: An autonomic mediator of affect. In Garber, J. A., & Dodge, K. A. (Eds.), *The development of affect regulation and dysregulation* (pp. 111–128). New York, NY: Cambridge University Press. doi:10.1017/CBO9780511663963.007

Porges, S. W. (1996). Physiological regulation in high-risk infants: A model for assessment and potential intervention. *Development and Psychopathology*, *8*, 43–58. doi:10.1017/S0954579400006969

Porges, S. W., & Byrne, E. A. (1992). Research methods for measurement of heart rate and respiration. *Biological Psychology*, *34*, 93–130. doi:10.1016/0301-0511(92)90012-J

Porges, S. W., Doussard-Roosevelt, J., & Maita, A. K. (1994). Vagal tone and the physiological regulation of emotion. *Monographs of the Society for Research in Child Development*, *59*(2–3).

Porges, S. W., Doussard-Roosevelt, J., Portales, L., & Greenspan, S. I. (1996). Infant regulation of the vagal brake predicts child behavior problems: A psychobiological model of social behavior. *Developmental Psychobiology*, *29*, 697–712. doi:10.1002/(SICI)1098-2302(199612)29:8<697::AID-DEV5>3.0.CO;2-O

Racine, E., Br-Ilan, O., & Illes, J. (2005). fMRI in the public eye. *Nature Reviews. Neuroscience*, *6*(2), 159–164. doi:10.1038/nrn1609

Raine, A., Reynolds, C., Venables, P. H., & Mednick, S. A. (1997). Biosocial bases of aggressive behavior in childhood: Resting heart rate, skin conductance orienting, and physique. In Raine, A., Brennan, P. A., Farrington, D. P., & Mednick, S. A. (Eds.), *Biosocial bases of violence* (pp. 107–126). New York, NY: Plenum.

Raine, A., Venables, P. H., & Mednick, S. A. (1997). Low resting heart rate at age 3 years predisposes to aggression at age 11 years: Findings from the Mauritius Joint Child Health Project. *Journal of the American Academy of Child and Adolescent Psychiatry*, *36*, 1457–1464. doi:10.1097/00004583-199710000-00029

Raine, A., Venables, P. H., & Williams, M. (1995). High autonomic arousal and electrodermal orienting at age 15 years as protective factors against criminal behavior at age 29 years.

Rajah, M. N., & McIntosh, A. R. (2008). Age-related differences in brain activity during verbal recency memory. *Brain Research*, *1199*, 111–125. doi:10.1016/j.brainres.2007.12.051

Richardson, D. C., & Spivey, M. J. (2004a). Eye tracking: Characteristics and methods. In Wnek, G., & Bowlin, G. (Eds.), *Encyclopedia of biomaterials and biomedical engineering* (pp. 568–572). Marcel Dekker, Inc.

Rousseau, J. (1979). *Emile or on education*. New York, NY: Basic Books. (Original work published 1762)

Roy-Charland, A., Saint-Aubin, J., & Evans, M. A. (2007). Eye movements in shared book reading with children from kindergarten to grade four. *Reading and Writing*, *20*, 909–931. doi:10.1007/s11145-007-9059-9

Scarborough, H. S., & Dobrich, W. (1994). On the efficacy of reading to preschoolers. *Developmental Review*, *14*, 245–302. doi:10.1006/drev.1994.1010

Scarr, S. (1992). Developmental theories for the 1990s: Development and individual differences. *Child Development*, *63*(1), 1–19. doi:10.2307/1130897

Schwartz, E. B., Granger, D. A., Susman, E. J., Gunnar, M. R., & Laird, B. (1998). Assessing salivary cortisol in studies of child development. *Child Development*, *69*(6), 1503–1513.

Scott, A. S., & Fong, E. (2004). *Body structures and functions*. Clifton Park, NY: Delamr Learning.

Shaywitz, B. A., Shaywitz, S. E., Blachman, B. A., Pugh, K. R., Fulbright, R. K., & Skudlarski, P. (2004). Development of left occipitotemporal systems for skilled reading in children after a phonologically-based intervention. *Biological Psychiatry*, *55*(9), 926–933. doi:10.1016/j.biopsych.2003.12.019

Shaywitz, S. E., Shaywitz, B. A., Pugh, K. R., Fulbright, R. K., Constable, R. T., & Mencl, W. E. ...Gore, J. C. (1998). Functional disruption in the organization of the brain for reading in dyslexia. *Proceedings of the National Academy of Sciences of the United States of American*, *95*(5), 2636-2641.

Shirtcliff, E., Granger, D. A., Booth, A., & Johnson, D. (2005). Low salivary cortisol levels and externalizing behavior problems: A latent state trait model in normally developing youth. *Development and Psychopathology*, *17*, 167–184.

Shonkoff, J., & Phillips, D. (2000). *From neurons to neighborhoods*. Washington, DC: National Academy Press.

Smider, N. A., Essex, M. J., Kalin, N. H., Buss, K. A., Klein, M. H., Davidson, R. J., & Goldsmith, H. H. (2002). Salivary cortisol as a predictor of socioemotional adjustment during kindergarten: A prospective study. *Child Development*, *73*, 75–92. doi:10.1111/1467-8624.00393

Suess, P. E., Porges, S. W., & Plude, D. J. (1994). Cardiac vagal tone and sustained attention in school-age children. *Psychophysiology*, *31*, 17–22. doi:10.1111/j.1469-8986.1994.tb01020.x

Technology. (2007). In *Merriam Webster's Dictionary* online. Retrieved from http://www.merriam-webster/dicionary.com/ technology

(n.d.)... *The American Journal of Psychiatry*, *152*, 1595–1600.

Tout, K., de Haan, M., Campbell, E. K., & Gunnar, M. R. (1998). Social behavior correlates of cortisol activity in child care: Gender differences and time-of-day effects. *Child Development*, *69*, 1247–1262. doi:10.2307/1132263

Tsujii, T., Yamamoto, E., Takahashi, T., Masuda, S., & Watanabe, S. (2009). Longitudinal study of spatial working memory development in young children. *Neuroreport*, *20*(8), 759–763. doi:10.1097/WNR.0b013e32832aa975

Vermer, H. J., & van IJzendoorn, M. H. (2006). Children's elevated cortisol levels at daycare: A review and meta-analysis. *Early Childhood Research Quarterly*, *21*, 390–401. doi:10.1016/j.ecresq.2006.07.004

Watamura, S. E., Donzella, B., Alwin, J., & Gunnar, M. R. (2003). Morning to afternoon increases in cortisol concentrations for infants and toddlers at child care: Age differences and behavioral correlates. *Child Development*, *74*(4), 1006–1020. doi:10.1111/1467-8624.00583

Watson, J. B. (1930). *Behaviorism*. Chicago, IL: University of Chicago Press.

Wentworth, N. (2008). Future orientation. In Haidth, M. M., & Benson, J. B. (Eds.), *Encyclopedia of infant and early childhood development* (pp. 562–574). Academic Press. doi:10.1016/B978-012370877-9.00068-2

Section 2

Bridging the Gap between Technology-Based Educational Research Methods and Child Development

Chapter 6
Bridging the Communication Gap through Video Research: The Preschool in Three Cultures Method

Yeh Hsueh
University of Memphis, USA

Joseph Tobin
Arizona State University, USA

ABSTRACT

Technology is a valuable tool for researchers of young children for many reasons. This chapter discusses the use of video as an ethnographic research tool for studying preschool education and offers insight into how video can be used to inform researchers, practitioners, and parents of young children. The approach referred to as video-cued multivocal ethnography is intended to highlight differences across cultures, and to reveal continuity and change in preschool education of three countries over the course of a generation. But this approach is also valuable for promoting teacher reflection on, and developing cultural understandings of how teachers' practice embodies the culture in which they live and work.

INTRODUCTION

Technology has changed the depth of research in early childhood classrooms in multiple ways. The use of video as a research tool helps bridge the communication gap between researchers, teachers, and parents in early childhood classrooms. Videos allow multiple viewing of the same interactions which generates meaningful dialogue among the community of teachers and researchers and gives insight into beliefs about educational cultures. This chapter focuses on one innovative approach to using video in early childhood education research, an approach that uses video not as data, but rather as a stimulus or cue for getting teachers and directors in different cultures to reflect on the thinking behind their practices. We have suggested calling this method

DOI: 10.4018/978-1-61350-059-0.ch006

Copyright © 2012, IGI Global. Copying or distributing in print or electronic forms without written permission of IGI Global is prohibited.

"Video-Cued Multivocal Ethnography," but it is better known as the *Preschool in Three Cultures method*, (Tobin, Wu, & Davidson, 1989; Tobin, Hsueh, & Karasawa, 2009). In this chapter we describe the video cued method we used in the two *Preschool in Three Cultures* studies, explain the antecedents we drew on in developing the method, and reflect on some factors that are key to using the method effectively. The conclusion suggests some ways that this method can be adapted for other uses in early childhood education.

Objectives

After reading this chapter the reader will be able to identify and discuss the role video technology plays in comparative early childhood education research, to have an in-depth understanding of how the method helps researchers obtain cultural information of preschool teachers, administrators, and parents of your children. The reader will come to know about how video can be used to inform teachers, administrators, parents and researchers about their cultural beliefs and practices in early childhood education. One important objective in introducing the *Preschool in Three Cultures* method is to shift the focus of the traditional academic educational research from privileging the researchers' voices to privileging teachers' perspectives. This approach not only contextualizes diverse perspectives, but also delves into the depth of implicit cultural meanings. In this chapter, the reader will become acquainted with the Preschool in Three Cultures method: Its major components and processes, the inspiring ideas behind its origin, and the role videos play in generating a multivocal dialogue and research questions. This chapter discusses how we use videos in interviews and how this can help teachers reflect on key issues in their teaching and beliefs about culture. The reader will:

- Develop an understanding of how the technology of video has and can impact research and teaching
- Develop an understanding of how video bridges the communication gap among researchers, teachers, administrators and parents

BACKGROUND: VIDEO TECHNOLOGY IN EDUCATIONAL ENVIRONMENTS

The first release of the technology of videotaping was in 1951 and was developed by John T. Mullin and Wayne R. Johnson. The first domestic videocassette recorders were launched in the early 1970s, but it was not until the Japanese systems, Sony's Beta (1975) and JVC's VHS, were launched, that videotape moved into the mass market. It was clear that this technology could be a valuable tool for education but it was unclear as to exactly how to use video tapes to support educational environments. The first use in educational environments was as an instructional tool and later as a tool for self evaluation of teaching. As technology evolved and cameras became easier to use, less expensive, and more common, models of research using videos developed and were accepted by the educational research community. By the 1980s videotaping had begun to be explored as a support tool for research. Collier and Collier (1986, p. 139) comment, "Film and video have become essential for the study of human behavior." One of the early studies which pioneered the use of video and how it has evolved as a research technology is described in this chapter. This narrative explains how this model supports not only research but the development of thoughtful communities of learners and professionals in the field of early childhood education.

Pioneering Use of Video in Comparative Early Childhood Education Research

The publication of Joseph Tobin, David Wu, & Dana Davidson's *Preschool in Three Cultures: Japan, China and the United States* in 1989 introduced a new approach to comparative research in early childhood education. This book, along with its companion video, attracted a wide range of readers including early childhood educators, parents of young children, anthropologists, sociologists and psychologists. The success of the book was due, to a great extent, to its innovative use of video technology. The comparisons of Japanese, Chinese, and American preschools presented in this study were anchored in a set of three videos made of ordinary days in a preschool in each of the three countries. The book features comments and reflections by insiders and outsiders responding to scenes in the videos. The text of the book weaves together a virtual dialogue made up of quotes from early childhood educators in multiple sites in each country talking about their notions of best practice, a dialogue which works to highlight the cultural nature of preschool education, emphasizing how preschools both reflect and help reproduce the larger cultures in which they are located.

Twenty years later, in 2009, Tobin, this time with colleagues Yeh Hsueh, and Mayumi Karasawa, published a sequel to the original study. The new book, *Preschool in Three Cultures Revisited: China, Japan and the United States,* added to the original study's focus on cultural difference a historical dimension, exploring how and why the early childhood educational approach of a country changes or stays the same over time. The new study uses the same video-cued comparative ethnographic method as the original, with some modifications intended to highlight continuity and change over the course of a generation.

These two studies demonstrate that reflective uses of video have the power not only to inform research, but also to help teachers, administrators and parents come to see their own taken-for-granted beliefs and practices in a new light, as well as to widen their horizons of what's possible by being exposed to approaches used in other cultures. This method of research has become well accepted and is considered valuable for early childhood professionals as the digital age brings cultures and communities closer together. The international application of this model allows insight into both common and unique characteristics of educational environments which gives researchers deeper insights into the cultural influences of early childhood.

The Preschool in Three Cultures Method

This method of video-cued comparative ethnography, or the *Preschool in Three Cultures* method, uses video not as data, but instead as a research tool for eliciting rich data, in the form of teachers' reactions and reflections. The steps of the method are straightforward: We first spend a few days in a selected preschool classroom in each country, becoming familiar with the daily routines and giving the teacher and children the chance to become comfortable with us and our camcorders. Then, using two camcorders and wireless microphones, we record a day in the classroom, from the children's arrival in the morning to departure in the late afternoon. We edit the 8-10 hours of footage we have shot down to 20 minutes. We then show this edited version to the teacher in whose classroom we videotaped and invite her to explain the events we have recorded and to reflect on the thinking behind her practices as seen in the video. We next use the video as an interviewing cue with other staff at the same preschool; then with early childhood educators at other preschools around the country; and finally with early childhood educators in the other two countries.

This approach allows educators to analyze and reflect within regions and among countries for a more comprehensive view of interactions in early childhood programs. The result is a video-cued multivocal conversation, a video-stimulated virtual dialogue, among early childhood educators.

The Development of the Preschool in Three Cultures Method

This method has multiple origins (Tobin, Wu, & Davidson, 1989; Tobin, Hsueh & Karasawa, 2009). The original idea of using videos as an interviewing cue was borrowed from the work of anthropologist Linda Conner and the ethnographic filmmakers Tim and Patsy Asch, who videotaped a Balinese shaman during a séance and then later showed her a film of herself in the state of trance and asked her to comment on her actions in the film (Asch, Conner, & Asch, 1983; Conner, Asch, & Asch, 1986).

In traditional ethnographic fieldwork, the anthropologist participated in activities of cultural insiders throughout the day and then, in the evening, she would ask her informants to reflect on and explain those activities by referring to her memory and notes. The Preschool in Three Cultures video-cued method condenses this daily observing and interviewing by replacing the observations made during extended fieldwork with a set of videos, which work to cue and focus reflections. Because this method replaces the long duration of fieldwork with a video-cued interviewing method, some anthropologists would argue that it does not meet the strict criteria of ethnography. On the other hand, we would argue that this method is nevertheless ethnographic because it focuses on ordinary events, positions culture as the central explanatory construct, privileging insider explanations and *emic* over *etic* analytic categories and theories (Spindler, 2000, xxii).

A second inspiration for the method came from the tradition in psychodynamic psychology of using ambiguous visual stimuli, for example, an inkblot, a photo, or a drawing, to reveal unconscious psychological processes (Henry, 1956). As an early predecessor, Henry A. Murray (1938) developed a method that he called "The Thematic Apperception Test" (TAT) in which he asked research participants to tell stories about drawings he selected, and then analyzed these participants' stories to reveal deep psychological issues in these individuals' thoughts and feelings. William Caudill (1962) adapted Murray's TAT method, changing it into the "picture interview." Instead of analyzing the individual's psyche, the picture interview became an ethnographic tool for analyzing cultural beliefs. For example, Caudill showed simple line drawings of scenes of interpersonal intimacy, such as scenes of children bathing together in a tub or of a man and woman sitting on a bed, to Japanese and American informants and asked them to tell him a story about each picture. He used these stories to analyze differences and similarities in the cultural patterning of physical and emotional intimacy between Japanese and American informants. In the Preschool in Three Cultures method, each scene in our videos is like a moving, noisy version of Caudill's drawings.

A third source for this method comes from Mikhail Bakhtin, a Russian literary theorist and social philosopher who introduced the terms multivocality and dialogism. As mentioned above, the Preschool in Three Cultures method is more formally called video-cued *multivocal* ethnography. Our method is in keeping with Bakhtin's term as well as a response to the call by James Clifford (1983) to recognize and emphasize the multivocality of ethnography as a research method. Bakhtin's notion of dialogism underlies our use of focus-group rather than individual interviews in most phases of the research, because we view meanings as arising out of dialogical interaction among speakers. We view our video-cued interviewing as a strategy, not so much uncovering pre-existing positions of our research participants as creating an occasion for research participants to co-construct meanings with each other as well as with us.

A fourth source of inspiration is Akira Kurosawa's movie *Rashomon* (based on a short story by Ryūnosuke Akutagawa) in which three people described differently a crime that took place on a path in the forest. Their accounts revealed their own experiences with the people involved in the crime. The discussions we held with early childhood educators following the viewing of our videotapes show that these audiences often have different understandings not only about what the teachers should do, but also about what transpired in watching the video. Like the participants and eyewitnesses in *Rashomon* who give different accounts of the same crime, our informants reveal something about themselves and their worldviews as they comment on our videos.

In the *Preschool in Three Cultures* method the videos are not data to be analyzed, but rather cues, stimuli, topics for discussion, and interviewing tools. The comments and explanations of our informants about the videos provide the data for our analysis. The use of video allows researchers and teachers to reflect on beliefs about teaching, learning and culture with a consistent picture of thinking. The technology allows researchers, teachers, and parents to view their thinking many times and communicate their understanding of cultural influences in early childhood classrooms.

The development support for the Preschool in Three Cultures method has two common features that are essential for data analysis. They all prioritize participants' perspectives and give validity to their explanations as cultural insiders, as people who are knowledgeable, but may not be articulate, about their own cultural practices. A second feature is to embrace multiple perspectives of the participants, including those of the researchers. Together, the informants and researchers co-construct a set of shared interpretations of the events recorded in the videos.

Diverse Perspectives on Key Video Scenes

Most approaches to research into the beliefs of early childhood teachers use questions, either in the form of oral interviews or written response questionnaires. A typical question might be "What is your philosophy of classroom management?" This is a difficult question for preschool teachers to answer because it is too abstract or can create a stress reaction as many teachers may associate this approach with a university exam question. This may influence the response giving the researcher a false understanding of beliefs. A second questioning approach would be to make it more concrete: "When a child in your class misbehaves, what do you do?" While this type of question attempts to clarify and give the teacher focus it remains ambiguous. Faced with this prompt one teacher may picture a child throwing food on the floor, a second teacher two girls squabbling over a teddy bear, and a third teacher two boys having a sword-fight with forks. These different events will tend to produce different levels of concern and therefore different responses in teachers. In our video-cued method, we show teachers a scene in a video in which, for example, a boy hits another boy, and we ask, "What would you do in this situation?" Scenes can be replayed numerous times as the teacher reflects on specific actions, thus reducing the possibility of premature inferences and conclusions and allows deeper understanding of the teacher's beliefs. Each scene in our 20-minute videos functions as a non-verbal question to stimulate a response that will provide insights into a participant's cultural and professional beliefs. We make sure to include in the video scenes that will stimulate a discussion of key topics in early childhood educational practice, topics including separation (scenes of children and parents saying goodbye in the morning); fighting (including not just the behavior of the fighting children but also the reactions of their classmates and teachers); misbehavior (for example, a child refusing to follow directions or share); mixed-aged play; and intimacy between teachers and children (for example, a teacher drying children with a towel after the swimming activity).

These and other scenes anchor the dialogue among participants in the focus group interviews as they interact with each other and the researchers. The video cues not only make the questions we are asking concrete and specific as discussed above, but also offer an identical referent for early childhood educators from different cultures to explain the same behaviors. This helps filter the analysis to focus more on beliefs rather than teachers trying to give perceived expected responses. This video-cued interviewing method has the advantage over questionnaires of being richer and more engaging. It also has the advantage over traditional ethnographic fieldwork interviews of allowing hundreds of informants from different cultural backgrounds to react to a set of common stimuli. This allows for identification of response patterns to make inferences about cultures as a whole rather than an array of individual perceptions.

Video and Interview Techniques

We employ several different strategies for using videos as interviewing cues. One technique is to hand the VCR controller or DVD player remote control to an informant, and to ask her to pause the video when she comes to a scene she wants to discuss or explain, an approach we most often use when conducting an individual interview with the teacher in whose classroom we shot the video. This allows our informant to share her thinking on issues she considers most important. When using this technique we also sometimes ask the teacher to pause the video to talk about a scene we want her to comment on. A second technique, which we use in focus group discussions with teachers, is for us to pause the video at the end of each key scene, and ask for reactions. The third technique is to play the video straight through, and then ask a series of questions, first giving the participants the chance to identity the scenes they are most eager to talk about and then following up with questions about scenes they do not spontaneously discuss. We most often show the videos straight through when first interviewing informants, so they can get an uninterrupted sense of the flow of events in the video and so as to not interrupt the drama and emotionality we build into the twenty minute videos, qualities which produce greater engagement and therefore more lively and thoughtful discussions. Stopping the videos to discuss scenes one by one is a technique we most often use for repeat interviews with key stakeholders, such as the directors and staff of the schools where the videos are shot. This more systematic discussion of each scene is especially effective for showing how educators' points of view shift over time, as in the case in the interviewing we did in China for Preschool in Three Cultures Revisited, where we re-interviewed teachers and directors three or more times between 2003 and 2008. In this way we had a chance to see how they were shifting in their perspectives along the rapid changes in Chinese early childhood education as reforms were implemented, embraced, resisted, and reassessed, and reconceived.

Ideally, when using the video-cued method, the researcher does not need to ask questions to initiate discussion because the video does this work for us. The videos in this sense lift from the shoulder of the researchers the burden of asking questions. For example, in one of our new videos there is a scene which shows a Japanese preschool teacher not intervening in a fight among girls over a teddy bear, Chinese and US teachers in our interviews cannot help but comment on this event, which inevitably produces a strong (critical) reaction. The Japanese teacher's non-intervention in a children's fight presents Chinese and US teachers with strange behavior in a familiar setting. Such moments of cultural dissonance are a key feature of ethnographic research which works to make the familiar strange and the strange familiar.

As cultural anthropologists, we are interested in learning about the cultural meaning system of the teachers in our study. This goal requires us to gain access to our informants' thoughts and feelings and to identity patterns not just of behavior but more importantly of meaning in the organization of their daily life. A central challenge of fieldwork is getting cultural insiders to talk about their values and beliefs they felt deeply and for them to see and reflect on the cultural dimensions of these values and beliefs. Video, thoughtfully produced (Tobin & Hsueh, 2007), can work effectively to cue and scaffold the process of cultural insiders identifying and sharing their thoughts and feelings about behaviors that are usually taken-for-granted and unremarkable. The scenes in the video of daily life in preschool classrooms in their own and others' cultures provide an anchor on which they can latch these thoughts and feelings. At the same time, the contextual richness and ambiguity of the scenes in the videos allow participants and the researchers to enter into a conversation that moves from particular issues to a wider discussion of cultural beliefs.

Video that Embeds and Generates Research Questions

This video method, as discussed above, in some ways collapses and shortens ethnography's traditional period of extended fieldwork. But the virtue of the method is not that it saves time or effort, but rather that produces rich insights. The method in the long run is not easier or faster than conducting a traditional ethnographic study because our method requires meticulous planning, repeated rounds of editing, ongoing consultation and negotiation with research participants, and repeated periods of interviewing, usually over the course of several years. The analysis and writing up of the meanings we uncover is a complex task, as our informants' reflections on the video need to be contextualized, interpreted, and combined with those of others, to eventually weave together a text which highlights both areas of agreement and diversity among practitioners within culture and across cultures.

The method allows and requires us to move back and forth between the concreteness of the events captured in our videos, the responses to these events of cultural insiders and outsiders, and the research questions we bring to the project, research questions that reflect our sense of key socio-cultural issues impacting preschools. For example, in the early 1980s when the first study Preschool in Three Cultures projects was being planned, a question on the minds of many educators and social scientists both inside and outside China was how the implementation of China's one-child-per-family policy was impacting Chinese society. A key research question of the first study was therefore how Chinese early childhood educators were responding to this dramatic change in the structure of families and therefore of society. The video shot at a preschool in Kunming of classes composed almost entirely of only-children and the dialogue stimulated by this video allowed for a nuanced discussion of various aspects of the impacts of the one-child policy. The Japanese side of the first study was informed by a great interest among social scientists and the lay public alike in the connections between Japanese education and Japan's economic success in the 1970s and 1980s. What were Japanese early childhood educators doing to prepare young children for the workforce and for becoming citizens of their rapidly post-modernizing society?

Preschool teachers, as practitioners and as cultural insiders, often introduce their own perspectives to the project, which help us identify important research questions about informants' cultural beliefs. We cannot predict such field-work-dependent questions before conducting the research, but often come out of our video-cued interviews with important new questions to pursue. In this sense, the videos help us generate new research questions based on our informants' perspectives we did not anticipate, perspectives that in turn become topics and focuses for subsequent interviews. For example, in the first study, Chinese early childhood educators explained many of the practices used by teachers as seen in our video of *A Day at Dong Feng* by using the concept of *guan*, which combines the meanings of the English words love, control, take responsibility, raise, train, and educate. This became a central concept in China chapter of the first book.

This question-generating aspect of the video-cued interviews, especially in the repeated interviews with key informants, is also conducive to capturing features of dynamic reforms in early childhood education. In 2002, the classroom teachers in our Sinanlu *you'eryuan* (preschool) video skillfully facilitated a group conversation among children about the conflict four children had just experienced during the period of socio-dramatic play. Many American and Chinese teachers praised the teachers in the video for taking the resolution of a conflict of a few to another level to benefit the larger group. However, in our return visit one year later, when we showed the same video scene to the classroom teachers, they informed us that their approaches had changed as their views shifted from the need for group debriefing as an educational process to the need for individual interest and learning that may not be beneficial to other children who were not involved in the conflict. Their thinking changed in their efforts to implement the curriculum reform in the city, a change that would be difficult to capture without the same video scene as a stimulus. The teachers' new perspective turned our attention to the fast-paced changes among Chinese preschool teachers as we conducted interviews in other major cities.

Adding a Diachronic Dimension

In *Preschool in Three Cultures Revisited* (Tobin, Hsueh, & Karasawa, 2009), we added to the original studies central concern with cultural comparison, a time dimension, as we explored how and why cultural systems of early childhood education stay the same and change over time. We used video-cued interviewing to get at questions of change over time in three ways. First, we showed teachers and directors at each school the videos we had shot their twenty years early and asked them to reflect on what had changed, what was still the same, and why. Secondly, we made a new videotape at each of the preschools where we had filmed a generation earlier, and we repeated the steps of the original method, using the new videos as cues for interviewing teachers and directors. Thirdly, to sharpen the focus on change, we made a second videotape in each country, of a preschool identified as exemplifying a new direction. We used these videos of new preschools, alongside the videos of preschools from the original study, as interviewing cues. This worked to provoke discussion in all three countries both about the direction of change and, as discussed below, about the typicality of the focus preschools in our study.

Typicality of the Samples

In the original study, we used as interviewing cues one video from each of the three countries, preschools that we claimed were typical only in the sense of not being atypical or extreme in their country in any obvious way. For the new study, as explained above, we videotaped days in two preschools in each country. We fully agree with those who would suggest that having two preschools per country is not an appreciable improvement over one, from the perspective of capturing the full range and diversity of approaches to early childhood education to be found in each country. We have grown accustomed over the years to the critique that the preschools we videotaped in each country may not be typical or representative.

Since we first presented the original study over 25 years ago, we have emphasized that the videos are not data, that we make no claims that the preschools in our videos are typical, and that we have an innovative, sophisticated method for addressing questions of typicality and variation (Tobin, 1992; Hsueh & Barton, 2006). Our study has a more systematic approach to the question of typicality and generalizability than do most. In our method, we address the question of typicality by showing the videotape we shot, for example, at Komatsudani Hoikuen in Kyoto, to teachers and directors in five other settings in Japan and asking these informants to tell us in what ways Komatsudani is like and unlike their preschool. When, for example, a preschool director in Tokyo tells us, "You should have videotaped in Tokyo, not in Kyoto, and in a public program rather than one run by a Buddhist temple, and in a *yoūchien* (nursery school / kindergarten) rather than in a *hoikuen* (daycare center)," her comments reveal not just variations in types of Japanese preschools, but also tensions and biases within the world of Japanese early childhood education, differences, tensions, and biases we then pursue and attempt to understand in subsequent rounds of interviewing.

Similarly, we showed the videos of the two Chinese preschool to preschool teachers and administrators in seven large Chinese cities and a dozen smaller cities. In this process we invited over 1000 early child educators to view and comment on the videos by asking them to tell us whether their preschools were like or unlike the school in the videos. In this way our method allows us to involve our informants in the task of judging typicality. The method also allows us to include the perspectives of a much larger number of participants than can traditional ethnographies.

Our approach allows not only to present a sense of the diversity and variation to be found in each countries' preschools, but also of what is widely shared. We suggest that this sharing of beliefs and practices reflects a combination of explicit factors (such as government curriculum mandates and national teacher certification requirements) and what we call "implicit cultural beliefs and practices," a phrase we use to refer to beliefs and practices that are widely shared within a nation despite the fact that they are not specified in government guidelines, written down in textbooks, or explicitly taught in schools of education (Tobin, 2010; Tobin, Hsueh, & Karasawa, 2009).

One example of such an implicit belief came to our attention as we reflected on why many Chinese early childhood educators criticized us for videotaping in Kunming, in the country's Southwest, rather than videotaping only in Beijing or Shanghai, where we could to feature model preschools that would showcase the best that China had to offer. We came to see this criticism as reflecting a deep-rooted cultural belief in presenting one's best face and in learning through emulating the best models available (Munroe, 1975; Li, 2003a, 2003b). Another example of an implicit cultural practice in China was the taken-for-granted reactions of approval of a scene in our video in which a child stand in front of the class and recites a story and then receives critiques on his storytelling from his classmates, practices that produced surprise and disapproval from many Japanese and American early childhood educators.

Research Video for Professional Development and Change

As researchers, our primary intent in using video as in interviewing tool in each of our studies has been to elucidate insider meanings and in this way to conduct comparative research. But over the years of conducting this research we have also received feedback from the teachers and directors who participated in the study suggesting that they not only enjoyed the process, but also learned something from it. These reactions alert us to the power of this method to be adapted for use in pre-service and in-service professional development of teachers.

Participants in our studies have told us that they learned something new both from watching videos of days in preschools in other countries and being introduced to the perspectives on the practices in the videos of educators who were insiders to these practices and also from watching videos of days in a preschools in their own country, and coming to see taken-for-granted beliefs and practices in a new light. In other words, this approach has the power both to make the exotic familiar and the familiar exotic.

One example of this process is that, by participating in our project, the Directors of Daguan *you'eryan* (preschool) in Kunming became conscious of the need to make changes in their views and practices. In our 1984 video of Daguan, we show a scene of children as a group squatting down together along a trough-like toilet. In the video we shot at Daguan twenty years later we see children joking and playing in the toilets, which are still troughs, but now with running water for flushing and with a dividing wall between the girls' and boys' sides. As we were wrapping up the study we learned from the Director that they planned to replace the trough toilets with sit-down toilets, and that they were considering putting in dividers to provide more privacy. Moreover the Director told us that our interviewing her about the toilets, combined with giving her a chance to see in our videos toilets in preschools in Shanghai, as well as in Japan and the US, had played a role in her decision to change the toilets. While we do not necessarily see these changes as improvements, and while we are a bit uncomfortable with the notion that our research worked to provoke change in one of our research sites, we are struck by the power of video-cued reflection to work as an agent of professional development.

Director Shi of Daguan *you'eryuan* has also shared with us how participating in our study has led her and her staff to also come to have a great appreciation of some of their own practices, and given them more resolve to draw on their traditions and knowledge as they forge their path forward. In other words, participating in our study has helped these educators both gain exposure to new ideas and to clarify their own values and aspirations.

In all three cultures, the experience of watching the videos has provided educators with a chance to rise above the fray of their daily practice and to clarify and rethink their beliefs. Some preschools in the United States used their participation in our research project as a way of meeting the accreditation requirement of participating in professional development activities. Many teachers and directors who have watched and discussed the videos have told us that this process is an interesting, entertaining, informative, and a thought provoking professional development experience.

ISSUES, CONTROVERSIES, PROBLEMS

The debate about what is and what is not appropriate research has a long history in education. Some argue that this over 100-year history of educational research started wrong foot that misdirected subsequent educational research, and that educational researchers are also in low status with a weak influence on social policy (Cf. Lageman, 2000). Within the field of educational research, there have been diverse arguments as well. Educational researchers often disagree along philosophical and methodological lines, Even though many share some common grounds concerning the general purposes and established methods, rarely does one study produce unequivocal and durable results.

Multiple methods, applied over time and tied to evidentiary results, are essential to establishing a base of scientific knowledge. Formal synthesis across studies is often necessary to explain the diversity of findings that characterize many fields. It takes time to build scientific knowledge and this knowledge changes as new information evolves. The multidimensional nature of research is often overlooked when we limit our thinking to one approach or data set. Scientific knowledge, whether in hard sciences, psychology or teacher education, requires a community or a network of researchers working together with established principles that guide scientific investigations. The use of video technology provides a visual record of research that can be used with researchers, teachers, and parents to connect verbal and physical cues to provide a deeper understanding of beliefs about culture in early childhood environments.

The premise of the Preschool in Three Cultures studies address the concerns of quality research design as it continues to add to a growing scientific knowledge base of what influences preschool environments from multiple dimensions and diverse perspectives. The community of practitioners and researchers is one of the powerful ideas from this method. The researchers join teachers, administrators and parents in grappling with their own taken-for-granted beliefs and practices in a new light, as well as to widen their horizons of what is possible by being exposed to approaches used in other places in their own culture and in other cultures. The method described in this chapter suggests that a multivocal conversation is necessary to allow researchers and practitioners alike to gain deeper insights into the values, beliefs, and the implicit cultural logic of early childhood educators, not just make assumptions on limited responses to interview and survey questions.

Three issues appear apparent in light of the Preschool in Three Cultures approach. The first is a critical issue in educational research in general and teacher education researcher in particular where researchers or professional facilitators share a pool of cultural assumptions with the participants they mean to study or help. Cultural assumptions are taken for granted that often do not warrant adequate objective distance to the researcher from the same culture to see the deeply embedded cultural logic in teachers' reasoning, thoughts and feelings. This problem of cultural blindness is complicated by the second issue in educational research in which researchers and teachers often have a power differential. Researchers are more privileged in their observations, instruments use, analysis, findings and especially conclusions. As a result, they control the discourse relevant to the research and frequently how teachers are supposed to change. Change is at the core of the third issue that is perennial in waves of educational reform in which teachers are often viewed as being resistant to reform although the success of a reform depends on teachers acting as reform agents. Can educational research practice overcome these problems in the 21st century educational arena? The Preschool in Three Cultures Approach suggested one possible direction that has been encouraged and advanced by the availability of video technology and an increasing understanding of the cultural roots of early childhood education of our times.

However, these issues and problems described above will continue to haunt us and they do not appear without controversies. This chapter addresses a most tenacious doubt heavily influenced by the 19th century scientific thought, a doubt about whether the sampling in the method of the preschool in each country is typical of all that country's preschools. Interestingly, this controversy is rooted in the three issues above and reflects conflicting positions in educational research. One side argues that it is methodologically mandatory to select a typical preschool for any comparative study. The other side counters that no preschool in each country is representative of all other schools in each country. It is the different perspectives and the identifiable underlying cultural beliefs and values that can inform us of the typicality in a cultural practice in early childhood education. Beneath the controversy here are the three longtime issues about what cultural and scientific assumptions one holds, who has the discourse power and who are the participants of a cultural community in study.

FUTURE TRENDS

As the educational arena continues to become more of a community rather than an array of isolated environments, it is more and more important to understand educators' cultural beliefs. Approaches to studying cultures and identifying how beliefs influence instructional practice is crucial to developing communities of researchers and learners. A large body of literature has pointed to the need in teacher education for researchers, teacher educators, and teachers to work together and maintain a sustained relationship in their curriculum innovations, pedagogical experiments and structuring reform efforts. The future of the Preschool in Three Cultures approach, armed with ever-improving video technology, may be conducive to transforming aspects of early childhood educational research in the future, especially its teacher education and professional development. In early childhood education across the world, one growing use of video is geared toward using classroom video as a key tool for stimulating and promoting teacher reflections of their professional practice. This trend is accompanied by the increased awareness that, in the age of globalization, we can gain many insights from cross-cultural research to heighten our awareness of deeply rooted beliefs, values and practice. Researchers, teacher educators and teachers in early childhood education have to look closely at the cross-cultural issues to increase their cultural sensitivity, not only because the world economy and technological advancement provide more means than ever for this end, but also because there is an ever-increasing necessity to understand our own cultural practice by looking at others'.

CONCLUSION

The use of video in early childhood classroom environments can support research and professional development. The Preschool in Three Cultures method is a field-tested research method, practically useful in understanding the beliefs, values and diverse practice of early childhood educators within and across culture, and in helping educators improving their teaching and care.

This chapter has described the video cued method we used in the two Preschool in Three Cultures studies, explained the intellectual inspirations in developing the method, and reviewed some essential elements for using the method effectively. This chapter also highlights the role of video in this innovative research method and reiterates that videos herein are not data in the method. The role of videos is to engage educators' thoughts, connect their thoughts and feelings with one another so they can co-construct and articulate their own cultural perspectives in practice. In this process, research and practice can come together for the improvement of early childhood education and for the improvement of our children's present and future life as world citizens.

Reflecting on the Preschool in Three Cultures Method and Early Childhood Education

This section gives you some questions and activities to help you think about how you can use some of the ideas from this chapter in your work.

Research

1. Video a typical day in your classroom. Also ask one early childhood educator from a different cultural community (i.e., from a different ethnic community or country) to do the same. Select scenes that you believe are stimulating or challenging to share with each other. Discuss how and why each of you responded to the video scenes from each other's community..Together you discuss what you have learned about your own beliefs in early childhood education.
2. Post your video clips to a group work site to generate discussions in your school group. Observe the interactions of colleagues and identify common themes in your school. Are there reoccurring patterns of ideas, beliefs, and proposed actions? If yes, what are they? Why?
3. Video for an hour a teacher's classroom that is located in a community different from your own. Select a few video scenes from the footage to interview the teacher in the video afterwards to learn her ideas about teaching and care for the young children in the class.

Reflect

1. Examine your beliefs about classroom interactions. Is it easy to identify the common core beliefs that you and your peers take for granted? What are they? Start a discussion of how these beliefs might influence your classroom interactions.
2. Think about the multivocal conversation used in this method. What are the advantages of this method in helping teachers think about their practice? How can this method be used in your school to support learning?
3. Describe your beliefs about early childhood education in Japan. How did you acquire information to form the beliefs? By reading books and viewing videos about Japanese preschool education video. Would they make you think differently from the beliefs you held before reading and viewing these materials?
4. One result from this study indicated that in China "a deep-rooted cultural belief in presenting one's best face and in learning through emulating the best models available." Is there any evidence in your experiences that this is a common idea across cultures? Why or why not?
5. As some early childhood education practices from a few Western countries become more and more globalized as "the best practices," how do you see your role as a contributor and practitioner in this globalization movement?

Practice

1. After analyzing a video of your "typical day" in your classroom, develop a list of things identified as "want to change" within your educational environment.
2. Take a video of your own classroom during certain key activities of the day. Show each episode to the children in the video. Ask them what they have noticed and what makes them think that way.

REFERENCES

Asch, T., Asch, P., & Connor, L. (1983). *Jero on Jero: A Balinese trance séance observed* [film]. Watertown, MA: Documentary Educational Resources.

Caudill, W. (1962). Patterns of emotion in modern Japan. In Smith, R. J., & Beardsley, R. K. (Eds.), *Japanese culture* (pp. 115–131). Chicago, IL: Aldine.

Clifford, J. (1983). On ethnographic authority. *Representations (Berkeley, Calif.)*, *1*(2), 118–146. doi:10.1525/rep.1983.2.1.99p0010p

Collier, J., & Collier, M. (1986). *Visual anthropology: Photography as a research method.* Albuquerque, NM: University of New Mexico Press.

Connor, L., Asch, T., & Asch, P. (1986). *Jero Tapakan: Balinese healer*. Cambridge, UK: Cambridge University Press.

Henry, W. (1956). *The analysis of fantasy: The thematic appreciation technique in the study of personality*. New York, NY: John Wiley & Sons.

Hsueh, Y., & Barton, B. (2006). A cultural perspective on professional beliefs of childcare teachers. *Early Childhood Education Journal*, *33*(3), 179–186. doi:10.1007/s10643-005-0042-2

Lagemann, E. C. (2002). *An elusive science: The troubling history of education research*. Chicago, IL: University of Chicago Press.

Li, J. (2003a). The core of Confucian learning. *The American Psychologist*, *58*, 146–147. doi:10.1037/0003-066X.58.2.146

Li, J. (2003b). U.S. and Chinese beliefs about learning. *Journal of Educational Psychology*, *95*, 258–267. doi:10.1037/0022-0663.95.2.258

Munro, D. J. (1975). The Chinese view of modeling. *Human Development*, *18*, 333–352. doi:10.1159/000271495

Murray, H. A. (1938). *Explorations in personality*. New York, NY: Oxford University Press.

Roush, R. (1971). *Research using the videotape recorder in teacher education*. Alexandria, VA: Association for Supervision and Curriculum Development.

Spindler, G. (2000). The four careers of George and Louise Spindler: 1948-2000. *Annual Review of Anthropology*, *29*, xv–xxxviii. doi:10.1146/annurev.anthro.29.1.00

Tobin, J. (1992). A dialogical solution to the problem of field site typicality. *City and Society*, *6*(1), 46–57. doi:10.1525/city.1992.6.1.46

Tobin, J. (2010, July). *The role of culture in early childhood education*. Keynote address at the Annual Conference of the Pacific Early Childhood Education Research Association, Hangzhou, China.

Tobin, J., & Hsueh, Y. (2007). The poetics and pleasures of video ethnography of education. In Goldman, R. (Ed.), *Video research in the learning sciences* (pp. 77–92). New York, NY: Erlbaum.

Tobin, J., Hsueh, Y., & Karasawa, M. (2010). *Preschool in three cultures revisited: China, Japan, & the United States*. Chicago, IL: The University of Chicago Press.

Tobin, J., Wu, D., & Davidson, D. (1989). *Preschool in three cultures: Japan, China & the United States*. New Haven, CT: Yale University Press.

Section 3
Bridging the Gap between Pedagogy and Technology

Chapter 7
Early Childhood Teachers:
Closing the Digital-Divide

Kevin Thomas
Bellarmine University, USA

Kathleen Spencer Cooter
Bellarmine University, USA

ABSTRACT

This chapter reviews the state of technology training for early childhood educators in teacher preparation institutions across the country. Using NCATE and NAEYC standards as benchmarks of practice, the chapter outlines some current issues and research on technology training at the preservice level, such as course sequence, textbook choice, content infusion, field experiences, et cetera. The chapter also outlines three technologies, Web 2.0, Google Earth, and the virtual manipulatives that are accessible, free to users, require little teacher training, and have evidence to support their instructional benefits. These three well-developed technologies can easily be introduced to students and teachers as exemplars of constructivist pedagogical technology in early childhood science and mathematics classrooms. Activities using each are included.

INTRODUCTION

Jessica is a five-year-old enchanted by dolphins. Last year she and her sisters sat in the splash zone of a water park and watched the dolphins perform with wet wonder. Since then, Jessica has viewed the video CD of her trip countless times as well as used the Internet on her family's computer to play dolphin games, learn dolphin facts, and download dolphin coloring book pages. For Halloween this year, she asked her mother to find a pattern on the Internet so as to make her a dolphin costume.

DOI: 10.4018/978-1-61350-059-0.ch007

Copyright © 2012, IGI Global. Copying or distributing in print or electronic forms without written permission of IGI Global is prohibited.

Together they perused a variety of sewing patterns to replicate a "real" dolphin. Jessica at five is clearly actively engaged in learning and exploring the virtual world all the while customizing the experience to suit her idiosyncratic interests and changing learning needs. To Jessica, technology is like electricity; it is a common and ubiquitous part of her everyday life.

Jessica is not unlike her young peers in her use of technology as a learning and exploration tool. Most children plug into a variety of technologies long before they enter school. According to the Kaiser Family Foundation (2003):

- Two-thirds of infants and toddlers watch a screen of some sort an average of two hours daily.
- Children under age six watch an average of about two hours of screen media a day, primarily TV and videos or DVDs.
- Children under age six are independent of adults in much of this activity. Consider that children are:
    - Turning on the TV by themselves (77%),
    - Asking for particular shows (67%),
    - Using the remote to change channels (62%),
    - Asking for their favorite videos or DVDs (71%),
    - Putting in their own music tapes or CDs (36%),
    - Getting on to the computer by themselves (33%),
    - Loading their own CD-ROMs (23%)
    - Asking for specific websites while on the Internet (12%).

Further, a report by the National Center for Education Statistics (NCES) cites 80% of kindergartners and children in grades 1-5 have used computers and 32% of kindergartners have used the Internet while 91% of children in grades 1-5 are Internet users (2009). This technological march, this digital Diaspora, now starts at an early age and is dramatically changing the everyday lives and learning experiences of young children. It is truly a profound cultural shift; a change in the very avenues of life and learning for our smallest learners.

This chapter will discuss resources for and approaches to training teachers in early childhood classrooms. We will focus on three tools which teachers can use in their classrooms which are available and teacher friendly. While teacher training programs provide coursework to assist professionals learn more about technology, this chapter is conceptualized as one for self-training. It is hoped that if you are a teacher who may have been avoiding the use of technology that this chapter will start you on the road to techno-teaching.

Objectives

After reading this chapter you will be aware of the important role you play in creating equal access to technology in the lives of all children in the United States. You should develop an awareness of how socio-economic environments can influence the learning potential of young children. The reader will:

- Develop a clearer understanding of what is happening with teacher training in the United States
- Learn about resources to support their teaching
- Develop a clearer understanding of the goals and standards for teachers in relation to technology

BACKGROUND: THE "SECOND" DIGITAL DIVIDE

The term "digital divide" refers to the vast difference in exposure to and use of technology between differing socioeconomic groups. This divide still exists (Fox, 2005; Judge, Puckett & Bell, 2006; National Center for Educational Statistics, 2006; Solomon, 2002; U. S. National Telecommunications and Information Administration, 2010). This is different from the communication- gap which exists between generations as it directly impacts children living in poverty in the United States.

We argue that teachers and others working in the world of education at both the practitioner and preservice levels have been slow to respond to this tremendous and irreversible cultural shift, thus creating a second and even more inequitable digital divide, the divide of technological opportunity. Many teachers/schools have not engaged fully with technology and its multiplicity of uses, let alone understand how the current generation of small learners interacts with technology to learn. This divide may call into question the cultural relevance of education.

This educational digital divide is one that can and must be scaled. It is truly a reciprocal relationship; as teachers scale this educational technological divide with their students, the other socioeconomic digital divide diminishes. It is therefore critical that teacher preparation programs design programs that assist the preservice educator to understand and embrace this important role.

Research informs us that schools play an important role in equalizing access to computers for children (DeBell and Chapman, 2003). African-American children (44%), Hispanic children (40%) and children from lower income households (41%) are considerably less likely to use a computer at home than white children (76%) or children from higher income families (83%). But in the school environment, virtually the same percent of all children have used a computer (55% of white children, 60% of African-American children, 43% of Hispanic children, 56% of high-income children, and 59% of low-income children).

Additionally, research has shown that schools lack socioeconomic technological equity with regard to the quality of technology as well as the instructional use of technology. The quality of the technology available at schools with higher percentage of students on free and reduced-price lunch lags behind that available to their more affluent peers. Furthermore, schools with high poverty students tend to use technology more for drill and practice than for higher order instructional purposes (Becker, 2000; National Center for Education Statistics, 2009).

Thus with technology paired with curricular expertise, teachers can help transcend both divides – the divide created by socioeconomic status and the educational technology divide. We will discuss two paths - both necessary for early childhood education to remain relevant. First to consider is preservice/inservice training. How are universities engaged in training or professional development of early childhood educators embracing and modeling technology that enhances learning? How are practicing teachers trained to evaluate technology in a world where technological advances constantly occur? How can teacher educators help create a mindset of "technological embrace" in early childhood educators? We will discuss the current research about technology training in teacher preparation programs that include what is included in technology classes offered, topics addressed in technology stand alone classes, technology as interwoven with curricular classes, and how field experiences can be reconsidered as technology training grounds.

Secondly, what are some technological tools available that pedagogically align with constructivist thinking and practices? How can these tools address standards and yet be user-friendly for educators in terms of accessibility, ease of use, student engagement, and researched learning outcomes? We will present three quality tools— virtual manipulatives, Google Earth, and Web 2.0 tools that should be included in early childhood training at the preservice level and in practice by early childhood educators particularly in science and mathematics.

Postsecondary Teacher Technology Training

Technology has radically changed our society and the world. The Partnership for 21st Century Skills (2008) reported, "Today's education system faces irrelevance unless we bridge the gap between how students live and how they learn" (p. 6). In recognition of the growing role technologies are playing in society, educational stakeholders have made technology a priority. In 1998, the International Society for Technology in Education (ISTE) released its National Educational Technology Standards for Students (NETS*S) followed in 2000 by the National Educational Technology Standards for Teachers (NETS*T). These standards were updated in 2007 and 2008 respectively. In 2001, the Enhancing Education through Technology Act component of No Child Left Behind (NCLB) was passed. Its primary goal was the use of technology in elementary and secondary schools to improve academic achievement (U. S. Department of Education, 2001). As of 2009, all fifty states had established technology standards for students and forty-six have technology standards for teachers (Education Week, 2010). Unfortunately, it would appear that teacher education preparation programs, despite the current emphasis placed on technology, have failed to prepare teachers to use technology in their classrooms (Cuban, 1999; Cuban 2001; Firek, 2003; Kay, 2006). In 1999, only 20% of the 2.5 million public school teachers reported feeling comfortable using computers in the classroom (National Center for Educational Statistics, 1999). A decade later, only 25% of teachers reported feeling adequately prepared to use technology in their classrooms (National Center for Educational Statistics, 2009).

Historically, teacher preparation programs have relied on a standalone technology course. These courses, which teach technology in a skill-based format primarily removed from the curriculum, are largely ineffective (O'Bannon & Puckett, 2009). The International Society for Technology in Education NETS*T and NETS*S has called on technology to become "an integral component or tool for learning and communication within the context of the academic subject areas" (ISTE, 2001, p. 17), and these standards have influenced some teacher preparation programs to adopt a more integrated approach to technology instruction; however, on whole, preservice programs have been resistant to change. A review of research concerning teacher preparation programs use of technology reveal that only:

- 44% integrate technology in all courses
- 29% use single technology course
- 27% model how to use technology
- 25% require collaboration among preservice teachers, mentor teachers and faculty
- 19% require preservice teachers to use technology in the field (Kay, 2006)

Teacher preparation programs reluctance or failure to properly integrate technology across the curriculum prevents teachers from developing the necessary technology pedagogical content knowledge to ensure that teachers feel confident in their use of technology for classroom instruction (Niess, 2005).

The authors of this chapter did an informal assessment of a variety of texts used in post secondary early childhood education classes at NCATE accredited institutions. The texts ranged in emphasis and topics, but generally could be considered entry-level early childhood curricular or pedagogical texts; they were not specific technology training texts. Of the sixteen surveyed, only one had extensive (more than five) technological resources listed with each topic. Several had pages specific to the use of technology, but in our opinion, overall technology got relatively short shrift and only transitory mention, particularly in science and mathematics.

Technology, Pedagogy and Content

Technology pedagogical content knowledge (TPCK) is an understanding of how these pedagogical, content and technological knowledge domains intersect to inform teachers in the selection of a particular technology that will be pedagogically sound in teaching content (Mishra & Koehler, 2006). TPCK is an extension of the pedagogical content knowledge (PCK) necessary for teachers to effectively teach (Shulman, 1986). Shulman emphasized the need for preservice teacher to not only learn pedagogy and content knowledge but also how one can be used to complement the other. With regard to PCK, Grossman identified four central components to ensure PCK in a teacher preparation program:

1. overarching conception of what it means to teach a particular subject;
2. knowledge of instructional strategies and representations for teaching particular subject matter topics;
3. knowledge of students' understandings, thinking, and learning in the subject area;
4. knowledge of curriculum and curriculum materials with learning subject matter (1989,1991).

The addition of technology to these four components reveals what technology pedagogical content knowledge preservice teachers would acquire if technology were appropriately infused throughout the curriculum: (1) an overarching conception of what it means to teach a particular subject integrating technology in the learning; (2) knowledge of instructional strategies and representations for teaching particular topics with technology; (3) knowledge of students' understandings, thinking, and learning with technology in a particular subject; (4) knowledge of curriculum and curriculum materials that integrate technology with learning in the subject area (Borko & Putnam, 1996).

In March 2010, the United States created The National Educational Technology Plan with the goal that

"Professional educators will be supported individually and in teams by technology that connects them to data, content, resources, expertise, and learning experiences that enable and inspire more effective teaching for all learners" (p 10).

To reach this goal, they suggest the following steps:

- Design, develop, and adopt technology-based content, resources, and online learning communities that create opportunities for educators to collaborate for more effective teaching, inspire and attract new people into the profession, and encourage our best educators to continue teaching.
- Provide pre-service and in-service educators with preparation and professional learning experiences powered by technology that close the gap between students' and educators' fluencies with technology and promote and enable technology use in ways that improve learning, assessment, and instructional practices.
- Transform the preparation and professional learning of educators and education leaders by leveraging technology to create career-long personal learning networks within and across schools, pre-service preparation and in-service educational institutions, and professional organizations.
- Use technology to provide access to the most effective teaching and learning resources, especially where they are not otherwise available, and to provide more options for all learners at all levels.
- Develop a teaching force skilled in online instruction. (p. 11)

As educators and researchers struggle to identify best practices in preservice preparation, there is one essential caveat best described by Iain McGilchrist (2009): "Every realm of academic endeavor is now subject to an explosion of information which renders those few who can really call themselves experts, experts on less and less" (p. 3). The message is clear; there can be no complete preparation in a domain where obsolescence is not only planned, but desired. There will be no technological advance that exists in its initial state for a sustained length of time. No professor or instructor can possibly teach or model all the technological advances that are available to teachers or learners. So the very instructional task is changing; professors must model those tools that have the characteristics of developmentally appropriate pedagogy NOT in order that teachers use only those tools, but rather that teachers learn how to choose and use technology in their classroom and lives. This is a vastly different mission.

TECHNOLOGY IN THE EARLY CHILDHOOD MATH AND SCIENCE CLASSROOMS

Elementary teachers no longer need to worry about the developmental appropriateness of technology. There is now ample research that demonstrates the ability of technology to facilitate learning in young children (Gillespie, 2004; Hutinger, Johanson, & Rippey, 2000; Sarama & Clements, 2002; Wright & Shade, 1994). The National Association for the Education of Young Children recognizes that young children find computers to be intrinsically motivating as well as promoting cognitive and social development (1996). Furthermore computer use promotes constructivist learning by increasing young children's spoken communication, initiation of interaction and cooperation (Haugland & Wright, 1997; Sivin-Kachala & Bialo, 2000). The acknowledgement of the benefits of computers in the early childhood classroom have charged early childhood educators with the responsibility of continuing to examine the impact of technology on their students and to utilize technology in their classrooms with their students (NAEYC, 1996).

Preparing preservice and practicing teachers to utilize technology in their classrooms is critical in math and science. National mathematics and science standards have made technology an essential aspect of curriculum and instruction (National Council of Teachers of Mathematics, 2000; National Science Educational Standards, 1996). Instruction of preservice mathematics and science should emphasize the classroom use of technology to support students' engagement and participation as well as how to leverage the power of current technologies to provides opportunities for students to acquire apply and extend learning as well as connect learning to authentic problems (Roblyer & Davis, 2008; Quellmalz, 1999).

By utilizing technologies like virtual manipulatives, Google Earth and Web 2.0 applications teachers can engage students in interactive authentic learning experiences and opportunities not commonly afforded them while at the same time providing the opportunity for student to develop 21st Century technology skills. These three tools will be discussed in detail in the following section to give teachers a better understanding of how to use them, additional resources to support these tools and examples of how these tools relate to national standards.

Three Technology Tools

Technology is essential in teaching and learning mathematics; it influences the mathematics that is taught and enhances students' learning (NCTM, 2000, p. 24).

When utilizing educational technology, teachers should not focus on the *technology*, but rather on its *educational* use—to support learning. After all, students do not learn from technology; students learn from thinking (Dede, 2007; Jonassen, Howland, Moore & Marra, 2003). What educational technology can do is provide teachers and students with a tool that supports constructivist learning through the facilitation of students ability to analyze the world, access information, interpret and organize their personal knowledge, and represent what they know to others" (Jonassen, 1994). Three exemplars of educational technologies are virtual manipulatives, Google Earth and Web 2.0. Though applicable across the early childhood curriculum, they are especially appropriate for mathematics and science instruction. All three technologies meet a number of NAEYC, NCTM, NSES, as well as ISTE standards. Furthermore, they are philosophically aligned with constructivist, inquiry-based learning theories (Association of Mathematics Teacher Educators' Technology Committee, 2005). Virtual manipulatives, Google Earth and Web 2.0 applications are also three technologies that transcend the traditional barriers to technology integration: access, time, training, technical support and funding.

Access

All three of these technologies are free Internet applications and can be accessed by teachers and students at school, home, or community technology centers. Teachers and families can use these tools to support learning of young children.

Time and Training

All of these tools are described in the literature as intuitive and "easy" to use; therefore, very little time is required to learn how to use them. Generally, these applications come with instructions (often with screen shots) for use. For the more difficult of the programs, like Google Earth, video tutorials are provided. In addition, Google Earth has an entire site, *Google Earth for Educators*, dedicated to the use of Google Earth in the classroom. Google Earth and virtual manipulatives as well as many of the Web 2.0 tools have complete, grade-level lessons plans already aligned with national standards (see Resources). For example, *Real World Mathematics* is a website that has complete lesson plans for using Google Earth in the K-12 classroom. Therefore, the use of these tools and their associated lesson plans could actually *save* teachers' time.

Technical Support

There are few if any technical issues associated with these applications on the users' end. virtual manipulatives and Web 2.0 applications are created and maintained by administrators and stored on the applications' server; therefore, users do not have to address any technical problems associated with them. Certainly users should test these technologies prior to use to make sure they function properly. Google Earth has two versions: downloadable or plug-in. The minimum system requirements for PC users are Windows 2000, Windows XP, or Windows Vista, a Pentium 3 with 256MB of RAM and 400MB hard drive free space; Mac user requirements are Mac OS X 10.4.0, Mac 1 GHz and 400MB hard drive free space. Google Earth provides numerous links, articles, videos and discussion forums for addressing potential technical problems.

Funding

There is no funding required for any of the applications; they are free. Thus these content rich applications are budget friendly. For example, three free applications that replace of items schools have previously had to purchase are:

- Owl Pellet (http://www.kidwings.com/owlpellets/flash/v4/index.htm): Virtual manipulative that allows students to virtually dissect an owl pellet.
- Scientific Calculator (http://web2.0calc.com/): Web 2.0 scientific calculator.

- Concept Maps (http://www.shambles.net/pages/school/mindmaps/http://think.ajsands.com/): Sites for creating online (printable) concept maps
- Virtual manipulatives can save schools funds by freeing them from purchasing their concrete counterparts.

Virtual manipulatives, Google Earth and Web 2.0 applications allow teachers to use technology appropriately in the mathematics and science class by facilitating teachers' use of the technology in context, to address worthwhile content and pedagogy, to take advantage of the technology, to connect content related topics, and to incorporate multiple representations (Garofalo, Drier, Harper, Timmerman & Shockey, 2000).

Tool One: Virtual Manipulatives

There is a great deal of research supporting the use of manipulatives in early childhood mathematics courses (Raphael & Whalstrom, 1989, Sowell, 1989, Suydam & Higgins, 1977). Traditional (static) mathematics manipulatives are concrete objects (e. g., chips, geoboards, cubes, square tiles, tangrams) designed to represent abstract mathematical ideas. Virtual (dynamic) manipulates are "interactive, Web-based visual representations of a dynamic object" (Moyer, Bolyard & Spikell, 2002, p. 373). They differ from their concrete counterparts in that they are manipulated on a computer screen using a mouse. Virtual manipulatives are often preferable to traditional manipulatives because they assist teachers in overcoming the major impediments for teachers' use of mathematics manipulatives: 1) lack of availability, 2) inordinate amount of time required to set them up and put them away, and 3) the inability of students to take them home for use (Lindroth, 2005). Also, the time saved setting up and putting away manipulatives can be utilized for additional instructional time or additional time interacting with the virtual manipulatives.

Many virtual manipulatives make use of Java *applets*. Java applets are applications created with the Java programming language that are embedded into a Web page and that allow the page to be animated. For example, the virtual manipulative scale below gives students a problem to solve. Students place coins on the scale and then click the "Weigh Coins" button to receive feedback (Figure 1).

Standards

Virtual manipulatives have the potential to assist early childhood teachers in meeting a number of NAEYC, NSES, NCTM and NETS*T standards. They can be used for the introduction and review of ideas, development of understanding by visually representing abstract concepts, scaffolding, and active engagement (Moyer, 2001; Bouck & Flanagan, 2010). Furthermore, virtual manipulatives are accessible to anyone with a computer and Internet connection. Virtual manipulatives facilitate the appropriate use of technology by introducing content in context, addressing worthwhile content and pedagogy, taking advantage of the technology, connecting content related topics, and incorporating multiple representations (Garofalo, et al., 2000).

Virtual manipulatives can teach content in the context of meaningful activities (NETS*T Std. 2). Many of the websites for virtual manipulative (see Resources) allow teachers to search by grade level and/or standard. Activities and lessons that are provided teach specific content standards. For example, one of the activities on the *Illuminations* site enables teachers to meet the NCTM Standard for PreK-2 Geometry by engaging students in creating and describing the attributes of geometric shapes as well as predicting the results of putting together and taking apart geometric shapes (NETS*T Std. 1c) (Figure 2).

Figure 1. Virtual manipulative with Java Applet

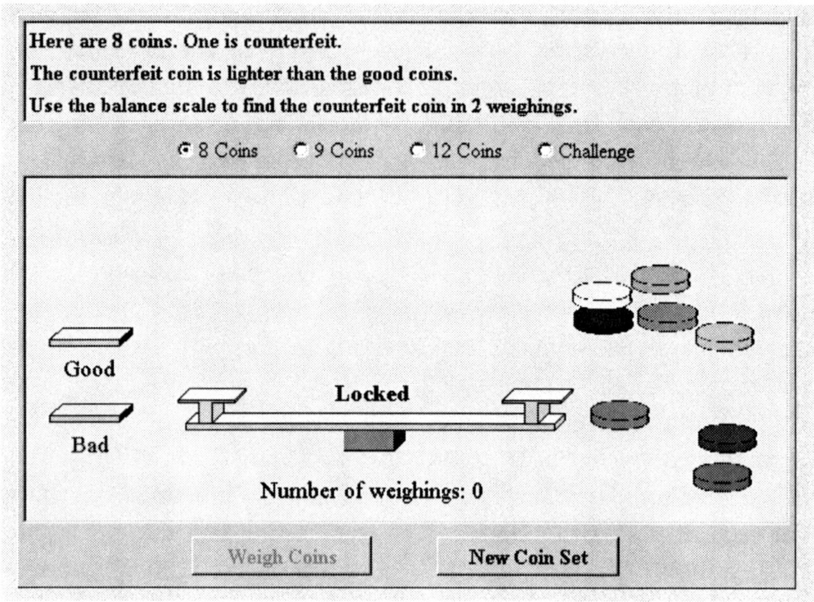

Figure 2. Virtual Geoboard

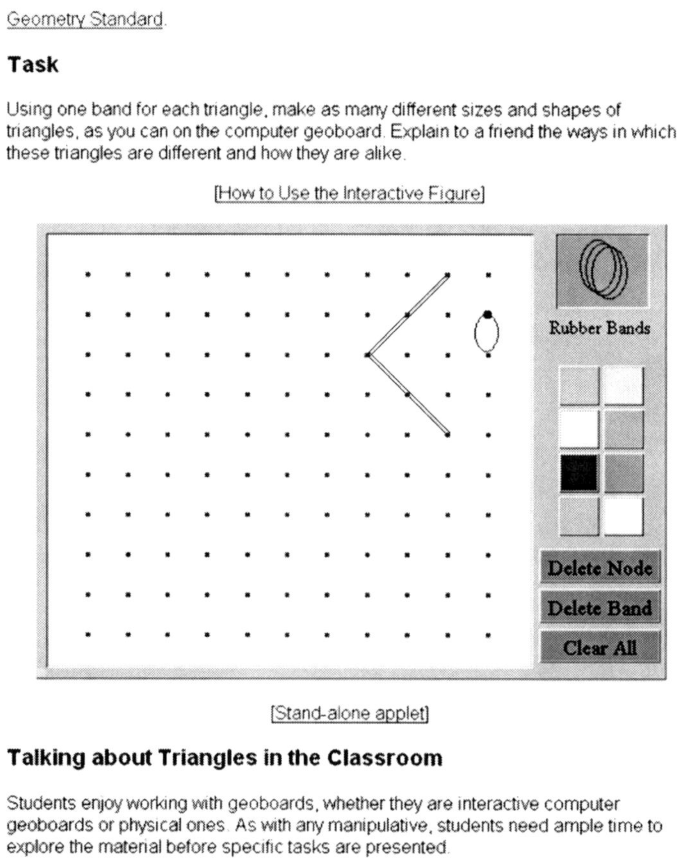

In addition, students can collaborate with a classmate to "Talk about Triangles in the Classroom" (NETS*T Std. 1c) and are given opportunities to extend their learning through creating polygons (NETS*T Std. 2a) (Figure 3). The web site gives teachers support for extensions of manipulative use like guiding "math talk" and ideas for discussion.

One of the many advantages of technology like virtual manipulatives is the ability to engage students in the content in authentic ways that are often not possible in the classroom. Virtual manipulatives allow students to be active learners and collaborate with others while interacting with dynamic, multimedia content that can appeal to a variety of different learners—visual, tactile, auditory (NETS*T Std. 2b). Teachers and students can personalize and individualize virtual manipulatives in order to differentiate instruction (NETS* Std. 2b, d). Furthermore, virtual manipulatives can provide immediate feedback to students (NETS*T Std. 2d). This feedback guides students in their use and understanding while freeing teachers to work with other students (NETS*T Std. 2b). Research has demonstrated the effectiveness of virtual manipulatives in improving achievement with low achieving students as well as students with disabilities (NETS*T Std. 2b) (Steen, Brooks & Lyons, 2006; Suh, Moyer & Heo, 2005).

Virtual manipulatives can take abstract concepts or those that would be otherwise difficult to demonstrate in the classroom and present them in engaging, interactive, dynamic activities while at same time, harnessing students' innate interest in computers (NETS*T Std. 1b, 3a). Moreover, they can differentiate, personalize and extend instruction by generating an unlimited number of examples of problems, with feedback, that students can access from school, home or anywhere with

Figure 3. Guiding "math talk"

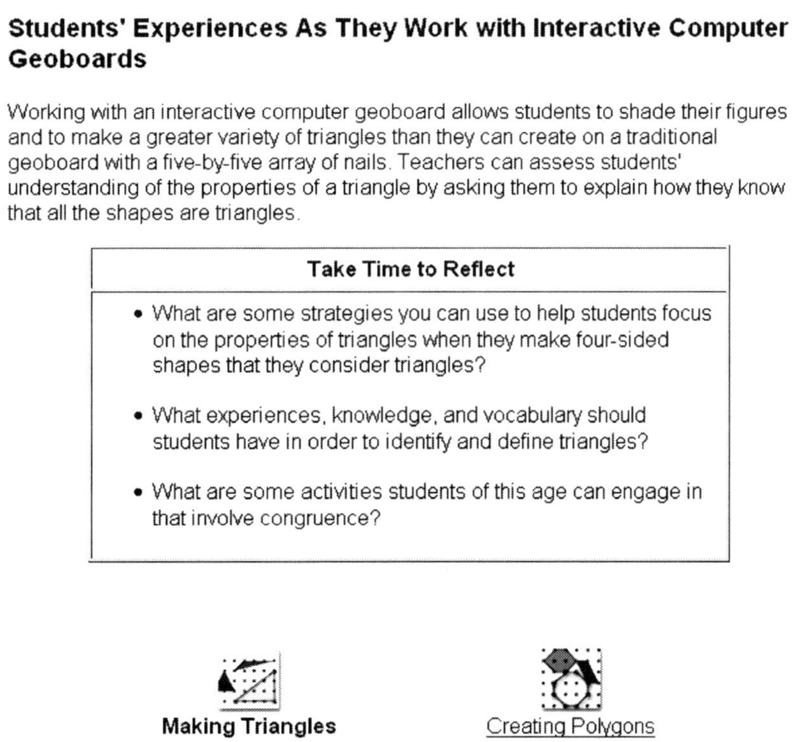

Students' Experiences As They Work with Interactive Computer Geoboards

Working with an interactive computer geoboard allows students to shade their figures and to make a greater variety of triangles than they can create on a traditional geoboard with a five-by-five array of nails. Teachers can assess students' understanding of the properties of a triangle by asking them to explain how they know that all the shapes are triangles.

Take Time to Reflect
• What are some strategies you can use to help students focus on the properties of triangles when they make four-sided shapes that they consider triangles? • What experiences, knowledge, and vocabulary should students have in order to identify and define triangles? • What are some activities students of this age can engage in that involve congruence?

Making Triangles Creating Polygons

Figure 4. Weather maker

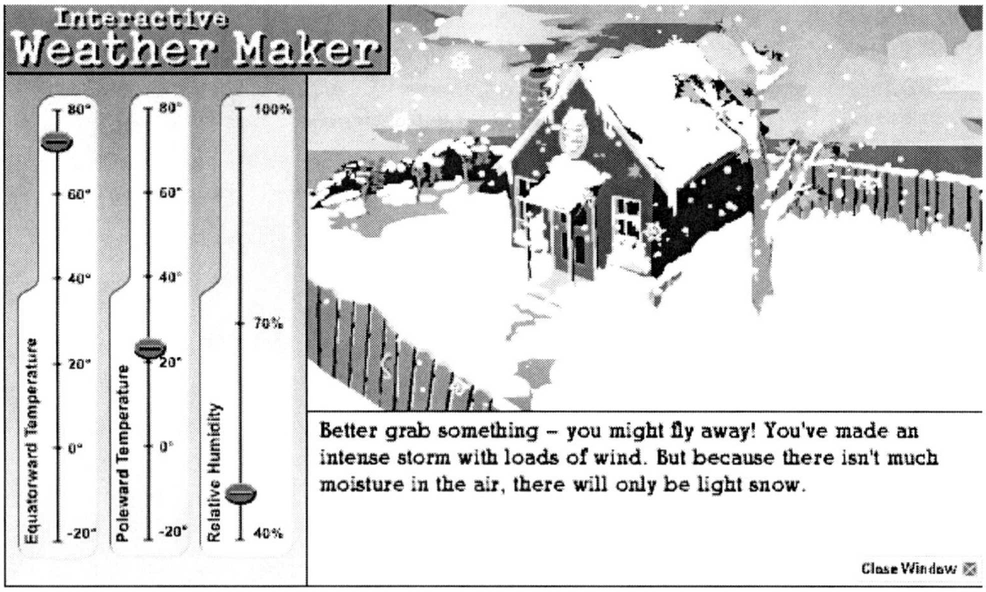

an Internet connection (NETS*T Std. 2). For example, this interactive science virtual manipulative allows students to create different weather by manipulating the temperature and humidity by moving the levers on the left and watch the weather change in the Flash movie on the right while receiving feedback in the paragraph below (NSES K-4.4). This allows children to see connections to conditions (humidity and temperature) and outcomes.

Examples

There are numerous online sites that provide free virtual manipulatives (see Resources). An excellent example is the *Illuminations* (http://illuminations.nctm.org/) website developed by the National Council of Teachers of Mathematics in partnership with Thinkfinity. *Illuminations* is divided into four categories: Activities, Lessons, Standards and Web Links. Presently, there are over 100 activities and over 500 lessons. The Activities, Lessons and Standards sections list all resources by grade and are searchable. The Lessons and Standards sections also align content by standards (Figure 5). Users can search by one or more grade level options and one or more standards. Search results show the grade, standards and whether there are any computer materials associated with the lesson. *Illuminations* also has a "Dynamic Paper" application that allows users to create their own interactive and printable mathematics activity (NETS*T Std. 1, 2).

Probably the most extensive collection of virtual manipulatives is the National Library of Virtual manipulatives (NLVM) (http://nlvm.usu.edu/en/nav/vlibrary.html). Developed by Utah State University in conjunction with the National Science Foundation, the NLVM offers a variety of virtual manipulatives appropriate for grades K-12. The site allows users to browse by grade or topic and each activity is linked to the NCTM Standards it addresses. The library, started in 1999, is continuing to be developed and refined through projects like the eNLVM project that creates interactive online learning units for mathematics (NLVM, 2010). However, there is an annual cost of $39.95 per computer station. Users can use the library for free for a trial period and any individual willing to "field test" one of

Figure 5. Illuminations selection page

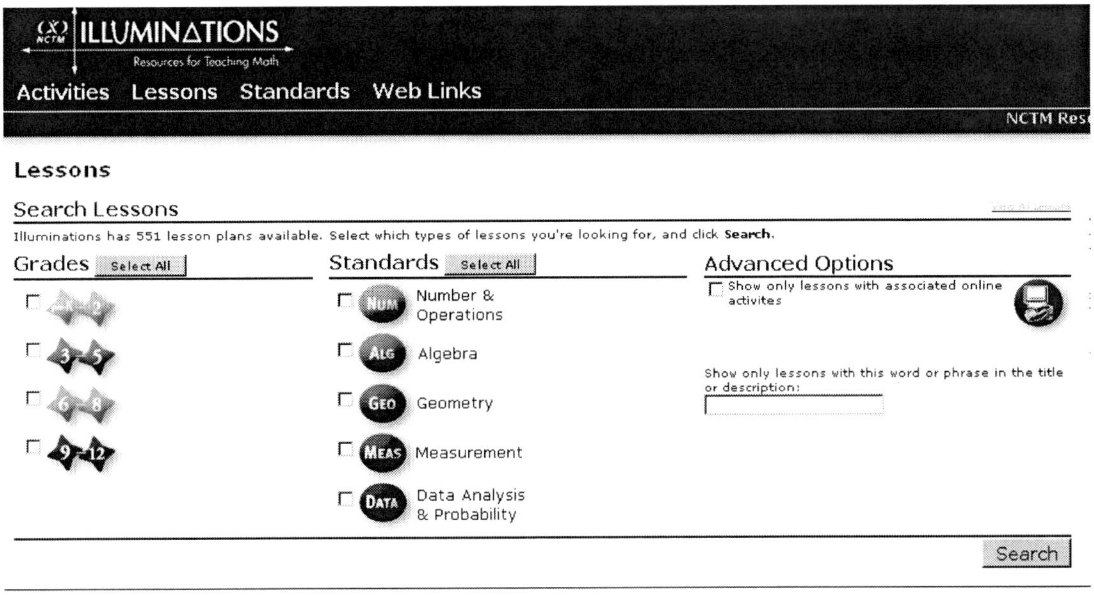

their modules can receive one free membership (Additional information is on the website).

The ability of manipulatives to support standards-based learning in the early childhood classroom is well documented. Virtual manipulatives, while realizing all the benefits of traditionally manipulatives, can extend their classroom benefits by allowing teachers to overcome traditional barriers associated with their classroom use. Virtual manipulates also surpass their concrete equivalent by better meeting the needs of diverse learners from school or home.

Additional Resources

Additional links to sites that provide a variety of instructional virtual manipulatives for early childhood mathematics and science:

Mathematics

1. eNLVM (http://enlvm.usu.edu/)
2. Inter*activate* (http://www.shodor.org/interactivate/activities/)
3. Learning Mathematics with Virtual manipulatives (http://www.cited.org/index.aspx?page_id=151)
4. Manipula Mathematics with JAVA (www.ies.co.jp/mathematics/java/index.html)
5. MathematicsTools (http://www.mathematicsforum.org/mathematicstools/)
6. Pythagoras' Theorem (http://www.dynamicgeometry.com/JavaSketchpad/Gallery.html)
7. The Geometry Applet (http://aleph0.clarku.edu/~djoyce/java/Geometry/Geometry.html)

Science

1. Owl Pellet (http://www.kidwings.com/owlpellets/flash/v4/index.htm)
2. K-2 Interactive (http://www.uen.org/k-2interactives/)
3. Wonderville (http://support.wonderville.ca/v1/home.html)
4. Utah Education Network: Science for grades 3-6 (http://www.uen.org/3-6interactives/science.shtml)

Tool Two: Google Earth

Geographic Information Systems (GIS) are computer-based systems that allow users to collect, organize, store, manipulate, analyze and display data with a geographic or spatial component (Baker & Case, 2000; Lamb & Johnson, 2010). Until the recent development of Internet-based programs like Google Earth, GIS have been expensive and technologically difficult to use. In contrast, Google Earth, a virtual globe created by satellite and aircraft images taken at different times, has an easy-to-use interface (Baker, 2005; Bodzin, 2008). All that is required is an Internet connection to download Google Earth to the user's hard-drive or users can use the Google Earth plugin. The newest version, Google Earth 5.0, provides a variety of information:

- Street names, country borders, 3D buildings, content from companies like the Discovery Channel, NASA and more
- 'Street View' provides digitally views a city
- Fly-over shows routes from above
- Historical timeline shows changes in satellite images over time
- Overlays show latitude and longitude lines
- Ruler tool enables measurement of distance between any two points on Earth
- Downloadable KML files enable tours of relevant sections of the planet (Hutcheson, 2009)

Google Earth also allows users to draw paths, add place marks, annotations and photos. 3-D typography allows users to view the geographic features of almost any location. For example, users can view Mount Saint Helens and use the terrain layer from the layers menu to superimpose 3-D overlay of the area typography. By placing the cursor anywhere on the image, users can see the latitude, longitude and altitude of the location (Siegle, 2007). Overlays are transparent images that can be placed over other images on Google Earth. Users can also create their own "image overlays" or use overlays created by others. Users could use overlays that were create to show the Gulf Coast after Hurricane Katrina to see a before and after view of the damage done by the hurricane.

For example the following image is used as the base to which children can select a menu of places and conditions to see how the local area was affected by the Hurricane.

The site was updated to allow children to see changes. For example the following update was available for children to explore the effects of the storm:

(September 2, 2005 Update) On the Google Earth Community BBS, over 100 image overlays have been processed. Be sure to only activate one image at a time so you do not overload your system.

- Biloxi Coast - Before
- Biloxi Coast - After
- New Orleans Before
- New Orleans After
- New Orleans Superdome - After
- 78 images of New Orleans Mississippi Coast - * images courtesy NOAA
- Image Overlay 1

Figure 6. Base image from Google Earth

- Image Overlay 2

Children can also use this site to see their community, their school, their home and other real world locations relative to their lives. Views of their school from a satellite can be compared to what they see and the children can dictate observations of their spatial relations to the online version. Google Earth also now has a number of additional tools: Google Ocean, Google Sky, Google Mars and Google Maps.

Standards

Traditionally, geographical information systems (GIS) have been too expensive or technologically difficult to use for most classroom applications. However, the emergence of Internet-based GIS like Google Earth as well as the ubiquity of broadband Internet, has made the use of GIS more common in the K-5 classroom. Although generally associated with geography and social studies, GIS enables teachers across disciplines to use them for inquiry-based activities. Early childhood mathematics and science teachers can use Google Earth to address NAEYC, NSES, NCTM and NETS*T standards by facilitating students' collection, analysis, and interpretation of real data (Patterson, 2007). In the process, students can develop critical analytical skills (Lamb and Johnson, 2010; Patterson, 2005).

One of the primary classroom benefits of technologies is their ability to meet standards through the creation of unique instructional opportunities (NETS*T Std. 1b). Google Earth is no exception. Virtually hovering above their community, students can recognize patterns and relationships in a unique environment (Patterson, 2007; Shin and Alibrandi, 2007) that assists in developing spatial analysis skills. Google Earth provides students with novel opportunities for research and authentic scientific investigations (NS.K-4.1) (Patterson, 2007). For example, Google Earth can be used by science teachers to facilitate student exploration of how humans obtain and use Earth materials as resources and in describing Earth's features and how human behavior changes the Earth's surface (NS.K-4.4) (Baker, 2005). Early childhood teachers can use it for mathematics instruction that supports students' analysis of data, probability, reasoning and proof (Patterson, 2007).

With Google Earth, these unique instructional opportunities allow content to be presented in the context of meaningful activities (NETS*T Std. 2). One of the hallmarks of this tool is its ability to engage students in real world, authentic learning. Google Earth can be used with PreK-2 students in developing understanding of numbers by having them find and count the number of houses/businesses around *their* school or use a ruler to measure the distance between the houses (NCTM). Likewise, Google Earth can help students distinguish natural objects from those made by man (NS.K4.5) or use resources like the Katrina example describe above to explore changes in the environment (NS.K-4.6). With regard to the latter, geospatial information systems like Google Earth aid students in developing a better understanding of the environment and improving decision making regarding the environment (Bodzin, 2008).

The characteristics of Google Earth also have the potential to increase access to mathematics and science for diverse learners (NETS*T Std. 2). Google Earth provides students with unlimited opportunities to locate evaluate and collect real data from resources that can be individualized and extended when needed. The visual nature of the program has also been show to engage, motivate and communicate to a variety of learners (Patterson, 2007). Google Earth's partnership with Discovery Communications and United Steaming has introduced multimedia to the application. Moreover, all of these benefits can be accessed outside of school.

Examples

There are a number of resources available for instructional ideas, lessons and other activities for Google Earth. Many of the materials are on sites, blogs and wikis created and maintained by teachers. A quality site is *Real World Mathematics* (see Resources). Developed by Thomas J. Petra, this site focuses on including Google Earth in the mathematics curriculum. It offers lesson ideas, examples and downloads that are aligned with national mathematics standards. Although the focus is on grades 4-12, there are lessons for younger students and lessons that can be modified for use with younger students. Lessons are constantly being added and teachers are encouraged to add lessons they have created. Lessons are categorized as: Concept Lessons, Project-Based Learning, Exploratory, and Measurement. All of the lessons identify the target grade levels, objectives, procedures and national standards the activity meets (Table 2). Additionally, each lesson has attached the corresponding KMZ file. KMZ files are "zipped kml (Keyhole Markup Language) files, which will start Google Earth and "fly" the user to a specified location (Google Earth, 2010).

Since Google Earth is a relatively new tool, there is little empirical evidence to support its use in the classroom; however, there has been wide body of applicable research on the use of other geospatial information systems for instructional purposes. This research supports the pedagogical soundness of GIS like Google Earth and their ability to increase student engagement, motivation and enthusiasm while creating contextually rich learning and interaction with content (Baker, 2005; Bodzin, 2008).

Additional Examples and Resources

- Crossing Boundaries (http://crossingboundariesproject.org/): biodiversity conservation.
- Discovery Education (http://www.google.com/educators/p_earth_discovery.html) creates online lessons and digital videos to supplement Google Earth.
- Google "Maps Mania" blog (http://googlemapsmania.blogspot.com)
- Google Earth & GPS Elementary Classroom Activities (http://www.amazon.com/Google-Earth-Elementary-Classroom-Activities/dp/1589128761)
- Google Earth and Discovery Education (http://www.google.com/educators/p_earth_discovery.html)
- Google Earth and Discovery Education (http://www.google.com/educators/p_earth_discovery.html)
- Google Earth Blog (http://www.gearthblog.com/reference.html)
- Google Earth Current Events (http://www.gearthhacks.com/dlcat11/Current-Events.htm)
- Google Earth for Educators (http://www.google.com/educators/p_earth.html): online interactive tools, curriculum resources, and lesson plans for teachers
- Google Earth Image Overlays (http://earth.google.com/support/bin/static.py?hl=en&page=guide.cs&guide=22373&topic=22376)
- Google Earth in the Elementary Classroom (http://cnx.org/content/m19821/latest/)
- Google Earth Lessons (http://gelessons.com/lessons/)
- Google Earth Lessons and Related Materials (http://delicious.com/library_chic/googleearth)
- Google Earth Ruler (http://earth.google.com/support/bin/static.py?hl=en&page=guide.cs&guide=22365&topic=23730&answer=148134)
- Real World Mathematics: Using Google Earth in the Mathematics Curriculum (http://www.realworldmath-

ematics.org/Real_World_Mathematics/ RealWorldMathematics.org.html)
- Screen Protractor (www.iconico. conVprotractor)
- Sea Turtle Project (http://www.seaturtle. org/tracking/explorer/): post data from tagged wildlife.
- The Atlas of Our Changing Environment (http://na.unep.net/digital%5fatlas2/ google.php): satellite images for the science classroom.
- The Cousteau Society (http://www.cousteau.org/expedition): images and video clips for use with Google Earth
- The Google Earth Community and Google's Keyhole mapping service, Bulletin Board Service (http://bbs.keyhole. com): data layers, supplementary readings, supporting photos and videos and a collaborative discussion forum

If you are considering using Google Earth in your library, you can apply for a free version of Google Earth Pro at Google Earth for Educators.

Tool Three: Web 2.0

Web 2.0 is a term used to describe a reinvention of the Internet. Initially, the Internet, Web 1.0, was a place where users went to static Web pages to consume content placed there by others; therefore, most users of the Internet functioned only as consumers of Web content. The emergence of Web 2.0 applications has changed individual's use of the Internet from static to dynamic. Today's Internet is a more democratic place where all users can participate as both consumers and creators of content. Characteristics of Web 2.0 applications facilitate the ability of users to create (YouTube), collaborate (wikis) and communicate (weblogs, podcast) on the Internet. Other characteristics of Web 2.0 applications are their emphasis on sharing content (SlideShare, Flcker), interactivity (Wikipedia) and social networking (Twitter, Facebook, Nings). These characteristics make Web 2.0 applications ideal for use in the classroom.

Web 2.0 applications are free and stored online, so they are accessible to anyone from anywhere with an Internet connection. All that is needed to create most Web 2.0 applications is an active email account. To sign up, create or use a Web 2.0 application, users go the applications web site. Users simply click on the "sign up" button, and they will be direct through a short series of steps, one of which will be to provide an active email account. After signing up, users are usually sent an email with a link that must be clicked to activate the account.

Most Web 2.0 applications have an administrator—usually the person who creates the account. The administrator has control over the content thus he can add, edit or delete content. The administrator also controls who else can add content and to what extent. Other users can be designated a degree of control ranging from administrative to simple viewer. Web 2.0 applications generally allow the administrator to designate security settings. These include but are not limited to making the application completely private, inviting those can view content, those can add content and specifying what content can be added (e.g., some weblog applications allow the administrator to block designated words). Web 2.0 applications are safe and secure if used properly, and their use in class is an excellent opportunity for teaching students about Internet safety.

Standards

In a sense, Web 1.0 was analogous to a teacher-centered, "sage on the stage" philosophy of instruction. If students had a question, they could go to the Internet to find the answer. Web 2.0 applications have created a more student-centered Internet aligned well with a constructivist philosophy of learning. In the Web 2.0 environment, "knowledge is decentralized, accessible, and co-constructed by and among a broad base of users (Greenhow, Robelia & Hughes, 2009, p. 247). Web 2.0 applications can assist teachers in meeting standards by engaging students in an environment that supports collaboration and communication in the creation and sharing of content (NETS*T Std. 1, 2). In addition, many Web 2.0 applications provide a platform for student reflection (NETS*T Std. 1c). Three classroom friendly examples of Web 2.0 applications for the classroom are weblogs, wikis and podcasts. Classroom weblogs can facilitate students' thinking skills and the construction of knowledge (Huffaker, 2005; Kagder & Bull, 2003; Oravec 2003; Richardson, 2005; Richardson, 2006; Wells, 2006). Weblogs also support student interaction (Brescia & Miller, 2006; Cobanoglu, 2006) and reflection (Brescia & Miller, 2006; Stiler & Philleo, 2003). Student created podcasts have been shown to increase motivation, higher-order thinking as wells as improving students' skills in writing and listening (Dlott, 2007; Halderson, 2006). An additional benefit of podcasting is their benefits to auditory learners (Smaldino, Russell, Heinich & Molenda, 2005).

Examples

There are literally hundreds of Web 2.0 applications and new ones are emerging daily. An online search is the starting point for researching and identifying applications for meeting classroom/curricular needs. Weblogs, wikis, and podcast are three Web 2.0 applications whose use in the classroom has been tested and supported by researchers and practitioners.

Weblogs

Weblogs are web pages that allow users to add content such as documents, images, audio, video, multimedia and hyperlinks. They differ from traditional static web pages by allowing users to post-comments. Comments are timed, dated and stored in reverse chronological order. Like other Web 2.0 applications, the content on weblogs is controlled by the administrator (creator of the weblog) who can disable the comments feature.

Weblogs have a number of applications in the classroom. Teachers can use them as a classroom webpage. They are free, easy to use, and technical problems typically addressed by the provider. Furthermore, the comments feature allows communication between teachers, students and parents. Teachers can create pages to post daily assignments and handouts. A page could also be created as a forum for student to ask questions and continue class discussion. Students in the mathematics classroom could use it to discuss solutions to difficult problems. In the science classroom, student could write reflections about a classroom activity. Weblogs provide a safe place for all students to contribute to the classroom conversation and provides an authentic audience for their writings.

Wikis

Like Weblogs, wikis support student construction of knowledge (Boulos, Maramba & Wheeler, 2006) and collaborative learning (Augar, Raitman & Zhou, 2004). Wikis are web pages that support a high level of interactivity. Users can place text, hyperlinks, images, audio, video and multimedia on wikis; however, unlike weblogs, wikis allow all users to add and edit content. All changes to the wiki can be viewed and if necessary, undone.

Wikis can be used in the classroom to support student collaboration on science projects, solving mathematics problems and creating projects. For example, students could use a digital camera to take pictures of different geometric shapes around the school (or find them online). They could then identify each shape and place them on the wiki to create a classroom collection of the shapes.

Podcasts

The term podcast is derived from the combination of iPod®/MP3 and broadcasting. A podcast is a digital recording, usually in an mp3 format, that is placed on the Internet for users to listen to online or download to an audio player (like an iPod®/MP3). All that is needed to create a podcast is a computer, a low cost microphone and a free audio recorder (see Resources). Podcast can be placed on the classroom weblogs or wikis for student access.

Students could create podcast in their science class to record their observations during an activity (e. g., an Owl pellet dissection or the daily activities of a classroom "pet" like a crawfish or anole).

The classroom application of these three tools is limited only by the imagination of the user. Any classroom activity could be enhanced through the ability of these tools to support collaboration, communication, content creation, and student reflection.

Additional Resources

Weblogs

- Edublogs (http://edublogs.org/): Weblog provider
- Blog Spot (www.blogspot.com/): Weblog provider
- Weblogs in Plain English (http://www.youtube.com/watch?v=NN2I1pWXjXI&feature=fvw): Short video by Lee LeFever from Common Craft that explains blogging.

Wikis

- WetPaint (http://wikisineducation.wetpaint.com/): Wiki Provider
- PBwork (http://pbworks.com/): Wiki provider
- Wikispaces (http://www.wikispaces.com/site/for/teachers): Wiki provider
- Wikis in Plain English (http://www.youtube.com/watch?v=vMgemQahuFM): Succinct, engaging explanation of wikis from Lee Lefever of Common Craft.

Podcast

- My Podcast (http://mypodcast.com/) Simple, free application for creating podcast
- Audacity (http://audacity.sourceforge.net/): Robust, free tool for creating and editing sound files that can be saved as podcast.
- Podcast in Plain English (http://www.youtube.com/watch?v=vMgemQahuFM): Another short video by Common Craft that explains podcasting.

CONCLUSION

This second digital divide, as we consider it, is more of an attitudinal and pedagogical challenge. Arguably, accessibility is still an issue particularly in schools serving children from poverty but there are quality technology tools that are low cost, pedagogically aligned, and standards based available. Ertmer (2005) suggests that educators have looked at technology training and its classroom uses somewhat backwards; she believes that for technology to truly become fluent in the life of the classroom, we must first examine how technology has a "fit" with what teachers and professors believe about how children learn and how we teach. Perhaps this is truly the task of the professorate in post secondary classrooms – finding that "fit" with pedagogy and content. We would also argue that open-minded technologically fluent professors must update their knowledge of what technology offers early childhood classrooms and model not only what is pedagogically sound, but also that habit of mind that delights in what can be.

Certainly post secondary instructors should look carefully at textbook adoptions is a starting point. Students and professors are often dependent on a text as a major portion of content and reading; thus adopting a text that considers technology as an integral piece to curriculum and practice in an early childhood classroom is critical.

Clearly students must SEE technology adapted to classrooms. Universities would well be advised to judge field placement opportunities for outstanding pedagogy certainly but also for technological activities that are consistent with early childhood philosophies challenging, and relevant to the lives of tech savvy children.

Principles abound for improvement of post secondary teacher technology training; we particularly like those offered by Hughes (2004) who pragmatically suggests that professors must present many accessible, low cost and pedagogically consonant technologies so as to not only entice the preservice teacher into the use of technology but also to begin to develop critical skills in evaluating technologies as an instructional tools.

The three tools we described here are models of exploration, constructivist learning and variety. Tools like these – accessible, easy to learn, facile in practice, free or low cost and pedagogically – are many. We believe that using well-designed mathematics and science tools such as those outlined here in teacher training and in classrooms are a start to a teacher's ease of use and persistence in learning the ever-evolving technologies for her students' growth.

In summary, technology is not a class, a course or a grade; it is integrated into all aspects of our lives. Schools can be exemplars of what equitable access to technology can do to scale the digital divide and open doors of opportunity for children whose access to technology is more limited in their out of school lives. Universities must prepare educators who are comfortable using technology, embrace technological change, and align their use of technology with the highest pedagogical standards. It is the teacher who is truly the linchpin assuring equity of access to quality technology that meets the highest standards of pedagogical practice. This is the loftiest mission of teaching technology in schools. Schooling may provide the only level playing field in the lives of children. It is not an add-on or a classroom learning station. It is a lifeline.

Reflecting on Early Childhood Teachers: Closing the Digital–Divide

This section gives you some questions and activities to help you think about how you can use some of the ideas from this chapter in your work.

Research

1. Set up two centers in your class. In one center provide actual manipulatives and in the other provide the computer version of the same activity. Collect data as to which activity was most used by the children.
2. After allowing your children to explore both centers check their understanding of the concept through interviews. Which approach best supported your teaching goals?
3. Children under age six are independent of adults in most technology interactions before they come to your classroom. Interview parents and children to develop a better understanding of what experiences your children bring to the classroom. Compare your information to the national data.

Reflect

1. How can you insure that all children have technological opportunity that supports the needs of children from lower socio-economic environments?
2. After reading this chapter you should have a better understanding of the role you play in technology learning. How do you see your role as a teacher and a learner?

3. In 2010, the United States created The National Educational Technology Plan with the goal that

"Professional educators will be supported individually and in teams by technology that connects them to data, content, resources, expertise, and learning experiences that enable and inspire more effective teaching for all learners" (p 10).

As an individual you cannot wait on someone else to do this for you. How can you accomplish these goals in your school?

Practice

1. Schools with high poverty students tend to use technology more for drill and practice than for higher order instructional purposes (Becker, 2000; National Center for Education Statistics, 2009). Analyze how you use technology in your class. Are you locked into drill or practice? Plan how you will provide a balance of technology activities in your work.
2. Students must SEE technology adapted to classrooms. Work with your colleagues to develop activities that allow children to SEE technology in action in your classrooms.
3. This chapter provides some of the national standards for technology. Use these standards to support your teaching and planning.
4. Part of your new role as teacher is a *teacher leader* who provides guidance and information for other teachers. How will you use the information in this chapter to better inform your colleagues and administrators about technology?

REFERENCES

Association of Mathematics Teacher Educators' Technology Committee. (2005). *Preparing teachers to use technology to enhance the learning of mathematics.* Position statement. Retrieved from http://www.citejournal.org/ vol9/iss1/mathematics/ article1.cfm

Augar, N., Raitman, R., & Zhou, W. (2004). Teaching and learning online with wikis. *Proceedings of the 21st Australasian Society for Computers in Learning in Tertiary Education (ASCILITE) Conference*, Perth, December 5-8, (pp. 95-104). Retrieved from http://www.ascilite.org.au/ conferences/ perth04/procs/pdf/ augar.pdf

Baker, T. R. (2005). Internet-based GIS mapping in support of K-12 education. *The Professional Geographer*, *57*(1), 44–50.

Baker, T. R., & Case, S. B. (2000). Let GIS be your guide. *Science Teacher (Normal, Ill.)*, *67*(7), 24–26.

Becker, H. J. (2000). Who's wired and who's not: Children's access to and use of computer technology. *The Future of Children: Children and Computer Technology*, *10*(2), 44–75. doi:10.2307/1602689

Bodzin, A. M. (2008). Integrating instructional technologies in a local watershed investigation with urban elementary learners. *The Journal of Environmental Education*, *39*(4), 47–57. doi:10.3200/JOEE.39.2.47-58

Borko, H., & Putnam, T. (1996). Learning to teach. In Berliner, D. C., & Calfee, R. C. (Eds.), *Handbook of educational psychology* (pp. 673–708). New York, NY: Simon & Schuster Macmillan.

Bouck, E. C., & Flanagan, S. M. (2010). Virtual manipulatives: What they are and how teachers can use them. *Intervention in School and Clinic*, *45*(3), 186–191. doi:10.1177/1053451209349530

Boulos, M., Maramba, I., & Wheeler, S. (2006). Wikis, blogs and podcast: A new generation of web-based tools for virtual collaborative clinical practice and education. *BMC Medical Education*, *6*(41). Retrieved from http://www.biomedcentral.com/ 1472-6920/6/41/.

Brescia, W. F., & Miller, M. T. (2006). What's it worth? The perceived benefits of instructional blogging. *Electronic Journal for the Integration of Technology in Education*, *5*, 44–52.

Cobanoglu, C. (2006). An analysis of blogs as a teaching tool as perceived by hospitality management students. *Journal of Hospitality, Leisure, Sport and Tourism Education*, *5*(2), 83–88. doi:10.3794/johlste.52.138

Cuban, L. (1999). High-tech schools, low-tech teaching. *Education Digest*, *64*(5), 53–54. Retrieved from http://web.ebscohost.com.avoserv.library.fordham.edu.

Cuban, L. (2001). *Oversold and underused: Computers in the classroom*. Cambridge, MA: Harvard University Press.

DeBell, M., & Chapman, C. (2003). *Computer and Internet use by children and adolescents in the United States, (NCES 2004-014)*. Washington, DC: U.S. Department of Education, National Center for Educational Statistics.

Dede, C. (2007). Information and communication technologies: Considerations of current practices for teachers and teacher educators. In N. C. Burbules (Ed.), *106th Yearbook of the National Society for the Study of Education, reinventing the role of information and communication technologies in education*, (pp. 11–38). Malden, MA: Blackwell.

Digital nation: 21st century America's progress towards universal broadband Internet access. Retrieved from http://www.ntia.doc.gov/press/ 2010/ DigitalNationReport_02162010. html

Dlott, A. M. (2007). A (pod)cast of thousands. *Educational Leadership*, *64*(7), 80–82.

Education Week. (January, 2010). *Quality counts report*. Retrieved from http://www.edweek.org/ ew/toc/ 2010/01/ 14/index.html

Ertmer, P. A. (2005). Teacher pedagogical beliefs: The final frontier in our quest for technology integration? *Educational Technology Research and Development*, *53*(4), 25–39. doi:10.1007/ BF02504683

Firek, H. (2003, April). One order of ed tech coming up... You want fries with that? *Phi Delta Kappan*, *84*, 596–597.

Fox, S. (2005). *Digital divisions*. Pew Internet and American Life Project. Retrieved from http:// www.pewiInternet.org/ Reports/2005/ Digital-Divisions.aspx?r=1

Garofalo, J., Drier, H., Harper, S., Timmerman, M. A., & Shockey, T. (2000). Promoting appropriate uses of technology in mathematics teacher preparation. *Contemporary Issues in Technology & Teacher Education*, *1*(1), 66–88.

Gillespie, C. W. (2004). Seymour Papert's vision for early childhood education? A descriptive study of preschoolers and kindergarteners in discovery-based, logo-rich classrooms. *Early Childhood Research and Practice, 6*(1).

Google Earth. (2010). *Spectacular satellite images of the world*. Retrieved on from http://www.kmzlinks.com/

Greenhow, C., Robelia, B., & Hughes, J. E. (2009). Learning, teaching, and scholarship in a digital age Web 2.0 and classroom research: What path should we take now? *Educational Researcher*, *38*(4), 246–259. doi:10.3102/0013189X09336671

Grossman, P. L. (1989). A study in contrast: Sources of pedagogical content knowledge for secondary English. *Journal of Teacher Education*, *40*(5), 24–31. doi:10.1177/002248718904000504

Grossman, P. L. (1991). Overcoming the apprenticeship of observation in teacher education coursework. *Teaching and Teacher Education, 7*, 245–257. doi:10.1016/0742-051X(91)90004-9

Halderson, J. (2006). Podcasting: Connecting with a new generation. *Middle Ground, 10*(1), 18–21.

Haugland, S. W., & Wright, J. L. (1997). *Young children and technology: A world of discovery*. Boston, MA: Allyn and Bacon.

Huffaker, D. (2005). The educated blogger: Using weblogs to promote literacy in the classroom. *AACE Journal, 13*(2), 91–98.

Hughes, J. (2004). Technology learning principles for preservice and in-service teacher education. *Contemporary Issues in Technology & Teacher Education, 4*(3), 345–362.

Hutcheson, G. (2009). *Google Earth in the elementary classroom*. Retrieved from http://cnx.org/ content/ m19821/1.2/

Hutinger, P., Johanson, J., & Rippey, R. (2000). *Final report: Benefits of comprehensive technology system in an early childhood setting: Results of a three-year study*. Macomb, IL: Western Illinois University, Center for Best Practices in Early Childhood.

International Society for Technology in Education. (2001). *National educational technology standards for teachers: Preparing teachers to use technology*. Eugene, OR: ISTE.

International Society for Technology in Education. (2007). *The ISTE national educational technology standards (NETS-S) and performance indicators for students*. Retrieved from http://www.iste.org/ Content/NavigationMenu/ NETS/ ForStudents/ 2007Standards/NETS_for_Students_2007_Standards.pdf

International Society for Technology in Education. (2008). *NETS for teachers 2008*. Retrieved on from http://www.iste.org/ Content/NavigationMenu/ NETS/ ForTeachers/ 2008Standards/ NETS_for_Teachers_2008.htm

Jonassen, D. (1994). Thinking technology: Towards a constructivist design model. *Educational Technology, 34*(4), 34–37.

Jonassen, D., Howland, J., Moore, J., & Marra, R. (2003). *Learning to solve problems with technology: A constructivist perspective* (2nd ed.). Upper Saddle River, NJ: Prentice Hall.

Judge, S., Puckett, K., & Bell, S. M. (2006). Closing the digital divide: Update from the early childhood longitudinal study. *The Journal of Educational Research, 100*(1), 52–60. doi:10.3200/JOER.100.1.52-60

Kaiser Family Foundation. (2003). *Fact sheet: The digital divide*. Retrieved from http://www.kff.org/ entpartnerships/ digitaldivide/index.cfm

Kajder, S., & Bull, G. (2003). Scaffolding for struggling students: Reading and writing with blogs. *Learning and Leading with Technology, 3*(12), 32–35.

Kay, R. H. (2006). Evaluating strategies used to incorporate technology into preserviceeducation: A review of the literature. *Journal of Research on Technology in Education, 38*(4), 383.

Lamb, A., & Johnson, L. (2010). Virtual expeditions: Google Earth, GIS, and geovisualization technologies in teaching and learning. *Teacher Librarian, 37*(3), 81–85.

Lindroth, L. K. (2005). *Technology in your classroom: How to find online mathematics manipulatives*. Retrieved from http://www.teachingk-8.com/ archives/ how_to/ how_tofind_online_mathematics_manipulatives.html

McGilchrist, I. (2009). *The master and his emissary*. New Haven, CT & London, UK: Yale University Press.

Mishra, P., & Koehler, M. J. (2006). Designing learning from day one: A first day activity to foster design thinking about educational technology. *Teacher's College Record.*

Moyer, P. S. (2001). Are we having fun yet? How teachers use manipulatives to teach mathematics. *Educational Studies in Mathematics*, *47*(2), 175–197. doi:10.1023/A:1014596316942

Moyer, P. S., Bolyard, J. J., & Spikell, M. A. (2002). What are virtual manipulatives? *Teaching Children Mathematics*, *8*, 372–377.

National Association for the Education of Young Children. (1996). *Technology and young children ages 3-8 (position statement).* Retrieved from www.naeyc.org/ files/naeyc/file/ positions/ PSTECH98.PDF

National Center for Educational Statistics. (1999). *A report on teachers' use of technology.* Retrieved from http://nces.ed.gov/ surveys/frss/ publications/2000102/

National Center for Educational Statistics. (2001). *The conditions of education*. Retrieved from http:// nces.ed.gov/ programs/coe/

National Center for Educational Statistics. (2006). *Rates of computer and Internet use by children in nursery school and students in kindergarten through twelfth grade: 2003.* (NCES 2005-111).

National Center for Educational Statistics. (2009). *Teachers' use of educational technology.* Retrieved from http://nces.ed.gov/ pubsearch/ pubsinfo.asp?pubid=2010040

National Center for Educational Statistics Office of Educational Research and Improvement. (2006). *Computer and Internet use stats in 2003*. U. S. Department of Education. Retrieved from http:// nces.ed.gov/ pubs2006/ 2006065.pdf

National Committee on Science Education Standards and Assessment, National Research Council. (1996). *National science education standards.* Washington, DC: National Academy Press.

National Council of Teachers of Mathematics (NCTM). *Principles and standards for school mathematics*. Reston, VA: NCTM.

Niess, M. L. (2005). Preparing teachers to teach science and mathematics with technology: Developing a technology pedagogical content knowledge. *Teaching and Teacher Education*, *21*, 509–523. doi:10.1016/j.tate.2005.03.006

O'Bannon, B., & Puckett, K. (2009). *Preparing to use technology: A practical guide to curriculum integration* (2nd ed.). Boston, MA: Allyn and Bacon.

Oravec, J. (2003, October). Blending by blogging: Weblogs in blended learning initiatives. *Journal of Educational Media*, *28*(2-3), 225–233.

Partnership for 21st Century Skills. (2008). *21st century skills, education and competitiveness: A resource and policy guide.* Retrieved from http://www.21stcenturyskills.org/ documents/ 21st_century_skills_education_and_competitiveness_guide.pdf

Patterson, T. C. (2007). Google Earth as a (not just) geography education tool. *The Journal of Geography*, *106*(4), 145–152. doi:10.1080/00221340701678032

Petra, T. J. (2010). *Real world mathematics*. Retrieved on from http://www.realworldmathematics.org/ Real_World_Mathematics/ RealWorld Mathematics.org. html

President's Committee of Advisors on Science and Technology, Panel on Educational Technology. (1997). *Report to the President on the use of technology to strengthen K-12 education in the United States*.

Quellmalz, E. (1999). The role of technology in advancing performance standards in science and mathematics learning. In Comfort, K. (Ed.), *Advancing standards for science and mathematics learning: Views from the field*. Washington, DC: AAAS.

Raphael, D., & Whalstrom, M. (1989). The influence of instructional aids on mathematics achievement. *Journal for Research in Mathematics Education, 20*(2), 173–190. doi:10.2307/749281

Richardson, W. (2005). Blog revolution: Expanding classroom horizons with web logs. *Technology and Learning, 26*(3), 48.

Richardson, W. (2006). *Blogs, wikis, podcasts, and other powerful web tools for classrooms*. Thousand Oaks, CA: Corwin Press.

Roblyer, M. D., & Davis, L. (2008, Winter). Predicting success for virtual school students: Putting research-based models into practice. *Online Journal of Distance Learning Administration, 11*(4). University of West Georgia, Distance Education Center.

Sarama, J., & Clements, D. H. (2002). Building blocks for young children's mathematical development. *Journal of Educational Computing Research, 27*(1&2), 93–110. doi:10.2190/F85E-QQXB-UAX4-BMBJ

Shin, E., & Alibrandi, M. (2007). Online interactive mapping: Using Google Earth. *Social Studies and the Young Learner, 19*(3), 1–P4.

Shulman, L. S. (1986). Those who understand: Knowledge growth in teaching. *Educational Researcher, 15*(2), 4–14.

Siegle, D. (2007). Moving beyond a Google search: Google Earth, SketchUp, Spreadsheets, and more. *Gifted Child Today, 30*(1), 24–28.

Sivin-Kachala, J., & Bialo, E. (2000). *2000 research report on the effectiveness of technology in schools* (7th ed.). Washington, DC: Software and Information Industry Association.

Smaldino, S. E., Russell, J. D., Heinich, R., & Molenda, M. (2005). *Instructional technology and media for learning* (8th ed.). Upper Saddle River, NJ: Prentice Hall.

Solomon, G. (2002). Digital equity: It's not just about access anymore. *Technology & Learning, 22*(9), 18–26.

Sowell, E. J. (1989). Effects of manipulative materials in mathematics instruction. *Journal for Research in Mathematics Education, 20*(5), 498–505. doi:10.2307/749423

Steen, K., Brooks, D., & Lyons, T. (2006). The impact of virtual manipulatives on first grade geometry instruction and learning. *Journal of Computers in Mathematics and Science Teaching, 24*(4), 373–391.

Stiler, G. M., & Philleo, T. (2003). Blogging and blogspots: An alternative format for encouraging reflective practice among pre-service teachers. *Education, 123*(4), 789–797.

Suh, J., Moyer, P. S., & Heo, H. (2005). Examining technology uses in the classroom: Developing fraction sense using virtual manipulative concept tutorials. *Journal of Interactive Online Learning, 3*(4), 1–21.

Suydam, M. N., & Higgins, J. L. (1977). *Activity-based learning in elementary school mathematics: Recommendations from research*. Columbus, OH: ERIC Center for Science, Mathematics and Environment Education, College of Education, Ohio State University.

U. S. National Telecommunications and Information Administration (NTIA). (2010).

U.S. Department of Education. (2001). *Policy documents: Elementary & secondary education.* Retrieved from http://www2.ed.gov/ policy/elsec/guid/states/index.html

U.S. Department of Education Office of Educational Technology. (March, 2010). *Draft: National educational technology plan. Transforming American Education: Learning powered by technology*. Retrieved from http://www.ed.gov/technology/netp-2010

Wells, L. (2006). Blog it: An innovative way to improve literacy. *Reading Today*, *24*(1), 40.

Wright, J. L., & Shade, D. D. (Eds.). (1994). *Young children: Active learners in a technological age*. Washington, DC: National Association for the Education of Young Children.

Chapter 8
Technology and Second Language Learning:
Developmental Recommendations for Early-Childhood Education

Nathan E. Ziegler
The University of Toledo, USA

Florian C. Feucht
The University of Toledo, USA

ABSTRACT

Technology is often viewed as a necessary component for the facilitation of learning, especially for second language learners in early-childhood education. However, integrating technology in the classroom is a difficult task. The existing literature often does not bridge the fields of technology, second language learning, and cognitive development in childhood. Therefore, the goal of this chapter is to develop a theoretical framework stemming from a critical literature review of conceptual and empirical works as they pertain to technology, second language learning, and cognitive development. This framework is used to describe conceptual issues and to identify educational implications for the use of technology in the second language classroom in early-childhood education. Furthermore, the chapter concludes with educational, conceptual, and methodological implications as they pertain to technology research and development in early second language classrooms.

DOI: 10.4018/978-1-61350-059-0.ch008

Copyright © 2012, IGI Global. Copying or distributing in print or electronic forms without written permission of IGI Global is prohibited.

INTRODUCTION: MR. JOHNSON'S LESSON

Sitting in front of brand new computers in the computer lab of a modern language school in South Korea were 30 bright eyed 7 year old English second language learners. Once the teacher, Mr. Johnson, settled the students down and got an internet web-browser running on each computer, he began his lesson plan. Previously, Mr. Johnson had taught the students the different state capitals of the United States in a history lesson designed to teach content-specific information in a second language. The learners had prior experience with learning English. They knew basic vocabulary, could ask questions about content, but they had trouble reading longer texts that consisted of much more complex meaning than statements such as "The chair is yellow" or "Hello, my name is Jin". Nevertheless, the teacher had two goals for this lesson plan. First, Mr. Johnson wanted to teach the students about the political geography of the United States. That is, there are 50 states that make up the United States. Additionally, Mr. Johnson wanted to teach the students about population size, capitals, and state flags. Mr. Johnson also wanted the students to explain their understanding of one state that they researched on the internet to the class. In the input section of the lesson plan, Mr. Johnson used two states as examples to help show the differences of the flags, populations, and capitals of each state. After the introduction phase, the teacher wanted to have the students research the states using the internet in the computer lab.

In the computer lab, the learners began searching the Internet for information on the states. Mr. Johnson had to focus much of his energy on keeping the students from using Korean websites to find the information. Throughout the class period, the learners became confused and began to play computer games instead of searching for the information regarding the state of their choice. Eventually, the teacher grew weary and frustrated and searched for the information for the students. Something went wrong. The type of technology that was used by Mr. Johnson was inappropriate for the early-childhood learners. Why did the students become so confused during the activity? Why did this part of the lesson plan seem to fail? What could he have done to use this type of technology more successfully?

In the following chapter, we will answer the following questions by looking at technology in the second language classroom from a developmental and methodological perspective. First, we establish a theoretical framework (see Figure 1) that looks at the relationship between cognitive development, second language teaching methods, and technology. More specifically, the framework aligns the different teaching methods and technology with Piaget's four level of cognitive development. To be used as a rubric, its purpose is to assist second language teachers in an early-childhood classroom in designing developmentally appropriate lesson plans with technology. Finally, we look at possible reasons why Mr. Johnson's lesson plan appeared problematic and suggest computer-based concept mapping as a more appropriate solution to working with technology in this teaching vignette. By the end of this chapter, it is our hope that teachers will be able to bypass some of the difficulties that Mr. Johnson faced in his lesson plan and for researchers to consider the framework to guide their study of second language learning.

Objectives

After reading this chapter the reader will have a better understanding of the interactive relationship between cognitive development, second language teaching methods, and technology. The reader will gain knowledge about why second language education is important to cognitive development and how language develops. The reader will:

- Identify the relationships between Cognitive Development, Second Language Methods, and Technology

Figure 1. Cognitive development, second language methods, and technology: An integrated framework to assist the second language teacher

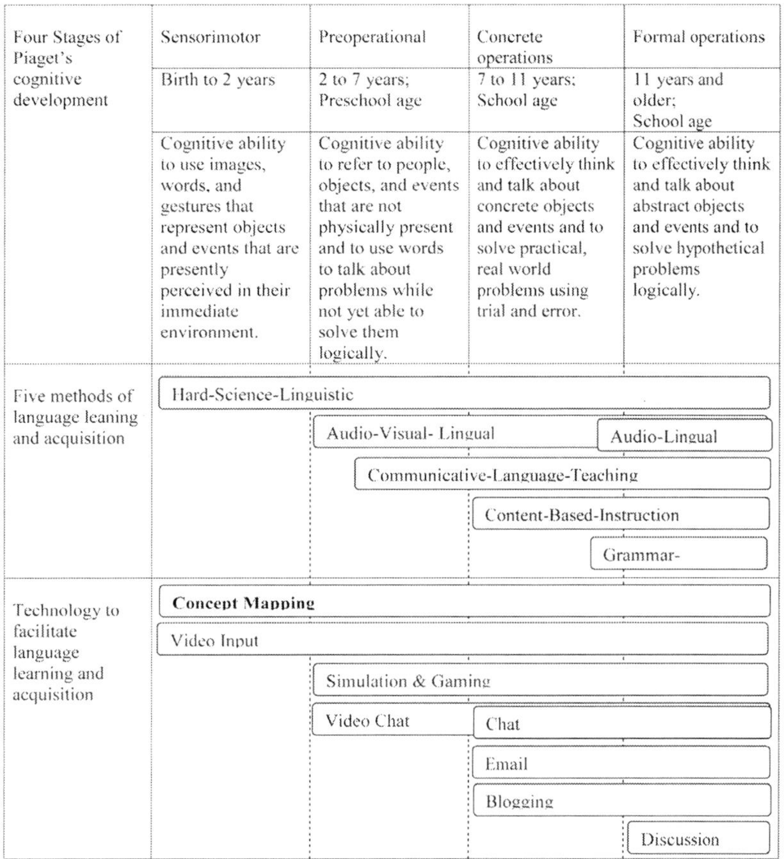

- Identify appropriate use of technology in second language classrooms
- Identify the importance of concept mapping to Second Language learners
- Develop an clearer understanding of how language develops and the important role they play in the future of second language learners

BACKGROUND: SECOND LANGUAGE LEARNERS

In the United States the issue of second language learners or English language learners (ELLs) has become very controversial. Unlike other countries where educational systems support multiple language learning, the United States still clings to the idea that all citizens should speak only one language. Many states, like Tennessee mandate "English only" in their schools and children coming to this and other states are labeled "special education" (SPED) and placed in environments that can limit their access to higher order curriculum vital to future success in mathematics and science education. Most "English only" states do not allow high stakes testing in these students home language which can dramatically influence the identification of the cognitive ability in these children. Other states like Texas and California have high percentages of ELL children in their schools and have learned alternative methods of serving these families and their needs, providing instructional materials and accountability tests in a variety of languages. Because the identification of SPED children starts in early childhood classrooms there is a clear need to better inform educators of young children about language and the importance of ELL instruction. The U.S. is home to more than 45 million Hispanics, making it the world's second-largest Spanish-speaking community after Mexico. Labeling this population as low cognitive functioning due to language could have serious implications for the future of the United States.

Technology has changed the world view of the importance of language in a Global Society. Simple applications like translation webs are available for all teachers. But more important the internet has opened the borders to all countries allowing communication in multiple languages. Technology has opened the gate for multilingual communities and if we are to move forward into the Global Society we need to think about the potential of multilingual students in our schools. The development of language in the rapidly growing population of second language learners in the United States is becoming a major concern as more and more immigrants move away from the border areas and into the "heartland" of America.

The Importance of Second Language Education

The acquisition and use of language is an important characteristic of human development and society. The development of a complex language system allows us to communicate and share our thinking and feelings with other people (Berk & Winsler, 1995). The major peak of language development occurs during early childhood and coincides with the rapid growth and maturation of the brain (Favell, Miller, & Miller, 2002; Lindfors, 1991; Kane & Sheingold, 1980; Sigelman & Rider, 2006). During the first years, children learn to recognize and produce the sounds of their own native language, speak two word sentences and later form simple sentences. Increasingly, they master the basic rules of grammar and syntax and acquire new vocabulary at an incredibly fast pace. At the age of six, the majority of children have acquired language proficiently (Clark, 2000; Sigelman & Rider, 2006).

While most existing theories consent in their description of language acquisition as a fast, complex, and systematic phenomenon, they often diverge in the explanations of its stimulating causes and mechanisms of change (Favell, Miller, & Miller, 2002; Sigelman & Rider, 2006). Most of these different perspectives seem to be rooted in the discussion of the influence of nature (innate) and nurture (acquisition) on language development (Favell, Miller, & Miller, 2002; Sigelman & Rider, 2006). Three main perspectives can be identified. First, the learning theory perspective explains that children acquire language by imitating what they hear and see and through reinforcement and punishment (e.g. Skinner, 1957). Second, the nativist perspective argues that the complexity of language systems in such a short time could only be explained if its development is biologically preprogrammed in children, for example that universal, grammatical knowledge of languages are inherited (e.g., Chomsky, 1968). Finally, the interactionist perspective explains language development as a result of a mutual influence of nature and nurture(e.g., Vygotzky, 1962), for example, the interplay of rapid brain development and linguistic stimulations within the environment. Despite these different perspectives, most theories describe language development as a dynamic process, complex, and systematic in its nature (Kane & Seingold, 1980).

Does the acquisition of a second language follow a similar and/or different developmental path to the first language? In general, research has shown that children who are proficient in their first language will acquire the second language in similar patterns and are able to transfer their knowledge of the first language to the second (Goodz, 1994; Pérez & Torres-Guzmán, 1996). In other words, children do not acquire a second language from scratch, but rather learn how their existing linguistic knowledge applies and integrates into a new language system (Bialystok & Hakuta, 1994; Tabors, 1997). Furthermore, there have been no negative effects identified in the cognitive development and academic performance of bilingual children in comparison to mono-linguistic children (Goodz, 1994). The performance within the second language system seems to be positively influenced by the academic performance and cognitive growth in the first language system, no matter if children are a minority student or not (Collier & Thomas, 1995). That is, if children struggle in their acquisition of their first language, they are also likely to experience problems in becoming fully literate and academically competent in the second language (Clark, 2000; Collier & Thomas, 1995; Sigelman & Rider, 2006).

Finally, there is some evidence that there is no best age when to learn a second language. Young children might benefit from their ability to recognize and pronounce the sounds of any language and, therefore, will be able to speak any second language accent free (Clark, 2000). However, if not practiced, young learners are more at risk to forget their first or second language than an adult learner who has acquired the first language proficiently and learned a second language intentionally. While there are no cognitive restrains in acquiring a second language, the active communication in, and not only exposure to, a second language, the perceived value of speaking a second language, (e.g., cultural pressure, prestige), and internal motivation are social factors that influence the speed and proficiency of the second language acquisition (Clark, 2000; McLaughlin, 1984).

Assumptions of Language

To provide the reader with a brief background on language theory, it is important to introduce current and traditional assumptions of language and language acquisition. Traditional theories of language assume that language is a real-world construct that people use to communicate. In this view, language is a complex system that is innately imbedded in each human being. Each person has a universal grammar that provides the foundation for how they communicate using language (Chomsky, 1968). Additionally, people are innately equipped with a language acquisition device that processes the received input and forms a generative grammar that enables the speaker to produce grammatically correct sentences (Chomsky, 1964). A few problems arise, however, from these fundamental theories of linguistics. First, Chomsky's idea of generative grammar attempts to scientifically observe an abstraction, which is a logical construct that exists in the mind of the participant, not in the external real world (Yngve, 1996). Under Chomsky's generative grammar theory, language has inherent meaning because it consists of real properties, which include verbs, subjects and nouns (1964, p. 29, 33). However, Yngve (1996) shows that language and grammar are abstractions that are not scientifically observable. Yngve further critically argues that the meaning of the sounds lies within participants of the communicative event. That is, our conceptualization of what language is only allows it to be a logical construct where the meaning lies in the minds of the participants. In educational terms, the learner needs to have a real-world context to associate the sounds and the text with the physical properties of the communicative event. Secondly, as Piaget (1980) showed, language is not solely innate. Piaget did believe in genetics and the notion of innateness, but he also believed that a person must learn language. That is, people do have the natural ability to produce and hear sounds and communicate, while they also must learn what the sounds refer to based on the context. In this view, people are not equipped with a universal grammar that filters the sounds to produce comprehensible output (i.e., sounds spoken, text, or physical behaviors used to communicate) and to understand input (i.e., sounds spoken, text or physical behaviors communicated by someone else).

Because language and grammar do not have real-world properties, it is important to look at the real-world properties of the communicative event when studying human communication. In Yngve's (1996) scientific framework for studying human communication in the real world, he defined a communicative event as a linkage which consists of the participants (i.e., the people), the props (i.e., the objects used in communication and that are referred to), the settings (i.e., the places where the communication is occurring), and the channels of communication (i.e., the energy flows--the sounds and the light waves). Using this framework for studying human communication, the sounds and the texts are correlated with the participant's behaviors, the props, the setting, and the outcome of the communicative event. Observing the communicative event rather than language allows the scientific examination of how people communicate, what they are referring to (the shared meaning of the participants), and to understand how their communicative abilities develop.

Most importantly, in the educational context of this chapter, understanding communication as a communicative event can help inform the second language methodology of the teacher and implementation of technology in a cognitively appropriate manner. That is, Yngve's definitions of props, settings, and channels of the communicative event allow for a direct, conceptual integration of technology in his linguistically approach while Chomsky's does not. For example, second language learners that are not yet able to thinking abstractly (e.g., preoperational level) will benefit from technology (e.g., video-recording) that shows all of properties of the communicative event, such as the sounds and texts, the participants, the setting, and the props. In the following section, we discuss how Piaget's model of cognitive development can inform a teacher's methodology in a developmentally appropriate manner.

COGNITIVE DEVELOPMENT AND LANGUAGE LEARNING

It is important to consider the cognitive development of the learner to ensure the success of the language learning method and to select the appropriate technology to enrich the promoted method. The reason for this is that not all methods and technology are equally suitable for young second language learners. For example, some methods require more abstract thought and some technology requires more complex skills than children at certain stages of their cognitive development are able to understand and/or carry out. Before introducing our framework that aligns cognitive development with methods of second language teaching and technology use, a brief overview of Piaget's model of cognitive development is provided next. Piaget described four stages of thought that are qualitatively different form each other: Sensorimotor, preoperational, concrete operational and formal operational stages (see Figure 1; Piaget, 1952; Sigelman & Rider, 2008). Children progress though these four stages in the same order but may differ in the timely occurrence of the stages. Towards the end of the sensorimotor stage (i.e., birth to 2 years), children develop the ability to develop mental representations or symbols of people, objects, and events in their immediate and concrete environment. They can communicate with and about them by pointing, gesturing, and using words or forming very basic sentences. During the preoperational level (i.e., 2 to 7 years), pre-school children learn language about people and objects that are not present and past or future events of their life. They can verbalize and solve simple, concrete problems that do not require any form of logical thought. During the concrete operational stage (i.e., 7 to 11 years), school children master the ability to effectively think and talk about concrete objects and events. They also acquire the skills to solve practical, real world problems using a trial-and-error approach. Finally, during the formal operational stage (i.e., 11 years and older), older school children and teenagers learn to think and talk at a more abstract level of thought. They become more skilled in solving hypothetical problems with an increasing number of components and solutions to them. At this stage, they are able to apply logic and deductive reasoning. These four stages of cognitive development are closely intertwined with language acquisition.

While the earlier literature review illustrated that a second language can be acquired any time during the life span, the different methods of teaching the second language assume and require specific levels of cognitive development (see Figure 1). For example, a student who is taught Spanish following the Grammar-Translation method must be able to think and talk about language at a meta-level. The ability to identify word categories, such as noun, verb, and object, and to apply grammatical rules to ensure a correct sentence structure requires abstract thought at the level of the formal operational stage of cognitive development. In contrast, for example, the method of Hard-Science Linguistics assumes that children can learn to communicate in a second language by immersing them in a language enriched learning environment. This method would allow a 4 year old child at the pre-operational stage to acquire Spanish by being exposed to it in a bi-lingual preschool. Learning Spanish by singing a song in Spanish or by listening to the teacher telling the story of a Spanish picture book does not require the child to think abstractly or analyze language at a meta-level. The need to match the cognitive developmental level of the child holds also true for the use of technology in second language learning (see Figure 1). For example, the teacher in the bi-lingual preschool could arrange weekly video chats with other four year old children in San Sebastián, Spain to talk about their favorite pets they brought to the classroom that day or to sing a song together. Although not yet being able to understand that their Spanish friends live in a different city and even country, the preschool children will still be able to improve their vocabulary and pronunciation by conversing through video chat because they will have all of the properties of the communicative event. While video chat is a technology suitable for most stages of cognitive development due to its concreteness of the conversation, the use of online discussion boards to facilitate a transatlantic discussion of an abstract problem, like global warming, with an "invisible" person would require the US and Spanish students in San Sebastián, Spain to think at a formal operational level and, therefore, to be more cognitively mature to make the use of this technology a success.

In Figure 1, we provide a cognitive development framework that juxtaposes Piaget's model of cognitive development with the different second language teaching methods and the various computer technologies that can be used to assist in second language instruction. While not all of the second language teaching methods or technologies are highlighted in this framework, a teacher could align his or her own methodological perspective and technologies in this rubric by looking at the orientation of the teaching method and technology with the different cognitive development stages. More specifically, we also provide an overview of some of the more prevalent second language teaching approaches, such as the Grammar-Translation, the Audio-Lingual and Audio-Visual-Lingual method, the Content-Based Instruction method, and the Communicative Language Teaching approach, and we introduce a newer second language approach: the Hard-Science Linguistics method. Finally, we will provide an in-depth explanation of how different technology would be appropriate with the different teaching methods and the cognitive development of the second language learners. Our hope is for second language teachers in early-childhood education to use this framework as a rubric to create different lesson plans and teaching strategies for their classrooms.

Second Language Teaching Methods

The following section provides a brief overview of different second language teaching methods and how they align with Yngve's (1996) theoretical framework for human communication, which will help guide the reader through the rubric because it provides the fundamental reasoning behind our juxtaposition of each teaching method with Piaget's model of cognitive development. Thus, we will provide a description and analysis of the Grammar-Translation method, the Audio-Lingual and Audio-Visual-Lingual method, the Content-Based Instruction approach, the Communicative Language Teaching approach, and the Hard-Science Linguistics approach. All of the approaches described below could greatly benefit from the use of technology in a developmentally appropriate manner, regardless of the linguistic or methodological orientation. As was previously mentioned, there are several, less prevalent approaches that are not mentioned in this chapter, such as the methods of Total Physical Response and Total Physical Response Storytelling.

Grammar-Translation Method

Since the notion of grammar was first introduced by the Stoics (Yngve, 1996) and became medium for second language instruction by the Ancient Greeks (Brown, 2007; Yngve, 1996), the Grammar-Translation method has remained one of the most used methods of second language instruction (Bachman & Palmer, 1996; Brown, 2007; Canale & Swain, 1980; Gass & Selinker, 2001; Oller, 1979; Purpura, 2004). With this method of language instruction, students typically learn and apply grammatical rules of the target language, such as conjugating verbs from the infinitive form to a different tense or judging the syntax of a written piece (Oller, 1979; Purpura, 2004). There has also been a tendency to teach the students the meaning of the words of a language by having them translate the word from the native language to the target language or vice versa (Brown, 2007).

The assumption that language and grammar exist as observable properties is important when seeing why traditional language instruction may not be appropriate for all levels of cognitive development. Under this approach, language is taught as a set of grammar rules and all the learner has to do is plug in the necessary word that complies with the specified grammatical rule. Thus, learners become accustomed to filling out grammar charts and learning how to conjugate verbs. They do not learn how to communicate in real-world contexts. Likewise, they are taught to translate a word from their native language to the target language. Usually, however, words do not translate exactly causing confusion later when the learner is trying to speak with native speakers. It is important to note that some teachers who primarily teach with this method may place the language learning in context, but they seldom deviate from such traditional views of language where it is a set of systematic rules that the learners must know. Nevertheless, there are older learners that are able to learn a language using this method. We argue that a language learner must be able to communicate about language at a meta-level in order to be a successful learner with this method. Furthermore, to acquire language at this abstract level of thinking (e.g., grammar) the learner must be able to perform at an advanced level of cognitive development (i.e., formal operations). In other words, learners at the lower stages of cognitive development (i.e.,, sensory motor, preoperational, concrete operations) have not yet developed the ability to think abstractly and therefore may not learn the second language effectively (see Figure 1).

Audio-Lingual Method and the Audio-Visual-Lingual Method

According to Brown (2007), the Audio-Lingual method entails that the learner is presented new material that is made available in audio form. The learner then is supposed to imitate the audio input and memorize the material. A great deal of effort is placed on repetition in this stage. For example, a learner may be presented with verbal and written input such as "President Barack Obama and First Lady Michelle Obama live in the White House". After hearing the input, the learner replicates these sounds several times. This may be done by simply repeating the sounds or by hearing the sounds, reading the text, and then saying the input.

The problem arises that learning is not made meaningful because the focus in on the 'correct' replication of sounds rather than communicating in real-world settings that involve the other components of communication (i.e., the props, the setting, the energy flows, the participants). Additionally, the Audio-Lingual method places a significant amount of emphasis on producing only error-free utterances, which is unrealistic considering native speakers of language produce error-ridden utterances[2] on occasion. Finally, because this method places a great deal of emphasis on memorizing abstracts (i.e., words) out of context, we believe that the learner must be at the formal operations level of cognitive development for the this method of instruction to be effective.

Taking it one step further, the Audio-Visual-Lingual method does attempt to add contextual aspects of communication with the Audio-Lingual method through the implementation of visual aids. According to Phillips (1968), this method is a "structured duplication of the way all children learn their first language, by the repeated aural-oral association of an object with its name or an action with its name, framed in an appropriate phrase or sentence" (p. 13). There are several useful aspects of this approach in comparison with the Audio-Lingual method. First of all, this method includes some of the real-world observable features of communication, such as the objects and the real-movements. For example, the learner is shown a book, hears the sounds /bUk/, and is encouraged to repeat the sounds. Likewise, a learner is shown the action of running, hears the sounds /rənniŋ/, and is encouraged to repeat the sounds.

While this method can be easily and effectively integrated into other second language teaching methods, there are other aspects of the communicative event that need to be included, such as related props, the other participants, and non-verbal aspects of communication. For this reason, we have juxtaposed Audio-Visual-Lingual method with the concrete operations level of cognitive development and higher because the learner is shown real-world objects in association with sounds that refer to them, while the learner does need a slightly higher level of cognition to be able to negotiate meaning using the Audio -Lingual method that does not feature a visual context (see Figure 1).

Content-Based Instruction

Content-Based Instruction has become increasingly popular over the last 35 years (Grabe & Stoller, 1997). Its focus on teaching second languages in immersion settings has been very provocative and appealing to many second language educators and researchers. Additionally, the focus of this method has been on the integration of content areas (e.g., math, science, history) into the second language curriculum of schools. Therefore, the Content-Based Instruction method argues for schools to integrate second languages into their main curriculum, thus giving the students more meaningful opportunities to learn a second language. Also appealing about this method for second language learning is the Vygotskian-perspective that has been applied to this theoretical framework. Content-Based Instruction gives students "many opportunities to negotiate the knowledge that they are learning (rather than simply interact or exchange information) and to extend their knowledge at increasing levels of complexity as more content is incorporated into the lesson" (p. 7). Thus, the learners are able to scaffold on their prior knowledge with an expert and move through the zone of proximal development.

There are many significant aspects of Content-Based Instruction that should be highlighted. First, this method begins integrating content into the second language curricula for early childhood in the beginning of their second language development. By approaching language learning in this fashion, the learners are more motivated and learn more. Second, this method promotes cooperative learning, which is beneficial when learning any subject, but is essential when learning to communicate. Through the collaborative learning process, the second language learners are able negotiate meaning together and it allows them to scaffold their learning with more advanced learners.

While there are clear and definite benefits to this method, it does not completely adhere to teaching real-world communication. This can be problematic for the early-childhood learner who is still developing cognitively and is not completely able to think abstractly. For this reason, Content-Based Instruction should be integrated into the curricula cautiously and appropriately (see Figure 1). Learners need to develop certain communicative abilities before they are able to learn specific content in a second language. However, that does not mean that educators should dismiss teaching content in a second language in schools. A teacher can teach math to second language early-childhood students by showing the action of adding two things together, saying the articulations that represent the equation, and show the result. For example, if the teacher is teaching the equation "1+1" and wants to teach it in a second language, the teacher could use apples as objects to add together. First, the teacher could say the articulation "These are apples" and point to the apples. Next, the teacher would count with the apples by saying "One apple, two apples" and would be pointing to the apples as he or she is saying the articulations. After the teacher has modeled counting with the learners, the teacher would then say "one apple plus one apple equals two apples". Here the teacher would give several examples of the apples being added together. Most importantly, the learners would be learning real-world communication while learning content at the same time. The teacher could also teach the same equation in the native language if necessary. Without the integration of the real-world objects into the lesson, the learners are not able to build on their prior knowledge (knowing what an apple is) and learn a new concept (adding two things together). Therefore, the Content-Based Instruction method would most adequately align with the concrete operations level of cognitive development and higher because the learners need to have some prior knowledge and skills in the school subject being studies (see Figure 1).

Communicative Language Teaching

Another very popular method of teaching second languages over the last 30 years is the Communicative Language Teaching method (Brown, 2007), which moves closer to the goal of teaching a learner how to communicate. Brown (2007) describes the overall goals of Communicative Language Teaching as a focus on all components of communicative competence, such as grammatical, discourse, functional, sociolinguistic, and strategic goals. The method also looks at teaching language in real-world contexts, with a focus on developing skills in unrehearsed contexts that are outside the classroom. Additionally, there is a focus on developing both fluency and accuracy in the language learners. Under this approach, the teacher should focus on fluency (e.g., flow of conversation) over accuracy (e.g., grammatical correctness) in order to maintain meaningful learning. That does not mean, however, that the teacher should ignore grammatical correctness. Finally, Brown highlights that the goal of the teacher should be to have the students construct meaning and facilitate the students' linguistic competence through the active participation of both the teacher and the student.

While there are many very positive aspects of this method, such as its emphasis on context-rich learning environments and engaged communication, many of the theories that influence the pedagogical goals of teachers who practice Communicative Language Teaching still assume that language and communication are different things. In reality this is true, since in fact language does not physically exist in the real world. But certain assumptions made in this field do assume that abstractions such as language and grammar in fact do physically exist and they still put primary emphasis on learning a language and not directly on the communicative behaviors of a target setting. For this reason, this approach is most suitable for language learners at the middle of the preoperational level of cognitive development and higher because there is still some emphasis, though quite small in comparison to other methods, on abstractions (i.e., grammar, translation). The learner at this level of cognitive development will, however, get plenty of real-world examples to make this a useful language teaching method.

Hard-Science Linguistics

The Hard-Science Linguistic method to teaching communication in a second language involves using real things or clear representations of real things, showing contrasts between objects and ideas, and giving the learner ample real-world contexts (Coleman, 2005). For example, when teaching non-native English speakers the teacher holds up a bottle and says 'this is a bottle', then the teacher holds up a bottle with different physical properties (maybe it is a green glass bottle instead of a clear plastic bottle) and says 'this is a bottle'. The teacher repeats this several times so the students can see how the physical properties of the objects vary but the sounds that describe them are the same. Then the teacher holds up a book and says 'this is a book' and then repeats the same process as with the bottles. Now the learner is learning that 'this is' is used when saying what something is, and is also learning the name of the objects (e.g., book, bottle).

It is necessary to point out that in order for this to be done effectively the second language learner must be provided with numerous examples of real objects that allow the learner to associate the speech articulation that the object represents with the possible variation in the objects' appearance. For example, if a second language teacher were to teach the learner how to describe a chair, the teacher would need to point to a hard wooden chair and say 'this is a chair'; then the teacher would point to a recliner that is soft and considerably larger and say 'this is a chair'. Next the teacher would contrast the object by pointing to an object with two seats that is also cushioned and relatively large and say 'this is a couch'. This process would continue with the different examples, so the learner would be able to identify the object appropriately.

To illustrate how this could possibly avoid confusion, one only needs to analyze how speakers of Chinese reference a chair. A native speaker of Chinese would reference a wooden object with one seat as 'yizi' which in English would be referred to as a 'chair'. However, a native speaker of Chinese would call an object with one seat that is soft a 'shafa' and likewise would call an object with two seats that is soft a 'shafa'. In English, the former of the two would be called a 'chair' and the latter of the two would be called a 'sofa' or a 'couch' depending on the dialect. Therefore, it is evident that we must show how native speakers can reference many objects with distinct physical characteristics with the same articulation and how objects that may have similar physical characteristics may be referenced with different articulations. Consequently, by providing a breadth of association for the learners (Coleman, 2006), the learners are able to learn to communicate like a native speaker of the target setting. Examples such as the one provided above can also be applied to other aspects of communication, such as describing emotions, actions, thoughts, and descriptions of real-world objects and actions.

One of the most appealing aspects of this teaching method is that it cuts across all stages of cognitive development. Because there is no emphasis on the abstractions of grammar and language, the learner in the sensory motor stage of cognitive development can start to learn a second language with this method because the learner is being presented with real-world examples in their immediate environment. And while it may seem that this method may seem too simplistic for the more cognitively advanced learners, these learners can still benefit from real-world input that is rich with context and has very little abstractions. Simply because formal operational learners are more able to learn abstract principles without the association to real-world constructs, does not mean that they will have trouble learning more concrete aspects of communication. Furthermore, the complexity of the real world context can be increased to match the cognitive developmental level of the learner. For example, learners can be exposed to a learning environment where they apply problem solving and are required to apply abstract thinking, for example a first aide course or completing an internship in a second language. In sum, we believe that this method may be the most useful second language method because it can be applied to all of the different stages of cognitive development.

Technology in the Second Language Classroom

Technology has aided the learning and instruction of second languages for decades and has become an integral part of the methodological structure of the language classroom. Currently, in classroom settings, technology is typically thought of as computer based (e.g., vocabulary learning software or online discussion boards). For example, computer programs such as Rosetta Stone and byki offer great opportunities for the second language learner. However, a technology is not limited to a typical desktop computer in a classroom, it can also include any equipment that requires electricity to operate (Brown, 2007) (e.g., leap frog learning technology). Non-computer based technology can include video-tapes and DVDs, and audio-tapes and CDs that are either self-made or commercially produced. While these essential pieces of technology still hold value, especially in environments that have financial limitations, computer-based technology has reshaped the possibilities of the second language classroom. In the next section, computer-based technology will be looked at from a cognitive development perspective to enhance the instructional practices of teachers of a second language and the learning for the second language learners. Therefore, different technologies will be discussed briefly and will be placed in juxtaposition to the different developmental stages of cognitive development and will be addressed from the different methodological perspectives that have been discussed above (see Figure 1).

Video Recording

With the accessibility of digital cameras and digital camcorders, creating videos for a second language classroom has never been easier. For the beginning second language learner, digital videos can be created to show real-world communication in accordance with the written texts that references the spoken articulations. Computer software, such as iMovie and Windows Movie Maker, make it easy for the teacher to record a video and then add the corresponding text to the video and most are often already installed when purchasing a computer. Additionally, a teacher can add texts that match the spoken sounds in the video (i.e., subtitles) so that the learners can learn to read while seeing the physical communication take place. Moreover, the teacher can replay the various parts of the video so that the learners can analyze the different aspects of the communicative event (e.g. spoken articulations, texts, physical objects like a bottle or book). Additionally, Chappelle (2007) points out that learners can negotiate meaning during the use of computer software because they are able to stop a video during input to slow the normal flow of conversation, which allows them to check their comprehension and repeat different aspects of the input if they indeed are having difficulties. Additionally, the learner is able to control when they ask for help, modify responses, repeat the material, and review it (Chapelle, 2007). Finally, students can create movies to tell personalized stories in a second language (Lotherington et al., 2008). Students can share these movies with each other and, therein, start using this form of digital media as an interactive communication tool.

The use of digital video cameras to teach communication in a second language (by the teacher) and to demonstrate communicative abilities in a second language (by the students) could be beneficial for learners at all four stages of cognitive development (see Figure 1). This is because the learners are presented with concrete examples of communication in real-world settings. Like the Hard-Science Linguistic method, learners at all stages of cognitive develop can understand the physical properties presented in the video (e.g., a boy throwing a ball) and the sounds that refer to that actions. For similar reasons, the Audio-Visual-Lingual method, the Content-Based Instruction method, the Communicative Language Teaching method, and the Hard-Science Linguistic method can find value in this technology. With the Audio-Visual-Lingual method, for example, the teacher can use videos to represent different speakers into a dialog, which would help the learners see and experience much richer communication strategies. Content-Based Instruction could also benefit from this type of technology. For example, the teacher could teach a history lesson in a second language by recreating an historical event in the target language. The students, likewise, could demonstrate their knowledge of the event and their ability to communicate in the second language by creating a video. With the Communicative Language Teaching method, the learners can see communicative events, create and participate in them, and they can isolate various aspects of the communicative event to better understand the different elements of communication.

With the Hard-Science Linguistic method, video cameras can be an essential part of any lesson plan. In a study by Ziegler (2007), video cameras were used to demonstrate input to the learners. The video-input included the speaker placing objects in different positions in relationship to other objects. First, the speaker picked up the object, pointed to it, said its name, and then began placing the object on, next to, or in another object while saying the articulation that represented that position, and then the speaker said the articulation that represented the other object (e.g., toy, toy on table, toy next to book). Meanwhile, the full string of texts (e.g. The toy is on the table) was subtitled at the bottom of the screen. The input lasted 10 minutes long and it showed several different objects in several different positions. The results of the study showed that this method of instruction benefited greatly from the use of video-recording to teach input, even though that was not the primary objective of the study. Learners that were shown the video had significantly higher scores on two different assessments (i.e., a task-based assessment and a grammar assessment) than did the learners that were taught the second language in person using the Grammar-Translation method.

Simulation and Gaming

Simulated learning environments (i.e., computer environments that look very similar to real-world settings) and learning games can help learners practice communicating in a simulated real-world environment. Schwienhorst (2002), for example, shows how virtual reality has the capacity of developing learning communities that help students communicate in real-world type settings and to become self-regulated and autonomous learners. Further, the learners in a virtual reality setting developed language and linguistic awareness through collaboration, interaction, and critical reflection (Schwienhorst, 2002). Moreover, according to Murray (1999) and Schwienhorst (2002), virtual reality benefits second language learners because it brings the learner into language contexts that are typically unreachable and it emphasizes the importance of socio-cultural contexts. He pointed out that this is because virtual environments support interaction, for they create a stress-free environment that encourages role-play without the embarrassment and apprehension that can play a factor in the physical classroom. Furthermore, virtual reality offers an environment that is authentic and provides the necessary realism that is needed when learning how to communicate in a second language. For example, programs similar to *Philippe* (Murray, 1999), and *WebQuest* (Simina & Hamel, 2005) can engage the learner in the communicative event and help them develop an understanding of the different properties of communication. According to Murray (1999), *Phillipe* "offers the possibility of inviting the learners into a fictional community where they can be immersed in the target language and actively participate in it culture" (p. 296).

While computer simulations and computer games are designed to appropriately accommodate different levels of language and cognitive development, they can be particularly helpful for the beginning stages of development and for early childhood second language learners because they give the learner a chance to explore simulated real-world environments that help them understand what the articulations and text of the second language mean in the given context. Additionally, simulated games make learning more fun for the early-childhood second language classroom because they offer a wide variety of intriguing and stimulating environments for children at the lower stages of cognitive development (e.g., pre-operational and concrete operational stages). As Corbeil (1999) argues, gaming gives the learner autonomy, makes learning enjoyable, and allows the learner to meet a challenge without the possibility of negative consequences that one may experience in the real world.

One of the main advantages of simulation and gaming in the early-childhood second language classroom is that it has many benefits for teaching the communicative properties of a non-native setting in environments that are typically impossible to experience for many younger learners. Therefore, the appeal of simulation and gaming for the Hard-Science Linguistic and Communicative Language Teaching method is very profound. First of all, simulated environments enable the teacher to isolate different properties of the communicative event. For example, assume that the second language teacher wants to teach directions. The teacher could use a computer gaming program where a 7-year old learner drives a car through a city in an attempt to accomplish certain goals, such as delivering a package to a certain location. If the learner does not follow the directions properly, the learner will not be able to accomplish the goal. Thus, after the teacher has taught directions in the lesson plan, the teacher could give directions to the learner (e.g., drive three blocks and take a right) and gives the learner a specific goal to accomplish. For the Content-Based Instruction method, simulations and games can be used very easily. For example, a teacher can use different gaming programs that teach math that make learning the subject matter applicable to the real-world and that help the learner associate the numbers in the second language with observable and easily manipulated math environments (Ke, 2008).

Chat

Internet based chat programs, both text and video, can provide learners with the opportunity to communicate with native speakers in authentic situations. Text chat, such as Instant Messenger and Microsoft Live, can create a self-regulatory and motivating environment where students are able to negotiate meaning with a native speaker. Video chat is a good way for students to also learn the non-verbal communicative behaviors of the target language setting in correlation with the spoken articulations. Chapelle (2007) showed that socio-constructivist language learning can occur with technology through computer-mediated communication, such as video and text chat. With text chat, for example, a learner can engage in communication with an expert (i.e., native language speaker) and can scaffold on their prior knowledge of the target language. While text chat does have some benefits, such as the ability to negotiate meaning and isolate different aspects of the communicative event, verbal chat has been shown to allow learners to fix errors they may have made with the native speaker who may give implicit and/or explicit feedback that occurs in the flow of conversation (Chapelle, 2007). Therefore, it gives the learner the chance to be guided by an expert in a more authentic setting than with text chat, which does not have the physical context to inform the learner. Second language learners can also use computer-mediated video chat where they speak to a native speaker using telecommunications. Programs such as Skype offer free and easy to use software that can be used as medium for telecommunication and video chat.

Text chat programs are most suitable for a learner who is moving from the middle stages of cognitive development (concrete operational) to stages of more abstract thought (e.g., formal operational) because the learner is presented with less of a real-world context (e.g., the concreteness of visual representations and manipulatives), while video chat allows for even younger learners to participate in synchronous communication due to the visual and concrete context of the video (see Figure 1).

Because chatting does not isolate parts of communication in the same manner as video recording does, it is a fruitful way for synchronous communication in a non-threatening environment. For the Content-Based Instruction method, chat could be used to facilitate discussion about different topics that are being studied. The teacher could also use this technology to have the students ask questions about the content and could use the chat to help gain a more thorough understanding of the content. However, this combination of technology and second language method learning requires the learners to be at a concrete operational level of cognitive development. They would need to understand the abstractness of chat, that is, communication with text without the concreteness of visuals, and have a good understanding of the content knowledge and skills learned in the school subject (see Figure 1). The Communicative Language Teaching method can benefit greatly from text and video chat. Here the teachers could simulate real world interactions by giving the students topics to discuss or scenarios to speak in or about. Finally, much like Communicative Language Teaching, the Hard-Science Linguistic method could use chat for simulation and discussion, but it is imperative that the learner has learned the target input (articulations that are the focus of the lesson plan) prior to using this technology.

Internet

The Internet can be a great tool for a language learner, but it must be used strategically and meaningfully. Randomly surfing web pages on the Internet (recall Mr. Johnson's history lesson in the vignette) can have little impact on language learners because they may not be presented with real-world constructs that help them observe the communicative behaviors with the setting, the props, and the outcome of the communicative event. Below are a few tools that can be used for language learners as they move from the beginning stages of language and cognitive development to the more advanced stages. Certainly the Internet as a service can be helpful for learners of all developmental levels; however, most web-pages may not be appropriate for second language learners at the beginning stages of cognitive development (i.e., sensory motor, preoperational). Instead of giving a view overview of the web-pages that teachers could use in the second language classroom, we will focus on a few tools that depend on the Internet to operate and how they fit in the framework (Figure 1).

E-Mail

One important aspect of the Internet is electronic mail or email. Similar to text chat, email can connect the language learner with native speakers. Email, however, gives the learner the chance to communicate asynchronously, which gives the learner the opportunity to analyze the text, think about the response, and negotiate meaning. For example, a student in Mr. Johnson's class could write an email to a government official requesting information about the political geography of the United States. Not only would the learner receive the appropriate information, but the learner would also be able to engage in meaningful communication. Additionally, the learner could spend time dissecting the information to gain a complete understanding of the material, assuming that the email was written at an educational level. It is important to point out, however, that email requires that the learners have developed the ability to communicate with writing. Learners at the sensory motor and preoperational levels of cognitive development will likely not benefit much from email because it will be very difficult for the learner to associate meaning to just the texts (see Figure 1). As the learners transition from the concrete operations level of cognitive development to the formal operations level of cognitive development, the learner will be able to increasingly communicate in writing about events in their immediate life (i.e., concrete operations) and more abstract concepts (i.e., formal operations).

Many of the teaching methods, therefore, line up with email if it is used at the appropriate level of cognitive development. For the Grammar-Translation method, the teacher can have the students write emails and assess them on their grammatical skills, or the teacher could have the students translate different email messages that the teacher has created for the lesson plan. With the Content-Based Instruction method, for example, the learner can write emails to experts in the field of study. While a young learner's conceptualization of the topic may be very simple, communicating with an expert may increase the students' motivation and could help make the learning experience more meaningful for the learner. Similarly, Communicative-Language Teaching and Hard-Science Linguistics both can take advantage of email because they both place emphasis on communication. For Hard-Science Linguistics, email can assist in long-running asynchronous dialogs between two learners or between the learner and the teacher. Under this method, though it is crucial that the learner have already gained an understanding for the communicative properties used to write the email (i.e., the shared abstractions that are referenced in the context of the email), students can use email in an informal context to communicate in a second language with a foreign e-pen pal.

Blogging

For the learner who is beginning to develop narrative storytelling abilities, both verbal and written, blogging can be a very useful tool. A blog is a web site where a person can write journals, share pictures, share comments and thoughts, and get feedback from peers. Blogs are typically free and are very easy to set-up. Additionally, blogs are great for learners who are entering an advanced level of language development because it gives them time to reflect on communication in a more abstract manner that was not able to be done in the earlier levels of second language development and cognitive development. Therefore, we suggest that blogging is most appropriate for the concrete and formal operation levels of cognitive development (see Figure 1). While we suggest that blogs would be more suitable for the older learner, the teacher can use them for younger learners (ages 7+) that are more advanced in their communicative abilities and assume ahead of time that the blogs will be less complex.

Many of the teaching methods that we have described so far can find value in blogging. For Communicative Language Teaching and Hard-Science Linguistics, narrative storytelling through blogs could be very useful because it gives the learner the chance to express themselves in a manner that would mimic real-world storytelling, only the learner would not receive immediate feedback from the person reading the blog. The Content-Based Instruction method could use blogs as a way for students to explain different concepts, whether they are historical, scientific, or mathematic, that have been learned in the given lesson. By having the students explain what was learned in their own words, the learners are given more autonomy and they are given the chance to practice communicating their ideas in the second language.

Discussion Boards

Another valuable tool for the second language learner who is moving into a more advanced level of communication and higher level of cognitive development is the discussion board. Discussion boards are online sites where students can engage in meta-cognitive problem solving, critical analysis, and argumentation. A learner, for example, can post their ideas on a certain subject, such as the oil spill in the Gulf of Mexico, and respond to other students' posts. By communicating this way, the second language learners can gain a more sophisticated understanding of the second language because they are required to present concepts that are abstract and not physically present. It is important to note, however, that discussion boards should be used diligently because they require the ability to understand the more abstract properties of communication. Thus, discussion boards should only be used with learners that are at the formal operations level of cognitive development (see Figure 1).

Discussion boards can be particularly useful for Content-Based Instruction, for they offer the opportunity for the learners to engage in meaningful discussion and to assist one another in the learning process. If the focus of the language teacher is to help the students gain a more thorough understanding of different content in a second language, the discussion board could be a very useful tool. Communicative Language Teaching and Hard-Science Linguistics could also find the use of discussion boards to be helpful simply because this technology promotes communication. Consequently, teachers must determine what level their students are and how well they communicate in a second language before deciding to use discussion boards in the early-childhood classroom.

Computer-Based Concept Mapping

One type of computer software that can be useful for second language learners who are moving through the beginning levels of cognitive development to the more advanced levels of cognitive development are computer-based concept maps. Concepts are "composed of nodes that represent concepts and links that connect nodes to represent the relationships between concepts" (Kwon and Cifuentes, 2009, p. 365) and can be used to develop reading comprehension abilities and a deeper conceptual understanding of the material. Software programs such as Cmap Tools and Kidspiration can create an interactive way for learners to understand the complexities and abstract properties of a language. In the next section of the chapter, concept mapping will be discussed as a possible solution to the problems that Mr. Johnson faced or as an alternative technology use in his second language classroom.

USING COMPUTER-BASED CONCEPT MAPPING TO DEVELOP SECOND LANGUAGE ABILITIES IN EARLY-CHILDHOOD LEARNERS

Mr. Johnson's Lesson Plan: What Went Wrong?

When using technology, it is necessary that teachers take into account the developmental level of the learners with respect to the method of second language learning as well as their choices of technology in support of their teaching. If students are presented with tasks that are too abstract and that include activities that require, for example, a formal operations level of thinking, the students will get frustrated rather than learning how to communicate in the second language. Therefore, when technology is used in the second language classroom, the technology should appropriately match the developmental cognitive ability of the learners.

In Mr. Johnson's class where the goal was to teach the students how to reference the political geography of the United States (i.e., the states, the capital, the population), he teacher could have used technology that shows as a picture of a state in correlation with the sounds and the texts that reference the particular state. That is, Mr. Johnson's Content-Based Instruction was geared towards learners at the formal operational level, when in fact they were actually transitioning from the preoperational to concrete operational level of cognitive development. The learners needed to have reached a level of abstract thinking that occurs at the formal operation level to engage and learn fully from the technology (i.e., web-based searching of the internet) in this activity. While Content-Based Instruction can be used for learners in the concrete operational level, the teacher should be diligent with what content is being taught and with what technology is being used to teach it. Additionally, if the learners have not yet moved to the higher levels of cognitive development, the learners will have trouble with writing that is void of physical contexts (i.e., pictures, drawings) because the written texts are too abstract for the second language learners. The learners needed to have reached a level of abstract thinking that occurs at the formal operation level to engage and learn fully from the technology (i.e., web-based searching of the internet) in this activity. Therefore, the teacher should have not used web-based search engines at this level because the learners were not able to think at this abstract level yet.

While Content-Based Instruction is suitable for learners in the concrete operational level, the selected technology or the complexity of using the technology as part of the task objective required a more advanced level of cognitive development. For this reason, Mr. Johnson should have made informed choices with what content is being taught, the cognitive development of his students, and with what technology is being used to teach it.

Next we introduce computer based concept mapping as a technique that that can be flexibly adapted by the teacher to the different developmental stages of cognition and language of the learner. Concept mapping can follow the learners along their developmental progression and be integrated, in unlike the majority of technologies, in teaching methods used in the field of language learning.

Growing Support for Concept Mapping

While there are many possible avenues that could be taken to improve Mr. Johnson's lesson plan and instructional strategies (i.e., behavior management, amount of information being taught), computer-based concept mapping could have been a useful technological tool that he could have used to prepare the students for the searching exercise. There are many benefits for computer-based concept mapping, which has been shown to develop reading comprehension abilities and create a deeper conceptual understanding of a second language (Kwon & Cifuentes, 2009). Anderson-Inman and Ditson (1999) and Royer and Royer (2004) showed that computer-based concept maps enable students to create organized conceptual ideas because they are easy to generate, easy to revise and they are not limited to space on papers (Kwon & Cifuentes, 2009).

Research on the effects of computer-based concept maps on second language acquisition is still growing and developing. Current research has shown that English second language learners provided with concept maps as a study strategy to develop reading comprehension did significantly better than students who were not provided with the same study strategy (Chularut & DeBacker, 2004). Chularut and DeBacker showed that concept mapping can have a positive effect on self-monitoring, knowledge acquisition, and self-efficacy. The researchers found that the higher English proficiency learners had more substantial gains in achievement than the lower English proficiency learners. One explanation Chularut and DeBacker suggest is that the learners could have reached a point where their abilities were no longer improving in their language learning and unassisted studying could have done very little to improve their achievement. A second reason is that lower level English proficiency learners (those that still have room to improve) may not have been cognitively prepared for providing such a conceptualization of the text. This shows the importance of assessing the learners' levels of cognitive development as they develop proficiency in a second language.

Finally, Ojima (2006) showed that concept maps do have a profound effect when used as a pre-task activity to improve a student's writing in the English second language classroom. However, there are certain limitations with this study. First of all, Ojima only looked at three participants in his study, which makes it hard to draw a generalization from his findings. Secondly, while his study does show that concept maps help generate ideas, he did not explore how concept mapping would help an English second language learner understand the abstract concepts in reading comprehension or disseminate knowledge that they read in the text. Nevertheless, this study does demonstrate that concept mapping can improve fluency on some level and accuracy in writing. However, there is little research that shows that learners develop better reading comprehension with concept maps because most research focuses on concept maps as an instructional tool rather than as an assessment tool (Oliver, 2009).

Moving from Concrete Representations to Abstract Communication

Computer-based concept mapping can be used to provide technology support in the second language learning of students at any stage of cognitive and language development. Beginning, sensory-motor learners depend on seeing objects (i.e., real-world observable properties) and hearing sounds simultaneously. At this level, learners have a difficult time making abstract generalizations of simple, concrete conceptualizations (see Figure 1; Son et al., 2008). For example, a young learner needs to hear the articulation "Barack and Michelle live in the house" while seeing a representation of Barack Obama, Michelle Obama, and a white house. With concept mapping computer software, such as Kidspiration, the educators and parents can create a concept map by using a picture of the Barack Obama, Michelle Obama, and the White House that can be read to them like a picture book. Figure 2 shows what a possible concept map may look like for a learner at this level. Here a picture chosen to represent Barack Obama and Michelle Obama[3] are shown in relationship to each other and in relationship to the White House, suggesting that they reside in that building.

As the language learner becomes more advanced and develops cognitively, the learner can begin to understand slightly more abstract conceptions (objects that are not physically present) and can therefore start associating sounds with texts and with the real-world representations of what they reference (see Figure 1). Therefore, the pre-

Figure 2. Sensorimotor concept map

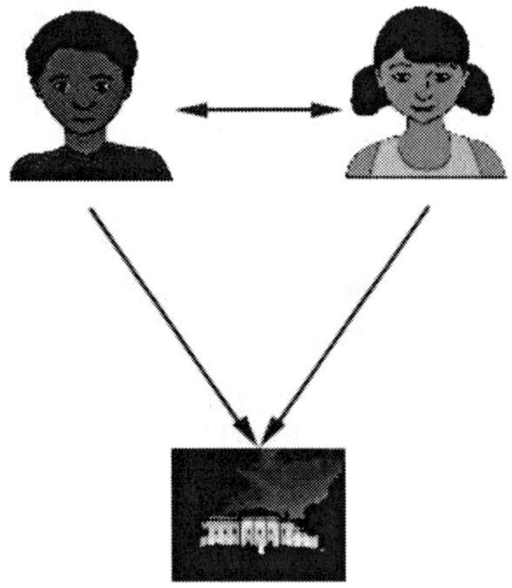

operational level learner can begin to read text, but this learner still needs to see the physical representation of the target input. Figure 3 demonstrates how a learner might create a concept map for the text "President Barack Obama and First Lady Michelle Obama live in the White House". Here the text "President Barack Obama" and a physical representation of him are shown in relationship to the text "First Lady Michelle Obama" and a physical representation of her are shown in relationship to the text "the White House" and a picture of the White House. Notice how the link labels "and" and "live in" represent the relationship of the pictures and the texts to one another.

The second language learner at the concrete operations level of cognitive development can begin to understand the abstract properties of communication (i.e., text, articulations), but is not yet able to focus on the naming conventions of language or analyzing language on a meta-cognitive level, such as abstract objects and relationships (see Figure 1). Therefore, the concrete operations learner can begin to understand language without the complete assistance of the physical representations (i.e., photos, video) of the articulations and text. Figure 4 shows what a concept map may look for a learner at this stage. It is important to point out that the learner at this stage of second language development may not understand the texts on a deeper level and may not see how those texts connect to other related concepts that have not been learned congruently with the target input.

As the second language learner moves into the formal operations of cognitive development, the learner begins to understand the abstract properties of longer texts, such as short stories and more complex dialogs (see Figure 1). Assuming the learner understands the majority of the target input in the text, the learner can use concept mapping tools to illustrate understanding and comprehension of the story and show the relationship between concepts within the story that were not directly discussed in the target input phase of the lesson plan. In this scenario, the learner shows how concepts that she or he sees are relevant to the text and can connect the ideas of the story together. Furthermore, the learner is choosing elements of the story that are relevant to him or

Figure 3. Preoperational concept map

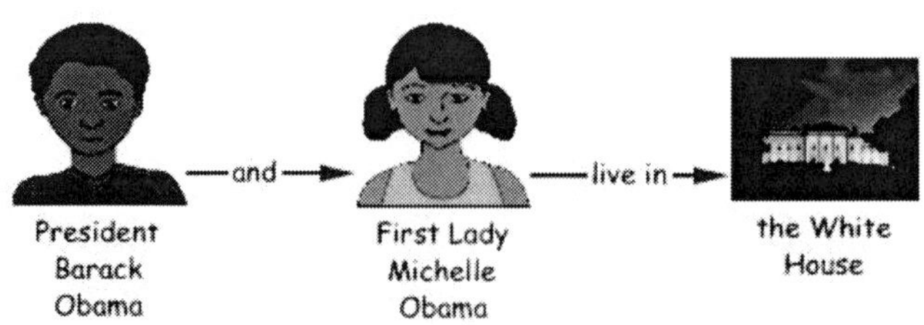

Figure 4. Concrete operations concept map

her at the moment they are creating the concept map. This creates a more meaningful learning experience because it allows the learner to focus on information, content, and language that are the most important or relevant to him or her. For example, in Figure 5, the learner can show the connection between Barack Obama, Michelle Obama, and the White House to Washington D.C., the capital of the United States. The learner can also demonstrate other knowledge of the United States by showing which state Barack Obama was born, Hawaii, and provide information about the state (e.g., Hawaii is the 50th state).

As the learner becomes more cognitively advanced, the teacher can use concept mapping with his students to analyze more complex forms of communication, both written and oral. That is, as the learner develops cognitively, she or he will be able to use more metacognitive strategies in a second language with the use of computer-based concept mapping. If the teacher is interested in teaching grammar principles of the target language, the learner at the formal operational level

Figure 5. Formal operations concept map in a second language

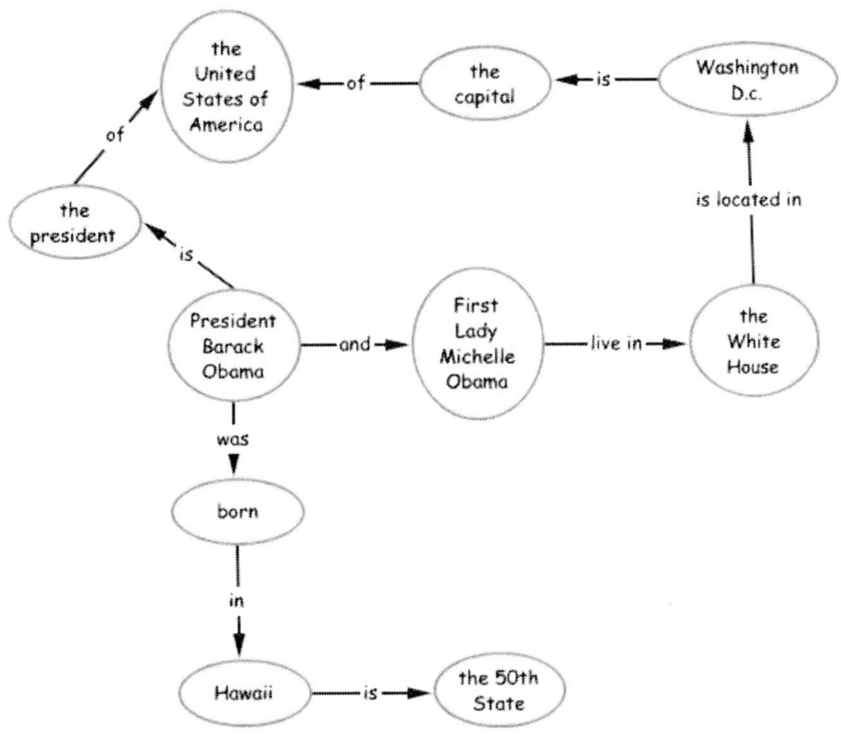

of development may be able to use concept mapping to understand the often complex and confusing grammatical rules that are presented to learners in the earlier stages of learning rather than the latter. Figure 6 shows how the sentence "President Barack Obama and First Lady Michelle Obama live in the White House" may be constructed in a concept map with the purpose of analyzing the sentence grammatically.

Because concept mapping requires the learners to actively construct meaning, they are continually building on their prior knowledge of the second language and they are using that knowledge to them understand the new forms of communication that they are learning. Therefore, it is imperative that teachers begin using concept mapping with the early-childhood language learner to help them develop, stage by stage, more abstract and complex forms of communication.

Concept Mapping as a Solution for Mr. Johnson's Lesson Plan

Looking back at the Vignette of Mr. Johnson's classroom, concept mapping could have been a useful tool to prepare his students for more abstract forms of communication. That is, if Mr. Johnson would have had his students build simple concepts linking the texts to pictures of the real-world constructs that they represent (i.e., the white house, the flag), the students may have been able to more fully understand what target information they were looking for and what it meant. More specifically, after Mr. Johnson taught the key input (i.e., the states, the white house, the flag, the capital), he could have taken his students to the computer lab to create concept maps of what they had learned. At this level of cognitive and linguistic development, the students could have built concept at the preoperational level, which could include a picture associated with the text (see Figure 3), or they could have created concepts at the concrete operations level where the students are connecting the target input with other concepts they have learned without the physical representations of the texts (see Figure 4). Once the students demonstrate an understanding, which can be evaluated from the concept maps that they have created, the students can then search for information regarding an individual state (assuming that the website they are looking at is appropriate for their level). As the students find information, they could even create concept maps of the information they find from the website to help them interpret and understand the information. Therefore, we argue that concept maps could really help scaffold the learners from one level to the next because the concepts enable the students to learn a second language at a level that is most appropriate for their level of cognitive development.

Process Tool and Instructional Approach

Not only can computer-based concept mapping be an adaptive tool for the different cognitive levels

Figure 6. Formal operations concept map for a grammar exercise

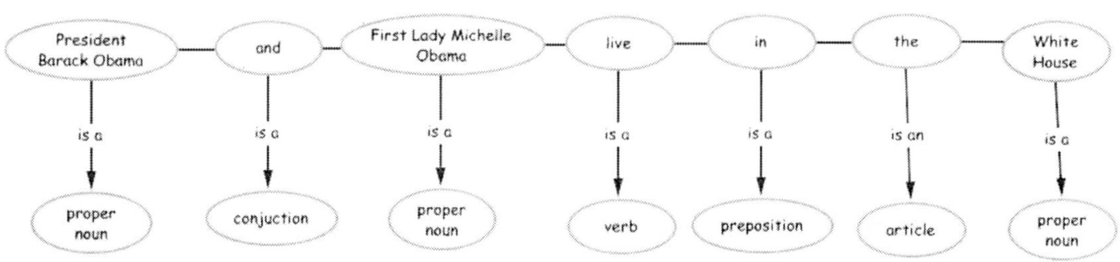

of development, it can also be used to assist with the aforementioned second language teaching methods. As was previously shown, teachers using the Grammar-Translation method can use concept mapping to dissect sentences and analyze the grammatical structure of each sentence (see Figure 6). This can certainly be done with a pencil and paper, but computer-based concept mapping can allow the learner to easily move around the different nodes and modify the concept map based on the desired complexity of the concept map from the teacher. For the Audio-Lingual and Audio-Visual Lingual methods, computer-based concept mapping can be used after the learners have learned the input (i.e., President Barack Obama and First Lady Michelle Obama live in the White House) to demonstrate understanding and comprehension of the material (see Figure 4). With the Content-Based Instruction method, the teacher could have the learner create computer-based concept maps to explain a recently learned concept and to connect the relationships between different concepts (see Figure 5). A teacher using the Communicative Language Teaching method could have the students demonstrate understanding as well, but this teacher can also have the learner show a simpler understanding of the material (see Figure 3 and Figure 4), or for the learner at a higher level of cognitive development, the learner can demonstrate the links between concepts at a higher, more abstract level (see Figure 5). Finally, the teacher using the Hard-Science Linguistic method can use concept maps at all levels and for various activities. The teacher could use this tool to show input (e.g., the teacher shows the picture of Barack Obama and Michelle Obama and the White) or have the learners communicate their understanding of the input by creating a concept map. As the learners become more advanced, the teacher can scaffold them to more create more complex concept maps.

Concept mapping could also be used as a valuable assessment tool for teachers in an early childhood second language classroom. Teachers could use concept maps as a summative assessment tool to see how much the learner has changed over the course of a specific period of time (i.e, one semester of a school year). By having the students generate concepts maps, the teacher can look at a learner's ability to comprehend and communicate in second language. For example, the teacher could have the students generate concepts maps of their knowledge of President Barack Obama in their second language. Based on the information that students provide and how well they link different concepts, the teacher can evaluate how much of the second language the learner understands in this context. Additionally, teachers can use concept mapping for pre- and post assessment to examine how much the learner's language ability has changed and improved over time. Concept mapping could also be very helpful as a formative assessment tool because it could give the teacher insight to the cognitive level of the language learner and could give the teacher information to assist in providing the learners with adequate feedback through their learning process. If the learners clearly understand the basic elements of second language communication at the sensory motor level, the teacher can encourage the learner to integrate texts into the concept map and show the relationship between those concepts as the learner moves to the preoperational level.

The focus on concept maps in this chapter has indicated that this approach can be used as a learning process tool for children, an instructional approach for the teacher and a mind map of learning for second language learners. The versatility of this tool supports teachers and learners. As with all tools the impact will be dependent on the teacher and how the mapping is applied.

FUTURE TRENDS

We suggest that more classroom research should be conducted to better understand the different aspects of second language learning in particular when technology is involved. It would be of interest to empirically validate aspects of our theory driven argumentation that certain methods of language learning and different types of technologies need to account for the cognitive development (see Figure 1) and cognitive load of the second language learner. To best investigate issues of this nature, Berliner (1991) suggested that researchers should be "technologically sophisticated and able to conduct instructional research in complex group settings" (p. 149). They need to be more conversant "in small sample, qualitative designs, and methods of cognitive psychology" (p. 150). Taking a step further, we argue that in particular micro-genetic research would be helpful as it allows not only to measure learning outcomes but also insights into the actual learning processes. For example, a lesson plan could be designed to introduce students to computer-based concept mapping. This lesson could encompass different scaffolds to account for students' cognitive development and load. By assessing students' language skills not only before and after, but also during the actual lesson, the researcher could gain insight into what aspects of the lesson plan are most conducive to students' language learning and their cognitive development.

Further research should be conducted to investigate the impact of concept mapping on the development of students' second language as they transition through the different cognitive levels (i.e., preoperational, concrete operations, and formal operations). Theoretically, computer-based concept mapping is predicted to increase the second language abilities of learners because it allows the material to be tailored to the appropriate cognitive level of development and thus meets the developmental needs of each learner, which is not the case of most technology. This theory, however, has not been tested empirically. Therefore, more research must be conducted to understand the impact of computer-based concept mapping on the development of language abilities as learners move through the different levels of cognitive development.

Cognitive Load

In the context of integrating technology into second language learning that appropriately accommodate the learners' cognitive development, there is the need to consider the impact of technology use on the cognitive load of the second language learner. Cognitive load is defined as the influence of learning and instruction on the working memory of students (e.g., Sweller, 1988; van Merriënboer & Sweller, 2005). For example, in the task to describe the everyday work of President Obama in a concept map will require a student to know what a concept map constitutes, the content of the map, and the knowledge and skill to successfully handle the concept mapping software. If a student is required to process all this information at the same time in his or her working memory, he or she will likely experience a cognitive overload. On the other hand, a student who has already proficiently acquired the skill of concept mapping using software and who can dedicate most of his or her attention to the content of the concept map will be less likely to experience a cognitive overload in the completion of the task. Now, beginning second language learners seem to be even more vulnerable to cognitive overload who are forced to translate content knowledge (i.e., everyday work of President Obama) and instructions (i.e., what to do and how to use the software) into their native and second language, respectively (e.g., Mayer & Moreno, 2003; Moreno, 2007).We argue that cognitive overload experienced in the context of second language learning might, therefore, not only hinder the acquisition of the new language, but might overtime cause in a student with a low frustration tolerance a disliking of second language learning and the second language itself. To overcome this problem, a teacher might consider scaffolding the task to reduce the cognitive load by teaching students the knowledge and skills of concept mapping sufficiently, before they are going to build a concept map in a second language and/or to provide instructions in the student's native language (e.g., Mayer & Moreno, 2003). We believe that the use of psychometric measures that assess cognitive load (Paas & van Merriënboer, 1993) could be instrumental in the development of technology-based instructions for second language learners. Ideally, the existing measures would need to be provided in a way that teachers would feel comfortable to use when instructions seem to fail or when testing out new technology-based approaches. Furthermore, to allow for a valid assessment the measures would need to be completed by students anonymously, as paper-pencil version, and probably translated into their native language to maintain a low cognitive load during their completion.

CONCLUSION

Technology can help create enriching, social interactive learning experiences for second language learners, especially those in early-childhood education. Even though technology can be a valuable resource, it must be used in a developmentally appropriate manner. Second language learners at the sensory motor, preoperational, and concrete level of cognitive development should be using technology that presents communication in a second language in real-world contexts. This is even true for the learner at the formal operations; however, if technology is too abstract, the learners will not be able to comprehend meaning behind the sounds and the texts. As the second language learner develops, they are able to understand more abstract aspects of communication and can use technology that facilitates their second language abilities at the formal operations and meta-cognitive level. Finally, it is important to consider how the teaching methods correspond with the learners' cognitive stage of development and the technology that is chosen to assist in instruction. In conclusion, it is our hope that the conceptual framework presented above (Figure 1) can be used as rubric for teachers of second languages in early-childhood education to help them choose the appropriate method of language instruction and technology.

Reflecting on Young Children, Second Language Learners and Technology

This section gives you some questions and activities to help you think about how you can use some of the ideas from this chapter in your work.

Research

1. The authors clearly support the use of Concept mapping in the classroom. Use the internet to create a concept web of what you have learned from this chapter.
2. Identify the relationships between Cognitive Development, Second Language Methods, and Technology. Add information from additional reading and net searches to support what you have learned.

Reflect

1. The major peak of language development occurs during early childhood and coincides with the rapid growth and maturation of the brain. What does this statement imply for early childhood education programs? How does this relate to second language learners in your classroom or school?
2. The assumption that language and grammar exist as observable properties is important when seeing why traditional language instruction may not be appropriate for all levels of cognitive development. This is another powerful concept from this chapter about language learning. Please explain what the author meant by this and give specific

examples from your experiences as a professional educator.

3. Figure 1, *Cognitive Development, Second Language Methods, and Technology: An Integrated Framework to Assist the Second Language Teacher* shows how language and cognitive development can be supported through technology. Compare and contrast your understanding of these ideas before and after you read this chapter. How has your thinking changed?
4. The authors discuss different approaches to teaching second language learners in the text. One of these, the Audio-Lingual method, has been popular in most foreign language classes in high schools. Think about classes you have had across the curriculum in your educational career. How many of these used a similar approach to teaching? Identify why each class was or was not supportive of your learning.

Practice

1. This chapter mentions the importance of learning how to communicate in real-world contexts. Discuss this with your peers and identify a list of ideas of how you can make your teaching relate more to real-world contexts. What changes or adaptations can you make in your classroom to support this approach to learning?
2. Compile a list of the five approaches to teaching English language learners mentioned in the text. Discuss which of these you have tried and which you consider successful and why. How do these approaches compare to the Dual Language approach recommended by many early childhood programs in the United States?
3. As the authors continue their discussion of cognition and second language learning they suggest different types of technology for use in your classroom. Create a chart of how you will adjust the suggested technology for the age group you work with. How do you think these tools will support learning not just for second language learners but all learners?
4. *Cognitive load* is becoming an accepted idea in many fields of learning. The hard part will be knowing how much work with second language learners is too much and when your work is not enough. One of the big advantages of technology is how it can support your individual learners in all fields. Plan how you and your colleagues will identify indicators of cognitive load overload and how you will use technology to support individual learners.

REFERENCES

Anderson-Inman, L., & Ditson, L. (1999). Computer-based concept mapping: A tool for negotiating meaning. *Learning and Leading with Technology*, *26*(8), 6–13.

Bachman, L. F., & Palmer, A. S. (1996). *Language testing practice*. Oxford, UK: Oxford University Press.

Berk, L., & Winsler, A. (1995). *Scaffolding children's learning: Vygotsky and early childhood education.* Washington, DC: National Association for the Education of Young Children. (ERIC Document No. ED384443)

Berliner, D. (1991). Educational psychology and pedagogical expertise: New findings and new opportunities for thinking about training. *Educational Psychologist*, *26*(2), 145–155. doi:10.1207/s15326985ep2602_6

Bialystok, E., & Hakuta, K. (1994). *In other words*. New York, NY: Basic Books.

Brown, H. D. (2007). *Teaching by principles: An interactive approach to languagepedagogy* (3rd ed.). White Plains, NY: Pearson Longman.

Canale, M., & Swain, M. (1980). Theoretical bases of communicative approaches to second language teaching and testing. *Applied Linguistics*, 1–47. doi:10.1093/applin/1.1.1

Chapelle, C. A. (2007). Technology and second language acquisition. *Annual Review of Applied Linguistics*, *27*, 98–114. doi:10.1017/S0267190508070050

Chomsky, N. (1964). *Current issues in linguistic theory*. London, UK: Mouton & Co.

Chomsky, N. (1968). *Language and mind.* New York, NY: Harcourt, Brace & World, Inc.

Chomsky, N. (1980). *Rules and representation.* New York, NY: Columbia University Press.

Chularut, P., & DeBacker, T. K. (2004). The influence of concept mapping on achievement, self-regulation, and self-efficacy in students in English as a second language. *Contemporary Educational Psychology*, *29*, 248–263. doi:10.1016/j.cedpsych.2003.09.001

Clark, B. A. (2000, November). First- and second-language acquisition in early childhood. In Issues in early childhood education: Curriculum, teacher education, & disseminationof information. *Proceedings of the Lilian Katz Symposium*, Champaign, IL.

Coleman, D. (2005). Language learning input and input for learning to communicate. *LacusForum*, *31*, 203–213.

Coleman, D. (2006). A formal integrated view of speech, gesture, gaze and its implications for learning. *LACUS Forum*, *32*, 163–172.

Collier, V. P., & Thomas, W. (1995). *Language minority student achievement and program effectiveness. Research summary on ongoing study*. Fairfax, VA: George Mason University.

Corbeil, P. (1999). Learning from the children: Practical and theoretical reflections on playing and learning. *Simulation & Gaming*, *30*(2), 163–180. doi:10.1177/104687819903000206

Flavell, J. H., Miller, P. H., & Miller, S. A. (2002). *Cognitive development* (4th, ed.). Englewood Cliffs, NJ: Prentice Hall.

Gass, S., & Selinker, L. (2001). *Second language acquisition: An introductory course*. Mahwah, NJ: Lawrence Erlbraum.

Goodz, N. S. (1994). Interactions between parents and children in bilingual families. In F. Genesee (Ed.), *Educating second language children: The whole child, the whole curriculum, the whole community.* Cambridge, UK: Cambridge University Press. (ERIC Document No. ED375641)

Grabe, W., & Stoller, F. L. (1997). Content-based instruction: Research foundations. In Snow, M. A., & Brinton, D. M. (Eds.), *The content-based classroom: Perspectives on integrating language and content* (pp. 5–21). White Plains, NY: Longman.

Inhelder, B., & Piaget, J. (1958). *The growth of logical thinking from childhood to adolescence.* New York, NY: Basic Books. doi:10.1037/10034-000

Kane, J. H., & Seingold, K. (1980). Language development: A complex, systematic, and natural process. *Early Childhood Education Journal*, *8*(2), 39–54. doi:10.1007/BF01628027

Ke, F. (2008). A case study of computer gaming for math: Engaged learning for gameplay? *Computers & Education*, *51*, 1609–1620. doi:10.1016/j.compedu.2008.03.003

Kwon, S. Y., & Cifuentes, L. (2009). The comparative effect of individually-constructed vs. collaboratively-constructed computer-based concept maps. *Computers & Education*, *52*, 365–375. doi:10.1016/j.compedu.2008.09.012

Lindfors, J. W. (1991). *Children's language and learning* (2nd ed.). Boston, MA: Allyn and Bacon.

Lotherington, H., Holland, M., Sotoudeh, S., & Zenten, M. (2008). Project-based community language learning: Three narratives of multilingual story-telling in early childhood education. *Canadian Modern Language Review, 65*(1), 125–145. doi:10.3138/cmlr.65.1.125

Mayer, R. E., & Moreno, R. (2003). Nine ways to reduce cognitive load in multimedia learning. *Educational Psychologist, 38*(1), 43–52. doi:10.1207/S15326985EP3801_6

McLaughlin, B. (1984). *Second language acquisition in childhood: Vol. 1. Preschool children* (2nd ed.). Hillsdale, NJ: Erlbaum. (ERIC Document No. ED154604)

Moreno, R. (2007). Optimising learning from animations by minimising cognitive load: Cognitive and affective consequences of signaling and segmentation methods. *Applied Cognitive Psychology, 21*(6), 765–781. doi:10.1002/acp.1348

Murray, G. L. (1999). Autonomy and language learning in a simulated environment. *System, 27*, 295–308. doi:10.1016/S0346-251X(99)00026-3

Ojima, M. (2006). Concept mapping as a pre-task planning: A case study of three Japanese ESL writers. *System, 34*, 566–585. doi:10.1016/j.system.2006.08.003

Oliver, K. (2009). An investigation of concept mapping to improve the reading comprehension of science texts. *Journal of Science Education and Technology, 18*, 402–414. doi:10.1007/s10956-009-9157-3

Oller, J. W. Jr. (1979). *Language testing at school.* London, UK: Methuen.

Paas, F. G. W. C., & van Merriënboer, J. J. G. (1993). The efficiency of instructional conditions: An approach to combine mental-effort and performance measures. *Human Factors, 35*(4), 737–743.

Pérez, B., & Torres-Guzmán, M. (1996). *Learning in two worlds* (2nd ed.). New York, NY: Longman.

Phillips, N. (1968). *Conversational English for the non-English speaking child.* New York, NY: Teacher College Press.

Piaget, J. (1952). *The origins of intelligence in children.* New York, NY: International University Press. doi:10.1037/11494-000

Piaget, J. (1980). The psychogenesis of knowledge and its epistemological significance. In Piattelli-Palmarini, M. (Ed.), *Language and learning: The debate between Jean Piaget and Noam Chomsky* (pp. 23–34). Cambridge, MA: Harvard University Press.

Purpura, J. E. (2004). *Assessing grammar.* Cambridge, UK: Cambridge University Press. doi:10.1017/CBO9780511733086

Royer, R., & Royer, J. (2004). Comparing hand drawn and computer generated concept mapping. *Journal of Computers in Mathematics and Science Teaching, 23*(1), 67–81.

Schwienhorst, K. (2002). Why virtual, why environments? Implementing virtual reality concepts in computer-assisted language learning. *Simulation & Gaming, 33*(2), 196–209.

Sigelman, C. K., & Rider, E. A. (2008). *Life-span human development* (6th ed.). US: Thomson/Wadsworth.

Simina, V., & Hamel, M. J. (2005). CASLA through a social constructivist perspective: WebQuest in project-driven language learning. *ReCALL, 17*(2), 217–228. doi:10.1017/S0958344005000522

Skinner, B. F. (1957). *Verbal behavior.* Englewood Cliffs, NJ: Prentice-Hall. doi:10.1037/11256-000

Son, J. Y., Smith, L. B., & Goldstone, R. L. (2008). Simplicity and generalization: Short-cutting abstraction in children's object categorizations. *Cognition, 108*, 626–638. doi:10.1016/j.cognition.2008.05.002

Sweller, J. (1988). Cognitive load during problem solving: Effects on learning. *Cognitive Science*, *12*(2), 257–285. doi:10.1207/s15516709cog1202_4

Tabors, P. (1997). *One child, two languages.* Baltimore, MD: Paul H. Brookes. (ERIC Document No. ED405987)

van Merriënboer, J. J. G., & Sweller, J. (2005). Cognitive load theory and complex learning: Recent developments and future directions. *Educational Psychology Review*, *17*(2), 147–177. doi:10.1007/s10648-005-3951-0

Vygotsky, L. S. (1962). *Thought and language.* Cambridge, MA: M.I.T. Press. doi:10.1037/11193-000

Yngve, V. H. (1996). *From grammar to science: New foundations for general linguistics*. Philadelphia, PA: John Benjamins Publishing Co.

Ziegler, N. E. (2007). *Task based assessment: Evaluating communication in the real world.* Master's thesis. Retrieved from http://etd.ohiolink.edu/ send-pdf.cgi/ Ziegler%20 Nathan %20E.pdf?acc_num=Toledo 1192757581

ENDNOTES

i Our summary of Piaget's stages is a brief account and geared towards aspects of language development; see elsewhere for a more detailed and comprehensive account of Piaget's (Piaget, 1952; Inhelder & Piaget, 1958.

ii The notion of utterances assumes that there is inherent meaning in sounds. Yngve (1996) argues that we must not refer to spoken sounds as utterances because this implies that language is physically real and not abstract. Instead, spoken sounds should be referred to as articulations because there is no assumption that articulations have inherent meaning.

iii While these pictures do not accurately represent Barack and Michelle Obama, they were the closest images in the software that was used to generate this concept map. Our hope, however, would have been to choose the actual pictures of the President and the First Lady. Nonetheless, the learners would likely be able to make an association between these two pictures and the real pictures of the President and First Lady if they were shown the cartoon pictures in association with the real pictures prior to engaging in the concept mapping activity.

Chapter 9
Science Technology and Young Children

Brian H. Giza
University of Texas at El Paso, USA

ABSTRACT

Teachers of young children have access to an ever increasing diversity of technology tools. This chapter provides a framework for evaluating and applying tools for science in all classrooms. It includes a series of vignettes that illustrate the application of technology in the context of a tools-task-strategy approach.

INTRODUCTION: TEACHING TOOLS, OR TEACHING THINKING?

Early childhood and primary level science teachers, especially novice science teachers, are confronted with a number of challenges when they try to integrate technology into the classroom. Sometimes the tools that they have are not appropriate for young children. Sometimes the tools that they have are not appropriate for anyone - they are obsolete hand-me-downs, computers and software passed from upper grades to the earlier ones. Fortunately, partly due to the reduction of costs of computers, school districts are beginning to equip early grades with computers that are of recent vintage. Even when the computers or other technology tools available are modern and grade-level appropriate, how can they best be used? Where can a teacher turn for ideas, for training, and for high-quality, teacher-tested strategies, for curricula that incorporate technology effectively?

The sustainability and fidelity of high-quality curricula in the classroom is not a new problem. In 1994 George W. Tressel, former head of the National Science Foundation's (NSF) programs on public understanding of science and pre-college curriculum development wrote a bleak assessment of the impact of NSF educational program interventions on improving science education. He noted that the NSF and other agencies had

DOI: 10.4018/978-1-61350-059-0.ch009

Copyright © 2012, IGI Global. Copying or distributing in print or electronic forms without written permission of IGI Global is prohibited.

spent billions in public expenditures and made little change in individual classrooms. Among the statements that he made in this key critique of science policy were: *"...after 30 years, there remains a wide gap between the massive scale of U.S. science education problems and the limited impact of most NSF projects"* (Tressel. 1994, p77). "*Three decades have seen little change in typical classroom practice and little overall impact on the average student*" (p84), and "*Teachers are still intimidated by the time, content and preparation demands of hands-on learning*" (p84).

A generation of students has started and finished school since Tressel wrote this bleak assessment of science reform in the United States. Despite the passage of years and the best efforts of well-meaning professional development programs, hands-on, inquiry-based instruction is still a pedagogical technique that is under-utilized. Tressel's quote that "*teachers are intimidated by the time...demands of hands-on learning*" is still a concern of educators today. The sad truth is there are wonderful inquiry-based curricula available, but that they too-often sit on the shelf because classroom teachers are not prepared to implement them effectively. The same can be said for technology tools in the classroom. One approach has been to purchase and implement a 'one-stop shop', a turn-key technology solution provided by a major provider, whether it is a textbook company, a computer products company, or a science supplies company. It simplifies the implementation for the school, but it includes a new set of hidden costs - it ties the teacher (and the school) into a single path, creating a form of 'product tunnel vision.' The school becomes increasingly connected to one product line, and it becomes less and less likely to explore diverse solutions that may present themselves in the fast-changing world of technology. Despite what the marketing representatives say - or even this author - there is no single product line or approach that has all the answers. A better solution is a well-developed campus or district committee that re-visits and renews the options available on a regular basis and involves the individual teachers in the use of tools and technology strategies. That is the most profitable answer to the question, "*where does a teacher turn to for high-quality curricula that effectively integrate technology*?" High quality curricula and training in their use are available from the NSF, from educational foundations such as the Concord Consortium, from private-public partnerships such as Thinkfinity or from educational development laboratories such as the Southwest Educational Development Laboratory (SEDL), but access to any curriculum is less important than the context in which it is used. Technology integration is most effective when the school collaborates internally to make the most of their technology resources, and when it works with the community to seek out training and support the needs of their teachers and students. George Tressel's concern about the lack of change in classroom practice is valid: although the resources for change can be provided from without, real educational transformation in science and technology must occur from within.

My belief that teachers are both the solution and the obstacle to implementing technology and science in the United States has influenced my decision to write this chapter. I have always had a strong sense of inquiry and interest in learning. I am currently a researcher but have teaching certificates in Composite Science, Life/Earth Science, Art, Dance, Theatre Arts and Geography and an endorsement in Gifted Education. I am currently a professor of technology and science education at the University of Texas. I strongly believe that our issues in science and technology are in part influenced by the environment of consumerism in the United States. We always seem to be looking for a quick fix to issues related to education and teacher training.

This chapter focuses on ways to assist that kind of engaged and active campus planning team - and provides advice and suggestions for the individual teacher who may or may not benefit from the resources that an effective support structure may give. To help users assess and integrate technology in pedagogically sound ways, we frame the use of technology in terms of *tools*, *tasks*, and *strategies*. We recommend that the user is best served when they first consider the *task* that they want to accomplish before they select the *tool* - and that they should consider the *strategy* (pedagogy) that they wish to use before they proceed into the using a particular tool for a task.

There is no magic answer - certainly there is no single tool that will automatically fulfill the instructional and learning style needs of every student in a pedagogically appropriate way. But there are ways to think about and apply the use of technology tools to creatively and effectively address individual and collective student needs. In this chapter we introduce some approaches to looking at tools and tasks to help educators incorporate technology into their teaching.

Objectives

After reading this chapter the reader should be able to select the proper technology tool in context of application of task-appropriate strategies that improve young students' understanding of concepts and motivation to learn. They will also be able to explain the difference between *tool-task coherence* and *tool-task independence*. Along the way they will learn about some major categories of technology tools and ways to use them with young children.

The reader will also:

- Develop an understanding of categories of tasks
- Develop an understanding of categories of tools
- Be able to apply strategies for identifying the right tool
- Be able to apply strategies for applying the right tool
- Be able to apply strategies for assessing how effectively a tool is being used.

BACKGROUND: TOOLS, TASKS AND STRATEGIES IN EARLY AND PRIMARY LEVEL SCIENCE EDUCATION

The International Society for Technology in Education National Educational Technology Standards for Students lists four general categories of technology tools (ISTE, 2007, 2008). These are summarized as follows in the online version of the standards: (1) Technology productivity tools, (2) Technology communications tools, (3) Technology research tools, and (4) Technology problem-solving and decision-making tools. These international standards are complemented by categories expressed at the regional, State, and even district or campus levels. There are other schemas that divide tools into categories - for years the author has divided tools into (1) data collection and analysis tools, (2) communication tools, (3) productivity tools, and (4) information retrieval and management tools. Each set of categories has its rationale. In the author's schema, digital cameras, data collection probes, and microscopes fall into one category because they are all tools that can be used for observing and acquiring data about the world. Technology productivity tools (such as word processors) are common to both schemas. But a product such as Microsoft PowerPoint (or its competitors, such as OpenOffice Impress) can actually fit more than one tool category. PowerPoint is usually included in the category of productivity tools - it is, after all, most commonly used as a tool for producing presentations. Or, perhaps it would best fit in the category of communications tools? Presentations are, after all, a form of communication, even if it is not a web-browser or email program (other tools commonly considered communications tools). But then, there are times when the versatile PowerPoint program can be used in different ways. Because PowerPoint can be used as a 'container' for multimedia artifacts, including audio, graphics, and video (in addition to text), and because it can link to a variety of other resources, such as spreadsheets or Acrobat files, it is sometimes used as a digital portfolio. PowerPoint is an easy-to-use aggregator of digital artifacts that, when properly organized, can be used as an information organization and storage tool. It is arguably as powerful as many proprietary digital portfolio tools - so it could logically be classified as an ISTE category "Technology decision-making tool" or in the author's "information retrieval and information management" tools category. Which category schema is used is not important. What is significant is the fact that PowerPoint may fit into more than one category - depending on the tasks to which it is applied.

PowerPoint's versatility makes it a good product for introducing the concepts of *tool-task independence* and *tool-task coherence*. These are two closely related viewpoints about the application of tools to tasks. We can use PowerPoint to illustrate the two viewpoints in this way. When PowerPoint is used in its traditional, common modality - as a presentation tool for enhancing lectures - it is *coherent* to its original, commonly understood tasks. There are plenty of books and workshops on how to use PowerPoint as a presentation tool. Some even note that, as is the case with the traditional blackboard (or its descendant, the interactive whiteboard) a tool is most powerfully used when it is in the hands of the student, instead of the teacher. PowerPoint used for presentations is an example of *tool-task coherence* - the tool is being used to accomplish its traditional task. But when PowerPoint is used as a repository or archive for student work, when each digital file is an aggregation of an individual student's scanned or acquired graphics, videos, sound files, and documents, it becomes adapted to a new task, one that is independent of its traditional use. This is an example of *tool-task independence*, and a mature tool-user, an experienced educator who can reflect upon and select the best tool(s) for a task is well served by being able to understand and be open to both points of view. A user who can operate from both points of view will have more options available to them, and a deeper understanding of what a tool can do.

Tool-task-coherence is the most common way that users interact with technologies. It approaches the use of a tool and a task in terms of a single dimension, the use of the tool as it has been promoted and designed. There is nothing wrong with that, but it is a base level of tool use. It reaches its peak when a user masters tool use. It can be seen as an analogue to the "application" level of the *Taxonomy of Educational Objectives* made famous as "Bloom's Taxonomy" in the 1950s (Bloom et al., 1956) or at the "applying" level of Anderson and Krathwohl's revised version of the taxonomy (Anderson, Krathwohl, et al., 2001; Krathwohl, 2002). Tool-task-independence adds additional dimensions and can be seen as the use of a tool at a higher level of capability, in creative ways that go beyond simple mastery. Tool-task-independence is the use of a tool in creative ways -- applying it to new tasks in ways that were not proposed by the tool's designers or marketers. It becomes possible when a user masters the application of a tool and understands its capabilities sufficiently well to extend it to new uses. To use as an analogy the terminology of the *Revised Taxonomy of Educational Objectives* described by Anderson and Krathwohl (2001), tool-task-independence is when a user can use a tool at higher levels, to analyze and evaluate the tool in the context of varied tasks and strategies and to use it creatively in new ways.

Consider another set of venerable tools that have been part of the technology of learning in classrooms for generations: The blackboard, or its modern analogue, the whiteboard (we shall deal with the descendant, the interactive whiteboard separately).In this case using the tool, a writing surface upon which a person can write and display ideas in front of a class, is well understood. When it is used in teacher-centered ways the teacher might simply writes out lecture notes or communications that are directed from the teacher to the student. When it is used in student-centered ways the teacher guides student writing on the board, assisting the student to express their ideas, eliciting an understanding of the student's thinking so that they may interact with that student and help mold their learning.

A more recent technology for displaying text (and other content) in the classroom is the interactive whiteboard (Gillen, 2008). There are several versions, but the basic premise is that a touch-sensitive surface can display and interact with content from a computer interface. There are products for turning regular whiteboards into surfaces of this kind, and much more sophisticated systems that either project content or display it internally on a touch screen. Whichever version is used is less important than HOW the technology is used. Some interactive whiteboards allow users to save user input, whether it is writing, doodles, or mathematical equations, to digital images that may be stored in the computer or sent across the Internet. The greatest power in this form of technology is not engendered by the use of the tool in the hands of the teacher, but, as was the case for the simple whiteboard or its predecessor the blackboard, the tool is most powerful when it frees up expression in the hands of students. As new display interfaces enter the educational community, it is important for users to remember that it is not the tool, but how it is used that gives it real power in learning settings.

Task Analysis and Affordability Analysis

There are other considerations that are critical in effectively applying technology in the classroom - at any grade level and in any content area. Among these are an understanding of the student and an understanding of the learning objective that one desires to accomplish. In educational technology the process of breaking down the instructional needs, matching them to learner capabilities, and identifying the most appropriate strategies is known as task analysis (Jonassen et al., 1999). It has been used in industry to generate and review production systems, and it has a venerable history in special education where it is one approach to developing the modifications that support learning in students with disabilities. Task analysis has a venerable heritage in information technology and instructional design. (John & Kieras, 1996; Jonassen et al., 1999; Jonassen & Carr, 2000). Teachers perform similar analyses of the learning tasks and tools available to them on a regular basis. Without delving into the theoretical underpinnings of task analysis, a simple method for doing this involves sitting down for a minute and listing the task that the teacher wants to accomplish, the tools available, and then making notes and a sub-list of the procedures and plans for accomplishing that task. A related concept is affordance analysis, which has nothing to do with the dollar cost of a technology. In affordance analysis the capability of a technology -- what it *affords* the user -- is categorized (Bower, 2008). For example, traditional computer-based spreadsheets afford the learner the ability to manipulate numbers in different scenarios. Web-based collaborative spreadsheets such as Google Docs afford users additional features, including the ability for workers to interact to explore scenarios from varied remote locations. But web-based tools are limited in applicability if all of the users that need them do not have access to the high-speed Internet connections required to get to them. As part of affordance analysis a list of the features of each version of the spreadsheet would be created so that the features could be used in designing or adapting a curriculum task. Affordance analysis would contribute, for example, to the decisions associated with engaging home-bound students in collaborative science activities. One tool (Google docs) would be appropriate in a setting in which all of the participants have access to high speed Internet at home. The other (a computer software-based spreadsheet) would be the choice if all of the users have computers, but some do not have Internet access at home.

Technology and Universal Design

David Rose, Anne Meyer, and their collaborators at the Center for Applied Special Technology (CAST) have led the development of a series of strategies for considering and responding to student learning needs by the appropriate application of technology. Their approaches, collectively referred to as "Universal Design for Learning" (UDL) were originally developed for use with students with disabilities, but were equally powerful and effective when used with 'traditional' students. They apply a social learning approach that takes into consideration three brain 'networks': The *recognition network* (which sees objects and places them in context), the *strategic network* (which determines how you will reflect on an object and gain information from it), and the affective network (which determines how closely you pay attention) (Rose & Meyer, 2002, Rose et al., 2005). UDL, developed to meet the needs of 'special learners' has had a fortuitous unintended consequence. All learners are special in the sense that all learners are unique, and UDL gives educators methods and materials for reaching learners in many new ways. Each of us brings a set of talents and challenges to every learning situation. UDL helps educators assess the unique talents and challenges and apply technology to maximize learning. In doing so UDL provides a wide set of tools that all learners can adapt to direct their own learning, providing many paths to achieving a goal. In an example outside of education, technology has made portable audio players almost ubiquitous. Although music was the driving force behind the iPod and its brethren, as an unintended development, audio books took off. Now many new automobiles feature MP3-compliant audio systems and truck stops have moved audio book displays into shelves that once were dedicated to baseball caps, tire gauges and country music. A previously niche industry, the educational audio lecture series (e.g.: *The Teaching Company*) has also taken off and those who desire to may listen to an educational text while cleaning house or driving across town. Parents may now complement classroom learning with appropriate audio lessons for their children. In this case, audio, a relatively little-used educational resource has been re-purposed in many new settings that the individual can choose to incorporate into their learning environments. This is Universal Design for Learning - the use of technology to provide educational content in a variety of ways and according to the individualized needs or desires of the learner. Understanding the varied tools available gives an educator a powerful new set of strategies for improving learning in their students. An educator who understands their tools well, and who has analyzed the learning tasks appropriately, now has a broader set of strategies available to target the learning needs of ALL of their students, whatever their gifts or challenges.

ISSUES, CONTROVERSIES, PROBLEMS

Many teachers in early grades are generalists and might feel uncomfortable teaching science. They often think that they must convey lists of facts - facts that they aren't sure that they themselves know. Actually, in the early grades the most important thing they can do to get the spark of inquiry burning in a young person is to encourage students to ask questions, and the systematically find out the answer to those questions. In the opinion of the author of this chapter, the most important thing that an educator of young children can do is to help those young minds learn to think like problem solvers.

Children at early ages experience science as part of their general sense of wonder about the world. As a science educator, it is the hope of the author that if we do nothing else that we nurture that sense of wonder and that we couple it with a burning desire to find out the reason why. To do so we need to help our children construct well-formed questions, questions that lend themselves to solutions through the tools and processes of science.

There are questions that we as educators are also obliged to ask. For example, the most important question a science education teacher can ask is "*What is it that I want my students to learn*?" Once they have an answer to this first question they might ask themselves: "*What resources are available to me to help me help my students master their learning goal*?" Among those resources are technology tools and the strategies to use them - we all are novices at first and mastery of any tool takes practice. A final framing question that follows after the "What resources are available" one is "*How can I use the resource in creative ways that will generate a positive, inquiry-based learning environment in which my students are challenged but not defeated*?" In answering these questions it might help to lay out a list of tools, tasks, and strategies. Here is one way to do so:

Make a table with four columns and as many rows as you need. In the first column write down what it is that you want students to learn (the task), and in the second column write down what tools are available for you to use. In the third column write down what pedagogy you would like to use (the strategy). In the fourth column write down what is keeping you from using a tool to accomplish the task using that strategy. The fourth column can guide you with concrete items to think about when considering one's own specific, discrete professional development needs.

Tools for Tasks and Strategies

To help facilitate the process of considering tools, tasks, and strategies we have provided some figures below to stimulate thinking about what is possible (Figure 1 and Figure 2). In each row of the figures are a few suggestions that an educator may use in planning technology use in their classroom, followed by notes and comments. Figure 1 looks at technology from the point-of view of the tool. In other words, it helps answer the question "*I have this set of tools - what can I do with them*?" Figure 2 looks at technology in terms of tasks. It helps answer the question "*I want to do this task, what tool or tools might I use to accomplish it?*" Also, if a tool is available in a cross-platform free version it is indicated in italics.

Tool Use Suggestions

Teachers using technology for data collection related to science have a number of options today. The hardware has become increasingly easy-to-use. Large environmental science curriculum programs such as GLOBE (Global Learning and Observations to Benefit the Environment) have advocated probeware use and included extensive online professional development in probeware in their protocols (Means et al., 2001).

Probes in the Early Childhood Classroom

The Concord Consortium (Concord.org, 2010), a leading proponent of technology integration in education has partnered with several probe instrument providers to develop recommendations, procedural guides, and pedagogical guides for teachers who wish to implement the use of probes at all grade levels, including in early childhood classrooms. The organization has developed several leadership initiatives for the use of probes in the classroom, including the Technology Enhanced Elementary and Middle School Science (TEEMSS) initiative (Metcalf & Tinker, 2003). Among the Consortium's strategies in the classroom integration of probes and sensors in science are partnerships with the well-respected Exploratorium (http://www.explarotorium.org) informal science education site, free and open-source software for data collection and analysis, the development of inexpensive probes, and teacher activity materials that integrate probes in inquiry-based science activities. They have also partnered with several of the major science

Figure 1. Tools and sample tasks for the elementary science classroom. Free and cross platform tools are noted in italics.

Tool/Tools	Task	Strategy	Comment
Digital cameras and presentation programs (*Gnu Image Manipulation Program 'GIMP'; OpenOffice.org Impress*)	*'Science Observations Collage'*; PowerPoint slideshow of plants and animals in our neighborhood	Life Science taxonomy: Students work with digital images that they acquire, rearranging them and integrating them into student work product that represents their understanding of native life forms in their local region.	This updates the venerable school activity in which students construct a photo album of living things from magazine photos. With the wide availability of digital imaging tools students can now collect images of living creatures with digital cameras and then sort them in a classroom activity. PowerPoint and OpenOffice Impress are good tools for collecting the images into slide pages. Tux Paint stamps provide an easy and fun way for teachers to introduce Life Science classification activities in early grades.
Audio recording software (*Audacity*) and web-based media players	Recording animal sounds; recording student presentations	Life Science taxonomy: Students go to an online location that features birdsongs or other wild animal sounds and download recordings of animals. Then they use sound recording/editing software to record short *'I am there'* podcasts in which they talk about the role of animals in ecosystems	There are several commercial sites that feature wild animal sounds, but there are also a number of good ones that are free including the British Library Board "*Listen to Nature*" site, and Cornell Laboratory of Ornithology's Macauley Library online archive. In some cases licenses permit students to download sounds for editing and use, in others they must pre-set a page in a browser or presentation link to play it.
Graphics editing (*Gnu Image Manipulation Program 'GIMP'; Tux Paint*	Creating and editing images of plants and animals	Life Science taxonomy: Students in grades K-2 use graphics programs to invent and construct an insect that is adapted to a particular niche. Students write "Niche notes" describing their niche and then	Tux Paint drawing tools provide an easy and fun way for teachers to work with graphics in early grades. Another well-regarded cross-platform graphics program for children is Canvastic (http://www.canvastic.com).

materials providers to ensure that their interfaces and activities are compatible with the available commercial tools. In this case a single organization has developed tools (temperature, light and other probes and sensors), applied them to tasks (classroom science data collection), and integrated their use with pedagogically-appropriate strategies (the TEEMSS activities). Many science equipment vendors sell probes that are compatible with TEEMSS activities, and a list of the vendors is available at http://probesight.concord.org/supplier/template_section.htm. This organization has taken things a step further and in their advocacy of making tools as widely available as possible they have developed a number of resources that will help educators build their own probes. Building your own probes is extremely empowering for teachers as well as upper-grade students, although it is certainly not an early childhood school student activity. Still, the easy-to-follow step

Figure 2. Tasks and early childhood and elementary science

Task	Sample Tool	Strategy	Comment
Classifying items in soil	Excel; iWork numbers	Students describe characteristics in soil that they observe. Lists can be reorganized into classification keys that may be constructed in various ways.	Generating a dichotomous key is a useful strategy in teaching observation skills among young children.
Collaborative writing with online software	Wikis, Google Docs	Students generate and collaborate upon the development of pages that describe their observations. Later they may extend and elaborate upon their work. Teachers can review the level of contribution of each individual student.	Several wiki sites provide free access to the wiki collaborative environments for students and educators. Many school districts are setting up Wiki software for student collaborations and to enable teachers to share conversations and plans with parents.
Assessing students during activities	Clickers	Students review a problem and submit their answers to the problem. Then the teacher reviews the answers, and guides the students to come to a consensus answer, using clickers to assess student understanding at each step.	Clickers are wireless remote instruments that permit individual students to submit responses that are aggregated in real time on a computer. When used as part of a constructivist question-prediction-confirmation strategy they can provide quick feedback to the teacher on student understanding of the steps in problem-solving.
Teaching writing with science	Online collaborative writing tools	Google Docs, Wikis	Students can share writing, and because some of these tools can highlight or mark individual contributions, teachers can track the collaborative process and ensure that work is shared equally.
Teacher assessment - supporting second language learners while building science skills	Tracking vocabulary words used by children	Spreadsheets (Excel, iNumber)	Spreadsheets allow teachers to track individual student use of vocabulary words and mastery of science tasks. In science vocabulary second language learners are presented with even greater challenges. Spreadsheets are one way of recording and tracking student progress.

by step instructions for building and using your own probes are included as part of the Concord Consortium's Information Technology in Science Instruction (ITSI) initiative (http://itsi.concord.org). The tools are made available in a variety of ways (by purchase from a variety of vendors, or via instructions on building them yourself), the tasks in which the tools may be used are realistic, content-driven ones, and the suggested strategies are pedagogically appropriate at a variety of grade levels, including the early science classroom.

Commercial or high-tech probes and probeware are not the only options available for incorporating data collection devices into the early science classroom. In Vignette 1 (below) a teacher uses a bit of initiative and common garden-supplier tools to integrate technology in inquiry-based science. Technology for detecting and evaluating conditions in the soil, air, and water are now commonly available for very low cost. Inexpensive commercial GPS units also have transformed the availability of science related activities.

Vignette 1: PH Probes in Early and Primary Level Classrooms

Mr. Owen has been a second grade teacher for a few years, and while seeking a Masters degree in science education he took a course in technology in the science classroom. He enjoyed working with data collection probes and data collection devices but was a bit concerned that all of the applications he learned about involved late middle school and high school level lessons. This year he was determined to use probes in his classroom. He had heard of the GLOBE program and looked it up online and was pleased to find training videos at the http://www.globe.gov site that he could download and watch. One showed how he could perform pH tests on soils. He downloaded the protocol instruction sheet from GLOBE but when he tried to obtain the sensors from his school science materials center he was disappointed to find that they were not available for his grade strand. Soil characterization was a key skill in his state science standard and he felt frustrated until he noticed a set of soil pH probes in the garden section of a neighborhood store. He made his case to his principal and was able to purchase five digital probes for under $100 with the Principal's admonition that he would "show the rest of the teachers how to use them in science projects." He adapted the GLOBE soil pH protocol activity to incorporate the commonly available probes and was able to teach calibration, data collection, and graphing along with the needed soil science content. He did not know it, but in terms of a tool-task-strategy viewpoint he was applying a tool (pH probe) to a task (engaging students in an inquiry based soil science activity) by adapting a commonly available resource (another tool, the GLOBE protocols online) to implement a strategy (hands-on inquiry-based science). He did so by reflecting upon the kind of technology he needed and adapting similar tools to replace the unavailable recommended tool.

Computers in the Early Grades

Robert Tinker, Director of the Concord Consortium has said "microcomputers and computer-based telecommunications offer flexible tools for communication, data acquisition, instrumentation, computation, analysis, and visualization. These tools empower students to do science, to undertake investigations of immediate interest and to build a durable understanding of the underlying science" (Tinker, 1991).

In the working lifetime of most of the readers of this text our world has been transformed by technology. The World Wide Web, originally a clever set of programs used by the developed as to organize and share documents on his computer (Berners-Lee & Frischetti, 1999) has grown into an information system that has expanded access to information to a degree unimagined by persons who grew up in the world of library index cards and land-line telephones. The addition of wireless networks to the mix has increased the utility and portability of the information resources available almost anywhere. While there are appropriate concerns about the content available online, most schools have found a compromise in the form of proxy servers that filter content and limit access to inappropriate sites. The World Wide Web, once a location in which resources were provided by a content manager (Web 1.0) has now been re-purposed to a location where individuals can create and manage their own content (Web 2.0). Examples of Web 2.0 environments are YouTube (and its educational equivalent, TeacherTube), Facebook and its social networking peers, Wiki-Pedia, and other Wikis (collaborative content creation sites). Many of the major players in technology have created sites for educators to experience training or to share ideas or to use collaboration tools online. Apple has the Classroom of Tomorrow- Today Initiative (http://ali.apple.

com/acot2/). Google has an 'apps for schools' and other education initiatives (http://www.google.com/educators), and Microsoft has a number of sites, including Microsoft Education Labs (http://www.educationlabs.com). There are also private/public partnerships that have led educational computing forward in less proprietary ways. Two examples of these are the Concord Consortium (http://www.concord.org) and the One Laptop per Child Initiative (http://laptop.org).

As the costs of computers have come down new education-friendly platforms have become available that make it possible for districts to provide a computer to each and every educator and student. The battle is on - will districts and educational purchasers commit to low cost and flexible netbooks, to touchscreen-enabled tablet computers, or will another technology - perhaps an extension of the smart phone - become the most practical tool for bringing computing power into the hands of every child? Time will tell, but it will not take long. The next few years will be interesting ones for computers in education. The way students get their information is also changing. Digital textbooks are entering the market and their ability to be delivered at lower cost and with a wide variety of ancillaries and online support sites make them likely to replace many textbooks in the near future. Standardized connectors such as the USB interface make it possible to connect data collection probes directly to low cost laptops, bypassing the data collection interfaces that formerly drove up the cost of science probeware kits. It is already possible for an early level educator to *engage* their students with a streaming video over a broadband connection in their classroom, and follow that with an *explore* activity that uses inexpensive data probes connected to the individual students' computers. The teacher might use an interactive whiteboard to *explain* and *evaluate* student understanding as the students transmit their responses to the teacher via clickers. The teacher can disaggregate the clicker-transmitted responses and use them to fashion individual projects for the students to pursue as *extensions* to the lesson. The 5E lesson cycle is well-suited to the classroom of the 21st century.

Vignette 2: Clickers for Evaluation

This year Mr. Kim's school provided him with a new tool for use with his first grade students. It was a set of clicker, small units that allow students to transmit answer choices wirelessly to his computer. At first he was suspicious. It seemed that the clickers were a technology that was designed to fit within the traditional teacher-directed instructional mode, but after experimenting a bit Mr. Kim began to see some other ways to use the tool. Today he wanted to explore the concept of machines with them. He wanted to make sure that he was not leaving any child behind at any step in his construction of the idea of a machine being a product of many interacting parts. He began by distributing his clickers to each table of three students. First, as an engage activity he projected a few moments of a video of some monster trucks from a recent news show, stopping it at a particularly exciting moment, one that clearly showed a truck with all of its exaggerated dimensions. Then he asked his first question: "Class, put your heads together and tell me: "how many parts make the truck go? Decide among your group and input your number into the clicker." Then he played a two minute piece of music on his computer to provide a 'timer countdown' for the reflection stage. When the music ended he checked his computer, and seeing that one group had not submitted their response he stepped over by them and gently helped them resolve their conflict. A moment later he had all of the responses in his computer's clicker software. He generated a bar graph and displayed it on his interactive whiteboard. There was a fairly wide distribution - from four to twelve, with three groups sending an answer of six. Equipped with the graph and the information about which group had submitted each answer he began eliciting explanations from each group. One group had said "five" so he chose a member of that group

(Sarah) and asked her to explain. Sarah looked at her group members and said "There are four wheels and an engine, that is five things." Mr. Kim thanked her and turned to the rest of the class. "Is that all that makes it go?" He asked. After rotating the questions around the groups he had elicited a much longer list: The driver, the gasoline, even the axle - this from a child whose parent owned a car repair shop. The next steps of the lesson extended into the presentation of the wheel as a simple machine, with a set of wheels that were round and some shaped like squares, or other polygons. The students had time to explore pushing and pulling the round and not-round wheels and generate ideas about the function of wheels. At various places in the lesson Mr. Kim would pause and ask students to collaborate and come up with a decision that was transmitted to his computer via the clicker. Mr. Kim was using the clickers as a tool for supporting a constructivist lesson that could have utilized simple 'raising of hands' but the clickers gave him additional data that provided him with insight into the thinking of individuals and of group dynamics.

Digital Imaging in the Classroom

Digital imaging can generally be divided into two categories: (1) acquiring or converting previously existing images into digital form, and (2) acquiring and storing new images. Scanners are the best known tool for the first category, and digital cameras are the best known tool in the second category. Individual images can be combined of course, so video also fits into these categories, almost always into category two, although cel-animation (e.g.: traditional animated cartoons) is an example of video produced in category one.

Cameras and the computer have become a match made in educational heaven. They can be used to 'fix' (store images of) the world in ways that permit students and educators to explore it in ways that were simply impossible in the past. Sometimes it is merely as an enhancement to a previously well-established lesson, sometimes it is by providing new windows into understanding that were unavailable without the capabilities of a digital imaging device and the software for processing and enhancing the images produced by the device. The capabilities provided by high-quality, low cost cameras are now being matched by high-quality, low-cost image-processing software. One of the best bargains available are open-source graphics programs such as Tux Paint (a delightful and free drawing program for children) and The Gnu Image Manipulation Program, or 'GIMP', a powerful but free graphics program with a dizzying array of sophisticated tools. The Gimp can even assemble image sequences into animations, making it useful for studying phenomena that take place over time, such as metamorphosis or plant growth (Giza, 2010).

Inexpensive webcams also provide a useful tool for the science classroom. They greatly enhance a classroom's view of the world - whether they are pointed out the window at a bird's nest in a tree, or at butterfly larvae going through their life cycle. The tools for capturing periodic images are almost always provided as part of the webcam software, and are now being provided as part of add-ons for many computer operating system (e.g.: the Windows XP Timershot Powertoy which is a free enhancement for Windows XP computers). Some vendors have even adapted webcam technology to microscopy and several inexpensive microscopes are available that can capture images directly to computers for editing as video or still images. In Figure 3 (below) an inexpensive DigitalBlue QX5 microscope has been trained on the wall of a container holding Painted Lady butterfly larvae. Windows Timershot was used to take an image through the side of the container every 60 seconds, and one image has been selected and brought into the GIMP graphics program for enhancement. The project is described in greater detail as Vignette 3, below.

Figure 3. A close-up of a Painted Butterfly larva acquired with an IntelPlay Qx5 microscope and Windows Timershot being edited with the Gnu Image Manipulation Program

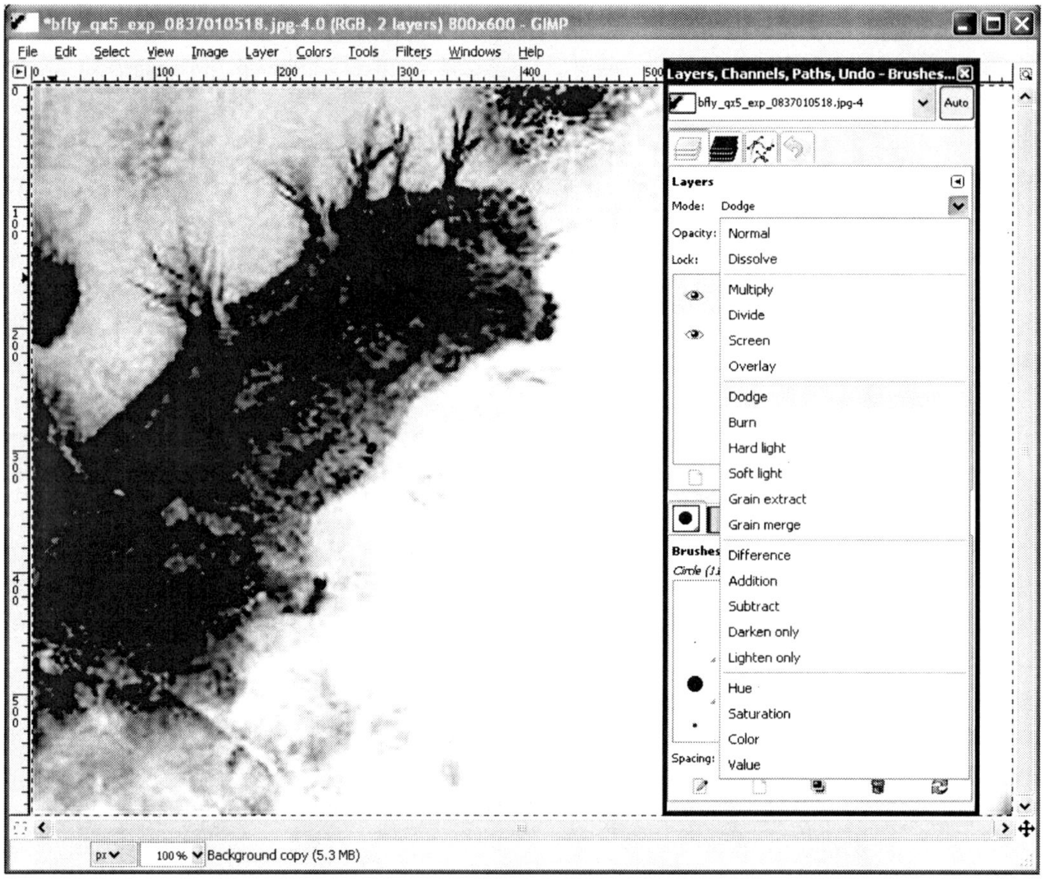

Vignette 3: Exploring Science with Image Sequences and Animation

In this activity Mrs. Robinson has obtained some butterfly larva and culture from her district's "live materials center". She has learned through prior experience that butterflies rarely emerge from their pupae at opportune times. So she has adapted a small plastic container and inserted a webcam into one end. The software that came with the webcam permits her to set up the camera to take an image periodically, one per minute (a free product for Windows XP, the Windows Timershot Powertoy will also do this). As the time approaches for the butterfly to emerge she will shorten the interval to two images per minute. JPEG format images take up very little space, and if she takes two pictures a minute for a month she will need between ten and thirty gigabytes for the 86400 images. That is a lot of space, but easily within the capacity of a modern computer. Her webcam becomes a "robot eye" watching over her class science project. Later she can select an interesting sequence of images, or even all of them, and import them into movie-making or animation software. In Windows a free and open source product called VirtualDub will import appropriately named image sequences and turn them into video. Windows MovieMaker will turn image sets into video as will Microsoft PhotoStory. A free product for Apple computers called FrameByFrame will do so as will many other commercial video production and animation products, including Apple QuickTime Pro. In this case Mrs. Robinson has a plethora of resources available for her to do "time-shifting." To accomplish her task she will need to understand her tools (culturing live insects, web-cams, software for image capture, and software for compiling image sequences to video); she will need to be able to apply her available technology to the task (digital observation of change over time). Of course she will need to do so in the context of a pedagogically-appropriate strategy. To ensure that students are engaged in all stages of the science activity she builds a daily observation protocol that begins with a KWL chart about metamorphosis and then has students record changes in the insect life stages and behaviors in their notebooks. Each day she briefly reviews images acquired by the time-delay webcam software and the class votes on their favorites for that day. The project culminates in individualized presentations that use student-selected images to describe the butterflies' life-cycle stages. At each major stage along the way, such as when the larvae begin attaching themselves to leaves and forming a chrysalis, she is able to access appropriate image sequences and review the process in greater detail than she could have if the students had been restricted to viewing the stages through the moments available during their class period.

Finding and Using Online Resources

As the amount of information available to us has increased it has become increasingly evident that mere information retrieval is not sufficient. Information evaluation is equally important. As certain search engines have come to dominate the process of seeking and finding answers to questions it should be noted that the top ten hits in a key word search are not going to provide appropriate answers to all questions. Consider the following exercise: Let's say that we want to find a recipe that uses Macintosh apples. If you use a major search engine and simply search on the term "apple" or "apple macintosh" you are not likely to find a useful hit among the first few thousands. But if you understand and can use Boolean filters (and, not, plus, minus) you can quickly find a recipe among the top search hits. Try constructing a more appropriate search string: "apple +recipe +macintosh -computer." The plus and minus filters restrict the search to the kinds of subjects you are interested in. Even more daunting is the task of evaluating the quality of resources on the web. Although it has greatly improved, many educators are extremely suspicious of the Wikipedia. Still it is an excellent place to start, and a strategy that begins with Wikipedia and that compares its findings to other sources is not a bad way to explore the answers to questions. It isn't just the ease of finding data, but the quality of the data, the trust that one can put into it that is a critical component for educators. That is why "Where did this information come from?" is a key question that every educator should ask whenever they are incorporating Internet research into a lesson.

Fortunately there are many highly regarded, trusted data repositories that can be incorporated into classroom lessons. They vary from enormous archives of historical artifacts such as the American Memory site at the Library of Congress online (http://memory.loc.gov), or museum collections like those of the Smithsonian Museum of Natural History online (http://www.mnh.si.edu/), to more dedicated sites such as bird song repositories. Two excellent locations for listening to bird songs from all over the world are the British Library Board's Listen to Nature site (http://www.bl.uk/listento-nature/main.html) and the Cornell Laboratory of Ornithology's Macauley Library online (http://macaulaylibrary.org). The sheer numbers of resources are daunting - and the strategy mentioned earlier in this chapter, that of taking a moment and listing tools, tasks, and strategies, will help an educator filter down to the kind of resources they need for a particular lesson. In vignette 4, below, the teacher incorporates online audio as an engage activity to help students visualize the life of birds with which they are unfamiliar. Then the students use graphics programs and search engines to develop story books that describe the environment of each bird.

Vignette 4: Building a Story Book

Mrs. Luna has been teaching 3rd grade for three years. She is very confident in her teaching and has received professional development in teaching 3rd grade science. She knows that in 3rd grade the National Science Education Standards (NSES) emphasize Life Science activities that support learning about "organisms and environments" (National Research Council, 1996, p. 106). She wants to try something that she saw in an educational technology conference she attended earlier in the year. She is fortunate to have relatively modern computers in her classroom - eight Apple Macintosh computers and ten small netbooks running Microsoft Windows. All of them are Internet-connected and multimedia-enabled. The problem is, she has sixteen students and although she has the luxury of having a small number of students and sufficient computers for each student, the computers are mixed between two operating systems. She wants to engage the children in the production of a story book about birds of the world in which the children describe the characteristics of each bird.

Mrs. Luna will do her project over three days, with a different set of activities on each day. She will use an adaptation of the well-established '5E' learning cycle: engage, explore, explain, elaborate, and evaluate. On the first day, her "bird classification' day she plans to engage her students by creating the list of birds and characteristics, and then have the children take turns reading about each bird. She will take her students online to visit a couple of Internet-based bird song archives and play the sounds of each bird. On day two her students will be 'exploring birds' through the use of Internet sites and another free, cross platform, and 'kid-friendly' graphics software product that integrates a collection of approximately 30 bird images. That product, Tux Paint can also play bird sounds or names while using the bird 'stamps'. Thankfully, since she has a mix of computers in her classroom Tux Paint can be obtained with versions that install to directories without administrator rights. She was able to get a version for both her Macintosh and for her Windows computers from http://www.Tux Paint.org. As part of their bird graphic, using Tux Paint's text tool each student must also incorporate a short description of the bird's environment. Mrs. Luna helps the students find this information at the bird song sites.

On the third day, her 'bird book' day, Mrs. Luna will have the students build a set of pictures around each bird. She will have students build the pictures in Tux Paint on the Macintosh computers, save them to png format (the native graphics file format supported by Tux Paint) and then import them to a presentation OpenOffice.org Impress, a free office presentation product similar to Microsoft PowerPoint. Once she has the images in OpenOffice she can create her multimedia picture 'book'. In a pinch she knows she can switch to using any of the computers for any of the steps - all of the software used is cross-platform and free, many using the user-friendly Gnu license that permits her to give the software away to her students (Gnu.org, 2008).

She knows that when working with third graders she will be dealing with short attention spans - and in the case of a couple of the children, VERY short attention spans. She also knows that these children have learned basic keyboarding and mouse skills. As is the case with all of her activities, planning is the key. She wants to integrate reading with her bird classification science activity - and technology is the vehicle for both the science and the reading objectives. When setting up the activity Mrs. Luna scribbled out a little chart for herself with a list of what the children would do and what she would do as part of her planning. The chart helps her stay on top of things in a class with many busy hands, and it also helps her set up the computers and keep track of time. When the class finishes the project she uses a USB thumb drive to copy the presentation onto each computer. When parent night comes around later that month she can sit each parent and their child in front of a computer, looking at the project (and others) while she spends time talking with individual parents about their own child's needs and accomplishments. It should be noted that Mrs. Luna used free and cross platform tools because of her mix of operating systems. There are appropriate proprietary tools (e.g.: Windows PhotoStory) that accomplish the same task within a single software - but that are not cross-platform. Mrs. Luna, a technologically proficient 'digital native' was confident enough to explore the options that individual tools gave her.

Remarks: Mrs. Luna is in a rare situation - enough computers for each student. They aren't all the same type, but by using high-quality, free, open-source, cross-platform software she can improve her ability to use them together in a common activity. Her colleague Mr. Allard works at a school with only one computer per class and so he must use a different strategy to accomplish the same task. He must work with the computer in a 'station' approach; setting up the tools and having students work on the computer in pairs over a more extended set of days. Each student still gets to use the computer in much the same way, but the entire process takes more days. That is satisfactory for him, since he integrates reading activities and kinesthetic 'bird plays' in his lessons. Each teacher is a master of their craft, integrating technology in ways that are adapted to their resources. The key is that they know what task they want to do (integrate images and sound in a life-science presentation created by the students), they understand the tools sufficiently well to be able to use each software tool effectively, and they can adapt their strategies to maximize the effectiveness of the tool and task in a learning exercise.

FUTURE TRENDS

Technologies available to the teacher will undoubtedly continue to become more and more common, as well as lowering in cost. This is a double edged sword -- as our world continues to create new tools teachers will be split between the need to adopt a tool and the need to teach in the most effective way they know. The answer lies in constant renewal of teacher skills, not just in technology but in all phases of our educational setting. We are doing a disservice to our students if we do not meet the challenge of learning along with them, engaging in a lifelong enhancement of our own educational skills. As new technologies present themselves, older technologies become transformed - audio recording and editing has been around for a long time, but the addition of online audio archives and web-based audio presentations (podcasts) has provided innumerable new ways for using audio to support learning. Each of the different categories of tools mentioned at the beginning of this chapter will be transformed in new ways in the near future. The key to using technology tools in new, but pedagogically sound ways, is to think about them in terms of the task and strategies and not to be tied down to their initial use.

CONCLUSION

It is not a particular tool, a particular task, or a particular strategy that will make a teacher successful in guiding student learning. An educator who is tool-task-independent will be ready to meet the inevitable technology changes that will take place in their classrooms, applying tools or other resources as needed in new ways as situations change. The secret, of course, is to constantly consider the vital question that frames each teacher's day as they enter their classroom: "*How can I use the resources at hand to maximize learning in ways that meet each student's needs*?"

Reflecting on Young Children, Science and Technology

This section gives you some questions and activities to help you think about how you can use some of the ideas from this chapter in your work.

Research

1. Technology can be expensive but you do not have to use expensive programs to teach science to children. Research available community and web-based resources and develop a list of free school and community resources that could support science learning in your classroom.
2. Interview teachers in your school about how they use technology when teaching science. Analyze this information according to frequency of use, types of technology, how it is used (teacher resource, teaching tool, or learning tool) and other. Prepare a report for your peers and administrators to better inform them what types if planning you need to do to prepare your school for the digital age.

Reflect

1. What is the difference in *tool-task coherence* and *tool-task independence* ? Reflect on how you have used technology in relation to these two categories. How has your thinking changed after reading this chapter?
2. Parents can support technology in your school. Organize a parent meeting to discuss technology and science learning. Ask for parents to help your school identify technology resources they would be willing to share. What kinds of expertise and experiences could your parents bring to the classroom? How can you best work with your parents to support technology in your classroom?
3. How can you use technology tools for communication with and about young children in your science teaching?
4. Look at your curriculum lesson plans, the ones you use every year like colors, seasons, family and so on. How have you used technology in your curriculum? Make a list of what you have been doing and plan for how you will alter your plans to include more technology.

Practice

1. What are some different ways you can use technology tools available in your school or home to teach science to young children?
2. Work with your colleagues to identify technology tools you can use for data collection and analysis?
3. Work with a colleague and plan how you will use technology to develop a *sense of wonder* in your school?
4. Analyzing web sites is very time consuming. How can you and your colleagues work together to develop a plan of sharing sites and information for your school?
5. A technology committee is a valuable group for your school and your teaching. How can you promote the development of this team in your school?

Online Resources

- Life Science Resources: British Library Board: *Listen to nature*. Many recordings of animals from around the world http://www.bl.uk/listentonature/main.html.
- Life Science Resources: Cornell Laboratory of Ornithology. *Macauley Library online*. An audio and video bird recordings archive. http://macaulaylibrary.org.
- Life Science Resources: *The Mangoverde World Bird Guide*. An audio bird recordings archive. http://www.mangoverde.com/birdsound/index.html.

- Software: PortableApps. Free and portable Windows software (portable software is software that usable without requiring administrative installation). http://portableapps.com.
- Software: OS X Portable Applications and portable Macintosh OSX software (portable software is software that usable without requiring administrative installation). http://www.freesmug.org/portableapps/
- Software: OpenOffice.org, a cross-platform, free productivity suite (also available in a portable version from PortableApps.org).
- Software: Tux Paint, an open source (free) cross-platform drawing software program for children. http://www.tuxpaint.org/
- Software: Drawing for Children, a free drawing program for children. Windows only. http://drawing.gamemaker.nl.
- Teacher resources: Thinkfinity, a lesson and teacher resource site that partners with the core education organizations (NCTM, AAAS, National Geographic Society, International Reading Association and others). http://www.thinkfinity.org.
- Teacher Resources: The Exploratorium, The museum of science, art and human perception. http://www.exploratorium.org
- Teacher Resources: The Regional Educational Development Laboratories home at http://ies.ed.gov/ncee/edlabs/.

REFERENCES

Anderson, L. W., Krathwohl, D. R., Airasian, P. W., Cruikshank, K. A., Mayer, R. E., & Pintrich, P. R. … Wittrock, M. C. (Eds.). (2001). *A taxonomy for learning, teaching, and assessing: A revision of Bloom's taxonomy of educational objectives*. Boston, MA: Pearson Education Group, Allyn & Bacon.

Berners-Lee, T., & Fischetti, M. (1999). *Weaving the Web: The original design and ultimate destiny of the World Wide Web by its inventor*. San Francisco, CA: HarperCollins Publishers.

Bloom, B. S. (Ed.). Englehart, M. D., Furst, E. J., Hill, W. H., & Krathwohl, D. R. (1956). *Taxonomy of educational objectives: The classification of educational goals, by a committee of college and university examiners. Handbook I: Cognitive domain*. New York, NY: Longmans, Green.

Bower, M. (2008). Affordance analysis - Matching learning tasks with learning technologies. *Educational Media International*, *45*(1), 3–15. doi:10.1080/09523980701847115

British Library Board. (n.d.). *Listen to nature*. Retrieved from http://www.bl.uk/ listentonature/main.html

Concord.org. (2010). *Probeware: Developing new tools for data collection and analysis*. Retrieved from http://www.concord.org/ work/themes/probeware.html

Cornell Laboratory of Ornithology. (n.d.). *Macauley library online. An audio and video bird recordings archive*. Retrieved from http://macaulaylibrary.org

Drawing for Children. (n.d.). *Drawing for Children, a free drawing program for children*. Retrieved from http://drawing.gamemaker.nl

Gillen, J., Littleton, K., Twiner, A., Staarman, J. K., & Mercer, N. (2008). Using the interactive whiteboard to resource continuity and support multimodal teaching in a primary science classroom. *Journal of Computer Assisted Learning*, *24*(4), 348–358. doi:10.1111/j.1365-2729.2007.00269.x

Giza, B. (2010). Strategies for the use of open-source graphics, animation, and video tools in STEM education. In C. Crawford et al. (Eds.), *Proceedings of Society for Information Technology & Teacher Education International Conference 2010,* (pp. 2722-2728). Chesapeake, VA: AACE.

Gnu.org. (2008). *Gnu licenses*. Retrieved from http://www.gnu.org/ licenses/ licenses.html.

International Society for Technology in Education. (2007). *ISTE national educational technology standards (NETS-S) and performance indicators for students*. Eugene, OR: International Society for Technology in Education.

International Society for Technology in Education. (2008). *ISTE national educational technology standards (NETS-T) and performance indicators for teachers*. Eugene, OR: International Society for Technology in Education.

John, B. E., & Kieras, D. E. (1996). The GOMS family of analysis techniques: Comparison and contrast. *ACM Transactions on Computer-Human Interaction*, *3*(4), 320–351. doi:10.1145/235833.236054

Jonassen, D. H., & Carr, C. (2000). Mindtools: Affording multiple knowledge representations in learning. In S. P. Lajoie (Ed.), *Computers as cognitive tools, vol. 2: No more walls* (pp. 165–196). Mahwah, NJ: Lawrence Erlbaum Associates.

Jonassen, D. H., Tessmer, M., & Hannum, W. H. (1999). *Task analysis methods for instructional design*. Mahwah, NJ: L. Erlbaum Associates.

Krathwohl, D. R. (2002). A revision of Bloom's taxonomy: An overview. *Theory into Practice*, *41*(4), 212–218. doi:10.1207/s15430421tip4104_2

Mangoverde. (n.d.). *The Mangoverde world bird guide*. Retrieved from http://www.mangoverde.com/ birdsound/index.html

Means, B., Penuel, W. R., Crawford, V. M., Korbak, C., Lewis, A., & Murphy, R. F. … Yarnall, L. (2001). *GLOBE Year 6 evaluation: Explaining variation in implementation*. Menlo Park, CA: SRI International. Retrieved from http://classic.globe.gov/ fsl/evals/ y6full.pdf

Metcalf, S. J., & Tinker, R. (2003). *TEEMSS: Technology enhanced elementary and middle school science*. Paper presented at the Annual Meeting of the National Association for Research in Science Teaching, March 23-26, 2003, Philadelphia. Retrieved from http://www.concord.org/ publications/files/ narst_teemss_paper.pdf

National Research Council. (1996). *National science education standards: Observe, interact, change, learn*. Washington, DC: National Academy Press.

Rose, D. H., & Meyer, A. (2002). *Teaching every student in the digital age: Universal design for learning*. Alexandria, VA: ASCD.

Rose, D. H., Meyer, A., & Hitchcock, C. (2005). *The universally designed classroom: Accessible curriculum and digital technologies*. Cambridge, MA: Harvard Education Press.

Tinker, R. F. (1991). Science for kids: The promise of technology. In K. Sheingold, L. Roberts & S. Malcom (Eds.), *Technology for teaching and learning. AAAS Forum Paper*. Washington, DC: American Association for the Advancement of Science (AAAS).

Tressel, G. W. (1994). Thirty years of improvement in precollege math and science education. *Journal of Science Education and Technology*, *3*(2), 77–88. doi:10.1007/BF01575187

Chapter 10
Mathematics Learning through the Use of Technology

Amy M. Smith
Pink Sky Education, USA

Amy R. Gentry
Shelby County Schools, USA

Sally Blake
Flagler College, USA

ABSTRACT

Technology can capture young children's attention, motivate them, and help them construct early mathematics concepts in meaningful ways. This chapter examines the nature of children's mathematics learning and how technology can support learning on three levels: (a) a teacher information resource; (b) teaching support; and (c) the learning process for children. It provides a description of how technology tools, when connected to sound inquiry-based pedagogy and formative assessment, can facilitate learning in today's increasingly technological world. Considerations for future research as well as a list of relevant, practical resources for teachers to experiment with in their own classrooms are included.

INTRODUCTION: CHARTER SCHOOL VIGNETTE

On a busy October day at Southern Avenue Elementary Charter School, Ms. Shepard's kindergarten children place an electronic popcorn popper at the end of a long roll of butcher paper taped to the floor. They measure the kernels in a measuring cup and pour them into the machine. Trying to bridle their excitement, they discuss their estimations concerning how far the popcorn will land after shooting out of the popping device. The "pop" button is pushed. Much conversation and collaborative problem solving quickly follow as the children observe that the popcorn does not follow their anticipated trajectory but instead pops randomly in all directions. They vote to move the popping machine to the middle of the paper. They furnish additional paper on the sides and then focus on measuring the distances of the popcorn and machine using their hands as tools of measurement. Together, they also count the

DOI: 10.4018/978-1-61350-059-0.ch010

Copyright © 2012, IGI Global. Copying or distributing in print or electronic forms without written permission of IGI Global is prohibited.

popcorn. Ms. Shepard documents the children's learning by taking pictures with her digital camera and recording their words on her laptop computer. All the while, she guides the children to think about and discuss their original hypotheses compared with the actual data collected and the differences in measurements. She also facilitates a conversation about how many kernels actually popped compared to the cup of kernels placed in the machine. The documentation will later serve as a foundation for thinking, learning and teaching as students and teachers revisit the experiment. For now, each child moves to a table to enjoy the edible manipulative while placing a mark on paper for every ten pieces eaten and reflecting on the experience in their journals.

A quick glance around the classroom reveals multiple applications of technology (besides the popcorn popper) that this creative teacher uses to facilitate her young students' development of early math skills. Learning is constructed within the context of inter-disciplinary, fun and meaningful activities that promote higher-order thinking skills. There are estimation jars sorted with differing colored popcorn kernels on a shelf with nearby corresponding printed-out bar graph. In one area of the room, kernels have been carefully placed in squares of a one-hundreds chart, and a nearby computer screen invites a pair of children to work on a similar interactive virtual manipulative hundreds chart. Ms. Shepard has also retrieved popcorn images printed from ClipArt and displays ordinal numbers and kindergarten-level math vocabulary words on them. A completed pie chart shows "Our Favorite Ways to Eat Popcorn" (i.e., with butter, with salt, with butter and salt, plain). The walls and shelves also hold child-created poems (typed with the help of older peers) from Word processing programs, popcorn songs and literature derived from the Internet. The words of children's theories in response to a question posed by the teacher are also evident: Why does popcorn pop? Next to the early theories are text and photos from http://www.tellmewhyfacts.com that supply the answer. (In short, when heated, pressure builds up from the steam of a small amount of water that exists inside the kernel). Finally, a hardcopy of a list of relevant hyperlinks that children can access to play popcorn-themed learning games is embedded on a popcorn themed bulletin board that depicts a web of disciplines and associated standards for learning.

The above vignette illustrates integrated learning opportunities for young children in mathematics, science and literacy supported by the use of technology. This activity uses technology in two ways, as a teacher information resource and as learning process tools for children to support exploration and conceptual development of mathematical skills and thinking. The use of multiple forms of data, graphing, counting and tallies and real materials allow children to think about multiple representations and communication, both important concepts in mathematics. The recording of this investigation through digital media provides data storage for future comparisons of similar investigations so children can identify patterns to make inferences from multiple observations and repeating conceptual activities to support learning. The use of real 3-dimensional objects and the transfer to 2-dimensional representatives through computer games and photos is another important element of mathematical thinking. The active exploration combined with the children's dialogue about the investigation included predictions, comparisons, actual data analysis and planning for adjustment of conditions support the ideas of Vygotsky (1978) through active discourse and social interaction. This teacher prepared a mathematically concept rich environment through the use of technology. Technology as a resource and a learning process tool is changing the educational environments in the field of early mathematics in the United States.

The world of mathematics can be an exciting exploration for the young child when combined with technology in a supportive mathematics rich learning environment. Hasselbring and Glaser

(2000) advocate that the primary goal of education is to help students apply skills and knowledge to solve real-world problems, and they explain that digital applications offer opportunities for students to do just this. This thinking is not uncommon among 21st century teachers of young children, as made evident by literature regarding the burgeoning use of classroom technology to inspire higher-order thinking that is associated with mathematical-related problem solving. In fact, with positive evidence from a growing number of research studies, the National Council of Teachers of Mathematics (NCTM) (2000) and the National Association for the Education of Young Children (NAEYC) (2006) support thoughtful use of technology incorporated in the regular learning environment as one of many vehicles for supporting learning.

This chapter was conceived by Sally Blake, Amy Smith and Amy Gentry to explore developmentally appropriate application of technological tools as a component of facilitation of early mathematics knowledge construction. Sally Blake has worked with this chapter in the capacity of a university faculty in early childhood science and mathematics. The authors will discuss both technology as a teacher information resource, a teaching support and a learning process tool in relation to mathematics. Amy Smith earned a Ph.D. in Educational Psychology and Research and has over 15 years of experience in early childhood education as a classroom teacher, college-level instructor, consultant, teacher trainer and researcher. She is currently president of Pink Sky Education in Atlanta Georgia. Amy Gentry earned a Master of Science in Education with a major in Instruction and Curriculum Leadership with a concentration in Early Childhood Education, and will be starting her first year of teaching in the second grade this fall. This team allows for a more comprehensive communication of mathematics and technology from different perspectives, university, consultation and practitioner views build a richer picture of the role of technology in mathematics.

The authors present information that focus on three applications of technology in mathematics: technology as a teacher resource, technology as a support tool for teaching and technology as process support for learning. The reader is probably familiar with the use of technology as a resource tool. The web has become a valuable resource for teachers. In the area of mathematics there are many sites that provide research, standards (guiding concepts for teaching), lesson plans, and clear definitions and examples of mathematics tools to help teachers enrich their work. The second application of technology for teaching includes the use of tools that support teachers' daily work to document, store, and allow comparisons of learning across the continuum of learning. The third and most important use of technology is as process support for learning. Traditional approaches to teaching mathematics focused on finding one answer or a product which did not support the development of mathematical thinking. Process refers to how children learn both mathematics and technology not just memorize words and formulas or operational applications. First we will discuss the recommended mathematics concepts for young children and how technology relates to these. Next we will discuss elements of effective technology-based teaching. We will include a discussion of some of the issues surrounding technology and mathematics for young children. We will conclude this chapter with examples from a charter school classroom and some recommended resources for teachers. In the United States many public schools have added Charter Schools which are primary or secondary schools that receive public money (and like other schools, may also receive private donations) but are not subject to some of the rules, regulations, and statutes that apply to other public schools in exchange for some type of accountability for producing certain results, which are set forth in each school's charter. Charter schools are opened and attended by choice. They evolved as part of the educational reform movements and allow experimental teaching.

For the sake of brevity, much of the information shared in this chapter is framed around a kindergarten (ages 4-5 in the United States) level; however, with simple modifications, the information can be applied to a range of learning differences. It is the intent of the authors to give examples that focus on the mathematics and technology rather than specific age levels. There are some ideas that would be appropriate across the age levels 3 to 9.

Objectives

After reading this chapter the reader should be able to identify the appropriate use of technology tools in relation to age or developmentally appropriate levels of young children in mathematics instruction. They should also develop enhanced planning approaches using technology as both a teacher resource and a learning process tool to support active learning environments. The reader should be able to:

- Identify the three main types of technology use in teaching mathematics
- Identify age appropriate use of technology
- Identify approaches to support technology in classrooms

BACKGROUND: CHANGING VIEWS OF MATHEMATICS IN EARLY CHILDHOOD CLASSROOMS

Children who learn that mathematics makes sense and who learn to trust their own abilities to make sense of it will be successful in developing mathematical competence. Developmental competence will occur as we increase the experiences that children have in mathematics (Richardson, 2000). While this is not new thinking it is one of the big ideas behind the importance of using technology as a teacher resource, technology as a support tool for teaching and technology as process support for learning.

Three reports of the National Academies address different aspects of education for very young children from a variety of perspectives (National Research Council, 2002). *From Neurons to Neighborhoods: The Science of Early Childhood Development* (National Research Council and Institute of Medicine, 2000) provides a detailed look at the many factors that influence development in very young children. *Eager to Learn: Educating Our Preschoolers* (NRC, 2001a) describes the current status of the programs in which young children are educated, setting that description in the context of recent contributions from the field of cognitive science. *Adding It Up: Helping Children Learn Mathematics* (NRC, 2001) closely examines mathematics learning and describes its facets. Each of these reports contributes to an evolving base of evidence that the early learning programs to which students are exposed are extremely important.

For many years, early childhood educators have relied heavily on their interpretations of Piaget's developmental stages when implementing mathematical instruction. Piaget's studies are interpreted as being dependent upon children's chronological ages and used to define what appropriate learning occurs at each stage of development. This may limit the experiences teachers provide for mathematical conceptual development or prevent teachers from building on the child's intuitive understanding of more sophisticated early mathematics conceptualization. Although children's understanding of mathematical thinking may seem simplistic at first, they may be capable of much more understanding than early childhood educators have typically allowed (Clements, 1998). Recent research studies such as those conducted by researchers Newcombe (2002) and Gelman (2004), challenges the interpretation of Piaget's work and believe his findings to be inconclusive. Children do not start learning mathematics in their middle and high school years. Their foundation for mathematical understanding is developed in a scaffolding process that starts in the early years. When typically developing children reach preschool, they are capable of negotiating their physical world with confidence, intuitively and informally, building their geometric and spatial ideas and skills (Hiele, 1999; Sarama & Clements, 2003) possibly indicating a more sophisticated level of understanding than previously believed.

The assumption of many educators that children are not capable of mathematical thinking has led them to teach at lower levels of thinking to include simple number recognition, naming of shapes, and counting. In a similar manner the use of technology has been considered as something that is "too hard" for young children. As these ideas began to change, teachers face many challenges as to how to better prepare young children for future academic success.

Learning Standards and Orientation to Learning

A standards-based approach to facilitating mathematics learning using technology is another element supported by research. Standards are established norms for instructional applications that have been developed by domain specific professional organizations in the United States. There are national standards and state standards which are required in all public schools. The National Council of Teachers of Mathematics (NCTM), the national professional organization for mathematics teachers, stated that alongside connections to data analysis and algebra, number and operations, geometry, and measurement are essential areas of study for young children. Fennell (2006) stated, "It is essential that these focal points be addressed in contexts that promote problem solving, reasoning, communication, making connections, and designing and analyzing representations" (p. 12). These are the building blocks of planning and assessing young children in mathematics. Figure 1 below includes the recommended focal points from NCTM for kindergarten age (4-5 years) children.

Figure 1 is reprinted with permission from *Curriculum Focal Points for Prekindergarten through Grade 8: A Quest for Coherence*, copyright 2006 by the National Council of Teachers of Mathematics. All rights reserved.

Teachers are expected to use these standards in all aspects of their work in mathematics. Teacher accountability is based on their children's successful understanding of these identified components and each grade level builds on the previous work.

Elements of Effective Mathematics Technology-Based Lessons

Technology, when integrated into school and real-life experiences can help children to think analytically, reinforce or facilitate learning new skills, engage and motivate, lead to cross-curriculum connections, promote math literacy, and offer opportunities for teachers to individualize instruction. Technology allows flexibility in instructional applications to support differentiated learning at different skill and developmental levels, is interactive, and provides useful means for authentic assessment (Lou, Abrami, and D'Apollonia, 2001; Silk, Higashi, Shoop & Schunn, 2010). Like any lesson with young children, those involving mathematics with technology connections should take place in the context of a "risk free environment" that focuses on children's interests and background experiences; one which provides ample time and a variety of opportunities to explore, communicate, and develop in-depth conceptual understanding. For example, by using programs that allow the creation of pictures with geometric shapes, children have demonstrated growing knowledge and competence in working with concepts such as symmetry, patterns, and spatial order when allowed to experiment or "play" with software applications (Sarama, 2004).

Children should be able to ask questions, experiment through play, and communicate and represent their thinking in many ways. The learning context should also support positive attitudes

Figure 1. Kindergarten standards

Kindergarten Curriculum Focal Points	Connections to the Focal Points
Number and Operations: Representing, comparing, and ordering whole numbers and joining and separating sets. Children us numbers, including written numerals, to represent quantities and to solve quantitative problems, such as counting objects in a set, creating a set with a given number of objects, comparing and ordering sets or numerals by using both cardinal and ordinal meanings, and modeling simple joining and separating situations with objects. They choose, combine, and apply effective strategies for answering quantitative questions, including quickly recognizing the number in a small set, counting and producing sets of given sizes, counting the number in combined sets, and counting backwards.	**Data Analysis:** Children sort object and use one or more attributes to solve problems. For example, they might sort solids that roll easily from those that do not. Or they might collect data and use counting to answer such questions as, "What is our favorite snack?" They re-sort objects by using new attributes (e.g., after sorting solids according to which ones roll, they might re-sort the solids according to which ones stack easily).
Geometry: Describing shapes and space: Children interpret the physical world with geometric ideas (e.g., shape, orientation, spatial relations) and describe it with corresponding vocabulary. They identify, name, and describe a variety of shapes, such as squares, triangles, circles, rectangles, (regular) hexagons, and (isosceles) trapezoids presented in a variety of ways (e.g., with different sizes or orientations), as well as three-dimensional shapes as spheres, cubes, and cylinders. They use basic shapes and spatial reasoning to model objects in their environment and to construct more complex shapes.	**Geometry:** Children integrate their understandings of geometry, measurement, and number. For example, they understand, discuss, and create simple navigational directions (e.g., "Walk forward 10 steps, turn right, and walk forward 5 steps"). **Algebra:** Children identify, duplicate, and extend simple number patterns and sequential and growing patterns (e.g., patterns made with shapes) as preparation for creating rules that describe relationships.
Measurement: Ordering objects by measurable attributes: Children use measureable attributes, such as length or weight, to solve problems by comparing and ordering objects. They compare the lengths of two objects both directly (by comparing them with each other) and indirectly (by comparing both with a third object), and they order several objects according to length.	

about learning mathematics through technology and develop higher-order thinking skills. The classroom environment is vital to the development of confidence and competence in mathematics and technology. Students need to see mathematics as a language, a tool, and an art form with which they can communicate ideas, solve problems, and explore the world around them.

Higher–Order Thinking (HOTS) and Teacher Talk

Lower level thinking has permeated most mathematics instruction in many schools. If we are to expect children to think mathematically, the development of higher order thinking is crucial. Along with the support for higher order thinking, there is a growing body of support for what we will call *"teacher talk"* which supports the com-

Figure 2. Church's adapted technology and Blake's mathematics talk connections to Bloom's taxonomy

Blooms Level	Church's Technology Talk	Blake's Mathematics Talk with Young Children
Creating	Programming, filming, animating, blogging, video blogging, mixing, podcasting, directing/producing, wiki-ing	Proposing new process, generating, creating, constructing, preparing, drawing conclusions, constructing, planning, designing, integrating, developing
Evaluating	Commenting, reviewing, posting, moderating, collaborating, networking, refactoring, (alpha and beta) testing	Identifying best solution, thinking to support, appraising, justifying, validating, comparing, concluding, rating, justifying, defending, explaining, estimating
Analyzing	Mashing, linking, tagging, validating, reverse-engineering, cracking	Predicting, identifying less than, greater than, equal to, contrasting, difference, pattern, repeating pattern, about, between, taller than, shorter than, wider than, narrower than, near, far, beside, between, inside, outside, above, below, in front, behind, over, under, top, bottom, left, right, closer, further, part, whole, one-half, one-quarter, one-third, first, last, pairs
Applying	Running, loading, playing, operating, hacking, uploading, sharing, editing	Counting backwards, counting forwards, counting on, skip counting, ordering, graphing, sorting, summing, tallying,

munication of mathematics and technology as teachers work with children.

In 2008 Churches adapted the work of Benjamin Bloom's mid-twentieth century Taxonomy of Cognitive Educational Objectives to connect technology verbs to levels of thinking to assist teachers in developing skills in "teacher talk" about technology. The vocabulary of technology, much of which is now in common use among the digital generation, is important to developing technology literacy. It is equally important for teachers to think about mathematics talk and what verbs and nouns support higher order thinking. Figure 2 identifies Church's technology associations and mathematics talk to Bloom's Digital Taxonomy.

Churches (2008) categorized the first of Bloom's higher order thinking skills as analytical in nature. This includes processes such as comparing, organizing, and integrating. Using technology to work with graphs and mind maps are examples of engaging in this level of thinking. The top levels of the revised hierarchy, creating and evaluation, requires hypothesizing, critiquing, judging, testing, experimenting. Evaluating the strengths of text or photos on a website or a speaker on a videoconference are examples of teacher evaluation. Children at this level combine the elements of the continuum of higher level thinking through investigations as they test ideas, revise variables, and argue their findings over time to support inferences. Technology allows children to keep running records of their investigations to support or disprove claims. Creating with technology, Churches explained, involves such activities as designing, constructing, planning, producing, and inventing. Publishing a class math book with a word processing application, developing a *PowerPoint* presentation, using online comic creation tools, or producing a video through *Movie Maker* are examples. Churches (2008) acknowledged collaborative skills such as negotiation, debate, commenting, questioning, contributing, networking, videoconferencing and emailing as important to the promotion of the process of higher order thinking and learning. It is important for the teacher to remember that these applications should be developed by children because the process, not the end product is what supports the thinking.

Supporting the Learning Process

To study the potential of technology as support for the learning process, Lim and Tay (2003) conducted interviews, observations, and focus group discussions to investigate the use of technology as process development sources to support higher order thinking with young children. Findings indicated children do engage in evaluation, analysis, and concept connections when using technology. They observed and recorded ideas as students interacted with activities from well-designed, thoughtful lessons incorporating such technology tools such as the CD-ROMs, PowerPoint presentations, simulations, on-line virtual realities, games, databases, teleconferencing and electronic whiteboards. The researchers concluded, "The objective of the lesson plays an important role in shaping the development of the lesson. Students are more likely to engage in higher-order thinking when the objective of the lesson is to do so" (Lim and Tay, 2003, p. 443). This indicates that the teacher must intentionally plan the inclusion of technology tools in their lessons to develop higher level thinking. The learning process tools support development of higher level thinking but the teacher's planning has to connect the applications to the objective.

To add further support for thoughtful technology use in lesson design, the position statement of the NAEYC is reiterated. Technology should not just be something "extra" but one of many strategies for teaching. Hubbell, a teacher of a Montessori school and author (2003) explained, "Different children have different learning styles and having a variety of vehicles through which to deliver and explore can only be beneficial" (p. 41). She uses technology to support the 3-to 2-dimensional representations in her math lessons starting with real manipulatives and then encourages children to use the computer with manipulative representations and simulations. Computers help by providing more-powerful and flexible "manipulatives" where the intentional and deliberate actions on the computer lead children to form mental images (Sarama, 2004). Computerized manipulative programs help children *link* previous experiences to more-explicit mathematical ideas. It helps *connec*t visual shapes with abstract numbers. Perhaps most important, it encourages children to *explore* mathematics through a variety of representations.

The research experiences of Butzin (2002) and Ainsa (1999) influenced further advocacy for a variety of modes for learning, including technology, literature, manipulatives, and paper and pencil activities. These multiple approaches support differentiated teaching considered important for addressing all learners in early childhood programs. The use of multiple representations addresses different learner preferences and support mathematical thinking.

Silk, Higashi, Shoop and Schunn (2010) also suggest that teachers help children focus on targeted math ideas and on the process of learning rather than the product. For example, teachers can encourage continuous examination of relationships between numbers and multiple ways of solving problems rather than focusing on one end answer. Similarly teachers need to think about the use of technology tools to support process rather than technology as end products. The data storage capabilities that technology supports give children and teachers a chance to reflect and analyze the learning and compare earlier understanding to new insights as they develop mathematical thinking. Comparisons of different approaches from individual children and teachers emphasize the process and how it can vary but still support higher order thinking.

Support for Social Development

Besides providing differentiated instructional approaches, NAEYC encourages teachers to promote collaboration around technology. Children need time to think about what they are doing, reflect, revisit, and talk about learning. Individuals construct their theories through language within social relationships. Searching for meaning with a community of peers means that children engage in activities that present support to one another and provide multiple conceptualizations and approaches to problem solving. This is the essence of social construction of knowledge (DeVries & Kohlberg, 1987; Vygotsky, 1978). The benefits of learning together with technology was affirmed by a meta-analysis of over one hundred empirical studies on the topic of small-group and individual learning orientations involving computer technology. The data showed that learning together had significant positive effects on individual student achievement, group task performance, and several other affective processes, such as constructive peer interactions, tenacity, and positive attitudes (Lou, Abrami, & d'Apollonia, 2001).

Support for Children's Interest

With these essential content areas in mind, it is also important to design mathematics lessons that are inspired by and capture children's interests. Silk, Higashi, Shoop and Schunn (2010) suggested basic principles for lesson design that integrate technology and mathematics teaching and learning in ways that work toward this goal, including motivating children and fostering deep learning by creating problem-based opportunities based on interests. One way to do this is to apply mathematics to solve every day, relevant problems. The issue with this approach is what are relevant problems with some children may not be relevant with other children depending on their home environments. As illustrated in the opening vignette of this chapter the teacher creates the environment and makes experiences relevant to the class to support learning.

Support for Investigations

One recommended instructional orientation is an inquiry-based or investigative approach to learning mathematics. The use of inquiry, while usually associated with science, can be adapted to support mathematics learning. Integration of literature, like *Mr. Archimedes Bath* by Pamela Allen encourages children to explore measurement, volume and spatial relationships as Mr. Archimedes and his friends try to work out why the water always overflows when they all have a bath. Children are naturally inquisitive; therefore inquiry-based learning when developed from their natural interest supports their intuitive way of understanding their world. The teacher role is to provide materials and start discourse as to the "why" of mathematics. Technology has expanded the types of materials for inquiry of mathematics. When children are actively engaged in their learning and are able to construct their own knowledge, the learning becomes more meaningful. Inquiry-based learning teaches children how to become life-long learners by questioning the phenomenon of the world around them, and discovering the answers to those questions. Yoder (2005) stated, "Inquiry-based and constructivist activities can invigorate teaching and motivate students to take charge of their own learning, understanding multiple perspectives, and develop high level reasoning skills" (p. 1). Therefore, for optimal learning to occur, teachers should use the interests and questions of their students along with available technology and incorporate it with the standards and curriculum according to their grade level.

Chang and Wang (2009) noted "With the assistance of modern technologies, it is likely that ideal inquiry learning environments, where students are encouraged to do a variety of exploratory activities can be built and applied in educational practices" (p.170). Technology adds a new dimension to exploration. Perhaps one of the largest gaps between generations is the use of technology as the information base for learning. The new generation of students is very comfortable with technology as a source of communication and information. The application of technology for inquiry investigations open global opportunities and comparisons among groups of children that were at one time limited to class or school bound perimeters.

Technology and Mathematics Assessment

Ongoing, authentic assessment (that is, pre-assessment, formative, and summative that is based on meaningful and relevant experiences) is another element of thoughtful, effective mathematics lessons that successfully incorporate technology. A word of caution here about assessment tools; an important idea for teachers is the use of a specific tool *does not* necessarily make the task or assessment authentic. Authentic assessment is generally used to evaluate performance or authentic tasks. It is different from traditional assessment approaches. Traditional assessments rarely allow teachers to evaluate higher level thinking. These forms of assessment are usually locked into assessment of recall. It is difficult to determine if a student can actually perform a task or what level of understanding a student has from lower level responses or actions. Authentic assessment of learning provides teachers with information about how a child understands and applies knowledge. Traditional assessment is usually isolated segments identifying what are considered important concepts but rarely connect to each other. Performance-based assessments in mathematics require children apply their knowledge and skills in context, not merely completing a task on cue.

In order to optimize learning experiences with applications of technology, Copley (2010) provided suggestions that teachers can use to collect and analyze evidence about what children know about mathematics, and she explained how to use this information to drive instruction. First, teachers should assess each child's knowledge, abilities and interests with the primary aim of benefiting the child. The Standards for Mathematics in section one provide a base for assessing the level of understanding. This requires a teacher to clearly identify the criteria that identifies successful learning. One approach developed in the early days of authentic assessment by Airasian (1991) is valuable to help teachers focus on coordinating assessment to mathematics teaching. We have added technology to the following process which should support teachers' thinking about criteria. Having clearly defined criteria will make it easier for teachers to remain objective during the assessment.

1. Identify the overall performance or task to be assessed, and perform it yourself or imagine yourself performing it. Identify what forms of technology can be used as a teacher resource and for the learning process support. Practice the technology so the task will be smoother.

2. List the important aspects of the performance or product. Identify what technology will support each level. Keep a running list of school wide technology and other resources.
3. Try to limit the number of performance criteria, so they can all be observed during a pupil's performance. Determine which criteria needs to be recorded for documentation either on video or audio or both.
4. If possible, have groups of teachers think through the important behaviors included in a task. Identify technology resources of individual teachers that can be shared and develop a schedule for use of shared technology tools.
5. Express the performance criteria in terms of observable pupil behaviors or product characteristics.
6. Arrange the performance criteria in the order in which they are likely to be observed.

Copley (2010) assessment should include many data sources and foci, including what children know (content), the processes they employ to use and understand mathematics, and their attitudes about mathematics. It is recommended that teachers use many assessment tools to evaluate different dimensions of learning and not attempt to evaluate all learning based on one type of instrument. Later in this section we identify additional technology applications to support assessment of mathematical learning.

Finally, assessment should encompass both children's learning and the teacher's instructional effectiveness (reflective practice that results in adjusting teaching strategies, as needed). Technology allows teachers to document store and reflect on progress across time. Videos give teachers the opportunity to see their interaction in classrooms and reflect on the learning environment.

Many mathematics assessment tools can be adapted for use with authentic assessment and technology. It is the responsibility of the teacher to develop instructional activities and tools that reflect both process and product opportunities. The start of authentic assessment is in the planning of authentic learning tasks. Technology provides support for developing, recording and some actual interactive assessment tools.

Teacher Resource and Process Technology Tools for Assessment in Mathematics

Technology provides some useful tools for assessment of mathematics with young children. Some of these can be considered both resources and process tools as well developed assessment evaluates the process of mathematical development as well as the indicators of success.

Rubric

One example of an assessment tool is a rubric, and teachers can customize them for any learning activity by using web sites such as http://www.rubistar.com. This and other web sites assist teachers' development of assessment instruments in mathematics and all domain specific areas. Performance assessments are recommended for mathematics because they support the idea that the learning process does not have clear-cut right or wrong answers. Rather, there are degrees to which a person is successful or unsuccessful. Teachers will need to evaluate the performance in a way that will allow them to take those varying degrees into consideration. This can be accomplished by creating rubrics. A rubric is based on children's real-world context and helps to determine the level of development of specific skills and understandings that are exhibited through teacher- (and child-) defined performance tasks. Specific criteria are used in relation to the performance task, which are used to evaluate the teaching and learning. These types of web based development support provides examples of rubrics, a drop down menu of suggested assessment categories, criteria for rating work samples, and an online depository to save rubrics which can be shared with all site users.

Figure 3. Checklist for preschool pre-mathematical concepts sets of classification (Kirova and Bhargava, 2002)

Concepts/Stages of Development	Sept.-Oct.	Dec.-Jan.	April-May
1. Able to group identical objects			
2. Sorts objects by 1 attribute—color, shape, size, material, pattern, texture			
3. Classifies by 2 attributes			
4. Classifies by 3 attributes			
5. Describes what has been done while classifying by 1, 2, or 3 attributes			
6. Explains what has been done while classifying by 1, 2, or 3 attributes			
7. Classifies according to function			
8. Describes and/or explains what has been done			
9. Classifies according to association			
10. Describes and/or explains what has been done			
11. Understands class exclusion			
12. Understands class inclusion			
13. Describes and/or explains what has been done			
14. Classifies by number			

KEY TO CHECKLISTS

✔	Demonstrates behavioral knowledge of the concept
✔✔	Demonstrates behavioral and representational knowledge of the concept
0	Demonstrates partial behavioral knowledge of the concept
00	Demonstrates partial representational knowledge of the concept
X	Does not demonstrate any kind of knowledge of the concept

Kirova and Bhargava (2002)

Another recommended web site for rubrics and resources of mathematics for young children is exemplars.com. This site has rubrics for Pre-k(ages 3-4) through grade level two (ages 7-8) developed on the NCTM standards for mathematics. There are a variety of rubrics that directly address process skills of young children in mathematics. The site also includes a many resources for teachers and support for different approaches to rubric use.

Checklist

A second example of tools for authentic assessment is a simple teacher-created checklist. Before a teacher can develop a checklist it is important to establish specific learning or process behaviors to use on a check list. Mathematics understanding checklists are different from behavior checklist and should be developed with conceptual evidence of understanding. One suggestion would be the NCTM standards. They can be used to create a checklist of the knowledge, skills, and concepts that we want children to learn and simply refer to the items on the list during daily activities. Below in Figure 3 is a checklist developed by Kirova and Bhargava (2002). It is a good model for developing a checklist for mathematics understanding. The example below is developed to identify sets of classification. Each mathematical concept will need a different checklist that supports key components related to the learning.

Checklists can be stored in mobile computers or on a personal digital assistant (PDA) which allows the teacher to use the checklist during observation of a child's play or lesson activity without having to depend on memory or bulky hard copy. These technology tools compress the documents and allow the teacher to move among children and more accurately record accomplishments. This allows for a more naturalistic observation of children.

Electronic Portfolio

An electronic portfolio is a comprehensive technology tool to study and document children's progress over time. Collaborative and individual work samples can be scanned, and the children's words, photographs, video and even music and graphics can be recorded. The e-portfolio can be stored and shared digitally and easily transferred to the teacher at the child's next grade level or even to another school if a child transfers. This allows teachers to identify areas of understanding and identify patterns of problems across years of instruction. Teachers can keep accurate records of a child's progress across the continuum of learning. The electronic portfolio allows parents and children to see their growth and learning as it evolved. The electronic portfolio requires little space and can easily be sent electronically to the next teacher or school.

Student Response System

Though currently relatively costly, another example of a tool for ongoing assessment is the student response system (often called clickers). This technology is available for the young learner and allows teachers to formatively assess for basic understanding and collect and store information both on a whole class and on individuals. The data are used to provide immediate feedback to children and to make adjustments in teaching. This tool allows teachers to identify patterns of learning and gives an overview of areas of strengths and weakness from which the teacher can assess their instructional approaches.

In sum, instructional technology can be an effective tool if it is one of a variety of teaching and learning experiences. It should focus on the objective of promoting higher level thinking skills, encourage the exchange of ideas, allow teachers to scaffold learning of children with many differences. Learning is facilitated when teachers adjust difficulty levels and teaching strategies based on assessment results, intentionally teaching standards-based skills and knowledge, and motivating learning by being guided by children's interest, questions, and desire to learn. The challenges of learning should be presented as fun, not as boring required learning that must be dealt with to move through the educational system.

These tools are examples of teacher resource, support and process tools that can assist in mathematics and all assessment in the classroom. The advantage is the compression of files which eliminates bulky paper documentation and allows for more efficient organization. The files allow better communication with other professionals. The PDAs are particularly valuable for work with young children when observing learning activities that are often in smaller groups and informal naturalistic settings.

TECHNOLOGICAL TOOLS AND APPLICATIONS TO TEACHING AND LEARNING IN MATHEMATICS: EXAMPLES FROM A CHARTER SCHOOL IN THE USA

Specific technology tools and ideas for integrating them into the early childhood classroom are described in the paragraphs below with connections drawn to the essential mathematics content areas, higher order thinking skills, and when appropriate, to a thematic unit on the topic of popcorn. The opening vignette to this chapter described an activity from this school. The following sections will explain how technology was used in this classroom. Of course, below is just a sample of available tools and ideas. These five popular technology tools are open-ended and lend themselves to diverse possibilities and outcomes. As technology changes these tools will be replaced by newer and more advanced tools. Many complement each other and can be used simultaneously. It is advisable to conduct introductory activities prior to the gradual release of responsibility to the children for using technology tools. Activities might encompass a discussion of expectations and explicit demonstrations.

Virtual Manipulatives

Web sites like the National Library of Virtual Manipulatives, http://nlvm.usu.edu/en/nav/vlibrary.html, has a large collection of digital "objects" for several grade bands, including prekindergarten through second grade. According to Moyer, Bolyard, & Spikell (2002), a virtual manipulative is "an interactive, Web-based visual representation of a dynamic object that presents opportunities for constructing mathematical knowledge" (p. 373). Virtual manipulatives are useful for addressing the five major mathematics standards areas: Number/Operations, Geometry, Measurement, and Algebra and Data Analysis. For example, to help children construct skills in Number and Operations, a variety of items can be manipulated while counting. These representations can be used to make comparisons between numbers to illustrate important concepts like more than, less than and equal to as children group and regroup sets. As stated by Jacobs and Crowley (2010), giving children experiences with manipulatives that help them to visualize numbers from one to 10 will help them begin to *subitize*, which they define as recognizing how many objects there are without actually counting each one.

To facilitate knowledge of numbers, a virtual chip abacus can also be manipulated by moving, removing, and exchanging chips that represent place value. Another example is illustrated by Ms. Shepard's kindergarten children described in the introductory vignette. The children use the virtual hundreds chart (as well as a paper-based chart) as another instrument for learning. Among its many uses, the children highlight numbers as they skip count by 2s, 5s and 10s.

To build geometry skills, children can make shapes and solve problems while creating geometric constructions. They can play with virtual tangrams or triangular Triominoes as they rotate, drag, group, flip, and create. Many geometric software applications allow for resizing shapes to experiment with ratio and congruent shapes. They can manipulate geoboards to explore area and perimeter and important measurement concepts based on spatial awareness. Algebraic thinking is explored when children use pattern blocks to manipulate geometric shapes to build patterns and then identify patterns. Children can count virtual money or answer questions using analog clocks. In the area of data analysis and probability, the virtual library site also houses a virtual spinner for children to access in order to explore chance and random choices. Finally, Ms. Shepard's class used the online resource to create virtual bar graphs to represent actual data from the investigation, recording actual kernels that popped in the popping machine as well as pie charts for preferences for popcorn preparation (salted, buttered, plain). The visual displays were printed and revisited with conversation using math talk (that is, more, less, equal).

HTML Links

The World Wide Web also hosts a plethora of simulations, virtual field trips, podcasts, and interactive educational games. Such links may be thoughtfully selected and incorporated into WebQuests, which are student-centered, inquiry-based collections of Internet sources intended to engage students in authentic performance tasks. Below are useful sites with corresponding, brief descriptions. They are divided into three categories:

1. General mathematic-related educational links,
2. Online popcorn math activities and ideas, and
3. A list of websites of authors of young children's books that concern the critical content areas of mathematics.

This list was compiled by Tammy Jones, a teacher and owner of a mathematics and technology education consulting company, and colleague of one of the authors of this chapter.

Teacher Resources: General Mathematics Websites

- **http://illuminations.nctm.org:** This site is a creation of National Council of Teachers of Mathematics' and is a free resource encompassing hundreds of Standards-based lessons and activities for teaching math skills.
- **http://www.kenttrustweb.org.uk/kentict/content/earlyict/:** Teaching and learning activities in the area of mathematics also comprise this website. Its developers include technology tools like digital cameras and images, online kaleidoscope, digital microscopes, simple paint programs, interactive white boards and provide ideas that can be used in whole or small group, both indoors and outdoors, and they have also included questions for teachers to pose to children to encourage higher order thinking.
- **http://www.ixl.com/:** This is a math-related site that teachers can use to help students improve skills in areas such as sorting, ordering, classification, data analysis, graphs, measurement, money, patterns, addition, subtraction, comparing, skip counting, and more. Students simply move the mouse over the appropriate level and skill, and then think about and respond to questions.
- **http://www.mrnussbaum.com:** Teachers can search dozens of interactive games, contests, virtual worlds, and moderated chat forums for helping children in grades kindergarten through eighth grades learn specific skills in numerous discipline areas, including mathematics.
- **http://www.sesamestreet.org/browseallgames:** This website gives children opportunities to build sorting and counting skills, and play with geometric shapes in games such as Bert's Bottle Caps, Identify Shapes with Big Bird, and Count Hats with Elmo and Zoe.

Digital Cameras and Movie Creators

One of the most obvious uses of digital photography is to document and communicate the children's learning progress. Ms. Shepard frequently captures learning in this way. For example, she took photos of the method one student used to place corn kernels on every even number, starting with two on the hundreds chart. She also photographed their works-in-progress (e.g., physical constructions with various open ended materials, including corn kernels) and used the video recording device on her camera to record the children's collaborative efforts at measuring distances of popped corn, debate about why popcorn pops, and their singing and movement associated with popcorn-related songs. She used these productions combined with the children's communication of their original poetry to create a class video. These documentations served as a basis of assessment and were used to further study the children' thinking and learning with the children themselves, with other teachers, and with family members. The video was replayed during group time, in planning meetings with colleagues, and at the end of the day pick-up routine as points of conversation about how to extend the learning experiences.

Digital cameras can also be used in other creative ways. With guidance, children can take and download photographs, measure and resize them to certain specifications, then include them in PowerPoint presentations for the class. Another popcorn-related activity is to encourage students to zoom in when taking photos of popcorn, download, print on heavy cardstock, and cut into large pieces to make puzzles. Children can exchange puzzles and work together to reconstruct them.

Interactive Whiteboard (IWB)

An interactive whiteboard is yet another tool that is gaining popularity in today's early childhood classroom. It is a touch-sensitive vertical surface connected to a computer and projector. The ways in which the electronic whiteboard technology can support the development of math skills was researched in a case study conducted by Wood and Ashfield (2008). The researchers collected and analyzed data from ten classroom observations, as well as teacher interviews and focus group discussions. The study revealed many benefits of interactive whiteboards, including student motivation, opportunities for teacher creativity in lesson design, and student creativity in problem solving and idea development. Wall, Higgins and Smith (2005) found that students perceive the interactive whiteboard to help with their concentration and attention to learning. Wood and Ashfield (2008) found that students engaged in analysis, evaluation, and communication of original ideas.

Teachers can use this tool to visually display information from Web sites, software, video, notes and data, PowerPoint presentations and give students opportunities to interact in countless ways. Free hand drawing, typing text, manipulating projected software applications, or working with online manipulatives that are projected on the screen are other possibilities. All can be saved, edited, and retrieved for revisiting skills and concepts, and the large screen and multimedia capability creates learning that is fun and motivating. The user can select different colored fonts to show odd and even numbers on a number line, display and work with a graphing grid, select and draw geometric shapes, and insert *ClipArt* images, photographs, music and sound effects, animation, video and hyperlinks (leading to interactive games, simulations or even puzzles). The possibilities are endless. Lim and Tay (2003) stated that more research is needed that include instruments for measuring associated higher order thinking skills. Similarly, while Wall, Higgins and Smith (2005) found interactive whiteboards to be motivational, they state more research is needed to comprehend students' understanding, remembering and thinking as it relates to instructional technology of this type.

A small, portable electronic whiteboard is a similar tool. As noted by Trueman (2004), a Maryland teacher and author, this wireless pad or mobile electronic whiteboard gives the teacher the ability to engage active student learning by using the pad with an electric pen to annotate and highlight anything projected from the computer, or to write and draw models which is displayed in real time on the screen. Likewise, if several of these portable devices are available, children can represent their thinking by doing these same activities while solving problems. This can be done from anywhere in the classroom, thus making active teacher monitoring and classroom management easier.

ISSUES, CONTROVERSIES, PROBLEMS: IS TECHNOLOGY NECESSARY TO DEVELOP MATHEMATICAL THINKING?

The original argument against the use of technology with mathematics started with the emphasis on hands-on activities for young children as needed for developmental learning and conceptual exploration of mathematics ideas. Part of this controversy came from the misunderstanding of the term "hands-on" on the part of educators. Many teachers took this literally and believed that learning only occurred when children used their hands to create or manipulate real objects. As better understanding of children's learning evolved the movement for "minds-on" learning began. It became apparent that just using hands with real objects did not necessarily build conceptual understanding in mathematics. When children are not actively engaged mentally there is little retention of concepts from any activity. It is the teacher's responsibility to plan and assess in a manner that will engage the learner. There are many technology-based programs that do engage thinking and motivate students to solve problems. Many teachers assume that young children learn mathematics by touching and moving concrete objects. In much of the talk about improving mathematics education, concrete objects, physical materials, or manipulatives have been seen as essential for mathematics learning. But mathematics is not tangible; it is a set of ideas. Mathematics in the early years does not need to be limited to the concrete or tangible. While Piaget is widely cited regarding the concreteness of children's thinking, what he meant by concrete was different from what people usually mean by it. No matter how well-designed, these manipulatives, in and of themselves, do not guarantee meaningful learning (Baroody, 1989). The use of materials is effective only when they are used to encourage children to think and make connections between the objects and the abstract mathematical idea. It is not so much important that they simply have their hands on, but rather that they have their minds on. Mathematics ideas are not in the manipulatives; they are in the child's mind.

The next issue in the mathematics education arena was concerns about the software used in schools. The early use was and some current use of technology software is clearly lower thinking level applications where children practiced drill. As a more balanced approach to mathematics became popular educators realized there is a need for some drill practice as long as conceptual development was the focus of mathematics instruction. There are many new web sites and software programs that allow children to solve problems and apply higher order thinking. Any web site or program developed through the NCTM like *Figure This* from NCTM http://www.figurethis.org/ Challenges, activities, and materials for teaching and families or *NCTM Illuminations* part of Marcopolo *project*http:// illuminations.nctm.org/ include multiple levels of activities to engage and develop conceptual understanding. The key is in the selection and use of any software.

Many teachers think computers are inappropriate learning tools for young children, especially for mathematics, as they involve no thinking and elicit mindless, random responses from children. Some even misunderstood the concrete nature of computer experiences as hands-on keyboard and mouse. In general, many teachers feel that computers isolate children and prevent social interactions and communications, and so fear that children will become antisocial.

Contrary to these beliefs, computers can be useful in teaching children mathematics, if used appropriately. In fact, computers have some unique advantages (Clements & Sarama, 2008). For example, computers increase children's flexibility with manipulatives as they can move (spatial exploration) or even resize (ratio and proportion) onscreen objects; often it is more difficult, or even impossible, to do these things with real objects. Onscreen objects do not pose the awkwardness of handling that real ones might. Another advantage is that children can save and retrieve their work on computers, and so can work on projects over a long period as they think through the meaning of mathematics connections. Computers can also provide immediate feedback.

Lee & Ginsburg (2009) advise that not all software designated for young children's mathematics education is age–appropriate or high quality. The same can be said of almost any educational material: manipulative, textbook, or television show. Teachers need to select wisely. They should not let colorful graphics; cute animation and music mislead them. Teachers need to critically review content and underlying objectives to evaluate what kinds of learning opportunities and experiences the software will provide for their young students. Drill and practice software may lead to gains in certain rote skills but not be as effective in improving children's conceptual understanding of mathematical ideas. It can easily end up being an electronic version of worksheets or flashcards. Discovery–based software may be valuable when children are encouraged to think and to apply mathematical ideas to solve problems or explain relationships.

In addition, effective use of computers can elicit, encourage and extend children's communication and collaboration in learning. As Clements (1999b) reports, computers serve as catalysts for social interaction. Children working at the computer solve problems together, talk about what they are doing, and help and teach friends. We do not mean to say computers should replace concrete objects or other real-life experiences or learning activities Lee, J.S. & Ginsburg, H.P. (2009). Rather, computers can extend the range of tools children use in their learning experiences. It makes as little sense to say that computers are bad for children as it does to say that books or manipulatives are good. It all depends on what kind of computer software and books and manipulatives are used, and how they are used.

The third and perhaps the largest issue with technology and mathematics for children is teacher training. Butzin (2002) and NAEYC (1996) agree that teacher training as well as equitable access and technical support are often obstacles to effective integration of technology in instruction. Butzin (2002) also contends, "The problem is that schools keep trying to retrofit new technologies into an outdated instructional model" (p.15). She points out that in classroom were didactic (teacher-focused) instruction dominates as the instructional model and a mindset resumes that computers are simply to "play on" after work has been completed, technology will not be a tool for constructivist, individualized, hands-on learning. Teachers have to practice using technology, plan for applications, and learn to discriminate between appropriate resources on the web if they are to become accomplished. This, like all other skills, requires time and support. Universities need to rethink their use of technology as instructional tools if teachers are to become competent and confident. Lecturing using a PowerPoint visual is really a limited approach to technology use in the university classroom.

The strength of technology far outweighs the issues that educators once had about technology and mathematics learning. As discussed in earlier sections of this chapter use of technology in the learning process has many benefits as does technology as a teacher resource and teaching source. It is no longer a question of whether technology should be used in a classroom but how it will be used.

FUTURE TRENDS

The literature on instruction and technology for young children suggests several areas for future exploration and possible barriers to overcome. Wartella and Jennings (2000) advocate a commitment to high quality Internet content by helping web developers to create programs that would best support cognitive development. They encourage new partnerships between schools, content providers, and government in efforts to create incentives for technology development to build on what we know from research about how children think and learn. Similarly, the position statement released by NAEYC (includes the request for teachers and parents to work together to advocate for more appropriate and useful technology applications for children (e.g., programs that promote collaboration, are responsive to cultural and learning differences, are nonviolent, and promote problem solving). Wood and Ashfield (2008) also make the case for the need for additional technology resources that are designed based on the social constructivist theory. The researchers believe that greater access to opportunities for social interactivity with a focus on the process of learning are needed in order to enhance learning and teaching in mathematics with technology.

Training is another area that will need to change for optimal future instructional technology usage (Hasselbring & Glaser, 2000; Fernandez and Luftglass, 2003; and Lim & Tay, 2003). Teachers must feel confident in their abilities and "know how" in using technology. They must be knowledgeable in technology-oriented math lesson design and implementation. Silk, Higashi, Shoop and Schunn (2010) explained, "...that just because the math is present in the activity, it doesn't mean that students will learn math" (p. 21). In other words, we cannot simply put technology tools in front of teachers and children and expect results. The future training of teachers will not be limited to specific software but will include use of tools to support learning, social networking with other teachers to share and compare technology to support mathematics, development for the children in their classrooms to work as a global community rather than in isolation, and open, flexible thinking about how technology fits in their work.

It should also be noted that the future of education increasingly enabled by technology does not imply that teachers' roles will be minimized. Rather, the 21st century will bring with it a proliferation of ways of helping children to learn, thus increasing opportunities for educators to learn, to take on a variety of roles, to reflect, and to grow as learning professionals. We will continue to need educators who are excited about learning about innovative tools so that they can inspire and transfer this excitement to young children.

CONCLUSION

This chapter provides a glimpse of some technological tools that many 21st century teachers are successfully integrating into their collections of instructional tools. There are so many more to explore, including game systems, MP3 players, electronic books, e-book readers, document cameras, Smartphones, student response systems, videoconferencing, and social networking systems. Children of the future may cue a digital playlist that conveys daily, customized, learning activities in mathematics (both online experiences and small group projects, for example) that build on individual learning levels, interests and questions, and preferred learning modalities. It will remain the knowledgeable teacher's responsibility to assess his or her students' needs and use professional judgment about the types of digital tools and activities that are appropriate to implement.

To conclude, early childhood educators can enrich each child's knowledge construction in the area of mathematical, higher order thinking with the help of technology. The potential of technology is unlimited as teachers not only use digital tools to build skills and knowledge but also to promote positive attitudes. Lim and Tay (2003) reported that when asked about technology in the classroom, one teacher explained to them that her objective was for her students "... to gather information from the Internet and later evaluate, organize and present findings" (p.444). The researchers acknowledged that this teacher was thoughtful in her instructional design, particularly in regard to the higher order thinking skills that she wanted to help her students develop. It is not about children pushing buttons or clicking a mouse. Learning is the result of the cognitive processes that are fostered by these 21st century tools.

Reflecting on Young Children, Mathematics and Technology

This section gives you some questions and activities to help you think about how you can use some of the ideas from this chapter in your work.

Research

1. Interview your colleagues about their thinking concerning how students learn mathematics. Analyze the results to determine if there are common ideas. Research resources to determine which of the approaches are supported through research.

Reflect

1. Educators of young children are often in conflict about their beliefs about child development and the new research on children's capabilities. How will you, as a professional, work to change your thinking about mathematics and technology as a resource, support and process tool in your classroom?
2. Work with a peer and list the myths about mathematics and technology that could be influencing your teaching. How can you change your teaching to better support the use of technology and mathematics in your classroom?
3. Analyze your room and how you can arrange the setting to allow children easy access to technology.

Practice

1. *Teacher Talk* is often hard to implement. It will require intentional identification and practice. Work with a peer and to plan and practice words to support learning in your classroom.
2. Work with your peers to develop rubrics that specifically identify developmental tasks in mathematics for young children. Store this in PDAs to prepare for your observational documentation of learning.
3. Identify components of each of the recommended mathematics areas: Number and Operations: Representing, comparing, and ordering whole numbers and joining and separating sets. Geometry: Describing shapes and space Measurement: Ordering objects by measurable attributes Data Analysis and Algebra. Use your school, state and national standards to prepare a list of each task children should be able to do to document competency.
4. Prepare checklists based on the above identified components and put them into your PDA or other technology tool for use in your classroom.
5. Prepare a list of resource tools that teachers can access when teaching mathematics. Separate your list into the NCTM recommended categories for easy support for each area.
6. Practice using technology as you plan for instruction.

REFERENCES

Ainsa, T. (1999). Success of using technology and manipulatives to introduce numerical problem solving skills in monolingual/bilingual early childhood classrooms. *Journal of Computers in Mathematics and Science Teaching*, *18*(4), 361–369.

Airasian, P. W. (1991). *Classroom assessment*. New York, NY: McGraw-Hill.

Anderson, L. W., Krathwohl, D. R., Airasian, P. W., Cruikshank, K. A., Mayer, R. E., & Pintrich, P. R. … Wittrock, M. C. (Eds.). (2001). *A taxonomy for learning, teaching, and assessing: A revision of Bloom's taxonomy of educational objectives*. Boston, MA: Allyn & Bacon, Pearson Education Group.

Butzin, S. M. (2002). Project CHILD (Changing how instruction for learning is delivered): The perfect fit for multimedia elementary schools. *Multimedia Schools*, *9*(6), 14–16.

Chang, C. Y., & Wang, H. C. (2009). Issues of inquiry learning in digital learning environments. *British Journal of Educational Technology*, *40*(1), 169–173. doi:10.1111/j.1467-8535.2008.00850.x

Churches, A. (2009, January, 4). *Bloom's digital taxonomy*. Retrieved April 11, 2010, from http://edorigami.wikispaces.com

Clements, D., & Conference Working Group. (2004). Part one: Major themes and recommendations. In D. H. Clements, J. Sarama, & A.-M. DiBiase (Eds.), *Engaging young children in mathematics education* (pp. 1-72). Mahwah, NJ: Lawrence Erlbum Associates.

Clements, D. H. (1999a). Concrete manipulatives, concrete ideas. *Contemporary Issues in Early Childhood*, *1*(1), 45–60. doi:10.2304/ciec.2000.1.1.7

Clements, D. H. (1999b). The effective use of computers with young children. In Copley, J. V. (Ed.), *Mathematics in the early years* (pp. 119–128). Reston, VA: National Council of Teachers of Mathematics.

Clements, D. H., & Battiste, M. (1992). *Electronic resources: 3D geometry in the 3rd grade: Sorting and describing polyhedra*. Retrieved July 11, 2007, from http://my.nctm.org/ erources/

Clements, D. H., & Sarama, J. (2008). Mathematics and technology: Supporting learning for students and teachers. In Saracho, O. N., & Spodek, B. (Eds.), *Contemporary perspectives on science and technology in early childhood education* (pp. 127–147). Charlotte, NC: Information Age.

Copley, J. V. (2010). *The young child and mathematics* (2nd ed.). Washington, DC: NAEYC/NCTM.

DeVries, R., & Kohlberg, L. (1987). *Programs of early education: The constructivist view*. New York, NY: Longman.

Fennell, F. (2006). *Curriculum focal points for prekindergarten through grade 8 mathematics*. Retrieved June 21, 2010, from http://www.nctm.org/ focalpoints

Fernandez, J. M., & Luftglass, M. (2003). Interactive whiteboards: A powerful learning tool. *Principal*, *83*(1), 63.

Gelman, R., & Brenneman, K. (2004). Science learning pathways for young children. *Early Childhood Research Quarterly*, *19*(1), 150–158. doi:10.1016/j.ecresq.2004.01.009

Hubbell, E. R. (2003). Integrating technology into the Montessori elementary classroom. *Montessori Life*, *15*(2), 40–41.

Kirova, A., & Bhargava, A. (2002). Learning to guide preschool children's mathematical understanding: A teacher's professional growth. *Early Childhood Research & Practice, 4*(1). Retrieved August, 2010 from http://www.ecrp.uiuc.edu/v4n1/kirova.html

Lee, J. S., & Ginsburg, H. P. (2009). Early childhood teachers misconceptions about mathematics education in the United States. *Australian Journal of Early Childhood*, *34*(4), 37–45.

Lim, C. P., & Tay, L. Y. (2003). Information and communication technologies (ICT) in an elementary school: Students' engagement in higher order thinking. *Journal of Educational Multimedia and Hypermedia, 12*(4), 425–451.

Lou, Y., Abrami, P. C., & Apollonia, S. (2001). Small group and individual learning with technology: A meta-analysis. *Review of Educational Research, 71*(3), 449–521. doi:10.3102/00346543071003449

Moyer, P. S., Bolyard, J. J., & Spikell, M. A. (2002). What are virtual manipulatives? [Online]. *Teaching Children Mathematics, 8*(6), 372–377. Retrieved from http://my.nctm.org/eresources/ articlesummary.asp?URI=TCM2002-02372a&from=B.

NAEYC. (1996). Position statement: Technology and young children – Ages three through eight. *Young Children, 51*(2), 4–12.

NAEYC. (2009). *Position statement: Developmentally appropriate practice in early childhood programs serving children from birth through age 8*. Retrieved May 5, 2010, from http://www.naeyc.org/ files/naeyc/file/ positions/position

National Council of Teachers of Mathematics. (2004). *Principles and standards for School Mathematics (2000-2004): A report published by the National Council of Teachers of Mathematics*.

National Mathematics Advisory Panel. (2008). *The final report of the National Mathematics Advisory Panel*. Washington, DC: U. S. Department of Education.

National Research Council. (1989). *Everybody counts: A report to the nation on the future of mathematics education*. Washington, DC: National Academies Press.

National Research Council. (2001). *Adding it all up: Helping children learn mathematics*. Washington, DC: National Academy Press.

National Research Council. (2001a). *Eager to learn: Educating our preschoolers*. Washington, DC: National Academy Press.

National Research Council. (2002). *Scientific research in education*. Washington, DC: National Academy Press.

National Research Council and Institute of Medicine. (2000). *From neurons to neighborhoods: The science of early childhood development*. Washington, DC: National Academy Press.

National Scientific Council on the Developing Child. (2007). *New science provides compelling framework for early childhood investment: Scientists chart path to improving outcomes in learning, behavior, and health for vulnerable children*. Retrieved August 9, 2009, from http://www.developingchild. harvard.edu/ content/

Newcombe, N. (2002). The nativist-empiricist controversy in the context of recent research on spatial and quantitative development. *Psychological Science, 13*(5), 394–401. doi:10.1111/1467-9280.00471

Richardson, K. (2000). *Mathematics standards for pre-kindergarten through grade 2*. Clearinghouse on Elementary and Early Childhood Education. (ERIC document EDO-PS00-11).

Sarama,J.(2004). Technology in early childhood mathematics: Building blocks as an innovative technology-based curriculum in engaging young children in mathematics: Standards for early childhood mathematics education.

Sarama, J., & Clements, D. H. (2003). Building blocks of early childhood mathematics. *Early Childhood Corner, 9*, 480–485.

Silk, E. M., Higashi, R., Shoop, R., & Schunn, C. D. (2009). Designing technology activities that teach mathematics. *Technology Teacher, 69*(4), 21–27.

Trueman, A. (2004). InterWrite SchoolPads take technology to a new level. *T.H.E. Journal*, *32*(1), 37.

Van Hiele, P. (1999). Developing geometric thinking through activities that begin with play. *Teaching Children Mathematics*, *5*, 301–317.

Vygotsky, L. (1978). *Mind in society: The development of higher psychological processes* (Cole, M., John-Steiner, V., Scribner, S., & Souberman, E. (Trans. Eds.)). Cambridge, MA: Harvard University Press.

Wall, K., Higgins, S., & Smith, H. (2005). The visual helps me understand the complicated things: Pupil views of teaching and learning with interactive whiteboards. *British Journal of Educational Technology*, *36*(5), 851–867. doi:10.1111/j.1467-8535.2005.00508.x

Wartella, E. A., & Jennings, N. (2000). Children and computers: New technology. Old concerns. *The Future of Children*, *10*(2), 31–43. doi:10.2307/1602688

Wood, R., & Ashfield, J. (2008). The use of the interactive whiteboard for creative teaching and learning in literacy and mathematics: A case study. *British Journal of Educational Technology*, *39*(1), 84–96.

Yoder, M. B. (2005, August). *Inquiry based learning using the Internet: Research, resources, WebQuests*. Paper presented at the 19th Annual Conference on Distance Learning and Teaching, Madison, WI.

Chapter 11
Technology for Young Children with Special Needs

Sara C. Bicard
University of Memphis, USA

David F. Bicard
University of Memphis, USA

ABSTRACT

Children come to early childhood programs with a wide range of learning abilities, languages, cultural backgrounds, and educational experiences. Most classrooms also include children with special needs or exceptional children, who differ from these typically developing children to such a degree that an individualized program of adapted, specialized education is required to meet their needs (Heward, 2009). This chapter provides a framework for the use of technology to assist these exceptional children in early childhood and primary level classrooms.

INTRODUCTION: EARLY INTERVENTION AND SPECIAL EDUCATION SERVICES FOR CHILDREN WITH DISABILITIES

In 1975 a landmark law, The Individuals with Disabilities Education Act (IDEA), was passed that provides for special education services in the United States. IDEA has been amended and reauthorized multiple times, most recently in 2004, and is the primary federal law that guides special education services for children through six principles: (a) *Zero Reject*, refers to the principle that schools must educate all students with disabilities regardless of the nature or severity of the disability and that no child may be excluded from a public education; (b) *Nondiscriminatory Identification and Evaluation*, refers to non-biased, multi-factored methods of evaluation that must be used to determine a disability and if so, whether special education services are warranted; (c) *Least Restrictive Environment* (LRE) refers to the principle that to the maximum extent appropriate, children with disabilities are educated

DOI: 10.4018/978-1-61350-059-0.ch011

Copyright © 2012, IGI Global. Copying or distributing in print or electronic forms without written permission of IGI Global is prohibited.

with children who do not have disabilities; (d) *Due Process*, means that safeguards are mandated and procedures are in place to protect the rights of children with disabilities and their parents; (e) *Parent Participation and Shared Decision Making,* refers to the principle that schools and local education agencies must collaborate with parents of students with disabilities when designing and implementing services, particularly with placement, goals and objectives, and related services; (f) *Free, Appropriate Public Education*, (FAPE) refers to the principle that all children with disabilities must be provided an appropriate education, outlined in an individualized family service plan for children ages birth to two years old or an individualized education program (IEP) for children ages 3 to 21, at public expense.

In early childhood programs the service provided to these exceptional young children is usually associated with *early intervention*. Early intervention refers to children of school age or younger who are discovered to have or be at risk of developing a handicapping condition or other special need that may affect their development. Approximately 3% of all children birth to three years old and 6% of all children ages 3 to 5 years old receive special education services in the United States (U.S. Department of Education, 2007). Disabilities that qualify for special education include physical disabilities, such as deafness or blindness; mental disabilities, such as Down's syndrome and autism; medical conditions, such as oxygen dependence or traumatic brain injury; learning deficits, such as dyslexia; and behavioral disorders, such as attention deficit hyperactivity disorder (ADHD) and conduct disorders.

Children who receive early intervention special education services are provided additional educational assistance for developmental delays such as speech and language delays, learning disabilities, intellectual disabilities like Down's Syndrome or Autism, and emotional and behavioral disorders. Regardless of a child's disability status, he or she is still expected to demonstrate progress towards attaining high levels of achievement according to the No Child Left Behind Act and IDEA.

Without the services mandated in IDEA, many children with disabilities would have difficulty accessing and participating in the instructional environment in public educational institutions. Particularly because curricular programs utilized in general education are intended for typically developing children and children with disabilities are not commonly considered in the research, development, and adoption process of curricular programs (Hitchcock & Stahl, 2003).

In order to accommodate for the specialized needs of children with disabilities the instructional environment must be adapted to include more accessible and research-based practices for children with disabilities and struggling learners. The challenge for early childhood teachers is to balance the current emphasis on higher standards and accountability with the requirements for special needs children in their classrooms. Technology is an advantageous tool that can provide a variety of resources allowing teachers to adapt the instructional environment for students with a wide range of learning abilities to maximize their progress toward achieving higher standards.

This chapter will approach the use of technology in early childhood programs through three types of applications: adaptation of existing computers and other technology (adapt); computer software programs to address particular skill deficits (address); and specialized technology used to assist the functioning of a child with disabilities (assist). To help users identify and integrate technology to support children with special needs we frame the use of technology in terms of *adapt*, *assist* and *address*.

Objectives

After reading this chapter the reader should be able to better understand the laws in the United States in regards to the education of young children with disabilities. They will learn about the support and importance of technology for children with special needs and how different forms of technology are used in classrooms.

The reader will

- Be able to clarify the teacher's role in early intervention for young children
- Be able to identify appropriate forms of technology to assist exceptional children in early childhood classrooms
- Be able to identify ways to adapt existing computers and other technology to support special needs children.
- Be able to identify specialized technology used to assist the functioning of a child with disabilities and
- Be able to identify computer software programs to address particular skill deficits.

BACKGROUND

The traditional approach to education of young children with disabilities is special education and related support services such as speech therapists, physical therapy, behavioral analysis is often misunderstood by schools, teachers, and parents. Special education services support children with disabilities in achieving individualized goals that may be perceived as different from the normal instructional environment and general curriculum. However, many of these individualized goals are sub-skills or components of the general curriculum and align with a standard set of expectations for what is considered a "normal" child. The approach to learning and the instructional approaches in the classroom are not adapted to address the abilities of children with special needs, instead teachers must identify how special needs goals relate to the instructional environment and general curriculum. For example, the expectation for all children to learn colors, letters, and shapes in early childhood programs can easily be approached for a student with a disability who has a language delay by allowing the child to point to the colors or give the proper shape to a teacher instead of identifying the colors by name.

The student and his or her academic and development goals and objectives should blend into and address the instructional environment so the problem-solving process is oriented around how the child can best access and communicate understanding of the instructional environment and general curriculum. There are several ways that technology can be utilized to increase the accessibility of general curriculum for students with disabilities. Existing computers and other technology can be adapted to make it more accessible, computer software programs can be utilized to address particular skill deficits, or specialized technology can be used to assist the functioning of a child with disabilities.

Definition and Selection of Assistive Technology (AT)

The Individuals with Disabilities Education Act (IDEA) of 2004 defines assistive technology as, "... any item, piece of equipment, or product system, whether acquired commercially off the shelf, modified, or customized, that is used to increase, maintain, or improve functional capabilities of a child with a disability" (20 U.S.C. §1401 [2004], 20 C.F.R. §300.5). Assistive technology can be thought of as any item that supports a child's ability to participate actively in his or her home, childcare program, school, or other community settings. It is a broad term that includes items ranging from something as "low tech" as a foam wedge for positioning to something as "high tech" as a power wheelchair for independent mobility. AT can include any tool, from low tech tools such as flexible drinking straws and pencil grips, to high tech tools that are complex electronic devices such as remote controls and speech synthesizers, that may increasing the daily functioning of children with disabilities (Parette & Murdick, 1998). A child with disabilities may need adaptive technology or assistive technology in the following areas to increase their independence and receive FAPE in the LRE: Mobility and positioning, augmentative and alternative communication, sensory (visual & assistive listening), environmental access (controls and manipulators), computers (computer based instruction and computer access), independent living (self care and self help), and socialization and exploration (adaptive toys, leisure/recreation) (Parette & Murdick, 1998; Rhodes & Seiler, 2007). Other examples of assistive technology for young children include items such as switch-operated toys, laminated picture boards, head pointers, specialized drinking cups, adapted spoons, augmentative and alternative communication (AAC) devices, apnea monitors, computers, crutches, and more (NECTAC, 2010). It is extremely important to note that a child's needs for assistive technology or supplementary aides and services such as remedial or adaptive technology must be considered when developing the child's IFSP (Individualized Family Service Program) or IEP (Individualized Educational Program). In addition, in most cases if the team decides adaptive equipment will benefit the student in accessing the general curriculum it the *responsibility of the school district to pay* for the assistive technology.

Identifying the Need for Assistive Technology Services

Not only does IDEA provide for use of these technologies in "educationally relevant settings", it also mandates assistive technology services including an evaluation of the child's needs based on assessment data, obtaining and individualizing devices to meet a child's needs, up-keep of devices, coordination of services and device use, and training or technical assistance for teachers, staff, family members, and the child. When considering assistive technology for a child with disabilities, the IFSP or IEP team usually consists of the child, the child's parents or guardians, the special education teacher, the general education teacher, a speech therapist, an occupational therapist, and sometimes an advocate who looks out for the needs of the child and family. To start the team reviews relevant psycho-educational assessment data, the child's present level of academic and functional performance level including strengths and weaknesses, the goals and objectives for the child, and the demands of the setting (Bryant & Bryant, 2003). The team then determines if assistive technology may assist the child in achieving appropriate goals and objectives in a learning environment that is, if not the general education setting, closest to the general education setting as possible. In making their decisions about assistive technology the team looks for assistive technology that enhance the strengths of the child and matches his or her needs (Chambers, 1997). If it is determined that an assistive technology device may help, an assistive technology evaluation is conducted by an assistive technology specialist. This evaluation may include ecological assessments that consider the contexts in which the device will be used, practical assessments during which the child actually utilizes the device while interacting with others, and ongoing assessment, which may take a variety of forms, but continues repeatedly over time (Bryant & Bryant, 2003).

Effective Assistive Technology Services

It is critical to involve families in the selection and assessment of assistive technology. First, parental involvement and shared decision making are mandated by law. A critical component of early intervention should be parent involvement and training (Mahoney & Kaiser, 1999). Second, parent and family goals, expectations for the child, and tolerance of assistive technology devices may be different than those of professionals working with the child. By taking their input and wishes into consideration when selecting assistive technology, device abandonment may be minimized. When an assistive technology device is abandoned or not utilized, it is an expensive mistake in terms of time and finances depending of the complexity of the device. To reduce the likelihood that a device is abandoned, parents and families should be consulted regarding their expectations of the child's independence, if they are willing to support the use of the device inside and outside the home (e.g., community settings such as restaurants and grocery stores), the degree to which the family wants the child to be accepted and the relationship to how the parents and child feel about the device (e.g., self-conscious), how soon they expect to see results from using the device, and willingness to attend training to facilitate use of the device (Alper & Raharinirina, 2006). Parents and families may have hesitations or concerns about assistive technology such as that the device's visibility in public, expense, the amount of time required for training, appearance that professionals have "given up" on the child learning to function independently, or that skills will not develop because of dependence on the device (Parette & McMahan, 2002). Proactively addressing parent and family concerns may facilitate their acceptance of assistive technology for their child.

TYPES OF ASSISTIVE TECHNOLOGY

There are many technologies that may function as assistive technology for children with disabilities. However, a technology will only serve this function for a child based on how well it meets the individual needs of the students. Assistive technology should support and enhance instruction, not distract from it. When appropriately used, assistive technology will also modify how the student receives or engages in instruction and with the environment to allow the most independence and success as possible. General areas in which assistive technology may be utilized to support children include computers, augmentative and alternative communication, mobility and positioning, sensory, environmental access, independent living, and socialization and exploration. However, early childhood educators report frequently utilizing assistive technology in the areas of communication and learning, specifically adaptations to computers (Judge, 2006).

Adapt, Address and Assist

To help users identify and integrate technology to support children with special needs we frame the use of technology in terms of *adapt*, *address* and *assist*. We will start this with discussion of adaptation, ways to modify computers to support learning of special needs children. The three types of AT are classified according to how children might best be served. Adapt refers to making an adjustment to current technology often already found in schools. Address refers to technology used to support learning by providing additional practice or information. Assist refers to technology that helps children work and navigate in educational environments

Adapt: Computers

Adaptive technology for computers involves modifying an existing technology such as a computer to make it easier to use for a child with disabilities. In addition, computers can be used to assist students with high-incidence disabilities with organization, note-taking, writing, productivity, access to reference materials, remediation of skills, and modifying instructional materials (Edyburn, 2006; Lahm & Morrissette, 1994).

Universal Access Features

Most children with disabilities have access to computers in their educational environments. However, modifications to the computer may make computers more user-friendly to children with disabilities. Many modifications such as the universal access feature, already exist within computers and only need to be turned on through the accessibility options in the computer settings or control panel. The computer display can be modified to provide high contrast in color schemes to increase the legibility for some children with vision impairments. Keyboard shortcuts or modifications change how a child interacts with the keyboard. For example, sticky keys will allow a child to press one key at a time instead of holding down a combination of keys to activate a function. Filter keys will change the rate of repetition or ignore multiple keystrokes if a key is held down. Toggle keys will provide a sound cue if options such as number lock, cap lock, etc. are activated on the keyboard. Sound modifications include altering sound notifications on the computer, which may be difficult for children with hearing impairments to hear, to include a visual warning such as a screen flash. A computer mouse can be modified so that the cursor can be moved through using the numeric keypad or increasing the size and blinking rate of the cursor. Serial keys allow for alternative input devices, discussed later in the chapter, to activate the computer. Information about universal access features for the two major computer operating systems, MicroSoft Windows (http://www.microsoft.com/enable/training/default.aspx) and Apple MacIntosh (http://www.apple.com/accessibility), are available on their websites.

Input Devices

Some students with disabilities will require alternative input and output methods for computers even with the use of conventional computer access and accessibility features. Some students with disabilities may require augmentations to the standard keyboard. These keyboard additions may include a keyguard that provides additional separation between keys to allow for easier keyboarding and limit accidental keystrokes, moisture guards to protect the keyboard from moisture such as drool, and key labels, either color coded or tactile, to prompt students which keys to activate. Pointing devices such as mouthsticks, hand pointers, head pointers, etc. can be used for direct selection of keys instead of fingers. Alternative keyboards that reduce or enlarge the size of the traditional keyboard may be more accessible for students with physical impairments. Mini keyboards are smaller than traditional keyboards and require less motion to activate the keys. Programmable keyboards are enlarged keyboards with additional spacing between keys. A key overlay may allow for specialized functions to be programmed for individual students.

Some students may have difficulty with keyboards all together and may find interface devices that allow alternative input devices to activate the keyboard and its functions to be more accessible. A touch screen is a device placed on the computer monitor that allows the child to touching the screen to activate keys, functions, or computer programs instead of the keyboard. Similarly, an onscreen keyboard is a visual of a traditional keyboard on the screen that enables a mouse or other pointing device to select the keys. Alternatives to the computer mouse include joysticks and trackballs that can be used to select items directly on the screen. The physical demands of standard keyboards are eliminated with use of touch screen and an onscreen keyboard.

A switch can also provide an input signal into the computer. Although switches vary in size and activation, the purpose is to simplify the physical response required of the child to produce an action on the computer or other battery operated or electronic device (e.g., battery operated toy, electronic communication board, CD players) (Johnston, 2003). Children younger than 1 year old with various disabilities have been able to successfully manipulate switches to activate toys, music, computer visual displays, and vibration (Campbell, Milbourne, Dugan & Wilcox, 2006). Switches can be activated through movement of the head, arms, legs, eyes, etc., or by electronic signals in the body, breathing actions, or phonation (e.g., voice or sounds). An example of a commonly used switch is the JellyBean Switch that looks like an oversized button that the child pushes to manipulate the computer or other electronic device. Operation of a switch can be momentary in that the switch is activated for as long as it is pressed, latched which requires multiple activations to turn on and off, and timed to turn itself on and off for a set period of time.

Although voice recognition systems have become more mainstream, they are still considered an adaptive technology in that they allow the child to operate the computer by speaking to it. Voice recognition systems have different characteristics that may lend themselves to better suit a child's particular strengths. A child must train the program to recognize his or her voice in a speaker dependent system. However, a speaker independent system recognizes a variety of speech patterns from different children without training. Independent systems maybe easier for children to use although number of words that the program recognizes may be limited. Another difference in voice recognition software is the required time delay between words spoken. In discrete systems a pause of less than one second between words while dictating is required. No pause between words, a more natural manner of speaking for most children, is required by continuous systems.

Output Devices

Some children may require the methods that computers provide information be modified to allow for easier text and figure access. Some students may require screen magnification in which enlarged characters are display on the monitor. If universal access features do not resolve issues that a child may have, a larger visual display may be achieved by using a larger monitor or software programs that are designed to specifically provide additional magnification.

An alternative to screen magnification is speech synthesis or screen reading, which provide synthetic or computerized spoken language of information displayed on a computer monitor. While most computers come with speakers to amplify sound, an additional internal board or chip inserted into the computer or an external hardware device may be required. There are many software options that provide speech synthesis or screen reading. Word prediction software may include speech output. Software is also available that only includes a speech synthesizer, such as DECtalk. Several different screen reader programs are also available (e.g., JAWS by Henter Joyce, Speech Stream by Text Help, OutSPOKEN by ALVA Access). Speech output programs may require the child to record words into the program to produce digitized speech or will utilize text-to-speech technology that converts letters and letter combinations to speech sounds.

Another manner in which computers provide information is through printers, which create hard copies of information stored or viewed on the computer. For some students simply enlarging the computer's printer type size will allow for easier access to the printed material. However for some students with severe visual impairments, a Braille embosser may be necessary. A Braille embosser transforms computer generated print into embossed Braille output (e.g., VersaPoint Due by Blazie Engineering).

These input and output devices have an enormous potential for assisting students with disabilities or other students who have difficulties reading and writing. For example, word prediction software can help students with LD reduce the impact of their "word finding", spelling, and basic grammar problems. As the computer will produce a likely word the student is trying to spell as a letter or word is entered, or after typing a sentence it will indicate grammatical errors, providing immediate feedback on writing. Speech synthesis features can also be used to model of oral reading through the children hearing pronunciations from computer speech and watching computer sound out words. Speech synthesis can be used to distinguish between reading and word calling and shows the impact of punctuation on meaning/logic with additional models of oral reading.

Address: Educational Software

There are three categories of general educational software: tutoring, practice, or simulation programs (Irvine Belson, 2003). Tutoring programs provide instruction on a select skill. Practice programs provide additional practice on a select skill and are frequently referred to as drill/skill programs. Simulation programs provide a simulation of environments from which the child to learn cause/effect relationships of a subject area among other things.

Most early childhood special educators report using computer software to reinforce a concept (Judge, 2001). Software applications designed for children with disabilities are usually referred to as remedial technology. This type of technology provides remedial instruction, teaching what the child needs to know in order to participate in general education curriculum as much as possible. Remedial instruction involves assessing the instructional needs of the child and basing instructional goals and objectives around the identified needs. Furthermore, complex tasks are task analyzed, or broken down into smaller, more doable tasks to provide instruction on the child's level and provide opportunities for him or her to succeed. Additional practice opportunities are provided with instructional feedback and appropriate reinforcers. Student performance is continuously assessed to determine if the child is making progress towards achieving the identified goal and objective. Remedial technology provides intensive practice, presents a topic in a different way, or provides a task analysis of the topic by requiring the child to master sub-skills prior to practice with more complex skills.

Advantages of Educational Software

Although education software should not take the place of teacher instruction, it does provide many advantages when working with young children with disabilities. When selected to match the learner's needs, educational software can individualize instruction for young children with disabilities by focusing on a specific skill or task, manipulating the pace of learning and the order and amount of skills presented, and providing immediate feedback while presenting instruction in an interesting and engaging manner. In addition, software can empower the children by providing the students with greater control over the learning environment so they can work at own pace. Another advantage is that the children are provided higher levels of active learning with some software packages. That is, a student is making many more academic responses than he or she would normally make in the same amount of time during instruction. Still further, software may provide additional opportunities to practice social skills when utilized with other peers (McCormick, 1987; Spiegel-McGill, 1989).

For many children, work completed on the computer provides less frustration than paper/pencil tasks. Some children are particularly bothered by frequently erasing mistakes on paper because although erased marks are still visible. Completing work on the computer allows for *cleaner work* in that once mistakes are deleted they are not visible. For example, a student creating a word web with *Kidspiration®* may make and delete many errors without them being visible on the final product. Whereas a child creating a word web with pencil and paper may erase many errors that are somewhat visible on the final product. In addition, many children are more comfortable working on the computer because instructional feedback provided from educational software may be perceived as less judgmental and more immediate than traditional sources of feedback.

However, as a word of caution, not all software packages provide high levels of active responses or practice on the relevant learning objectives. It is up to the teacher or IEP/IFSP team to make critical evaluations of curricular materials with the focus on the important skill the student is supposed to master.

Selecting and Evaluating Educational Software

First and foremost, children's instructional needs should drive the selection process for educational software. When uniformly applied to educational software being considered for adoption in a classroom, all of the following information will aid teachers in identifying education software that has the most potential for effectively teaching children.

Many school districts will provide general educational software, but sometimes software programs do not meet the needs of the child with disabilities. Since educational software programs rarely align themselves with national or state learning standards, the primary factor in selecting educational software to remediate deficits of students with disabilities should be the degree to which it matches the instructional objective. Additionally education software may vary in the quality of graphics, sounds, animation, audience, instructional soundness, and assessment capabilities. It is critical that a teacher carefully select educational software that will enhance and support their instruction and meet the needs of their students. It is important to remember that educational software and other computer programs can be used different ways with different children because certain aspects of a software program will be more beneficial than others for each individual child.

Software publishers, educational organizations, and websites provide information about educational software programs on the internet. Publishers may list curriculum areas and academic levels and provide demonstration versions of the software on their websites. Educational and parent organizations often provide evaluations of educational software online. These sources can provide helpful information, however the best way to determine if educational software will meet the needs of your student with disabilities is to personally test it out.

When evaluating educational software, be sure to note the name, version, price, and publisher in case you decide to purchase the educational software. The following are important considerations in selecting educational software for your students (Irvine Belson, 2003). First, determine if the program is compatible with the computer in your classroom by looking at the hardware requirements.

Next, identify the content area and the type of knowledge the software is designed to teach and evaluate the degree to which it addresses specific areas of need. It is important to preview software programs to determine the content area and skills taught and not to "judge a book by its cover." For example, the software program may be marketed as mathematics software but may actually be a computer game that tangentially uses numbers to move the game along and does not actually teach or provide practice on math skills. Remember, the purpose of the software is to provide practice to aid in memorization of basic math facts, understanding basic principles, or problem solving.

Teachers should carefully analyze the process and type of instruction programmed in the software. Software that contains a task analysis component and integrated learning systems, systems that monitor the students' progress and provide teachers with detail reports on a student's skill development, can be very useful for determining what aspect of the task is difficult for the student. Many students with disabilities need explicit instruction to be successful. Direct Instruction (DI), a published curriculum containing very explicit instruction is carefully sequenced, highly structured curriculum utilizing rapid pacing, active student responding, and scripted lessons. Although DI is mainly published by SRA® in paper form, there are websites and software to provide this type of instruction such as *Headsprout Reading*®, which adapts instruction in vivo based on student responses. Another example of software utilizing a task analysis approach, Access to Math (Don Johnson Incorporated) allows for individualized worksheets with specific types of math problems to be created.

Software should be instructionally sound. As you may recall from the introduction the work of teachers is to find ways to support the same learning as found in the general curriculum for special needs children. Teachers should evaluate software for the presence of the elements described below. If these elements are not featured in the software, it will not be as effective in teaching the desired skill or concept as software that does contain the features.

- Clarity of instructional antecedents (e.g., direction, question, problem) presented.
- Availability of prompts (e.g., cues, hints) before the student is required to respond.
- Adequacy of "think time" between the presentation of the instructional antecedent and when the child is required to respond and minimal time between presentations of each instructional antecedent.
- The type and frequency of student response required. Effective educational software should provide a high level of student engagement or active student responding (ASR). Children should be required to progress through the software program by responding to instructionally relevant stimuli instead of simply clicking the mouse to move through the program. A software program that requires high amounts of observable, measurablestudent responding will be more effective than one with lower levels of ASR.
- Type and amount of feedback and error correction provided. The more specific and frequent the feedback, the more effective the instruction.
- The stimuli to which students are responding. Teachers should not assume that children are always responding to instructionally relevant stimuli in the software. If not properly designed, other elements in the software program may allow students to answer correctly but not because they have acquired the target skill. For example, if the software designed to present numbers in a maze and students must connect the numbers in order to exit the maze, there should be multiple ways out of the maze with only one of the ways with the correct number sequence. If there were only one way out of the maze, children could simply respond to the maze and not to the order of numbers but still respond correctly.
- Instructional strategies (Stokes & Bauer, 1977) and practice opportunities for maintenance and generalization of skills. Children are more likely to maintain and generalize skills if provided multiple and real-life examples, allowed to practice the skill in "natural" situations, and taught skills until fluent.

Another critical variable in evaluating software is the ease of use. Software will not be an effective instructional tool if it is difficult to access and use. Students should be able to independently operate the software without a lot of teacher supervision. Teachers should pay particular attention to the clarity and accessibility of instructions. The program should provide clear directions and prompts for students to utilize the program. Clearly written user guides will aid the problem solving process should issues arise when using the software in the classroom. A user guide should be readily available to the teacher. If you cannot locate your paper copy, the guide should also be posted online at the company's website. Even the best written user guide can be difficult to interpret; therefore technical support offered online or by phone can reduce a teacher's frustration if problems arise.

Particularly important for early childhood is the degree to which the software is developmentally appropriate for the children. Teachers should analyze the vocabulary, graphics, layout, and design of the software to ensure a match between the developmental level of the children and audience for which the program was designed. If the program is not interesting or stimulating to the student, it will not provide successful instruction.

When students use software to produce a permanent product, such as writing a story or creating a graphic organizer, the degree of open-endedness and flexibility of the software should be assessed. A range of options such as availability of templates, import and export capabilities, creating original work, and changing difficulty levels will allow teachers to more closely match the software to the child's needs. The feature to save work or level in a program can reduce the frustration for many children with disabilities as they may not be able to finish the assignment or program at one sitting.

The technical soundness of the software program should also be considered by teachers. The appearance of the program such as animations, sounds, and colors should facilitate student interest but not distract from instruction. Hypermedia or different kinds of media relating to a topic should allow children to move in a nonlinear fashion from one segment to another (e.g., image links that take you to new sections or pages of information). Hypermedia can benefit children with reading and commutation difficulties (Boone & Higgins, 1993; Nelson & Materson, 1999). As mentioned earlier, integrated learning systems, systems that track student progress and performance are very beneficial for teachers, especially if the program provides detailed reports on a student's skill development. Printable progress reports may be sent home to parents or used to document progress towards instructional goals and objectives for students with disabilities.

Finally, quality software will be inclusive of diversity. The software should be free of gender, ethnic, religious, or sexual bias. Software should not contain assumptions about people from different backgrounds. Sources of prejudice may subtle and not blatantly obvious. Teachers should carefully examine content and characters portrayed in the software to ensure diversity is appropriately represented.

Assist: Augmentative and Alternative Communication Devices

Augmentative & Alternative Communication (AAC) is "an area of clinical practice that attempts to compensate (either temporarily or permanently) for the impairment and disability patterns of individuals with expressive disorders (i.e., the severely speech-language and writing impaired)" (AHSA, 1989). A wide range of strategies and methods are used to assist children who have difficulties speaking or writing to communicate. An AAC system consists of symbols or vocabulary, a method to select symbols or vocabulary, and a method for transmitting the symbol or vocabulary to a communicative partner. An AAC system may be utilized to augment or add to a child's existing ability, such as utilizing a device to supplement a child's existing speech because it is not understandable. An alternative system is utilized to communicate through nonvocal means.

AAC components may be unaided and not require any equipment such as sign language or cued speech. In other cases, a physical aid or device may be required. Aided techniques require an external device or piece of equipment such as picture exchange communication system (PECS), communication books or boards, or voice output communication aids (e.g., speech synthesizers). The foundation of any aided AAC is the symbol system. Ideas and concepts are represented by symbols in aided techniques and function as spoken words. Therefore, choosing symbols is extremely important to successful communication by a child utilizing an aided AAC system.

Selecting Symbols

Many factors impact the types of symbols chosen for an AAC system such as a child's cognitive, linguistic, visual, and perceptive abilities. The child's strengths and weaknesses in these areas will impact the complexity or abstractness of the symbols selected, style, size, and number of symbols selected. Symbols themselves can range from simple to complex such as actual objects, photographs, drawings, or written words. Abstract symbols, those with icons that may have multiple meanings (e.g., a picture of the sun could represent hot, circular, yellow, happy) or the alphabet, are the most flexible and allows for a wider range of communication opportunities. The detail, outline, color, and background color are stylistic elements of symbols that should be selected based on functionality and personal preferences and needs of the child (e.g., a child with visual impairments may benefit from simple black and white illustrations instead of pictures with many details and low color contrast). Teachers should continuously evaluate the stylistic choices of symbols to ensure that a child can effectively identify and select the symbol. When determining the size, spacing, and positioning of pictures a child's visual and motor needs should be considered. For children with visual or motor impairments, larger pictures may be easier to see, recognize, and select than smaller pictures. Especially when dealing with young children with disabilities, it may be necessary to teach the child how to utilize the AAC system with concrete representations or large (e.g., full page) symbols and gradually reduce the size of the symbols to no less than 2 inches. While a teacher may search for images on the internet to use as symbols, there are several online resources for symbols. *Boardmaker*® software by Mayer-Johnson is commonly used for a source of symbols. *Boardmaker*® is a teacher utility program, software that makes a teacher's job easier, to create symbols for high-tech and low-tech AAC systems. Essentially, it is a catalog of digital picture communication symbols that can be used for AAC systems, picture activity schedules, and other language development activities. The symbols can be presented alone or with words or only words. Students with visual impairments may find it easier to perceive symbols created using software programs and quality printers than hand drawn or copied symbols, as software generated symbols typically results in clearer symbols.

Selecting vocabulary that symbols represent is critical to the success of an AAC system. Symbols should empower the child and allow them to impact the environment around them by what they communicate. Symbols represent vocabulary that child will need to frequently utilize in a variety of settings with additional symbols added as the child masters existing symbols in the AAC system (Blackstone, 1988; Fallon & Light, 2001). To identify frequently used vocabulary, teachers should identify common feelings and emotions and the activities in which a child engages. These are then prioritized based on frequency of engagement and student interest. A teacher can identify words used in an activity by listening to other peers as they engage in the activity and/or by generating a list of possible words that may be required to engage in the activity. Of the words generated, the teacher again prioritizes which words are most frequently used and important to the activity. Teachers should select a balance of words that include a variety of verbs and nouns associated with the activity (and adjective and adverbs depending on the ability of the child). Symbols are then selected for the words.

The ultimate goal of selecting vocabulary that symbols represent is that the child can engage in naturalistic, rich, and varied types of communication (e.g., make a positive or negative comment, ask a question, maintain a conversation, and make a demand). Vocabulary should match the personality of the child and be age appropriate. The challenge for teachers is to select words/phrases that will be functional in situations as they arise. Phrases and sentences may be appropriate depending on the functioning level of the child and facilitate more natural communication (e.g., Where is ___?, I want ___). In addition, initiation (e.g., hello, excuse me), clarification (e.g., I don't understand, that's not what I mean), rejection (e.g., I don't want to, I don't like), conversation starters (e.g., I have a baby sister. Do you?), and conversation maintainers (e.g., tell me more) statements will add to the richness of communication as the child is capable of understanding and selecting.

Selection Techniques for Aided Communication Systems

The method that a child selects a symbol to communicate to a partner should be based on the child's motor strengths and needs. Direct selection is an efficient selection technique and the easiest for children to learn. Symbols may be selected directly by utilizing physical movement to point to the desired symbol (e.g., finger-pointing, pointing with a head or mouth stick, eye-gazing at symbol). It may be necessary to reduce the number of symbols if a child is struggling with the physical effort involved with selecting a symbol. When using a high-tech AAC system, physical effort may also be reduced through electronic direct selection, pressing keys on a standard or modified keyboard or other adaptive input device to select the symbol. Non-scanning switches also allow for direct selection and are programmed with specific messages. The child activates the specific switch to communicate the desired message (e.g., red button states "I need to go to the restroom." Blue button states, " I am hungry.").

Another selection technique involves the child selecting a symbol when a scanner (e.g., communication partner, computer, electronic AAC device) identifies the desired symbol. A communication partner may point to individual symbols until the child responds with a facial, motor, or vocal response to indicate the desired symbol has been selected. With high-tech systems, symbols are displayed on the face of the device or computer screen and the child selects a choice by activating a switch or key on keyboard when symbol is highlighted or lit up. Many devices feature different methods of scanning symbols (e.g., by rows, columns, etc). Some children with visual impairments may require auditory scanning, naming the symbols aloud. When dealing with a child with a more complex symbol system, auditory scanning should name the category of symbols, then each symbol in the category selected.

Adapt, Address, and Assist: Aided AAC Devices

AAC systems may include low-tech and high-tech devices. Non-electronic systems such as communication board, communication books, picture schedules or displays are considered low-tech devices. These systems should be utilized first due to their flexibility and cost. Low-tech devices display symbols in a variety formats to allow children to select the desired symbol. When selecting an appropriate format for a child, teachers should consider the accessibility of frequently used symbols, ease of use, portability, unobtrusiveness of format.

Low-Tech Aided Devices

A communication board is a single display of symbols and may range in size and number of symbols based on the child's physical and visual abilities and repertoire of vocabulary, but is usually fits in the child's lap or on a tray. Similarly, a communication book is a compilation of symbol displays arranged in categories that allow for a larger vocabulary. Symbols on each individual display or page in the communication book relates to a specific topic or activity. Communication boards and books should be of a size and construction that is portable to other locations, unobtrusive to activities, does not call undue attention to the child, durable, and require minimal physical and cognitive effort to produce timely communication. Picture Exchange Communication System (PECS) is a non-electronic aided system based on Skinner's analysis of verbal behavior that was designed for young children with autism. PECS involves a child selecting pictorial representations and delivering to a communicative partner to communicate.

High-Tech Aided Devices

Electronic AAC devices are similar in basic functions as low-tech devices, but have several features not available with low-tech options. Many electronic AAC devices utilize a membrane keyboard and overlay of symbols for the child to select from. A variety of symbol overlays can be created as the child's vocabulary expands. The amount of vocabulary that may be programmed into the device varies on the device's memory.

When a child selects a symbol, the device may display and/or speak the word or phrase represented by the symbol. High-tech devices may have speech output options such as digitized speech, recorded human speech, or synthesized speech, speech produced electronically through text-to-speech software program within the device. With these options the quality of speech such as smooth speech or more robotic-like speech, and female or male voices may be selected based on user preference. Although electronic devices are more expensive than non-electronic devices, they may be more advantageous for children in that they provide increased independence because the device scans for symbols and speech output may be customized to reflect the child's age.

Arranging Symbols for Aided AAC Devices

When creating communication boards, communication books, or keyboard overlays, the arrangement of symbols should be based on the child's cognitive, linguistic, visual, and perceptive abilities and range of motion, the selection technique, and frequent communication situations (Dell et al., 1998). Related symbols (e.g., similar topics, parts of speech, important messages, messages specific to certain activities) should be grouped together in rows or columns. The most important and frequently used symbols should be arranged so that they are the easiest for the child to select. Color-coding symbols may also enhance the organization. Related symbols could contain the same color or have the same color board or background. Depending on the child's functioning level, providing symbols of the alphabet or numbers may allow them to participate in more spontaneous communication that picture symbols may not address.

Teaching a Child to Utilize AAC Devices

One instructional method that has been successful in teaching children to use AAC devices is enhanced milieu teaching (EMT) or naturalistic instruction (James, Bicard, & Bicard, 2010; Olive et al., 2007; Schepis, Reid, Behrmann, & Sutton, 1998). EMT consists of engaging the child in activities that require communication, interacting with the child to model and prompt new language, and providing positive reinforcement when the child uses new language in appropriate contexts (Hancock & Kaiser, 2002). For example, if a child expresses an interest in wanting to play with a fire truck by reaching over a peer to retrieve it, the teacher may use physical prompting to show the child how to select the correct symbol on the AAC device and then immediately reward the child by providing access to the fire truck. As the child consistently selects the correct symbol in similar communication situations, the teacher reduces the restrictiveness of the prompt to gently guiding the student to select the symbol, then to gesturing to the symbol, and finally verbally encouraging the child to select the symbol. In the end, the participants were incidentally engaged in communication by placing desired object out of reach and taught to use the AAC through most-to-least prompting in naturalistic settings and communication scenarios. This procedure resulted in four non-verbal children, two diagnosed with autism and two diagnosed with mental retardation, spontaneously requesting items using an AAC. Two of the four children actually began to verbalize requests in the special education classroom and other settings and untrained situations within the school (James, Bicard, & Bicard, 2010). It is also important to train communication partners with the system so that they can identify and interpret the communication attempt.

AAC uses a variety of techniques to supplement a child's abilities to communicate. It is highly recommended to train the child and provide access to AAC system as early as possible. Utilizing an AAC system does not preclude a child from developing speech. Actually the opposite may be the case and AAC systems may enhance speech and language development.

ISSUES, CONTROVERSIES, PROBLEMS

In 2000 the two biggest barriers identified by consumers were lack of information and knowledge about appropriate AT, and lack of funding to purchase the needed AT (National Council on Disability, 2000). These two issues continue to present problems for technology use with special needs children and professionals. The current system places the burden on the individuals or families who need AT. They have to find out what is out there, navigate the system and funding streams, and know their rights and fight for them. The few success stories that were found in a survey from the National Council on Disability found the successes occurred only after the parents or individuals became experts at the law and government procedures, spent months fighting the many systems, went through a legal battle, or lobbied legislators. For many, the battle does not seem worth the reward. Unfortunately, the rapid acquisition of educational technology has not sufficiently addressed the needs of students with disabilities. Access for students with disabilities is just beginning to be identified as an important factor when purchasing educational technology.

It is the responsibility of the school district to pay for needed technology when a child enters their schools. This places an added burden on schools often struggling with budgets. The cost of addressing each individual child's needs often demand special staff, material and technology. Because of this many schools avoid or delay assistive technology purchases. The general rule is that the AT device remains the property of the school. Under this general rule, the device remains with the school upon the student's departure. The school can spend thousands of dollars on equipment to have it stored after a child leaves the school, sitting in a storage room not used. Currently, public dollars are being spent on technology for schools, community centers, libraries, and other public entities without clear policy guidance regarding accessibility. As a result, individuals with disabilities frequently find themselves unable to use the newly installed technology and the public agency is left scrambling trying to fix the access problem--usually at significant cost. In addition, in far too many instances, the public entity asks a "special" disability program, with already limited funding, to bear the cost of fixing the access problem. For example, some states and schools are requiring special education budgets to bear the costs of accessibility adaptations for educational technology rather than utilizing general educational technology dollars to provide access. This would be similar to requiring special education to fund the cost of an elevator when building a new school facility. Accessibility costs should be included in overall technology budgets, not shuffled off to special funding sources. One solution for struggling school districts would be for Uncle Sam to provide funding to establish a statewide loan network that could provide 30-, 60-, or 90-day loans to determine the practicality of a device in the environments in which it will be used. The bank could be maintained with rental fees based on the cost of the equipment. A "statewide warehouse of assistive technology" (SWAT) would allow the equipment that was tried on a loan basis to stay with the student user if the device proves itself to be appropriate for the student's needs. Keeping the device that works would eliminate long delays in acquiring the device and not require reprogramming. The learning curve for the student, teacher, parents, and others involved in the child's education would not be interrupted. The district could then pay the SWAT for the device (already in use by the student) and SWAT could purchase a new device for the warehouse, hopefully at a negotiated volume-buying discount.

Another barrier to the use of advanced telecommunications for students with disabilities in public schools include special education teachers not sufficiently trained to use equipment; insufficient evaluation and support services to meet special technology needs; too few computers with alternative input-output devices; too few computers available to students with disabilities; and school administrators not seeing telecommunications as relevant for many students with disabilities (National Center for Education Statistics, 2000). This issue still exists in schools and little has been done to correct the training of teachers in many states. This issue includes: the lack of trained, qualified professionals to evaluate what AT was appropriate; the difficulty finding and trying out AT; the red tape and bureaucracy of public programs and insurance companies; the difficulty of keeping pace with technology developments; the lack of maintenance and support; and the lack of access to AT in other areas, such as housing and transportation. Training should provide awareness-level information for practitioners in all disciplines along with consumers and advocates. Training should also develop expertise-level competency in sufficient numbers of providers to meet growing consumer needs. One solution would be for Colleges of Education and teacher training programs to integrate their technology, early childhood, and special education programs and courses to train teachers how to use technology to support these children.

FUTURE TRENDS

The development and use of technology has changed the opportunity for children with special needs in many ways. Twenty years ago these children were often placed in "special" homes or isolated in classrooms away from "normal" children. As educators find more approaches to serving the needs of special education children through technology the instructional environment will continue to change. Teacher training institutions will adapt their degree programs to prepare all teachers to work with these children and all children through technology that supports learning. The crucial question is how teachers adapt instruction, not water down instruction, to insure all children are given the opportunity to reach their potential? The answer lies in the preparation of teachers and developing new models of training that support conceptual planning for education.

CONCLUSION

This chapter provides an overview of assistive technology in early childhood education, specifically computer technology and AAC. All children with disabilities may have areas of need in which assistive technology will help to promote independence (see Alper & Raharinirina, (2006) for a more extensive review of assistive technology for all children with disabilities). When deciding on what type and kind of assistive technology to use to enable a child with a disability to access the general curriculum it is important to keep in mind the processes of shared decision making and parental involvement. The parents and family are the child's first teacher and are the ones who will be around long after the child has left the early education setting. The number one goal for the use of technology for young children with special needs is to provide them with a compensatory means of accessing the general curriculum with as much success as possible.

Reflecting on Young Children and Assistive Technology

This section gives you some questions and activities to help you think about how you can use some of the ideas from this chapter in your work.

Research

1. Acceptance of special needs children by their peers is another important aspect to support learning. How will you insure that your classroom environment is one where respect for these children is enhanced? You may want to video segments of your teaching and reflect on your interactions with special needs children to insure you are not giving your class unintentional impressions that you consider them incapable of learning.

Reflect

1. Think about your classroom and the physical environment you have developed for your students. What adaptations do you need to make to insure children with special needs have equal access to materials?
2. How can you as a professional find resources to use in your classroom that will provide special needs children the assistive technology needed to support learning?
3. Teachers often think they are being supportive of SPED children when they lower expectations in their classrooms. Think about your beliefs about special needs children. What assumptions have you made about their abilities to learn and how have these changed after reading this chapter?
4. The parent interaction with you and their children is vital to the success of all children. Identify ways parents can become full partners in your classroom. What types of activities could you implement to bring parents into your room to assist learning?
5. Teacher training programs rarely change at the pace of technology development. How can you, in your school, learn about new technologies to better serve your children?

Practice

1. Parents often have problems accepting their child needs special help to succeed in schools. Work with your peers to develop parent information presentations and brochures that will better education parents in your school.
2. What technology do you already have in your class or school that can be adapted for use with special needs children?
3. Advocacy for children with special needs is an important part of your work. Parents, of course are one component but the need to educate colleagues, administrators and your community about SPED issues is also important. Develop a community action plan that addresses key information about assistive technology for children.
4. Work with your peers to develop a budget for assistive technology for your teaching environment. Meet with your administrators to identify these materials and ways to really make this happen in your school.

REFERENCES

Alper, S., & Raharinirina, S. (2006). Assistive technology for individuals with disabilities: A review and synthesis of the literature. *Journal of Special Education Technology*, *21*, 47–64.

Blackstone, S. (1988). Vocabulary selection: Current practices and a glimpse at the future. *Augmentative Communication News, 7*(5).

Boone, R., & Higgins, K. (1993). Hypermedia basal readers: Three years of school-based research. *Journal of Special Education Technology*, *12*(2), 86–106.

Bryant, D., & Bryant, B. (2003). *Assistive technology for people with disabilities*. Boston, MA: Allyn & Bacon.

Campbell, P. H., Milbourne, S., Dugan, L. M., & Wilcox, M. J. (2006). A review of evidence on practices for teaching young children to use assistive technology devices. *Topics in Early Childhood Special Education*, *26*(1), 3–13. doi: 10.1177/02711214060260010101

Chambers, A. C. (1997). *Has technology been considered? A guide for IEP teams*. Reston, VA: Council of Administrators of Special Education and the Technology and Media Division of The Council for Exceptional Children.

Dell, A., Disdier, A., Goldman, A., & Mervine, P. (1998). The teacher's role in augmentative communication. *Tech-NJ Bulletin Board, 9*(1). Retrieved from http://www.tcnj.edu/~technj/win98/trainingmod.html

Edyburn, D. L. (2006). Assistive technology and mild disabilities. *Special Education Technology Practice*, *8*(4), 18–28.

Fallon, K., & Light, J. (2001). Enhancing vocabulary selection for preschoolers who require augmentative and alternative communication. *American Journal of Speech-Language Pathology*, *10*, 81–94. doi:10.1044/1058-0360(2001/010)

Hancock, T. B., & Kaiser, A. P. (2002). The effects of trainer-implemented enhanced milieu teaching on the social communication of children with autism. *Topics in Early Childhood Special Education*, *22*(1), 39–54. doi:10.1177/027112140202200104

Heward, W. L. (2009). *Exceptional children* (9th ed.). Upper Saddle River, NJ: Pearson.

Hitchcock, C., & Stahl, S. (2003). Assistive technology, universal design, universal design for learning: Improved learning opportunities. *Journal of Special Education Technology*, *18*(4), 45–52.

Irvine Belson, S. (2003). *Technology for exceptional learners*. Boston, MA: Houghton Mifflin.

James, S. R., Bicard, S. C., & Bicard, D. F. (2010). *The effects of enhanced milieu teaching and a voice output communication aid on the rate and generalization of demanding during classroom free play*. Unpublished manuscript, Instruction and Curriculum Leadership Department, The University of Memphis, Memphis, Tennessee.

Johnston, S. S. (2003). Making the most of single switch technology: A primer. *Journal of Special Education Technology*, *18*(2), 47–50.

Judge, S. (2001). Computer applications in programs for young children with disabilities: Current status and future directions. *Journal of Special Education Technology*, *16*(1), 29–40.

Judge, S. (2006). Constructing an assistive technology toolkit for young children: Views from the field. *Journal of Special Education Technology*, *21*(4), 17–24.

Lahm, E., & Morrissette, S. (1994, April). *Zap 'em with assistive technology*. Paper presented at the Annual Meeting of The Council for Exceptional Children, Denver, CO.

Mahoney, G., Kaiser, A., Girolametto, L., MacDonald, J., Robinson, C., & Spiker, D. (1999). Parent education in early intervention: A call for a renewed focus. *Topics in Early Childhood Special Education*, *19*(3), 131–140. doi:10.1177/027112149901900301

McCormick, L. (1987). Comparison of the effects of a microcomputer activity and toy play on social and communication behaviors of young children. *Journal of the Division for Early Childhood, 11*, 195–205.

National Council on Disability. (2000). *Federal policy barriers to assistive technology*. Retrieved from http://www.ncd.gov/newsroom /publications/2000/ assisttechnology.htm

Nelson, L., & Materson, J. (1999). Computer technology: Creative interfaces in service delivery. *Topics in Language Disorders*, *19*(3), 68–86. doi:10.1097/00011363-199905000-00007

Olive, M. L., de la Cruz, B., Davis, T. N., Chan, J. M., Lang, R. B., O'Reilly, M. F., & Dickson, S. M. (2006). The effects of enhanced milieu teaching and a voice output communication aid on the requesting of three children with autism. *Journal of Autism and Developmental Disorders*, *37*(8), 1505–1513. doi:10.1007/s10803-006-0243-6

Parette, H. P., & Murdick, N. L. (1998). Assistive technology and IEPs for young children with disabilities. *Early Childhood Education Journal*, *25*(3), 193–198. doi:10.1023/A:1025661329039

Parette, P., & McMahan, G. (2002). What should we expect of assistive technology? Being sensitive to family goals. *Teaching Exceptional Children*, *35*(1), 56–61.

Rhodes, L., & Seiler, R. (2007). *Assistive technology for infants and toddlers with disabilities: A handbook for parents and caregivers*. Moscow, ID: Idaho Assistive Technology Project.

Schepis, M. M., Reid, D. H., Behrmann, M. M., & Sutton, K. A. (1998). Increasing communicative interactions of young children with autism using a voice output communication aid and naturalistic teaching. *Journal of Applied Behavior Analysis*, *31*(4), 561–578. doi:10.1901/jaba.1998.31-561

Spiegel-McGill, P., Zippiroli, S., & Mistrett, S. (1989). Microcomputers as social facilitators in integrated preschools. *Journal of Early Intervention*, *13*, 249–260. doi:10.1177/105381518901300306

Stokes, T. F., & Baer, D. M. (1977). An implicit technology of generalization. *Journal of Applied Behavior Analysis*, *10*, 349–367. doi:10.1901/jaba.1977.10-349

U.S. Office of Special Education Programs. (2007). *Individuals with Disabilities Education Act* (IDEA) data (Tables 1-14, 8-14). Washington, DC: Author. Retrieved from http://www.ideadata.org

Section 4
Bridging the Gap between Policy and Practice

Chapter 12
Bridging the Gap between Policy and Implementation:
Preschool Education in Mexico, Latin America and Spain

Jorge Lopez
University of Texas at El Paso, USA

ABSTRACT

The last decade brought major change to the Mexican educational system as sweeping reforms across all levels were implemented. In particular the early years of education became the focus of legislation to increase quality, open access, and improve curriculum. Mexico captured international attention when it became the first country to make it obligatory for the State to provide pre-school education services for children 3 to 6 years of age and required parents to see that their children attend a public or private pre-school. This chapter explores the gap between policy and implementation of early childhood and technology reform. This sweeping reform is one of the first international attempts to support early childhood education at this level.

INTRODUCTION

It is not enough for the teacher to love the child. She must first love and understand the universe. She must prepare herself, and truly work at it.
-Maria Montessori

DOI: 10.4018/978-1-61350-059-0.ch012

During the last decades Mexico brought international focus to the educational systems as the Law of Mandatory Pre-schooling made Mexico the only country in the world with mandatory education for 3-year olds. The reform policies were influenced by the changing economic policies as Mexico surged forward in development of technology related industries. As Mexico continued to move

Copyright © 2012, IGI Global. Copying or distributing in print or electronic forms without written permission of IGI Global is prohibited.

toward a more technological state it was vital that the schools keep up by preparing the children of Mexico for global economy.

Preschool education has existed in Mexico for over 120 years, but it has been the last lustrum that Mexico became an educational research laboratory to study policy and implementation. *The Law of Mandatory Pre-schooling* (2002) made Mexico the only country in the world with mandatory education for all young children and demanded sweeping reform of preschool education. This chapter discusses this reform in Mexico from the perspective of practitioners and citizens, their views of what has happened to this important attempt to provide young children educational opportunity. It also includes current information about the use of technology in Mexico, Spain and the Latin American Countries (LACs).

The first section examines the issues when *top down reform* (decisions about policy made by politicians or governing agencies) is implemented. This section includes a description of the Mexican preschool system, its composition and structure, this chapter explores the purposes of the overall reform, its new curriculum and challenges. It reviews the philosophy, competencies, and some of the peripheral tasks that are being implemented as support to the reform, such as training program for educators, new school programs, and community efforts I will discuss how technology has evolved in the light of the new reforms and how policy and implementation often clash in reality. It will discuss the gap between policy and implementation of reform efforts in an attempt to help teachers better realizes the importance of their role in political decisions

The second section of this chapter includes results of a survey concerning the use of technology in Spanish speaking countries administered in 2010 with Spanish-speaking educators from Mexico, Latin American countries and Spain through the Latin American branch of the World Association of Early Childhood Educators (AMEI-WAECE). The countries are considered a representative sample of Spanish speaking groups in the field of early childhood education.

The Importance of Early Childhood

First I want to explain how I, a nuclear physicist, have developed such passionate interest in and support for the field of early childhood education. My involvement in young children's education started in a rather unusual way, as explained in the opening Montessori epigraph, I indeed learned to love and understand the universe first. My background includes B.S., M.S. and Ph.D. degrees in Physics as well as over two decades of research in research centers and universities in North America, Europe and South America. But it was not until the mid-nineties that I realized what the cornerstone of a good scientific education is. And let me be precise as a scientist and define "good education" as one that is gradual, painless, solid, and lasting; one that caters to the natural curiosity of the children and becomes a permanent part of their way of thinking. A "good education" is needed as we integrate technology into the lives of young children. Technology is here and will continue to influence all aspects of learning for children. We are the ones who must provide the support and access, the burning interest and inquiry for technology. The following vignette is one that is true and one I believe can be applied to technology and young children.

Early Influences on Conceptual Understanding

Dr. Judith Rosenthal, while studying the impact science programs for non-English speakers in the US, interviewed me as a product of the InterAmerican Science Program of the University of Texas at El Paso. As it is rare to find a Hispanic physicist and even more to find one with a Ph.D. degree, (Rosenthal, 1996) Dr. Rosenthal began dissecting my past to better understand what influenced my career choice. The first key influence she identified was that I am not Hispanic in the usual US ethnic sense, but I am Mexican born and raised in Mexico and a typical product of the Mexican educational system of the 60's. The second –and crucial— observation Dr. Rosenthal made was that following the official Mexican education programs I started toying with science in 3rd grade, and never stopped until I graduated from the *preparatoria*, a type of public prep high school typical in Mexico at the time. By my 11th and last year I had completed three formal years of physics, two of chemistry, one of biology, many years of math, including two of calculus, as well as technical drawing (three years), machinist instruction (two years), and more. All of this, she concluded, had been influenced by the countless hours of scientific games playing with electricity, magnetism, etc. as a child. This, I believe, constituted the cornerstone of my scientific education. This to me is the basis for development of inquiry, investigation, and the motivation to continuously learn and intellectually explore options of thinking. This is analogous to the use of technology games in the new generation of students. The use of technology can inspire, motivate and support the development of problem solving abilities in children.

Dr. Rosenthal strongly influenced my awareness of the importance of the experiences young children have as they develop their thinking. I no longer believe the university level of instruction can generate and develop the level of thinking needed for higher order problem solving from a blank slate, I am now convinced that a mediocre (in the sense of average) college student cannot change their problem solving approach or develop a passion for inquiry with remedial plans, textbooks in color, peer led teaching, recitations, clickers, and the many simplistic interventions I and others in science have tried during reform efforts over the last fifteen years. While these approaches may have increased the number of high grades in one semester of classes there was no long term evidence that we improved the understanding, thinking or motivation of these students. By the time a student arrives at a university without the proper background, opportunities and support in the early years, he/she will be lacking not only the understanding from six years of science missed in high school, but more importantly will be lacking the mental structure she/he never had the opportunity to develop in early childhood programs and elementary school. For these students science, at best, will be a job but never a passion. I believe this will apply to the implementation of technology. The interest, inquiry and motivation for life-long learning start in the early childhood and elementary classroom. The exploration of science and technology must start in the early years if children are to develop the mental structures to support higher order thinking. This makes the role of these teachers key to the future development of citizens who can really make informed decisions, contribute to the global society, and face the challenges of an increasingly technological society. We live in a society exquisitely dependent on science and technology, in which hardly anyone knows anything about science and technology.

While working at the University of Texas at El Paso –and to support my own two children— I began to search for how to teach science to K-6 kids, but finding a lack of science-based material for the pre-K level, I became interested in developing it. There were many programs called "science" but these were often lacking in real science concepts, developed to entertain children, often build on misconceptions or misunderstanding of scientific principles. While there are many materials for science and young children few are accurate in relation to science or developed with scientists, many who still cling to the outdated notion that science learning starts in high school and at the university and are only for the "Smart" kids. Science and technology does not belong to the elite few but to all children. Technology can be a major influence on the development of thinking. During my experiences it became my belief that the early years are the most important for development of thinking, and with funding of the National Science Foundation (NSF) I began developing science activities for preschool children and became involved in two of the local preschool centers, predominantly with children of Hispanic origin from homes identified as lower socio-economic in the United States I now spent much of my time developing lesson plans for preschool teachers, and refine them through teacher training workshops. Some of these activities are being used in Mexico and Chile with preschool children.

Key to these activities is the materials used in these lessons as well as the linguistic skills employed, particularly in this border area where the Hispanic and Anglo culture not only meet, but more often crash. With respect to materials, the guiding light in my design of activities has been accessibility for instructors; with respect to language, I do away with patriotic taboos and adhere to Woody Allen's physicist rule: "whatever works".

But this chapter is not about what I do, but more about what is done in Mexico in preschool education now. In spite of my rich experience of the 60's, let me warn the reader that reforms in the 80's died away with many of the ingredients that cemented the scientific cornerstone in my generation. The issues discussed in this chapter are not border bound but ones that are evident in all countries as we become a more united global community through the opportunity technology provides we find issues with learning and thinking become universal. The intent is for readers to identify common issues and work towards solutions and support technology reform in early childhood from an international perspective. As you read I think you will find many common themes that will relate to your country and the issues of technology, early childhood and reform. In each section of this chapter I have included the intent and then the reality of reform in early childhood education and technology. What we say and what we do seem to be two very different realities in educational environments.

Can this change? If we all work as a team to implement the changes needed in early childhood and technology we stand a better chance of making this a reality for all children. It is from my experiences in higher education and my own children that I have formed my belief that the early and elementary years in children's lives are the defining time for developing inquiry, confidence levels and a life-long passion for learning. Technology provides the means in a variety of ways by improving communication, allowing for exploration through images we could only visualize at one time, opening new fields in research and learning.

Objectives

After reading this chapter the reader should be able to identify and compare issues between the policy and implementation of early childhood reform efforts in relation to technology. They will be able to use this information to compare and analyze reform in their home countries and be able to identify common issues among communities which can be used to inform policy and practice from an international perspective. Lessons learned from this chapter can help teachers become stronger advocates for reform, reflect on change and their role, and find solutions to closing the gaps between policy and implementation in their educational institutions. The reader will:

- Identify implementation policy in education and analyze ways to support and supplement technology resources
- Develop a better understanding of their role in policy change
- Develop a clearer understanding of how educators and communities can make technology available in classrooms and schools.

This next section is a snapshot of the reform efforts in Mexico used as an example of the gap between policy and implementation. This chapter is not developed to criticize the Mexican system or any other attempt at reform but to analyze the gap between policy and implementation of reform efforts in early childhood. If we try nothing we learn nothing, even when the lessons are painful we must continually analyze and revise our efforts if we are to support the learning of young children and teachers. This chapter is about the reform realities, what happens when *top down* mandates and politics precede resource availability and teacher training. It is also about how communities and educators found ways to bring technology to the young children of Mexico and how we compare to other Spanish speaking countries in relation to technology.

BACKGROUND

To carry out the education we pursue, we make use of a series of activities that respond to the interests and needs of the little students, as they constitute as well defined plan of the work needed for the physical moral, mental, emotional and social development in the most harmonic and necessary form. -Laura Zapata (1876–1963), Mexican Pioneer Preschool Educator

Technology in Mexico

The Mexican economy has expanded to become the ninth largest in the world. The industrial sector has been the driving force behind much of this progress. Through the National Development Plan for 2001-2006, the government launched the Program for the Competitiveness of the Electronics and Hi-tech Industries (PCIEAT). The program's goal was to put the country in the top five electronics manufacturers in the world through a variety of strategies, including developing local providers of electrical and electronic components, promoting the transition from analogue to digital technology, creating marketable technology nationally, and increasing investment in the tech sector. Business, academia, and the government were collaborating on the initiative, which included the development of the domestic market, the strengthening of the local IT industry, the provision of technological education, the establishment of a solid legal framework, and the promotion of techno related exports among its key goals. The drive for digitalization was seen as crucial to create a stronger internal market for software and related services, which would in turn make Mexico more competitive internationally.

The national e-Mexico initiative was further raising awareness of the power of technology and fostering the development of the internal market. Led by the Ministry for Communications and Transport, its main objective is to create widespread online access to information, to encourage rapid community development, particularly among marginalized communities. The government and state enterprises were also increasingly going digital and tending to buy software and solutions from local suppliers. The stage was set to bring Mexico into the global digital community.

Mexico is one of the few Latin American countries that does not impose censorship of internet use. Mexico has approximately 25 million Internet users and continues to increase the demand for broadband Internet services. Mexico is the country with the most internet users in Latin America, and in August 2005 Cisco Systems, the industry leader in Internet backbone routing equipment, said they see Mexico and other Latin American countries as the focal point for growth in coming years, with Mexico receiving the biggest chunk of their investments, identifying it as a *hypergrowth* market for equipment suppliers. Additionally looking at the historical growth for the period from 2001 to 2005 we see broadband Internet jump from 0.1 subscribers per hundred population to 2.2 subscribers per hundred population, a growth of 2200% in just 5 years. The stage was set for technology reform in Mexico.

Preschool Education in Mexico

Kindergarten education started in Mexico in 1883, the first normal school was founded in Mexico in 1887 and its first specialization into preschool started in 1910 (Galván Lafarga, 2009). In 1921 preschool teachers were incorporated into the federal system of education, the first preschool conference was held, and the number of preschools in the country had grown to over twenty. In 1957 Mexico hosted the meeting of the World Organization for Early Childhood Education and by the 60s the number of pre-schools in the country surpassed 3,000. In 1984 studies in preschool education were included at the university level and by 2002-2003 there were about 200 private and public Normal Schools (OECD, 2006).

In Mexico preschool has evolved into what today constitutes the *preprimaria*, literally "previous to primary school" and consisting of three years, one a playgroup for 3 to 4-year olds to develop social interactions, and two of more formal preschool type of education for 4 to 6-year olds. Preschool is offered through three program types: general, indigenous and community courses, and it is under the Federal Government (through SEP), State Governments, and private schools – about 10% of the preschools are private (OECD, 2006). Most children (88.1%) are enrolled in the general pre-school program in both urban and rural areas, while the indigenous program serves 8.4% of children and the Community pre-schools in rural communities enroll the remaining 3.5%. Education for the more than 6 million indigenous children is offered solely by the Federal Government with educators trained in the more than 80 dialects (SEP 2009) and with material prepared in 52 native tongues.

The largest providers of preschool education in Mexico are the Child development Centers knows as CENDI (Centro de Desarrollo Infantil). The CENDI program started in 1990 more as nurseries than preschools, but soon developed a dual structure that accommodates infants starting from 45 days of age to 3 years old and preschoolers from 3 to 6 years old. All CENDIs operate under the programs established by the Secretary of Education. Such programs emphasize, among others, the use of technology as tools to face future challenges (English language and computers), and to allow artistic and physical potentialities, such as music, dance, painting, and sports (Rodríguez Martínez, 2002).

In 2002-2003 over 3.6 million of a total of 6.5 million children (55%) were enrolled in one of these programs; over 81% of 5-year olds were registered in preschool or primary school. In comparison 55% of children of Mexican immigrant families living in the United States were enrolled in similar programs. A report on preschool enrollment indicated that preschool enrollment rates in Mexico were also higher than those for children in white U.S. native-born families (Hernandez et al. 2007). This indicates that the start of the preschool reform is on track to serve our children. It was believed (Zehr, 2007) that such high attendance in Mexican preschools was influenced by the fact that preschool in Mexico is free and supported by policy for all children. We considered this indicates that we were providing the access to education that would change the future of our country.

The Mandate

The 2002 Law of Mandatory Pre-schooling made pre-school education for all 3 to 6-year olds mandatory by 2009. This placed preschool under the auspices of the Federal Secretary of Education (OECD, 2006). Currently, Mexico –the only country in the world with mandatory education for 3-year olds— has several systems of childhood education operating under the SEP, Secretary of Social Development (SEDESOL), the Mexican Institute of Social Security (IMSS and ISSSTE), the National System for Integral

Figure 1. Model for Mexico's preschool program

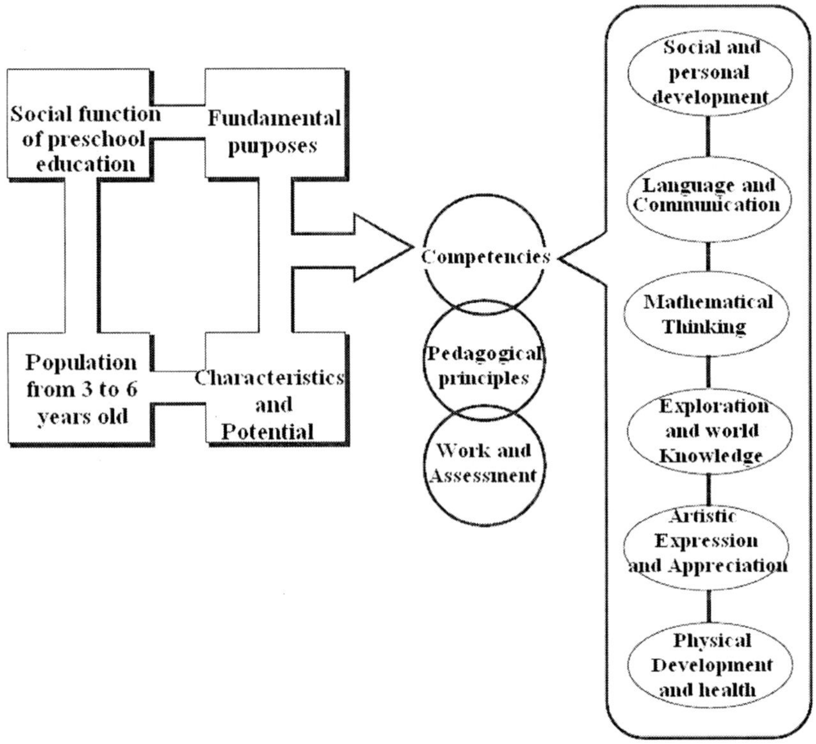

Family Development (DIF), the National Council for Educational Promotion (CONAFE), as well as other state and private schools and nurseries. The model for the preschool reform identified six key areas of focus. Figure 1 is the planning model for policy in preschool reform.

The six areas of focus for preschool children were:

1. Personal and social development,
2. Language and communication,
3. Mathematical thinking,
4. Investigation and knowledge of the world,
5. Artistic expression and appreciation, and
6. Health and physical development.

The Planning

The 2002 law influenced a new program for pre-school education in Mexico which was introduced in 2004 (SEP, 2004). This program, known as the "Educational Reform of Pre-School Education", incorporated many revisions of pilot programs implemented between 2002 and 2004 throughout the country. This revision included stakeholders and practitioners input based on their experiences and recommendations with regional meetings and a series of observations in schools to identify best practice. The new program also reviewed models being used in other countries, as well as results of Mexican research projects, especially those catering to the different indigenous groups living in Mexico.

The 2004 program goals were identified as:

- To acquire confidence in the mother tongue, understand the main functions of written language, acknowledge variations in the language and dialects, and learn to use the different means of mass commu-

nication such as printed and electronic media.
- To develop mathematical notions for counting, comparing, estimating, etc.
- To support development of investigations of natural phenomena and the experimentation, questioning, and discussions about them.

SEP planned to introduce a training program for educators and administrators, envisioning new university coursework, and a media campaign to inform the parents of children about the changes and expectations. The program "Schools of Quality" (Programa de Escuelas de Calidad, PEC) was added in 2005 to support quality improvement in public schools through collaborative work among parents, teachers and school authorities. The plan had many strong components to upgrade education across the continuum from preschool through the university.

In 2007 SEP commissioned researchers from Harvard to analyze the development of policy in these early years (2000-2006) of the Mexican reform. The study focused on preschool expansion, quality improvement and curricular reform (Yoshikawa, 2007). Researchers reviewed the educational policies according to access, quality and equity, and found that the reform resulted in rapid increases in enrollment, without an increase on the national averages of class sizes, but with some increase of the percentage of preschools with average student-adult ratio of 30 (from 12% in 2001 to 18% in 2005). The average increase in structural indicators of quality was relatively small due to increases in numbers of preschools. The study also concluded that the new curriculum was more demanding and challenging and required high levels of teacher initiative and reflective practice, as well as more and more specialized teacher training.

ISSUES, CONTROVERSIES, PROBLEMS: IMPLEMENTATION

People who thought that the question about technology in education was whether there should be a computer in every classroom have had their eyes opened to the idea that something much bigger is at stake. –Seymour Papert (2000)

In striking contrast to the emphasis the Mexican early childhood reform places on language and communication, it flagrantly ignores the role of technology in preschool education in Mexico. No master plan or teacher training programs were introduced to bring the youngest Mexicans closer to information and communications technologies. The technology reform that has come to the early childhood programs in Mexico comes from the educators, parents and business community.

Mexico's early childhood reform is now mature enough as to serve as a case study. The intention of the reform was clearly meant to bring the children of Mexico into the Global Community, preparing our children to be competitive in the new world economy. The absence of technology goals in this preschool plan is a paradox in light of the importance technology now plays in global competition and the dramatic economic technology plan in place in this country. Mexico embarked on a mandated modernization plan in education but the implementation, without adequate resources and support, met many obstacles. Among these were lack of physical facilities to house millions of new preschoolers, facilities that were not technology friendly, lack of resources, and limited support for technology training. The reform demands from the policy mandated by the Federal and State governments forced private day care owners to implement programs in hundreds of new and unsafe preschools manned by unprepared *express* educators. The term *express educator* refers to teachers who were thrown into classrooms with limited and often inadequate preparation to fill the demand for expansion. This explosive combination caused at least one tragedy that made the international news as educators grappled with the need for facilities and teachers.

The incorporation of technology in preschool education in Mexico has been a slow process independent of the usual forces of change in Mexican education. Different from other curricula modifications, and in spite of being identified as a goal in the 2004 Program Reform, *cf.* p. 14 in (SEP, 2003), there has been no master plan to introduce technology in the preschool classrooms, nor a teacher training program. The policy was in place with few resources and support structures for the K-16 educational continuum and even less in the preschool reform. The closest official implementation attempt to support early education came as part of a 2000-2006 Federal administration program named e-Mexico, which was designed to bring Mexicans closer to information and communications technologies. This project was developed to provide digital centers for the citizens of Mexico in all areas, urban, rural, and indigenous populations to allow access to technology for the general public. The policy was intended to provide technology access to all children and families. The reality was that without training and educational focus the general population was unprepared to use this resource.

Implementation: E-Mexico

Due to the economic and social conditions of the country, the information technology continues to be a tool out of reach for a large percentage of the population. The program e-Mexico, initiated by the Federal Government in 2003, created thousands of "Digital Community Centers" (DCCs) to allow public access to Internet throughout the country in schools, libraries, health centers, post offices and government buildings. In 2004 there were 3200 available public technology sites and the number of DCCs more than doubled by the end of the decade. The intention was access to technology across all populations, a *Field of Dreams* approach. This *if we provide it they will come* program was well intentioned and clearly technology reform without access will fail.

Portals for E-Mexico on many topics were created and, although the program focused on the community at large, it did have a portal on education, e-Learning (www.e-mexico.gob.mx/wb2/eMex/eMex_eEducacion), which informed the public about educational services by different academic institutions, public organizations and private enterprise. One section was devoted to early education and had information about program types, support for early educational programs and general early childhood development information.

In addition the preschool web site, the e-Learning portal provided a number of web pages to cover a minimum set of educational themes (www.e-mexico.gob.mx/wb2/eMex/Mex_Preescolar_y_Primaria) including language skills (alphabet in Spanish and English, calligraphy, reading, stories, etc.), math, science, video, etc., Although by itself a useful tool, it is not as developed as other dedicated official (e.g. www.educarchile.cl or www.educ.ar) or private portals (www.aulainfantil.com).

Reality

Unfortunately, the ambitious e-Mexico program did not receive support from the Secretary of Education (Hofmann & García-Cantú, 2008) and has not reached all of its objectives. At present, plans are being developed to introduce Wi-Fi connectivity in schools across the country. The sophistication of these web sites indicates that Mexico does indeed have a technological society that supports education for our children. However the reality has fallen short of the intended plans. The introduction of educational technology into the Mexican preschools has happened mostly by the interest of the educators, community and local business themselves without the support of the federal and state governments.

Challenges: Politics and Policy

I am guilty for trusting,

I am guilty for paying my taxes,

I am guilty for voting,

I am responsible for the death of my son!

–Roberto Zavala, Father of Santiago Jesús who died in the tragedy of the ABC preschool (Osorno 2010)

Mexico took the plunge to the modernization of the preschool education without full consideration of implementation reality and after several years the consequences of the gap between policy and implementation are beginning to appear. The national goals for technology were admirable as were the mandates for education of all young children. Few would argue the good intentions of policy makers on both accounts but without an infrastructure to support these goals the policies began to crack.

As there were not enough schools for the millions of new customers, the sudden demand to make preschool mandatory put the country on a crossroads. Unable to provide facilities from the self-imposed demand, the Federal government turned to the private sector to satisfy the policy. Without a checks and balance system in place to insure proper supervision or planning, new preschools and day care centers began to crop up throughout the country creating implementation and practice issues. This included a massive wave of hiring of *express* (unprepared) educators. These educators had little or no training in development or pedagogy of young children but were hired to meet the demand for increased staffing of child facilities. Each of these steps –implemented in a hurry— left ample opportunities for errors which caused tragedies that made the international news. On June 5, 2009 a short-circuit triggered a fire that consumed the "ABC" nursery in Hermosillo, in the State of Sonora in Mexico, killing 49 and injuring 74 children ages newborn to six years old.

According to Osorno, 2010, the fire took place in a grubby industrial warehouse rented out by a private group to provide the legally-required childcare services to workers' children. The old warehouse had toxic and inflammable walls and blocked emergency exits. It had been licensed as an IMSS service provider in 2001 and again in 2006; its certification by Hermosillo's Fire Department just days before the tragedy was later found to be a mere copy of a 2005 bill and to have been issued without an inspection.

In addition to the preschool reform the Fox administration (2000-2006) initiated a strategy to move part of the government childcare operations to private hands due to the increase in numbers without an established infrastructure for public expansion. The urgent privatization of government day care centers to meet the need for increased facilities often ignored the safety standards to the point of sacrificing children's lives to meet mandated policy. Often high ranking politicians and their close relatives seemed to be the group who gained the most from the precipitous preschool reform efforts of President Vicente Fox. This tainted the reform efforts in the community.

In March, 2010, a report by an investigative commission of the Supreme Court of Justice found IMSS outsourcing of childcare services illegal and named 17 people for violating the individual rights of the children that died in the tragic fire. The investigation also found that of the 1,480 outsourcing contracts signed by the IMSS, only 14 had met all the legal requirements. Among those cited was the governor of Sonora. Investigations also point to negligence by authorities and influence trafficking on the part of the owners, one of whom is a close relative of Mexican President Felipe Calderon (Ross, 2009).

Gustavo Leal, a professor at the Autonomous Metropolitan University in Mexico City blames the practice of private subcontracting for the tragedy (Cruz Martínez, 2010). The ABC Center is only one of over 1500 such private facilities that have been privatized by the IMSS since 2000. By reducing costs, the yearly cost per child was reduced from 3800 pesos to 2100 with a subsequent deterioration in food quality, medical services, educational programs, and safety. In Sonora, 79 out of 87 government day care centers have been sold off, and at least 13 owners have family ties with the governor.

The rush to increase facilities to serve children while cutting implementation costs raises many questions about the system and the political involvement in reform. Top down reform developed by the government and school governing agencies often depend on top level administrators to support the plans and implement changes. While clearly well intentioned this approach leaves the reform policy open to interpretation and allows political relationships the opportunity to influence implementation.

The staffing presents another issue for implementation in educational environments. The increase in express *educators*, according to Professor Miguel Angel Castillo, will result in the emerging problem of having substandard preparation for the upcoming generation of Mexican teachers (Castillo, 2009). One response to the educational reform was the private certification agency Center for the Assessment of Higher Education (CENEVAL) offering certification exams to students interested in becoming preschool educators without prior training. Anyone who can pass the exam becomes a certified preschool teacher. Castillo concludes, "this new crop of Felipe Calderon's express teachers guarantees three things: Mexico will maintain the last places in education in the world scale, the national development will continue being stuck, and Mexican children will continue living in a permanent state of vulnerability."

One of the major challenges for the Mexican preschool education continues to be the reality of implementation to serve children from 3 to 5 as mandated and the training of the number of teachers that are required by the increase in demand (López & López, 2010). It is up to the Mexican education community to resolve these issues before more active (*e.g.* fires) or passive (*e.g.* underdevelopment) tragedies occur. As the epigraph that opens this section and as the title of Diego Osorno's book (Osorno, 2010) implies: we all are to blame for these disasters.

The influence of politics on educational policy is not isolated to Mexico. For decades the presidential elections in the United States have included educational reform as a major issue with little progress made in schools. As advocates for children we must take responsibility for who is elected to guide our countries educational polices. According to the US Census Bureau 2000 census, the "Number of all teachers in the United States" is 6.2 million and it estimated this number has grown. When you add in the family of these professionals the potential for voting could make a major impact on political elections. Our policies come from state and national government officials who are elected by the population. This gives teachers a voice in policy if teachers will take the responsibility of becoming advocates for change. The changing role of teachers as a political presence is needed if practitioners are to monitor change. Teachers may need to rethink their importance in the educational policies made in their country. Changing from problem identifiers to problem solvers through active involvement rather than passive acceptance can change the power structures of education.

Often the intention of politicians and policy makers is for the good of a group but implementation of large reform efforts can become diluted as officials and educators struggle to meet the demands. Few would argue against education for all children but the reality of large scale reform requires adequate resources, training, quality assurance standards and practical plans developed by practitioners and stakeholders to insure successful change. When one or more of these support systems is missing efforts can not only be diminished but harm children.

Technology in Mexico, Spain and Latin American Countries

In this section we will discuss the results of a technology survey implemented by the Latin American branch of the World Association of Early Childhood Educators (AMEI-WAECE) to collect information about the Latin American Countries (LACS), Spain and Mexico in regards to technology use with predominantly Hispanic origin countries. The survey provides us with a snapshot of the use of technology in the Americas and in Spain which can be compared with information from Mexico to provide a pictures a large percentage of predominantly Hispanic origin countries. In addition comparisons with computer use in the United States when appropriate have been included in the narrative to provide a baseline for estimation of progress and access of technology use in preschool programs. It is important to note that most technology in preschools in Mexico still come from donations from industry, community partners and educators while other countries have educational funds to support technology.

Technology in Preschools in Mexico, Latin American Countries (LACS) and Spain

While Papert (2000) acknowledged that the number of computers per school is a simplistic data set when analyzing technology success with schools I am providing a comparison among Mexico, Spain, and the LACs but acknowledge that the number of computers does not correlate to the use and quality of technology applications. The presence of computers does indicate the possible opportunity for student interaction and use these tools.

Figure 2 shows the enrollment of preschoolers in early childhood programs by country and the percentage of each school by enrollment number. The majority of preschools in Spain have a significantly lower class size in comparison to Mexico and Latin America.

Figure 2 indicates that most of the schools in Spain have an enrollment of 50 children or less, and that a sizable group of Mexican educators, 25%, work in preschools with large student populations of 100 to 200; such percentage gets reduced to about half in Spain. LACs also have more schools with smaller enrollment but do compare with Mexico's percentage of schools serving 100-200 children. In the United States program enrollment sizes are smaller with a recommended teacher-child ration of 1:8 by the National Association for the Education of Young Children (NAEYC). OECD (2006) found the teacher-child ratio to be 1:30 in the Mexican Schools. Current ratios in Spain and the LACs were not available but one report from the 90's indicated a 2:21 ratio in Spain. Overall the Mexican schools have larger program size and a smaller teacher to student ratio.

Figure 3 represents the number of computers in these schools and the percentage of schools with the identified number range.

Spain reported no preschools without computers while Mexico and other LACs have fewer than 25% of preschools with no computers, these results –however– might be due to the fact that

Figure 2. Early childhood enrollment by country

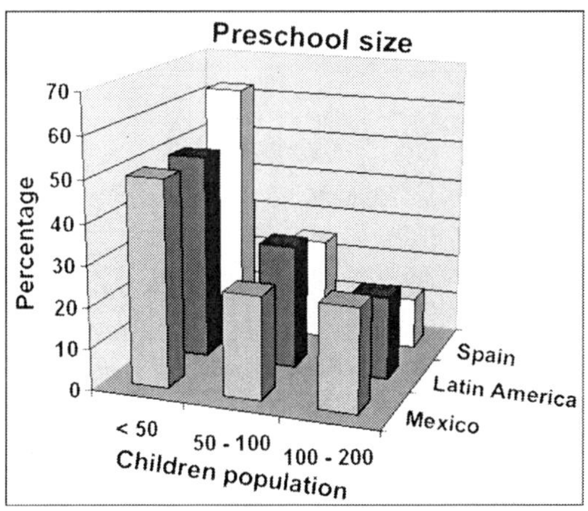

Figure 3. Comparison of number of computers in schools and % of schools with each number

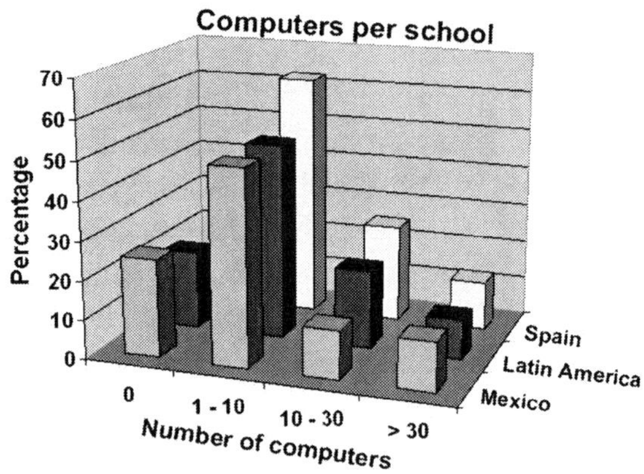

the survey was completed electronically and respondents had to have access to computers to answer it. In spite of this, taking the results at face value would place Mexico –in the best of cases— a good decade and a half behind the level of development of the United States which reported at least one computer in every class as early as 1997, but in line with the statistics of low-income and minority students in the US during the same period (Coley et al., 1997). More current information from the United States compares computers, internet, hand-held computers and lending laptops to students, areas which have not studied in Mexico due in part to the e-Mexico system which was planned to insure technology access for all.

The above figure identifies hand-held computers are personal digital assistants, such as Palm Pilots or Pocket PCs. Schools were asked to include all hand-held computers provided for instructional purposes, including those available for loan, but to exclude laptop computers. The number of students to instructional computers with internet access was computed by dividing the total number of students in all public schools by the total number of instructional computers with internet access in all public schools (including schools with no internet access).

Combining the information of Figures 2 and 3 one can estimate the number of students served by computer in Mexico, Spain and the LACs. Figure 5 shows a comparison of the ratios of student–to–computer in the countries being investigated. Excluded from the chart are the cases of schools without computers (about 7% in LACS) and those with ratios larger than 10 students per computer,

Figure 4. Number of public school students per instructional computer with internet access and percentage of public schools providing hand-held or laptop computers, by locale: 2005 (United States)

		Percent of schools		
		Providing hand-held computers for instructional purposes		
Locale	Number of students per instructional computer with internet access	To teachers	To students	Lending laptop computers to students
Total	**3.8**	**17.2**	**8.1**	**10.0**
City	4.2	19.2	8.6	6.8
Suburban	4.3	15.7	10.2	10.1
Town	3.3	14.0	6.1	10.5
Rural	3.0	18.5	6.9	11.9

U.S. Department of Education, National Center for Education Statistics, Fast Response Survey System (FRSS), "Internet Access in U.S. Public Schools, Fall 2005," FRSS 90, 2005.

which constitute between 15 to 20% of the total in Americas and in Spain. The chart shows that preschools with resources and experience with the use of computers in education prefer to allocate one computer per every five children. It is not clear from the survey if computer ratios are a result of limited funding or based on intentional selection of the number of computers for educational support. When compared to the information from the United States we see that their schools offer a variety of computers for teacher and students, an idea that is not evident in the Mexican, Spanish, and LACs schools. The United States also provides "check out" computers for students which is another approach not evident in the Spanish speaking countries.

The above figure includes computers and software in schools but is not illustrative of the technology available to many young children in their homes. One can safely say that in Mexico technology arrived to the classrooms a bit later than it first appeared in the teacher's and children's homes. Preschool educational technology such as computers and software, TV sets and video players, WII, Nintendo and similar video games, photography and video cameras, and computer projectors, are becoming common in schools. Most urban preschools have several of the above mentioned technology available although few have developed well laid out plans for its use.

In Mexico funding for the acquisition of technology usually comes from the operational funds of the school, or from private donations. While CENDI No. 2 in Ciudad Juárez bought four educational computers with State money, the private school "Asociación Civil Bermúdez" received its 10 computers as a donation from industry. Educators in Mexico often use teachers' or parents' personal technology in their classrooms to enhance learning. A glance at the national situation of the number of computers in preschool in Mexico is presented in Figure 3 in comparison, again, to other LACs and Spain. As it can be seen in Figure 5, the number of computers in schools in Spain is higher than in Latin America, and the median of computers per school is between 1 and 10.

Other Results of Interest

Other questions in the survey indicate that about three quarters of the preschools with computers in Mexico have a room dedicated for educational use of the computers, the rest of the schools tend to have one computer per classroom. In other Latin American countries these numbers drop to 61% for schools with computer rooms, and 23%

Figure 5. Estimates of the ratio of students-to-computer in Mexico, other Latin American countries and Spain

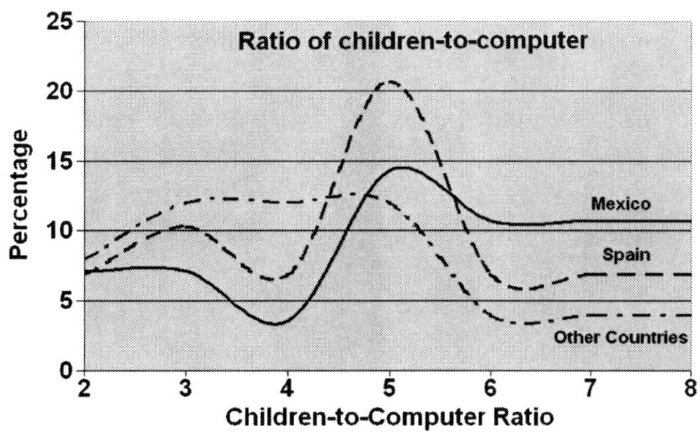

and 15% for schools with one or two or more computers per classroom, respectively; for Spain the numbers are 31%, 38% and 31% for the same items. The schools still have a central location for computer use which requires scheduling and allows limited time for use by children.

The most common student arrangement in Mexico and other LACs is of one or two children per computer selected by 75% and 25% percent of the respondents, respectively; these percentages are 12.5% and 87.5 in Spain. Some educators described the use of "corner computers" for simultaneous use of up to four kids during other educational activities, yet others mentioned the use of computers with smart boards for use by the educators with the whole class. Most instructors combine the use of computers with other amenable activities simultaneously; a smaller percentage (between (14 to 33%) manage to combine them with posterior educational tasks.

Most teachers –between 50% to 77%– learned the use of computers for educational purposes by themselves, while a fraction –ranging from 22% to 40%– had formal education courses on the subject, or received training at work –between 10% and 17%. The survey also found that there is a general consensus that the use of computers for educational purposes is well adapted to the curricula, beneficial to preschool education, and that there are good software packages that can be used at the preschool level; none commented on the type of software being used, such as drill-and-practice software, discovery-based, etc. This indicates the beginning of acceptance of technology in preschool classrooms however it also reveals the need for teacher training in the applications of technology.

It must be remarked that the survey failed to inspire comments related to the intrinsic benefits of the use of computers in the classroom. No instructors, for instance, remarked the assessment virtues of the computer that provide teachers with a "window into a child's thinking process" (Weir et al., 1982), or allow performing ongoing observations to chart children's learning progress (Cochran-Smith et al., 1988). This indicates there is still much work to be done in the area of teacher training and the use of technology as a learning process tool.

On the issue of gender differences, approximately 25% of the Mexican educators saw that boys tend to have a stronger preference for the use of computers as compared to girls, while instructors from other LACs and Spain did not detect major differences. None commented on the different learning abilities such as risk taking for boys nor girls' intellectual quickness and acuity as reported in (Yelland 1994). This indicates a change in the perceptions of gender differences from 1994 in relation to technology.

The results of this study indicate that technology is becoming a presence in preschool classrooms in Mexico, Latin American Countries and Spain. While progress in Mexico still lags behind these countries and the United States there is a clear indication that preschool programs are slowing moving into the digital age.

FUTURE TRENDS

The examples in this chapter are from Mexico, Spain and Latin American countries and the United States but they are far from exclusive to this area of the world. This chapter has identified specific issues we are facing in Mexico under the belief that all countries may be facing similar problems. The following includes current conditions and how we see the future changes concerning key issues in this chapter.

Privatization

Without proper supervision or planning, new preschools and day care centers began to crop up throughout the country with obvious disregard for educational plans and safety. This resulted in tragedy when the lives of children were lost.

Standards for facilities must be implemented and followed-up through inspections and other mechanisms to insure where children are support reform efforts. The future will provide guidance for implementation of technology through a realistic plan that balances implementation with resources and training.

Access

The access to technology issue is common in Mexico and all countries. How do we all insure children have access to technology regardless of socio-economic status, language and ethnicity? I believe that technology is one of the great equalizers for education among all groups of people. It does not make judgments and provides equal information. The future will support access for all citizens to educational technology.

Resources

Support and resources for technology is clearly another issue. The reality of funding in many countries is that there is little money to support technology reform. While all countries are increasing technology use in private homes these tools are not filtering into schools at the rate of new development. Schools continue to fall behind the global use and understanding of technology. Each generation of technology tools become more affordable and will as the global digital age expands. Allocation of funds for outdated teaching tools will be moved to support technology in schools.

Training

The reform in Mexico brought a massive wave of hiring of *express* (unprepared) educators. New training programs that envision the future, not what has always been, must be developed if our teachers are to meet the challenge of integrating technology into early childhood classrooms. Traditional coursework in teacher training programs *have* to be upgraded to include technology as both a teaching tool and an ever evolving process for learning. Teachers will have to rethink how they maintain current information in their teaching and classrooms. The future teacher training will include all applications of technology as a teaching resource, support for teaching and as a process for learning.

CONCLUSION

As technology becomes more common internationally all countries must prepare their teachers and children to use and understand technology. Many reform efforts do not address the actual implementation of new demands. The early childhood reform often ignores technology and makes broad general requirements with little or no support for educational systems to make the requirements a reality.

The influence of politics and politician's campaign promises and mandates are unlikely to disappear in the future. It is up to individuals and professional organizations to monitor and support reform that is well planned and demand the support and resources to make technology happen. The "good education", one that is gradual, painless, solid, and lasting; one that caters to the natural curiosity of the children and becomes a permanent part of their way of thinking is vital for the future of our global society. The technology reform in Mexico has come from the individual commitment of the population, not the decrees from the higher levels of government. Commitment to this change has to come through individual and professional organizations. We cannot blame or depend on politicians to make this a reality for our children. Nor can we continue to blame politicians we have supported and elected to guide educational policy.

If we truly support the idea that the early years of education are the most important for building and sustaining the love of learning then we must take responsibility for quality teacher training and availability of resources to support these programs. Demanding more but not better preschools only creates a new set of issues and problems for the future of our children. Reform, for the sake of reform is a dead end street.

Reflecting on Young Children and Policy and Implementation

This section gives you some questions and activities to help you think about how you can use some of the ideas from this chapter in your work.

Research

1. Search mandated policies for young children and technology in your state. Prepare a chart that lists the policy versus the reality from your school site. Make a Venn diagram to illustrate how these policies are related and what has been implemented.
2. Interview your colleagues about their involvement in policy decisions and their voting patterns in elections. How many are active advocates for your field?

Reflect

1. How can you, as a professional, influence policy and practice in your school that will solve some of the implementation issues with technology for young children?
2. The Law of Mandatory Pre-schooling in Mexico was a strong statement for the belief in the importance of early education. What evidence do you have about support for preschool in your region?
3. What implementation issues influence the reality of reform?
4. As you read this chapter there are some key issues about the importance of early childhood education. What are these key issues? How do these issues relate to your job?

Practice

1. What can you do in your school to communicate the importance of early childhood technology use for the future success of young children? Prepare information for parents, colleagues and administrators that informs them of implementation issues in your school.
2. Organize awareness teams and a networking system to inform stakeholders of issues in early childhood education.
3. Become active advocates for reform in technology education. Recruit peers, family and friends to vote for important policy decisions.
4. Prepare a support paper for the need for technology in early childhood education and send to your policy makers in your school system.

ACKNOWLEDGMENT

The author thanks the help of Miguel Ángel Castillo, Miguel Ángel Pérez, Policarpo Chacón Ángel, and the members of the World Association of Early Childhood Educators that participated in the survey.

REFERENCES

Castillo, M. A. (2009, Oct. 9). La educación preescolar: Entre las maestras express y la vulnerabilidad. *Observatorio Ciudadano de la Educación*. Retrieved from www.observatorio.org/ colaboraciones/2009/ Oct09-MiguelAngel-Castillo -EducPreesc.pdf

Cochran-Smith, M., Kahn, J., & Paris, C. L. (1988). When word processors come into the classroom. In Hoot, J. L., & Silvern, S. B. (Eds.), *Writing with computers in the early grades* (pp. 43–74). New York, NY: Teachers College Press.

Coley, R. J., Cradler, J., & Engel, P. K. (1997). *Computers and classrooms: The status of technology in U.S. schools*. Princeton, NJ: Educational Testing Service.

Galván Lafarga, L. E. (2009). *In De las escuelas de párvulos al preescolar, una historia por contar*. Retrieved from http://biblioweb.dgsca.unam.mx /diccionario/htm/articulos/ sec_25.htm

Hernandez, D. J., Denton, N. A., & Macartney, S. E. (2007, November). *Children in immigrant families-The U.S. and 50 states: National origins, language, and early education. Children in America's newcomer families*. Retrieved from http://mumford.albany.edu /children/img/ Research_brief_1.pdf

Hofman, A., & García-Cantú, M. (2008). *Una estrategia nueva para el acceso universal en México. Política Digital, 45*. August-September.

Leal, G. (2010). *Subrogación, causa del incendio en la guardería*. Retrieved from www.jornada.unam.mx

López, J., & López, M. E. (2010). Technology and preschool education in Mexico: A country in transformation. In Blake, S., & Izumi-Taylor, S. (Eds.), *Technology for early childhood education and socialization: Developmental applications and methodologies*. Hershey, PA: IGI Global.

Manheim, K. (1936). *Ideology and utopia*. New York, NY: Harcourt, Brace.

NAEYC. (2009). *Position statement: Developmentally appropriate practice in early childhood programs serving children from birth through age 8*. Retrieved May 5, 2010, from http://www.naeyc.org/files/ naeyc/file/positions/ position%20 statement %20Web.pdf

OECD. (2006). *Starting strong II: Early childhood education and care.* ISBN 92-64-03545-1

Osorno, D. E. (2010). *Nosotros somos los culpables*. Mexico, DF: Grijalbo Mondadori. ISBN 9786073100670

Papert, S. (2000). *From lunch boxes to laptops: The Governor King Initiative*. Retrieved from www.papert.org/articles/ laptops/laptops_master.html

Rodríguez Martínez, G. (2002). *CENDI, report to OAS*. Retrieved from www.oas.org/udse/ readytolearn/quee.html

Rosenthal, J. W. (1996). *Teaching science to language minority students*. Bristol, PA: Multilingual Matters Ltd.

Ross, J. (2009, Jun. 22). *Sacrificed on the altar of neoliberalism*. Pacific Free Press. Retrieved from www.pacificfreepress.com/ news/1/4307-abcs-for- mexicos-poor-kids-sacrificed- on-thealtar-of- neoliberalism.html

SEP. (2003). *Fundamentos y características de una nueva propuesta curricular para la educación preescolar*. Retrieved from www.reformapreescolar.sep.gob.mx /actualizacion/programa/ fundamentos.pdf

SEP. (2004). *Programa de educación preescolar 2004*. ISBN 970-767-023-1

SEP. (2009). *La estructura del sistema educativo mexicano: Dirección general de acreditación, incorporación y revalidación, SEP, 2009*. Retrieved from www.sep.gob.mx/work/sites/ sep1/ resources/LocalContent/ 127650/2/sistemaedumex09.pdf

Weir, S., Russell, S. J., & Valente, J. A. (1982). Logo: An approach to educating disabled children. *BYTE*, *7*, 342–360.

Yelland, N. (1994). The strategies and interactions of young children in Logo tasks. *Journal of Computer Assisted Learning*, *10*, 33–49. doi:10.1111/j.1365-2729.1994.tb00280.x

Yoshikawa, H., et al. (2007). *Early childhood education in Mexico expansion, quality improvement, and curricular reform*. United Nations Children's Fund (UNICEF). ISSN: 1014-7837

Zehr, M. A. (2007, April 12). Preschool attendance: More likely in Mexico than in the United States. *Education Week*. Retrieved from http://blogs.edweek.org/edweek /learning-the-language/2007/04/ preschool_attendance_more_like_1.html

Compilation of References

Adam, E., Klimes-Dougan, B., & Gunnar, M. R. (2007). Emotional and social regulation of the adrenocortical response to stress. In Coch, D., Dawson, G., & Fischer, K. W. (Eds.), *Human behavior and the developing brain: Atypical development* (2nd ed., pp. 264–304). New York, NY: Guilford Press.

Ainsa, T. (1989). Effects of computers and training in Head Start curriculum. *Journal of Instructional Psychology, 16*, 72–78.

Ainsa, T. (1999). Success of using technology and manipulatives to introduce numerical problem solving skills in monolingual/bilingual early childhood classrooms. *Journal of Computers in Mathematics and Science Teaching, 18*(4), 361–369.

Airasian, P. W. (1991). *Classroom assessment*. New York, NY: McGraw-Hill.

Alper, S., & Raharinirina, S. (2006). Assistive technology for individuals with disabilities: A review and synthesis of the literature. *Journal of Special Education Technology, 21*, 47–64.

Althusser, L. (1970). *Lenin and philosophy and other essays (B. Brewster translation)*. New York, NY: Monthly Review Press.

American Optometric Association. (2010). *Impact of computer use on children's vision*. Retrieved from http://www.aoa.org/ x5379.xml

Amso, D., & Johnson, S. P. (2005). Selection and inhibition in infancy: Evidence from the spatial negative priming paradigm. *Cognition, 95*, B27–B36. doi:10.1016/j.cognition.2004.08.006

Anderson, S. W., Bechara, A., Damasio, H., Tranel, D., & Damasio, A. R. (1999). Impairment of social and moral behavior related to early damage in human prefrontal cortex. *Nature Neuroscience, 2*, 1032–1037. doi:10.1038/12194

Anderson, L. W., Krathwohl, D. R., Airasian, P. W., Cruikshank, K. A., Mayer, R. E., & Pintrich, P. R. ... Wittrock, M. C. (Eds.). (2001). *A taxonomy for learning, teaching, and assessing: A revision of Bloom's taxonomy of educational objectives*. Boston, MA: Allyn & Bacon, Pearson Education Group.

Anderson-Inman, L., & Ditson, L. (1999). Computer-based concept mapping: A tool for negotiating meaning. *Learning and Leading with Technology, 26*(8), 6–13.

Andreassi, J. L. (2007). *Psychophysiology: Human behavior and physiological response* (5th ed.). Mahwah, NJ: Lawrence Erlbaum Associates.

Apple, M. W. (2007). Foreword in J. A. Van Galen & G. W. Noblit (Eds.), *Late to class: Social class and schooling in the new economy*. Albany, NY: State University of New York Press.

Ariès, P. (1962). *Centuries of childhood* (Baldick, R., Trans.). London, UK: Jonathan Cape.

Asch, T., Asch, P., & Connor, L. (1983). *Jero on Jero: A Balinese trance séance observed* [film]. Watertown, MA: Documentary Educational Resources.

Aslin, R. N. (2007). What's in a look? *Developmental Science, 10*(1), 48–53. doi:10.1111/j.1467-7687.2007.00563.x

Aslin, R. N., & McMurry, B. (2004). Automated corneal-reflection eye-tracking in infancy: Methodological developments and applications to cognition. *Infancy, 6*, 155–163. doi:10.1207/s15327078in0602_1

Aslin, R. N., & Salapatek, P. (1975). Saccadic localization of visual targets by the very young human infant. *Perception & Psychophysics*, *17*, 293–392. doi:10.3758/BF03203214

Association of Mathematics Teacher Educators' Technology Committee. (2005). *Preparing teachers to use technology to enhance the learning of mathematics*. Position statement. Retrieved from http://www.citejournal.org/vol9/iss1/mathematics/ article1.cfm

Augar, N., Raitman, R., & Zhou, W. (2004). Teaching and learning online with wikis. *Proceedings of the 21st Australasian Society for Computers in Learning in Tertiary Education (ASCILITE) Conference*, Perth, December 5-8, (pp. 95-104). Retrieved from http://www.ascilite.org.au/conferences/ perth04/procs/pdf/ augar.pdf

Azevedo, R. (2005). Using hypermedia as a metacognitive tool for enhancing student learning? The role of self-regulated learning. *Educational Psychologist*, *40*(4), 199–209. doi:10.1207/s15326985ep4004_2

Bachman, L. F., & Palmer, A. S. (1996). *Language testing practice*. Oxford, UK: Oxford University Press.

Baillargeon, R. (1994). How do infants learn about the physical world? *Current Directions in Psychological Science*, *3*(5), 133–140. doi:10.1111/1467-8721.ep10770614

Baker, E. L., & O'Neil, F. (2003). Evaluation and research for technology: Not just playing around. *Evaluation and Program Planning*, *26*(2), 169–176. doi:10.1016/S0149-7189(03)00008-9

Baker, T. R. (2005). Internet-based GIS mapping in support of K-12 education. *The Professional Geographer*, *57*(1), 44–50.

Baker, T. R., & Case, S. B. (2000). Let GIS be your guide. *Science Teacher (Normal, Ill.)*, *67*(7), 24–26.

Bakhtin, M. (1984). *Rabelais and his world*. Bloomington, IN: Indiana University Press.

Bakhtin, M. (2009). *The Bakhtin reader: Selected writings of Bakhtin, Medvedev, Voloshinov*. London, UK: Bloomsbury.

Bandura, A. (2001). Social cognitive theory and mass communication. *Media Psychology*, *3*, 265–299. doi:10.1207/S1532785XMEP0303_03

Bandura, A. (1986). *Social foundations of thought and action: A social cognitive theory*. Englewood Cliffs, NJ: Prentice Hall.

Barazzoni, R. (2000). Brick by brick [*Aprile" people's nursery school of Villa Cella*. Reggio, Emilia, Italy: Reggio Children.]. *Histoire (Paris)*, XXV.

Barlow, D. (2010). The teachers' lounge. *Education Digest*, *75*(6), 65–68.

Barnes, B. (1988). *The nature of power*. Urbana, IL: University of Illinois Press.

Barron, B., Walter, S. E., Martin, C. K., & Schatz, C. (2010). Predictors of creative computing participation and profiles of experience in two Silicon Valley middle schools. *Computers & Education*, *54*(1), 178–189. doi:10.1016/j.compedu.2009.07.017

Barry, E. S. (2006). Children's memory: A primer for understanding behavior. *Early Childhood Education Journal*, *33*(6), 405–411. doi:10.1007/s10643-006-0073-3

Barthes, R. (1967). *Elements of Semiology. (A. Lavers & C. Smith translation)*. London, UK: Jonathan Cape.

Battro, A. M., Fisher, K., & Léna, P. J. (2008). *The educated brain: Essays in neuroeducation*. New York, NY: Cambridge University Press. doi:10.1017/CBO9780511489907

Becker, H. J. (2000). Who's wired and who's not: Children's access to and use of computer technology. *The Future of Children: Children and Computer Technology*, *10*(2), 44–75. doi:10.2307/1602689

Bennis, W. (2003). *On becoming a leader*. New York, NY: Basic Books.

Berk, L., & Winsler, A. (1995). *Scaffolding children's learning: Vygotsky and early childhood education*. Washington, DC: National Association for the Education of Young Children. (ERICDocument No. ED384443)

Berliner, D. (1991). Educational psychology and pedagogical expertise: New findings and new opportunities for thinking about training. *Educational Psychologist*, *26*(2), 145–155. doi:10.1207/s15326985ep2602_6

Berners-Lee, T., & Fischetti, M. (1999). *Weaving the Web: The original design and ultimate destiny of the World Wide Web by its inventor*. San Francisco, CA: HarperCollins Publishers.

Bialystok, E., & Hakuta, K. (1994). *In other words*. New York, NY: Basic Books.

Bickham, D. S., Vandewater, E. A., Huston, A. C., Lee, J. H., Caplovitz, A. G., & Wright, J. C. (2003). Predictors of children's electronic media use: An examination of three ethnic groups. *Media Psychology*, *5*, 107–137. doi:10.1207/S1532785XMEP0502_1

Bilton, N. (2010, March 1). Connecting your car, socks and body to the Internet. *Bits Blog, NYTimes.com*. Retrieved from http://bits.blogs.nytimes.com/ 2010/03/01/ connecting-your- car-socks-and- body-to-the-Internet /

Blackstone, S. (1988). Vocabulary selection: Current practices and a glimpse at the future. *Augmentative Communication News, 7*(5).

Bloom, B. S. (Ed.). Englehart, M. D., Furst, E. J., Hill, W. H., & Krathwohl, D. R. (1956). *Taxonomy of educational objectives: The classification of educational goals, by a committee of college and university examiners. Handbook I: Cognitive domain*. New York, NY: Longmans, Green.

Bodzin, A. M. (2008). Integrating instructional technologies in a local watershed investigation with urban elementary learners. *The Journal of Environmental Education*, *39*(4), 47–57. doi:10.3200/JOEE.39.2.47-58

Boone, R., & Higgins, K. (1993). Hypermedia basal readers: Three years of school-based research. *Journal of Special Education Technology*, *12*(2), 86–106.

Boring, E. G. (1942). *Sensation and perception in the history of experimental psychology*. New York, NY: Appleton-Century.

Borko, H., & Putnam, T. (1996). Learning to teach. In Berliner, D. C., & Calfee, R. C. (Eds.), *Handbook of educational psychology* (pp. 673–708). New York, NY: Simon & Schuster Macmillan.

Bornstein, M. (1985). Habituation as a measure of visual information processing in human infants: Summary, systematization, and synthesis. In Gottleib, G., & Krasnegor, N. (Eds.), *Development of audition and vision during the first year of postnatal life: A methodological overview* (pp. 253–295). Norwood, NJ: Ablex.

Bouck, E. C., & Flanagan, S. M. (2010). Virtual manipulatives: What they are and how teachers can use them. *Intervention in School and Clinic*, *45*(3), 186–191. doi:10.1177/1053451209349530

Boulos, M., Maramba, I., & Wheeler, S. (2006). Wikis, blogs and podcast: A new generation of web-based tools for virtual collaborative clinical practice and education. *BMC Medical Education*, *6*(41). Retrieved from http://www.biomedcentral.com/ 1472-6920/6/41/.

Bourdieu, P. (1984). *Distinction: A social critique of the judgment of taste*. Cambridge, MA: Harvard University Press.

Bourdieu, P. (1986). The forms of capital. In Richardson, J. (Ed.), *Handbook of theory and research for the sociology of education*. New York, NY: Greenwood.

Bower, M. (2008). Affordance analysis - Matching learning tasks with learning technologies. *Educational Media International*, *45*(1), 3–15. doi:10.1080/09523980701847115

Bransford, J., Brown, A., & Cocking, R. (2000). *How people learn: Brain, mind, experience and school*. Washington, DC: National Academy Press.

Brasic, J. R., Wong, D., & Eroglu, A. (2007). PET scanning in autism spectrum disorders. *E-Medicine Journal*. Retrieved from http://www.emedicine.com/ neuro/ topic440.htm

Brescia, W. F., & Miller, M. T. (2006). What's it worth? The perceived benefits of instructional blogging. *Electronic Journal for the Integration of Technology in Education*, *5*, 44–52.

British Library Board. (n.d.). *Listen to nature*. Retrieved from http://www.bl.uk/ listentonature/main.html

Bronson, G. W. (1974). The postnatal growth of visual capacity. *Child Development*, *4*(5), 873–890. doi:10.2307/1128073

Bronson, G. W. (1982). Structure, status, and characteristics of the nervous system at birth. In Stratton, P. (Ed.), *Psychobiology of the human newborn* (pp. 99–118). Chichester, UK: Wiley.

Brown, J. S., Collins, A., & Duguid, P. (1989). Situated cognition and the culture of learning. *Educational Research, 18*, 32–42.

Brown, H. D. (2007). *Teaching by principles: An interactive approach to languagepedagogy* (3rd ed.). White Plains, NY: Pearson Longman.

Bryant, D., & Bryant, B. (2003). *Assistive technology for people with disabilities*. Boston, MA: Allyn & Bacon.

Buckingham, D. (2007). *Beyond technology: Children's learning in the age of digital culture*. Malden, MA: Polity.

Buckingham, D., & Scanlon, M. (2001). Parental pedagogies: An analysis of British edutainment magazines for young children. *Journal of Early Childhood Literacy, 1*(3), 281–299. doi:10.1177/14687984010013003

Buckingham, D. (1998). *Teaching popular culture*. London, UK: UCL Press.

Buckingham, D., & Sefton-Green, J. (1994). *Cultural studies goes to school: Reading and teaching popular media*. London, UK: Taylor and Francis.

Buckingham, D., & Sefton Green, J. (2004). Structure, Agency and pedagogy in children's media culture. In Tobin, J. (Ed.), *Pikachu's global adventure: The rise and fall of Pokémon*. Durham, NC: Duke University Press.

Buckleitner, W. (1999). The state of children's software evaluation, yesterday, today and in the 21st century. *Information Technology in Childhood Education Annual*, 211–220.

Bus, A. G., Van, I., Jzendoorn, M. H., & Pellegrini, A. D. (1995). Storybook reading makes for success in learning to read. A meta-analysis on intergenerational transmission of literacy. *Review of Educational Research, 65*, 1–21.

Butzin, S. M. (2002). Project CHILD (Changing how instruction for learning is delivered): The perfect fit for multimedia elementary schools. *Multimedia Schools, 9*(6), 14–16.

Calkins, S. D., & Dedmon, S. E. (2000). Physiological and behavorial regulation in ten-year-old children with aggressive/destructive behavior problems. *Journal of Abnormal Child Psychology, 28*(2), 103–118. doi:10.1023/A:1005112912906

Calkins, S. D., & Keane, S. P. (2004). Cardiac vagal regulation across the preschool period: Stability, continuity, and implications for childhood adjustment. *Developmental Psychobiology, 45*(3), 101–112. doi:10.1002/dev.20020

Campbell, M. (2010). Collaborations between librarians and faculty in a digital age. *Education Digest, 75*(6), 30–33.

Campbell, P. H., Milbourne, S., Dugan, L. M., & Wilcox, M. J. (2006). A review of evidence on practices for teaching young children to use assistive technology devices. *Topics in Early Childhood Special Education, 26*(1), 3–13. doi:10.1177/02711214060260010101

Canale, M., & Swain, M. (1980). Theoretical bases of communicative approaches to second language teaching and testing. *Applied Linguistics*, 1–47. doi:10.1093/applin/1.1.1

Cashell, B. (2007). *Report for Congress: "Who are the Middle Class?"* Retrieved from http://www.policyarchive.org/ handle/ 10207/bitstreams /4472.pdf

Castillo, M. A. (2009, Oct. 9). La educación preescolar: Entre las maestras express y la vulnerabilidad. *Observatorio Ciudadano de la Educación*. Retrieved from www.observatorio.org/ colaboraciones/2009/ Oct09-MiguelAngelCastillo -EducPreesc.pdf

Caudill, W. (1962). Patterns of emotion in modern Japan. In Smith, R. J., & Beardsley, R. K. (Eds.), *Japanese culture* (pp. 115–131). Chicago, IL: Aldine.

Chakravarti, S., Srivastava, S., & Mittnacht, A. J. C. (2008). Near infrared spectroscopy (NIRS) in children. *Seminars in Cardiothoracic and Vascular Anesthesia, 12*(1), 70–79. doi:10.1177/1089253208316444

Chambers, A. C. (1997). *Has technology been considered? A guide for IEP teams*. Reston, VA: Council of Administrators of Special Education and the Technology and Media Division of The Council for Exceptional Children.

Chambliss, J. J. (1982). Aristotle's conception of childhood and the poliscraft. *Educational Studies, 13*, 33–43.

Chang, C. Y., & Wang, H. C. (2009). Issues of inquiry learning in digital learning environments. *British Journal of Educational Technology*, *40*(1), 169–173. doi:10.1111/j.1467-8535.2008.00850.x

Chapelle, C. A. (2007). Technology and second language acquisition. *Annual Review of Applied Linguistics*, *27*, 98–114. doi:10.1017/S0267190508070050

Chen, E., Cohen, S., & Miller, G. E. (2010). How low socioeconomic status affects 2-year hormonal trajectories in children. *Psychological Science*, *21*(1), 31–37. doi:10.1177/0956797609355566

Chin, E. (1999). Ethnically correct dolls: Toying with the race industry. *American Anthropologist*, *101*(2). doi:10.1525/aa.1999.101.2.305

Chin, E. (2001). *Purchasing power: Black kids and American consumer culture*. Minneapolis, MN: University of Minnesota Press.

Chomsky, N. (1964). *Current issues in linguistic theory*. London, UK: Mouton & Co.

Chomsky, N. (1968). *Language and mind*. New York, NY: Harcourt, Brace & World, Inc.

Chomsky, N. (1980). *Rules and representation*. New York, NY: Columbia University Press.

Chugani, H. T., & Phelps, M. E. (1986). Maturational changes in cerebral functions in infants determined by 18FDG positron emission tomography. *Science*, *231*, 840–843. doi:10.1126/science.3945811

Chugani, H. T. (1994). Development of regional brain glucose metabolism in relation to behavior and plasticity. In Dawson, G., & Fisher, K. W. (Eds.), *Human behavior and the developing brain* (pp. 153–175). New York, NY: Guliford Press.

Chularut, P., & DeBacker, T. K. (2004). The influence of concept mapping on achievement, self-regulation, and self-efficacy in students in English as a second language. *Contemporary Educational Psychology*, *29*, 248–263. doi:10.1016/j.cedpsych.2003.09.001

Churches, A. (2009, January, 4). *Bloom's digital taxonomy*. Retrieved April 11, 2010, from http://edorigami.wikispaces.com

Clark, B. A. (2000, November). First- and second-language acquisition in early childhood. In Issues in early childhood education: Curriculum, teacher education, & disseminationof information. *Proceedings of the Lilian Katz Symposium*, Champaign, IL.

Clarkea, A. R., Barrya, R. J., McCarthyb, R., & Selikowitzb, M. (1998). EEG analysis in attention-deficit/hyperactivity disorder: A comparative study of two subtypes. *Psychiatry Research*, *81*(1), 19–29. doi:10.1016/S0165-1781(98)00072-9

Clements, D. H., & Sarama, J. (2003). Young children and technology: What does the research say? *Young Children*, *58*(6), 34–40.

Clements, D. H. (1999a). Concrete manipulatives, concrete ideas. *Contemporary Issues in Early Childhood*, *1*(1), 45–60. doi:10.2304/ciec.2000.1.1.7

Clements, D. H. (1999b). The effective use of computers with young children. In Copley, J. V. (Ed.), *Mathematics in the early years* (pp. 119–128). Reston, VA: National Council of Teachers of Mathematics.

Clements, D. H., & Sarama, J. (2008). Mathematics and technology: Supporting learning for students and teachers. In Saracho, O. N., & Spodek, B. (Eds.), *Contemporary perspectives on science and technology in early childhood education* (pp. 127–147). Charlotte, NC: Information Age.

Clements, D. H., & Battiste, M. (1992). *Electronic resources: 3D geometry in the 3rd grade: Sorting and describing polyhedra*. Retrieved July 11, 2007, from http://my.nctm.org/ erources/

Clements, D., & Conference Working Group. (2004). Part one: Major themes and recommendations. In D. H. Clements, J. Sarama, & A.-M. DiBiase (Eds.), *Engaging young children in mathematics education* (pp. 1-72). Mahwah, NJ: Lawrence Erlbum Associates.

Clifford, J. (1983). On ethnographic authority. *Representations (Berkeley, Calif.)*, *1*(2), 118–146. doi:10.1525/rep.1983.2.1.99p0010p

Clinton, B. (1997, February 4). *What new brain research tells us about our youngest children*. Conference presented at White House Conference on Early Childhood Development and Learning, Washington D.C. Colombo, J. (2001). The development of visual attention. *Annual Review of Psychology*, *52*, 337–367.

Cobanoglu, C. (2006). An analysis of blogs as a teaching tool as perceived by hospitality management students. *Journal of Hospitality, Leisure, Sport and Tourism Education*, *5*(2), 83–88. doi:10.3794/johlste.52.138

Cochran-Smith, M., Kahn, J., & Paris, C. L. (1988). When word processors come into the classroom. In Hoot, J. L., & Silvern, S. B. (Eds.), *Writing with computers in the early grades* (pp. 43–74). New York, NY: Teachers College Press.

Coleman, D. (2005). Language learning input and input for learning to communicate. *LacusForum*, *31*, 203–213.

Coleman, D. (2006). A formal integrated view of speech, gesture, gaze and its implications for learning. *LACUS Forum*, *32*, 163–172.

Coley, R. J., Cradler, J., & Engel, P. K. (1997). *Computers and classrooms: The status of technology in U.S. schools*. Princeton, NJ: Educational Testing Service.

Collier, J., & Collier, M. (1986). *Visual anthropology: Photography as a research method*. Albuquerque, NM: University of New Mexico Press.

Collier, V. P., & Thomas, W. (1995). *Language minority student achievement and program effectiveness. Research summary on ongoing study*. Fairfax, VA: George Mason University.

Concord.org. (2010). *Probeware: Developing new tools for data collection and analysis*. Retrieved from http://www.concord.org/ work/themes/probeware.html

Connor, L., Asch, T., & Asch, P. (1986). *Jero Tapakan: Balinese healer*. Cambridge, UK: Cambridge University Press.

Cook, D. (2004). *The commodification of childhood: The children's clothing industry and the rise of the child consumer*. Durham, NC: Duke University Press.

Copley, J. V. (2010). *The young child and mathematics* (2nd ed.). Washington, DC: NAEYC/NCTM.

Corbeil, P. (1999). Learning from the children: Practical and theoretical reflections on playing and learning. *Simulation & Gaming*, *30*(2), 163–180. doi:10.1177/104687819903000206

Cordes, C., & Miller, E. (2000). *Fool's gold: A critical look at computers in childhood*. College Park, MD: Alliance for Childhood.

Cornell Laboratory of Ornithology. (n.d.). *Macauley library online. An audio and video bird recordings archive*. Retrieved from http://macaulaylibrary.org

Council for Research Excellence. (2009). *Video consumer mapping study*. Retrieved from http://www.researchexcellence.com/ VCMFINALREPORT_4_28_ 09.pdf

Croissant, J. (1998). Growing up cyborg: Development stories for postmodern children. In Davis-Floyd, R., & Dumit, J. (Eds.), *Cyborg babies: From techno-sex to techno-tots* (pp. 285–298). New York, NY: Routledge.

Cross, G. (1997). *Kids' stuff: Toys and the changing world of American childhood*. Cambridge, MA: Harvard University Press.

Cross, G. (2004). *The cute and the cool: Wondrous innocence and modern American children's culture*. New York, NY: Oxford University Press.

Cruz, F. M. F., & Snider, S. L. (2009, November). Storying with technology: Using the multiple literacies of the new technology and media landscape to connect with young learners. *Contemporary Issues in Early Childhood*, *10*(4).

Cuban, L. (2001). *Oversold and underused: Reforming schools through technology, 1980-2000*. Cambridge, MA: Harvard University Press.

Cuban, L. (1999). High-tech schools, low-tech teaching. *Education Digest*, *64*(5), 53–54. Retrieved from http://web.ebscohost.com.avoserv. library.fordham.edu.

Cuban, L. (2001). *Oversold and underused: Computers in the classroom*. Cambridge, MA: Harvard University Press.

Curren, R. (2003). *A companion to the philosophy of education: Blackwell companions to philosophy*. Hoboken, NJ: Wiley-Blackwell.

Damasio, A. R. (2005). The neurobiological grounding of human values. In Changeux, J. P., Damasio, A. R., Singer, W., & Christen, Y. (Eds.), *Neurobiology of human values* (pp. 47–56). London, UK: Springer Verlag. doi:10.1007/3-540-29803-7_5

Davis-Floyd, R., & Dumit, J. (1998). *Cyborg babies: From techno-sex to techno-tots*. New York, NY: Routledge.

De Certeau, M. (1994). *The practice of everyday life*. Los Angeles, CA: University of California Press.

De Kloet, E. R. (1991). Brain corticosteroid receptor balance and homeostatic control. *Frontiers in Neuroendocrinology*, *12*, 95–164.

DeBell, M., & Chapman, C. (2003). *Computer and Internet use by children and adolescents in the United States, (NCES 2004-014)*. Washington, DC: U.S. Department of Education, National Center for Educational Statistics.

DeCaro, J. A., & Worthman, C. M. (2007). Cultural models, parent behavior, and young child experience in working American families. *Parenting, Science and Practice*, *7*(2), 17203. doi:10.1080/15295190701306953

DeCaro, J. A., & Worthman, C. M. (2008). Culture and the socialization of child cardiovascular regulation at school entry in the US. *American Journal of Human Biology*, *20*(5), 572–583. doi:10.1002/ajhb.20782

Dede, C. (2007). Information and communication technologies: Considerations of current practices for teachers and teacher educators. In N. C. Burbules (Ed.), *106th Yearbook of the National Society for the Study of Education, reinventing the role of information and communication technologies in education*, (pp. 11–38). Malden, MA: Blackwell.

Dell, A., Disdier, A., Goldman, A., & Mervine, P. (1998). The teacher's role in augmentative communication. *Tech-NJ Bulletin Board, 9*(1). Retrieved from http://www.tcnj.edu/~technj/ win98/trainingmod.html

Desimone, L. (1999). Linking parent involvement with student achievement: Do race and income matter? *The Journal of Educational Research*, *93*, 11–30. doi:10.1080/00220679909597625

DeVries, R., & Kohlberg, L. (1987). *Programs of early education: The constructivist view*. New York, NY: Longman.

Dewey, J. (1997). *How we think*. Mineola, NY: Dover.

Digiovanni, L., Schwartz, S., & Greer, C. (2009). I think, iPod(cast), I learn: Using digital media and podcasting in teacher education. In I. Gibson, et al. (Eds.), *Proceedings of Society for Information Technology & Teacher Education International Conference 2009* (pp. 1812-1819). Chesapeake, VA: AACE.

Digital nation: 21st century America's progress towards universal broadband Internet access. Retrieved from http://www.ntia.doc.gov/press/ 2010/ DigitalNationReport_02162010. html

Dlott, A. M. (2007). A (pod)cast of thousands. *Educational Leadership*, *64*(7), 80–82.

Drawing for Children. (n.d.). *Drawing for Children, a free drawing program for children*. Retrieved from http://drawing.gamemaker.nl

Dreyfus, H. L., & Spinosa, C. (2002). Highway bridges and feasts: Heidegger and Borgmann on how to affirm technology. In Dreyfus, H., & Wrathall, M. (Eds.), *Heidegger re-examined: Art, poetry and technology* (*Vol. III*, pp. 175–193). New York, NY: Routledge.

Du Gay, P., Hall, S., Janes, L., & Negus, K. (1997). *Doing cultural studies: The story of the Sony Walkman*. Thousand Oaks, CA: Sage Publications.

Duncan, G. J., & Brooks-Gunn, J. (2000). Family poverty, welfare reform, and child development. *Child Development*, *71*(1), 188–196. doi:10.1111/1467-8624.00133

Education Week. (January, 2010). *Quality counts report*. Retrieved from http://www.edweek.org/ ew/toc/ 2010/01/ 14/index.html

Edyburn, D. L. (2006). Assistive technology and mild disabilities. *Special Education Technology Practice*, *8*(4), 18–28.

Elkind, D. (1998). *All grown up and no place to go: Teenagers in crisis*. Cambridge, MA: Da Capo Press.

Ellul, J. (1964). *The technological society* (Wilkinson, J., Trans.). New York, NY: Vintage Books.

Epstein, J. L. (1987). Parent involvement: What research says to administrators. *Education and Urban Society*, *79*, 119–136. doi:10.1177/0013124587019002002

Ertmer, P. A. (2005). Teacher pedagogical beliefs: The final frontier in our quest for technology integration? *Educational Technology Research and Development*, *53*(4), 25–39. doi:10.1007/BF02504683

Essex, M. J., Klein, M. H., Cho, E., & Kalin, N. H. (2002). Maternal stress beginning in infancy may sensitize children to later stress exposure: Effects of cortisol and behavior. *Society of Biological Psychiatry*, *52*, 776–784. doi:10.1016/S0006-3223(02)01553-6

Evans, G. W., & English, K. (2003). The environment of poverty: Multiple stressor exposure, psychophysiological stress, and socioemotional adjustment. *Child Development*, *74*(4), 1238–1248.

Evans, G. W., & Schamberg, M. A. (2009). Childhood poverty, chronic stress, and adult working memory. *Proceedings of the National Academy of Sciences of the United States of America*.. doi:10.1073/pnas.0811910106

Evans, M. A., & Saint-Aubin, J. (2005). What children are looking at during shared storybook reading? *Psychological Science*, *16*(11), 913–920. doi:10.1111/j.1467-9280.2005.01636.x

Evans, M. A., Saint-Aubin, J., & Landry, N. (2009). Letter names and alphabet book reading by senior kindergartners: An eye movement study. *Child Development*, *80*(6), 1824–1841. doi:10.1111/j.1467-8624.2009.01370.x

Evans, M. A., & Saint-Aubin, J. (2010). An eye for print: Child and adult attention to print during shared book reading. In Aram, D., & Korat, O. (Eds.), *Literacy development and enhancement across orthographies and cultures* (pp. 43–53). London, UK: Springer. doi:10.1007/978-1-4419-0834-6_4

Evans, M. A., Saint-Aubin, J., & Roy-Charland, A. (2006, June). *Reading pictures: Preschoolers eye fixations on illustrations during shared book reading*. Colloquiam presented at Royal Netherlands Academy of Arts and Sciences, Amsterdam.

Fabes, R. A., Martin, C. L., & Hanish, L. D. (2004). The next 50 years: Considering gender as a context for understanding young children's peer relationships. *Merrill-Palmer Quarterly*, *50*(3), 260–273. doi:10.1353/mpq.2004.0017

Falbel, A. (1991). The computer as a convivial tool. In Harel, I., & Papert, S. (Eds.), *Constructionism* (pp. 29–37). New Jersey: Ablex Publishing.

Fallon, K., & Light, J. (2001). Enhancing vocabulary selection for preschoolers who require augmentative and alternative communication. *American Journal of Speech-Language Pathology*, *10*, 81–94. doi:10.1044/1058-0360(2001/010)

Fantz, R. L. (1958). Pattern vision in young infants. *The Psychological Record*, *8*, 43–47.

Fantz, R. L. (1961). The origin of form perception. *Scientific American*, *204*, 66–72. doi:10.1038/scientificamerican0561-66

Fantz, R. L. (1963). Pattern vision in newborn infants. *Science*, *140*, 296–297. doi:10.1126/science.140.3564.296

Fennell, F. (2006). *Curriculum focal points for prekindergarten through grade 8 mathematics*. Retrieved June 21, 2010, from http://www.nctm.org/ focalpoints

Fernandez, J. M., & Luftglass, M. (2003). Interactive whiteboards: A powerful learning tool. *Principal*, *83*(1), 63.

Firek, H. (2003, April). One order of ed tech coming up... You want fries with that? *Phi Delta Kappan*, *84*, 596–597.

Flavell, J. H., Miller, P. H., & Miller, S. A. (2002). *Cognitive development* (4th, ed.). Englewood Cliffs, NJ: Prentice Hall.

Fleer, M. (1999). *Technology for children: Developing your own approach*. Sydney, Australia: Prentice Hall.

Fleer, M. (2001). *Science for children: Developing a personal approach to teaching*. Frenchs Forest, New South Wales, Australia: Pearson.

Foucault, M. (1980). *Power/knowledge: Selected interviews and other writings 1972-1977* (Gordon, C., Ed.). London, UK: Harvester.

Fox, S. (2005). *Digital divisions*. Pew Internet and American Life Project. Retrieved from http://www.pewiInternet.org/ Reports/2005/ Digital-Divisions.aspx?r=1

Franchak, J. M., Kretch, K. S., Soska, K. C., Babcock, J. S., & Adolph, K. E. (2010). Head-mounted eye-tracking of infants' natural interactions: A new method. *Proceedings of the 2010 Symposium on Eye Tracking Research & Applications*, Austin, Texas.

Frazel, M. (2007). K12 online conference. *Beyond the Horizon: The Online Journal of Adventures in Genealogy, Technology, and Research*. Retrieved from http://midgefrazel.net/blog/ 2007_09_01 _midgefrazel_archive.html

Freire, P. (1970). *Pedagogy of the oppressed*. New York, NY: Continuum.

French, J., & Raven, B. (1959). The bases of social power. In Cartwright, D. (Ed.), *Studies in social power* (pp. 150–167). Ann Arbor, MI: The University of Michigan.

Froebel, F. (1886). *Autobiography of Friedrich Froebel* (Michaelis, E., & Moore, H. K., Trans.). London, England: Swan, Sonneschein and Co.

Galván Lafarga, L. E. (2009). *In De las escuelas de párvulos al preescolar, una historia por contar*. Retrieved from http://biblioweb.dgsca.unam.mx /diccionario/htm/ articulos/ sec_25.htm

Galyon-Keramidas, C., & Collins, B. C. (2009). Assistive technology use with the birth to three population: A rural perspective. *Rural Special Education Quarterly*, *28*(1), 38–48.

Gandini, L. (2002). The story and foundation of the Reggio Emilia approach. In V. R. Fu, A. J. Stremmel, & L. T. Hill (Eds.) (2002). *Teaching and learning: Collaborative exploration of the Reggio Emilia approach*. Upper Saddle River, NJ: Merrill Prentice Hall.

Garmezy, N., Masten, A. S., & Tellegen, A. (1984). The study of stress and competence in children: A building block for developmental psychopathology. *Child Development*, *55*, 97–111. doi:10.2307/1129837

Garofalo, J., Drier, H., Harper, S., Timmerman, M. A., & Shockey, T. (2000). Promoting appropriate uses of technology in mathematics teacher preparation. *Contemporary Issues in Technology & Teacher Education*, *1*(1), 66–88.

Gass, S., & Selinker, L. (2001). *Second language acquisition: An introductory course*. Mahwah, NJ: Lawrence Erlbraum.

Gebhardt-Seele, P. G. (1985). *The computer and the child: A Montessori approach*. Rockville, MD: Computer Science Press.

Gee, J. P. (2005). Learning by design: Good video games as learning machines. *E-learning*, *2*(1), 5–16. doi:10.2304/ elea.2005.2.1.5

Gee, J. P. (2003). *What video games have to teach us about learning and literacy*. New York, NY: Palgrave McMillan.

Gee, J. P. (2004). *Situated language and learning: A critique of traditional schooling*. New York, NY: Routledge.

Gee, J. P. (2007). *What video games have to teach us about learning and literacy* (2nd ed.). Palgrave Macmillan.

Geissinger, H. (1997). *Educational software: Criteria for evaluation*. Retrieved from http://www.ascilite.org.au/ conferences/perth97/ papers/Geissinger/ Geissinger.html

Gelman, R., & Brenneman, K. (2004). Science learning pathways for young children. *Early Childhood Research Quarterly*, *19*(1), 150–158. doi:10.1016/j. ecresq.2004.01.009

Ghiraldelli, P. Jr. (2000). The fundamentals of Gepeto's philosophy of education: Neopragmatism and infancy in the postmodern world. *Educational Philosophy and Theory*, *32*(2), 201–207. doi:10.1111/j.1469-5812.2000. tb00444.x

Gibboney, R. (2006). Intelligence by design: Thorndike versus Dewey. *Phi Delta Kappan*, *88*(2), 170–178.

Gibbons, A. N. (2007). *The matrix ate my baby*. Amsterdam, The Netherlands: Sense Publishers.

Gillen, J., Littleton, K., Twiner, A., Staarman, J. K., & Mercer, N. (2008). Using the interactive whiteboard to resource continuity and support multimodal teaching in a primary science classroom. *Journal of Computer Assisted Learning*, *24*(4), 348–358. doi:10.1111/j.1365-2729.2007.00269.x

Gillespie, C. W. (2004). Seymour Papert's vision for early childhood education? A descriptive study of preschoolers and kindergarteners in discovery-based, logo-rich classrooms. *Early Childhood Research and Practice, 6*(1).

Gilutz, S., & Nielsen, J. (2002). *How children use the Web. 70 design guidelines from usability studies with kids using websites*. Fremont, CA: Nielsen Norman Group.

Giza, B. (2010). Strategies for the use of open-source graphics, animation, and video tools in STEM education. In C. Crawford et al. (Eds.), *Proceedings of Society for Information Technology & Teacher Education International Conference 2010,* (pp. 2722-2728). Chesapeake, VA: AACE.

Glister, P. (1997). *Digital literacy*. New York, NY: John Wiley and Sons.

Gnu.org. (2008). *Gnu licenses*. Retrieved from http://www.gnu.org/ licenses/ licenses.html.

Godden, D. R., & Baddeley, A. D. (1975). Context-dependent memory in two natural environments: On land and underwater. *The British Journal of Psychology*, *66*(3), 325–331. doi:10.1111/j.2044-8295.1975.tb01468.x

Goodz, N. S. (1994). Interactions between parents and children in bilingual families. In F. Genesee (Ed.), *Educating second language children: The whole child, the whole curriculum, the whole community.* Cambridge, UK: Cambridge University Press. (ERIC Document No. ED375641)

Google Earth. (2010). *Spectacular satellite images of the world*. Retrieved on from http://www.kmzlinks.com/

Gough, N. (2004). RhizomANTically becoming-cyborg: Performing posthuman pedagogies. *Educational Philosophy and Theory*, *46*(3), 253–265. doi:10.1111/j.1469-5812.2004.00066.x

Grabe, W., & Stoller, F. L. (1997). Content-based instruction: Research foundations. In Snow, M. A., & Brinton, D. M. (Eds.), *The content-based classroom: Perspectives on integrating language and content* (pp. 5–21). White Plains, NY: Longman.

Granger, D. A., Weisz, J. R., & Kauneckis, D. (1994). Neuroendocrine reactivity, internalizing behavior problems, and control-related cognitions in clinic-referred children and adolescents. *Journal of Abnormal Child Psychology*, *103*, 267–276.

Greenberg, M. T., & Snell, J. L. (1997). Brain development and emotional development: The role of teaching in organizing the frontal lobe. In P. Salovey & D. J. Sluyter (Eds.), *Emotional development and emotional intelligence: Educational implications* (pp. 93 119). New York, NY: BasicBooks.

Greenfield, A. (2006). *Everyware: The dawning age of ubiquitous computing*. CA: New Riders.

Greenfield, P., & Yan, Z. (2006). Children, adolescents, and the Internet: A new field of inquiry in developmental psychology. *Developmental Psychology*, *42*, 391–394. doi:10.1037/0012-1649.42.3.391

Greenhow, C., Robelia, B., & Hughes, J. E. (2009). Learning, teaching, and scholarship in a digital age Web 2.0 and classroom research: What path should we take now? *Educational Researcher*, *38*(4), 246–259. doi:10.3102/0013189X09336671

Grimmett, S., & McCoy, M. (1980). Effects of parental communication on reading performance of third grade children. *The Reading Teacher*, *33*, 303–308.

Grossman, P. L. (1989). A study in contrast: Sources of pedagogical content knowledge for secondary English. *Journal of Teacher Education*, *40*(5), 24–31. doi:10.1177/002248718904000504

Grossman, P. L. (1991). Overcoming the apprenticeship of observation in teacher education coursework. *Teaching and Teacher Education*, *7*, 245–257. doi:10.1016/0742-051X(91)90004-9

Gunnar, M. R., & Donzella, B. (2002). Social regulation of the cortisol levels in early human development. *Psychoneuroendocrinology*, *27*, 199–220. doi:10.1016/S0306-4530(01)00045-2

Gunnar, M. R., Larson, M. C., Hertsgaard, L., Harris, M. L., & Brodersen, L. (1992). The stressfulness of separation among nine-month-old infants: Effects of social context variables and infant temperament. *Child Development*, *63*, 290–303. doi:10.2307/1131479

Gunnar, M. R., Sebanc, A. M., Tout, K., Donzella, B., & Van Dulmen, M. M. H. (2003). Peer rejection, temperament, and cortisol activity in preschoolers. *Developmental Psychobiology*, *43*, 346–358. doi:10.1002/dev.10144

Gunnar, M. R. (2001). The role of glococorticoids in anxiety disorders: A critical analysis. In Vasey, M. W., & Dadds, M. R. (Eds.), *The developmental psychopathology of anxiety* (pp. 143–159). New York, NY: Oxford University Press.

Haas Dyson, A. (1997). *Writing superheroes: Contemporary childhood, popular culture, and classroom literacy*. New York, NY: Teacher's College Press.

Hackman, D. A., & Farah, M. J. (2009). Socioeconomic status and the developing brain. *Trends in Cognitive Sciences*, *13*(2), 65–73. doi:10.1016/j.tics.2008.11.003

Haith, M. M. (1966). The response of the human newborn to visual movement. *Journal of Experimental Child Psychology*, *3*, 235–243. doi:10.1016/0022-0965(66)90067-1

Haith, M. M. (1969). Infrared television recording and measurement of ocular behavior in the human infant. *The American Psychologist*, *24*, 279–283. doi:10.1037/h0028419

Haith, M. M. (1980). *Rules that babies look by: The organization of newborn visual activity*. Hillsdale, NJ: Lawrence Erlbaum Associates, Inc.

Haith, M. M. (2004). Progress and standardization in eye movement work with human infants. *Infancy*, *6*, 257–265. doi:10.1207/s15327078in0602_6

Haith, M. M. (1994). Visual expectations as the first step toward the development of future-oriented processes. In Haith, M. M., Benson, J. B., Roberts, R. J. Jr, & Pennington, B. F. (Eds.), *The development of future-oriented processes* (pp. 11–38). Chicago, IL: The University of Chicago Press.

Halderson, J. (2006). Podcasting: Connecting with a new generation. *Middle Ground*, *10*(1), 18–21.

Hall, S. (1999). Encoding, decoding. In During, S. (Ed.), *The cultural studies reader*. London, UK: Routledge.

Hancock, T. B., & Kaiser, A. P. (2002). The effects of trainer-implemented enhanced milieu teaching on the social communication of children with autism. *Topics in Early Childhood Special Education*, *22*(1), 39–54. doi:10.1177/027112140202200104

Hargittai, E. (2010). Digital na(t)ives? Variation in Internet skills and uses among members of the net generation. *Sociological Inquiry*, *80*(1), 92–113. doi:10.1111/j.1475-682X.2009.00317.x

Hastings, E., Karas, T., Winsler, A., Way, E., Madigan, A., & Tyler, S. (2009). Young children's video/computer game use: Relations with school performance and behavior. *Issues in Mental Health Nursing*, *30*(10), 638–649.. doi:10.1080/01612840903050414

Hatzinger, M., Brand, S., Perren, S., von Wyl, A., von Klitzing, K., & Holsboer-Traschler, E. (2007). Hypothalamic-pituitary-adrenal (HPA) activity in kindergarten children: Importance of gender and associations with behavioral/emotional difficulties. *Journal of Psychiatric Research*, *41*, 861–870. doi:10.1016/j.jpsychires.2006.07.012

Haugland, S. (1992). The effect of computer software on preschool children's developmental gains. *Journal of Computing in Childhood Education*, *3*(1), 15–30.

Haugland, S. (1995). Selecting or upgrading software and websites in the classroom. *Early Childhood Education Journal*, *32*(5), 329–340. doi:10.1007/s10643-005-4401-9

Haugland, S. (1999). What role should technology play in young children's learning? Part 2. *Young Children*, *54*(6), 26–31.

Haugland, S. W. (1999). The newest software that meets the developmental needs of young children. *Early Childhood Journal*, *26*(4), 73–82.

Haugland, S. W., & Wright, J. L. (1997). *Young children and technology: A world of discovery*. Boston, MA: Allyn and Bacon.

Haugland, S. (2000). Computers and young children. Champaign, IL: ERIC Clearinghouse on Elementary and Early Childhood Education. Retrieved from http://ceep.crc.uiuc.edu/ eecearchive/ digests/ 2000/haugland00.pdf

Hayhoe, M. M. (2004). Advances in relating eye movements and cognition. *Infancy*, *6*(2), 267–274. doi:10.1207/s15327078in0602_7

Healey, J. (1998). *Failure to connect: How computers affect our children's minds – For better or worse*. New York, NY: Simon and Schuster.

Heidegger, M. (1977). The question concerning technology. In Heidegger, M. (Ed.), *The question concerning technology and other essays* (pp. 1–49). (Lovitt, W., Trans.). New York, NY: Harper & Row.

Heinrichs, J. H., & Lim, J. (2010). Information literacy and office tool competencies: A benchmark study. *Journal of Education for Business*, *85*(3), 153–164. doi:10.1080/08832320903252371

Henry, W. (1956). *The analysis of fantasy: The thematic appreciation technique in the study of personality*. New York, NY: John Wiley & Sons.

Hernandez, D. J., Denton, N. A., & Macartney, S. E. (2007, November). *Children in immigrant families-The U.S. and 50 states: National origins, language, and early education. Children in America's newcomer families*. Retrieved from http://mumford.albany.edu /children/img/Research_brief_1.pdf

Heward, W. L. (2009). *Exceptional children* (9th ed.). Upper Saddle River, NJ: Pearson.

Hitchcock, C., & Stahl, S. (2003). Assistive technology, universal design, universal design for learning: Improved learning opportunities. *Journal of Special Education Technology*, *18*(4), 45–52.

Hodge, R., & Trip, D. (1986). *Children and television: A semiotic approach*. Palo Alto, CA: Stanford University Press.

Hoffman, B., & Spatariu, A. (2008). The influence of self-efficacy and metacognitive prompting on math problem-solving. *Contemporary Educational Psychology*, *33*(4), 875–893. doi:10.1016/j.cedpsych.2007.07.002

Hoffman, B., & Nadelson, L. (in press). Motivational engagement in video gaming: A mixed methods study. *Educational Technology Research & Development, 57*(6).

Hofman, A., & García-Cantú, M. (2008). *Una estrategia nueva para el acceso universal en México. Política Digital, 45*. August-September.

Honda, Y., Nakato, E., Otsuka, Y., Kanazawa, S., Kojima, S., Yamaguchi, M. K., & Kakgi, R. (2010). How do infants perceive scrambled face? A near-infrared spectroscopic study. *Brain Research*, *1308*, 137–146. doi:10.1016/j.brainres.2009.10.046

Hong, S. B., & Trepanier-Street, M. (2004). Technology: A tool for knowledge construction in a Reggio Emilia inspired teacher education program. *Early Childhood Education Journal*, *32*(2), 87–94. doi:10.1007/s10643-004-7971-z

Horn, C., Bruning, R., Schraw, G., & Curry, E. (1993). Paths to success in the college classroom. *Contemporary Educational Psychology*, *18*, 464–478. doi:10.1006/ceps.1993.1035

Hough, L. (2007) Handhelds, avatars, and virtual aliens. *Retrievedfrom*http://www.gse.harvard.edu/ news_events/ed/2007/ fall/features/ handhelds.html

Howard-Jones, P. A., Taylor, J. R., & Sutton, L. (2002). The effect of play on the creativity of young children during subsequent activity. *Early Child Development and Care*, *172*(4), 323–328. doi:10.1080/03004430212722

Hsueh, Y., & Barton, B. (2006). A cultural perspective on professional beliefs of childcare teachers. *Early Childhood Education Journal*, *33*(3), 179–186. doi:10.1007/s10643-005-0042-2

Hubbell, E. R. (2003). Integrating technology into the Montessori elementary classroom. *Montessori Life*, *15*(2), 40–41.

Huffaker, D. (2005). The educated blogger: Using weblogs to promote literacy in the classroom. *AACE Journal*, *13*(2), 91–98.

Huffman, L. C., Bryan, Y., del Carmen, R., Pederson, F., Doussard-Roosevelt, J., & Porges, S. (1998). Infant temperament and cardiac vagal tone: Assessments at twelve weeks of age. *Child Development*, *69*, 624–635.

Hughes, J. R., DeLeo, A. J., & Melyn, M. A. (2000). The electroencephalogram in attention deficit-hyperactivity disorder: Emphasis on epileptiform discharges. *Epilepsy & Behavior*, *1*, 271–277. doi:10.1006/ebeh.2000.0073

Hughes, J. (2004). Technology learning principles for pre-service and in-service teacher education. *Contemporary Issues in Technology & Teacher Education*, *4*(3), 345–362.

Hunnius, S. (2007). The early development of visual attention and its implications for social and cognitive development. *Progress in Brain Research*, *164*, 187–209. doi:10.1016/S0079-6123(07)64010-2

Hunnius, S., & Geuze, R. H. (2004). Developmental changes in visual scanning of dynamic faces and abstract stimuli in infants: A longitudinal study. *Infancy*, *6*, 231–255. doi:10.1207/s15327078in0602_5

Hutcheson, G. (2009). *Google Earth in the elementary classroom*. Retrieved from http://cnx.org/ content/ m19821/1.2/

Hutinger, P., & Johanson, J. (2000). Implementing and maintaining and effective early childhood comprehensive technology system. *Topics in Early Childhood Special Education*, *20*(3), 159–173. doi:10.1177/027112140002000305

Hutinger, P., Johanson, J., & Rippey, R. (2000). *Final report: Benefits of comprehensive technology system in an early childhood setting: Results of a three-year study*. Macomb, IL: Western Illinois University, Center for Best Practices in Early Childhood.

Immordino-Yang, M. H. (2007). A tale of two cases: Lessons for education from the study of two boys living with half their brains. *Mind. Brain and Education*, *1*(2), 66–83. doi:10.1111/j.1751-228X.2007.00008.x

Immordino-Yang, M. H., & Damasio, A. R. (2007). We feel, therefore we learn: The relevance of affective and social neuroscience to education. *Mind. Brain and Education*, *1*(1), 3–10. doi:10.1111/j.1751-228X.2007.00004.x

Immordino-Yang, M. H. (2009in press). Our bodies, our minds, our selves: Social neuroscience and its application to education. In Feifer, S., & Rattan, G. (Eds.), *The neuropsychology of emotional disorders*. Middletown, MD: School Neuropsychology Press.

Inhelder, B., & Piaget, J. (1958). *The growth of logical thinking from childhood to adolescence*. New York, NY: Basic Books. doi:10.1037/10034-000

In-Stat. (2008). *Continued growth in the worldwide market for portable, electronic based edutainment toys* (Report No. IN0804073ID) Retrieved from http://instat.com/ newmk.asp

International Society for Technology in Education. (2001). *National educational technology standards for teachers: Preparing teachers to use technology*. Eugene, OR: ISTE.

International Society for Technology in Education. (2007). *The ISTE national educational technology standards (NETS-S) and performance indicators for students*. Retrieved from http://www.iste.org/ Content/ NavigationMenu/ NETS/ ForStudents/ 2007Standards/ NETS _for_Students_2007_Standards.pdf

International Society for Technology in Education. (2008). *NETS for teachers 2008*. Retrieved on from http://www.iste.org/ Content/NavigationMenu/ NETS/ ForTeachers/ 2008Standards/ NETS_for_Teachers_2008.htm

International Society for Technology in Education. (2007). *ISTE national educational technology standards (NETS-S) and performance indicators for students*. Eugene, OR: International Society for Technology in Education.

International Society for Technology in Education. (2008). *ISTE national educational technology standards (NETS-T) and performance indicators for teachers*. Eugene, OR: International Society for Technology in Education.

InTime. (2001). *Integrating new technologies into the methods of education*. Retrieved from http://www.intime.uni.edu/

Irvine Belson, S. (2003). *Technology for exceptional learners*. Boston, MA: Houghton Mifflin.

Ito, M., Horst, H., Bittanti, M., Boyd, D., Herr-Stephenson, B., & Lange, P. G. … Robinson, L. (2008). Leaving and learning with new media: Summary of findings from the digital youth project. *MacArthur Foundation. Retrieved from*http://digitalyouth.ischool.berkeley.edu/ iles/report/ digitalyouth-WhitePaper. pdf

James, A., Jenks, C., & Prout, A. (1998). *Theorizing childhood*. New York, NY: Teachers College Press.

James, W. (1981). *The principles of psychology*. Cambridge, MA: Harvard University Press. (Original work published 1890)

James, S. R., Bicard, S. C., & Bicard, D. F. (2010). *The effects of enhanced milieu teaching and a voice output communication aid on the rate and generalization of demanding during classroom free play*. Unpublished manuscript, Instruction and Curriculum Leadership Department, The University of Memphis, Memphis, Tennessee.

John, B. E., & Kieras, D. E. (1996). The GOMS family of analysis techniques: Comparison and contrast. *ACM Transactions on Computer-Human Interaction*, *3*(4), 320–351. doi:10.1145/235833.236054

Johnson, G. M. (2010). Internet use and child development: Validation of the ecological techno-subsystem. *Journal of Educational Technology & Society*, *13*(1), 176–185.

Johnson, M. H. (1994). Covert visual attention and the control of eye movements in early infancy. In Umilta, C., & Moscovitch, M. (Eds.), *Attention and performance XV* (pp. 291–310). Cambridge, MA: MIT Press.

Johnston, S. S. (2003). Making the most of single switch technology: A primer. *Journal of Special Education Technology*, *18*(2), 47–50.

Jonassen, D. (1994). Thinking technology: Towards a constructivist design model. *Educational Technology*, *34*(4), 34–37.

Jonassen, D., Howland, J., Moore, J., & Marra, R. (2003). *Learning to solve problems with technology: A constructivist perspective* (2nd ed.). Upper Saddle River, NJ: Prentice Hall.

Jonassen, D. H., Tessmer, M., & Hannum, W. H. (1999). *Task analysis methods for instructional design*. Mahwah, NJ: L. Erlbaum Associates.

Jonassen, D. H., & Carr, C. (2000). Mindtools: Affording multiple knowledge representations in learning. In S. P. Lajoie (Ed.), *Computers as cognitive tools, vol. 2: No more walls* (pp. 165–196). Mahwah, NJ: Lawrence Erlbaum Associates.

Judge, S., Puckett, K., & Bell, S. M. (2006). Closing the digital divide: Update from the early childhood longitudinal study. *The Journal of Educational Research*, *100*(1), 52–60. doi:10.3200/JOER.100.1.52-60

Judge, S., Puckett, K., & Cabuk, B. (2004). Digital equity: New findings from the Early Childhood Longitudinal Study. *Journal of Research on Technology in Education*, *36*(4), 383–396.

Judge, S., Puckett, K., & Bell, S. M. (2006). Closing the digital divide: Update from the early childhood longitudinal study. *The Journal of Educational Research*, *100*(1), 52–60. doi:10.3200/JOER.100.1.52-60

Judge, S. (2001). Computer applications in programs for young children with disabilities: Current status and future directions. *Journal of Special Education Technology*, *16*(1), 29–40.

Judge, S. (2006). Constructing an assistive technology toolkit for young children: Views from the field. *Journal of Special Education Technology*, *21*(4), 17–24.

Justice, L. M., & Ezell, H. K. (2002). *The syntax handbook*. Eau Claire, WI: Thinking Publications.

Justice, L. M., Skibbe, L., Canning, A., & Lankford, C. (2005). Pre-schoolers, print and storybooks: An observational study using eye movement analysis. *Journal of Research in Reading*, *28*(3), 229–243. doi:10.1111/j.1467-9817.2005.00267.x

Kafai, Y., & Harel, I. (1991). Children learning through consulting: When mathematical ideas, knowledge of programming and design, and playful discourse are intertwined. In Harel, I., & Papert, S. (Eds.), *Constructionism* (pp. 111–140). New Jersey: Ablex Publishing.

Kahn, P. H., Jr., Friedman, B., Perez-Granados, D. R., & Freier, N. G. (2004). *Robotic pets in the lives of preschool children*. CHI, 24-29 April, Vienna, Austria, (pp. 1449-1452).

Kaiser Family Foundation. (2003). *Fact sheet: The digital divide*. Retrieved from http://www.kff.org/ entpartnerships/ digitaldivide/index.cfm

Kajder, S., & Bull, G. (2003). Scaffolding for struggling students: Reading and writing with blogs. *Learning and Leading with Technology*, *3*(12), 32–35.

Kane, J. H., & Seingold, K. (1980). Language development: A complex, systematic, and natural process. *Early Childhood Education Journal*, *8*(2), 39–54. doi:10.1007/BF01628027

Kay, R. H. (2006). Evaluating strategies used to incorporate technology into preserviceeducation: A review of the literature. *Journal of Research on Technology in Education*, *38*(4), 383.

Ke, F. (2008). A case study of computer gaming for math: Engaged learning for gameplay? *Computers & Education*, *51*, 1609–1620. doi:10.1016/j.compedu.2008.03.003

Keesing-Styles, L. (2002). A critical pedagogy of early childhood education: The Aotearoa/New Zealand context. *New Zealand Research in Early Childhood Education*, *5*, 109–121.

Kenway, J., & Bullen, E. (2001). *Consuming children: Education entertainment advertizing*. Philadelphia, PA: Open University Press.

Kinder, M. (1991). *Playing with power in movies, TV and video games*. Los Angeles, CA: University of California Press.

Kinder, M. (1999). *Kids media culture*. Durham, NC: Duke University Press.

Kindlon, D., Mezzacappa, E., & Earls, F. (1995). Psychometric properties of impulsivity measures: Temporal stability, validity and factor structure. *Journal of Child Psychology and Psychiatry, and Allied Disciplines*, *36*, 645–661.

Kirova, A., & Bhargava, A. (2002). Learning to guide preschool children's mathematical understanding: A teacher's professional growth. *Early Childhood Research & Practice, 4*(1). Retrieved August, 2010 from http://www.ecrp.uiuc.edu/ v4n1/kirova.html

Kirschbaum, C., & Hellhammer, D. H. (1994). Salivary cortisol in psychoneuroendocrine research: Recent developments and applications. *Psychoneuroendocrinology*, *19*, 313–333. doi:10.1016/0306-4530(94)90013-2

Kishiyama, M. M., Boyce, W. T., Jimenez, A. M., Perry, L. M., & Knight, R. T. (2009). Socioeconomicdisparities affect prefrontal function in children. *Journal of Cognitive Neuroscience*, *21*(6), 1106–1115. doi:10.1162/jocn.2009.21101

Kline, S. (1993). *Out of the garden: Toys, TV, and children's culture in the age of marketing*. London, UK: Verso.

Knowles, M. (1975). *Self-directed learning: A guide for learners and teachers*. New York, NY: Association Press.

Kobayashi, C., Glover, G. H., & Temple, E. (2007). Children's and adults neural bases of verbal and nonverbal theory of mind. *Neuropsychologia*, *45*(7), 1522–1532. doi:10.1016/j.neuropsychologia.2006.11.017

Krathwohl, D. R. (2002). A revision of Bloom's taxonomy: An overview. *Theory into Practice*, *41*(4), 212–218. doi:10.1207/s15430421tip4104_2

Kwon, S. Y., & Cifuentes, L. (2009). The comparative effect of individually-constructed vs. collaboratively-constructed computer-based concept maps. *Computers & Education*, *52*, 365–375. doi:10.1016/j.compedu.2008.09.012

Kyiosaki, R., & Lechter, S. (2000). *Rich dad poor dad: What the rich teach their kids that the poor and middle class do not*. New York, NY: Business Plus.

Lagemann, E. C. (2002). *An elusive science: The troubling history of education research*. Chicago, IL: University of Chicago Press.

Lahm, E., & Morrissette, S. (1994, April). *Zap 'em with assistive technology*. Paper presented at the Annual Meeting of The Council for Exceptional Children, Denver, CO.

Lamb, A., & Johnson, L. (2010). Virtual expeditions: Google Earth, GIS, and geovisualization technologies in teaching and learning. *Teacher Librarian*, *37*(3), 81–85.

Lankshear, C., Peters, M. A., & Knobel, M. (1996). Critical pedagogy and cyberspace. In Giroux, H., Lankshear, C., McLaren, P., & Peters, M. A. (Eds.), *Counternarratives: Cultural studies and critical pedagogies in postmodern spaces* (pp. 149–188). New York, NY: Routledge.

Lareau, A. (2003). *Unequal childhoods: Class, race, and family life*. Berkeley, CA: University of California Press.

Lave, J., & Wenger, E. (1991). *Situated learning: Legitimate peripheral participation*. Cambridge, UK: Cambridge University Press.

Leal, G. (2010). *Subrogación, causa del incendio en la guardería*. Retrieved from www.jornada.unam.mx

Lee, S. J., Bartolic, S., & Vandewater, E. A. (2009). Predicting children's media use in the USA: Differences in cross-sectional and longitudinal analysis. *The British Journal of Developmental Psychology*, *27*, 123–143. doi:10.1348/026151008X401336

Lee, S. J., & Spires, H. (2009). What students think about technology and academic engagement in school: Implications for middle grades teaching and learning. *AACE Journal*, *17*(2), 61–81.

Lee, J. S., & Ginsburg, H. P. (2009). Early childhood teachers misconceptions about mathematics education in the United States. *Australian Journal of Early Childhood, 34*(4), 37–45.

Legendre, A. (2003). Environmental features influencing toddlers' bioemotional reactions in day care centers. *Environment and Behavior, 35*, 523–549. doi:10.1177/0013916503035004005

Lemish, D. (2007). *Children and television: A global perspective*. Malden, MA: Blackwell Publishing.

Levy, R. (2009). You have to understand words...but not read them: Young children becoming readers in a digital age. *Journal of Research in Reading, 32*(1), 75–91. doi:10.1111/j.1467-9817.2008.01382.x

Lewin, C. (2000). Exploring the effects of talking books software in UK primary classrooms. *Journal of Research in Reading, 23*(2), 149–157. doi:10.1111/1467-9817.00111

Li, X., & Atkins, M. S. (2004). Early childhood computer experience and cognitive and motor development. *Pediatrics, 113*(6), 1715–1722. doi:10.1542/peds.113.6.1715

Li, J. (2003a). The core of Confucian learning. *The American Psychologist, 58*, 146–147. doi:10.1037/0003-066X.58.2.146

Li, J. (2003b). U.S. and Chinese beliefs about learning. *Journal of Educational Psychology, 95*, 258–267. doi:10.1037/0022-0663.95.2.258

Lim, C. P., & Tay, L. Y. (2003). Information and communication technologies (ICT) in an elementary school: Students' engagement in higher order thinking. *Journal of Educational Multimedia and Hypermedia, 12*(4), 425–451.

Lind, K. K. (2005). *Exploring science in early childhood* (4th ed.). Clifton Park, NY: Thomson Delmar Learning.

Lindfors, J. W. (1991). *Children's language and learning* (2nd ed.). Boston, MA: Allyn and Bacon.

Lindroth, L. K. (2005). *Technology in your classroom: How to find online mathematics manipulatives*. Retrieved from http://www.teachingk-8.com/ archives/ how_to/ how_tofind_online_mathematics_manipulatives.html

Ljung-Djarf, A. (2008). The owner, the participant and the spectator: Positions and positioning in peer activity around the computer in pre-school. *Early Years, 28*(1), 61–72. doi:10.1080/09575140701846487

López, J., & López, M. E. (2010). Technology and preschool education in Mexico: A country in transformation. In Blake, S., & Izumi-Taylor, S. (Eds.), *Technology for early childhood education and socialization: Developmental applications and methodologies*. Hershey, PA: IGI Global.

Lotherington, H., Holland, M., Sotoudeh, S., & Zenten, M. (2008). Project-based community language learning: Three narratives of multilingual story-telling in early childhood education. *Canadian Modern Language Review, 65*(1), 125–145. doi:10.3138/cmlr.65.1.125

Lou, Y., Abrami, P. C., & Apollonia, S. (2001). Small group and individual learning with technology: A meta-analysis. *Review of Educational Research, 71*(3), 449–521. doi:10.3102/00346543071003449

Lubar, J. F., Swartwood, M. O., Swartwood, J., & O'Donnell, P. H. (1995). Evaluation of the effectiveness of EEG neurofeedback training for ADHD in a clinical setting as measured by changes in T.O.V.A. scores, behavioral ratings, and WISC-R performance. *Applied Psychophysiology and Biofeedback, 20*(1), 83–99.

Luecken, L. J., & Lemery, K. S. (2004). Early caregiving and physiological stress responses. *Clinical Psychology Review, 24*, 171–191. doi:10.1016/j.cpr.2004.01.003

Luke, A., & Luke, C. (2001). Adolescence lost/childhood regained: On early intervention and the emergence of the techno-subject. *Journal of Early Childhood Literacy, 1*(1), 91–120. doi:10.1177/14687984010011005

Luke, C. (1999). What next? Toddler netizens, Playstation thumb, techno-literacies. *Contemporary Issues in Early Childhood, 1*(1), 95–100. doi:10.2304/ciec.2000.1.1.10

Lynch, S. A., & Warner, L. (2004). Computer use in preschools: Directors' reports of the state of the practice. *Early Childhood Research and Practice, 6*(2). Retrieved from http://ecrp.uiuc.edu/ v6n2/ lynch.html

Lyotard, J.-F. (1999). *The postmodern condition: A report on knowledge* (Bennington, G., & Massumi, B., Trans.). Minneapolis, MN: University of Minnesota Press.

Mahoney, G., Kaiser, A., Girolametto, L., MacDonald, J., Robinson, C., & Spiker, D. (1999). Parent education in early intervention: A call for a renewed focus. *Topics in Early Childhood Special Education, 19*(3), 131–140. doi:10.1177/027112149901900301

Mandese, J. (2008). MediaPost Publications OMG! UM finds Web 2.0 breeding consumers 2.0, social media attains critical mass. *Online Media Daily*. Retrieved from http://www.mediapost.com/ publications/?fa=Articles.show Article&art_aid=85025

Mangoverde. (n.d.). *The Mangoverde world bird guide*. Retrieved from http://www.mangoverde.com/ birdsound/ index.html

Manheim, K. (1936). *Ideology and utopia*. New York, NY: Harcourt, Brace.

Marcus, G. (1995). Ethnography in/of the world system: The emergence of multisite ethnography. *Annual Review of Anthropology, 24*, 95–117. doi:10.1146/annurev.an.24.100195.000523

Marsh, J. (2002). Electronic toys: Why should we be concerned? A response to Levin & Rosenquest (2001). *Contemporary Issues in Early Childhood, 3*(1), 132–138. doi:10.2304/ciec.2002.3.1.3

May, J. (2010). *James May's toy stories*. London, England: Conway Publishing.

Mayer, S. (2005). The early evolution of Jean Piaget's clinical method. *History of Psychology, 8*(4), 362–382. doi:10.1037/1093-4510.8.4.362

Mayer, R. E., & Moreno, R. (2003). Nine ways to reduce cognitive load in multimedia learning. *Educational Psychologist, 38*(1), 43–52. doi:10.1207/S15326985EP3801_6

Mayfield, M. I. (2005). Children's museums: Purposes, practices and play? *Early Child Development and Care, 175*(2), 179–192..doi:10.1080/0300443042000230348

McCann, H. S., & Miller, K. F. (2008, July). *Word learning and shared book reading: An analysis of eye movements*. Poster presented at the Annual Meeting of the Society for the Scientific Study of Reading, Asheville, NC.

McCormick, L. (1987). Comparison of the effects of a microcomputer activity and toy play on social and communication behaviors of young children. *Journal of the Division for Early Childhood, 11*, 195–205.

McGilchrist, I. (2009). *The master and his emissary*. New Haven, CT & London, UK: Yale University Press.

McLaughlin, B. (1984). *Second language acquisition in childhood: Vol. 1. Preschool children* (2nd ed.). Hillsdale, NJ: Erlbaum. (ERIC Document No. ED154604)

McLeod, J., & Vasinda, S. (2009a). Electronic portfolios: Perspectives of students, teachers and parents. *Education and Information Technologies, 14*, 29–38. doi:10.1007/s10639-008-9077-5

McLeod, J., & Vasinda, S. (2009b). Web 2.0 affordances for literacies: Using technology as pedagogically strong scaffolds for learning. In Kidd, T., & Chen, I. (Eds.), *Wired for learning: An educator's guide to Web 2.0*. Charlotte, NC: Information Age Publishing.

McLeod, J., & Lin, L. (2010). A child's power in game-play. *Computers & Education, 54*, 517 527.

Means, B., Penuel, W. R., Crawford, V. M., Korbak, C., Lewis, A., & Murphy, R. F. ... Yarnall, L. (2001). *GLOBE Year 6 evaluation: Explaining variation in implementation*. Menlo Park, CA: SRI International. Retrieved from http://classic.globe.gov/ fsl/evals/ y6full.pdf

Metcalf, S. J., & Tinker, R. (2003). *TEEMSS: Technology enhanced elementary and middle school science*. Paper presented at the Annual Meeting of the National Association for Research in Science Teaching, March 23-26, 2003, Philadelphia. Retrieved from http://www.concord.org/ publications/files/ narst_teemss_paper.pdf

Miller, D. J., & Robertson, D. P. (2010). Using a games console in the primary classroom: Effects of Brain Training programme on computation and self-esteem. *British Journal of Educational Technology, 41*(2), 242–255. doi:10.1111/j.1467-8535.2008.00918.x

Milne, A. A. (2007). *The house at Pooh Corner*. London, England: Egmont.

Miriam-Webster Dictionary. (2010). *Enculturation*. Retrieved from http://www.merriam-webster.com /dictionary/ enculturation

Mishra, P., & Koehler, M. J. (2006). Designing learning from day one: A first day activity to foster design thinking about educational technology. *Teacher's College Record.*

Mitchell, L. M. (2007). Using technology in Reggio Emilia-inspired programs. *Theory into Practice*, *46*(1), 32–39. doi:10.1080/00405840709336546

Molnar, A. (2005). *School commercialism: From democratic ideal to market commodity*. New York, NY: Taylor and Francis Group.

Montessori, M. (1995). *The absorbent mind*. New York, NY: Holt Paperbacks.

Moos, D. C., & Azevedo, R. (2009). Self-efficacy and prior domain knowledge: To what extent does monitoring mediate their relationship with hypermedia learning? *Metacognition and Learning*, *4*(3), 197–216..doi:10.1007/s11409-009-9045-5

Moreno, R. (2007). Optimising learning from animations by minimising cognitive load: Cognitive and affective consequences of signaling and segmentation methods. *Applied Cognitive Psychology*, *21*(6), 765–781. doi:10.1002/acp.1348

Moyer, P. S. (2001). Are we having fun yet? How teachers use manipulatives to teach mathematics. *Educational Studies in Mathematics*, *47*(2), 175–197. doi:10.1023/A:1014596316942

Moyer, P. S., Bolyard, J. J., & Spikell, M. A. (2002). What are virtual manipulatives? *Teaching Children Mathematics*, *8*, 372–377.

Moyer, P. S., Bolyard, J. J., & Spikell, M. A. (2002). What are virtual manipulatives? [Online]. *Teaching Children Mathematics*, *8*(6), 372–377. Retrieved from http://my.nctm.org/ eresources/ articlesummary.asp?URI= TCM2002-02372a&from=B.

Munro, D. J. (1975). The Chinese view of modeling. *Human Development*, *18*, 333–352. doi:10.1159/000271495

Murray, H. A. (1938). *Explorations in personality*. New York, NY: Oxford University Press.

Murray, G. L. (1999). Autonomy and language learning in a simulated environment. *System*, *27*, 295–308. doi:10.1016/S0346-251X(99)00026-3

NAEYC. (1996 b). NAEYC position statement: Technology and young children-Ages three through eight. *Young Children*, *51*(6), 11–16.

NAEYC. (1996). Position statement: Technology and young children – Ages three through eight. *Young Children*, *51*(2), 4–12.

NAEYC. (1996). *Technology and young children – Ages 3 through 8*. Washington, DC: National Association for the Education of Young Children.

NAEYC. (2009). *Position statement: Developmentally appropriate practice in early childhood programs serving children from birth through age 8*. Retrieved May 5, 2010, from http://www.naeyc.org/files/ naeyc/file/positions/ position%20statement %20Web.pdf

Nakato, E., Otsuka, Y., Kanazawa, S., Yamaguchi, M. K., & Kakigi, R. (2009). When do infants differentiate profile face from frontal face? A near-infrared spectroscopic study. *Human Brain Mapping*, *30*(2), 462–472. doi:10.1002/hbm.20516

National Association for the Education of Young Children. (1996). *Technology and young children ages 3-8 (position statement)*. Retrieved from www.naeyc.org/ files/naeyc/ file/ positions/PSTECH98.PDF

National Center for Educational Statistics. (1999). *A report on teachers' use of technology*. Retrieved from http://nces.ed.gov/ surveys/frss/ publications/2000102/

National Center for Educational Statistics. (2001). *The conditions of education*. Retrieved from http://nces.ed.gov/ programs/coe/

National Center for Educational Statistics. (2006). *Rates of computer and Internet use by children in nursery school and students in kindergarten through twelfth grade: 2003*. (NCES 2005-111).

National Center for Educational Statistics. (2009). *Teachers' use of educational technology*. Retrieved from http:// nces.ed.gov/ pubsearch/ pubsinfo.asp?pubid=2010040

National Center for Educational Statistics Office of Educational Research and Improvement. (2006). *Computer and Internet use stats in 2003*. U. S. Department of Education. Retrieved from http://nces.ed.gov/ pubs2006/ 2006065.pdf

National Committee on Science Education Standards and Assessment, National Research Council. (1996). *National science education standards*. Washington, DC: National Academy Press.

National Council of Teachers of Mathematics (NCTM). *Principles and standards for school mathematics*. Reston, VA: NCTM.

National Council of Teachers of Mathematics. (2004). *Principles and standards for School Mathematics (2000-2004): A report published by the National Council of Teachers of Mathematics*.

National Council on Disability. (2000). *Federal policy barriers to assistive technology*. Retrieved from http://www.ncd.gov/newsroom /publications/2000/ assist-technology.htm

National Mathematics Advisory Panel. (2008). *The final report of the National Mathematics Advisory Panel*. Washington, DC: U. S. Department of Education.

National Research Council. (1996). *National science education standards: Observe, interact, change, learn*. Washington, DC: National Academy Press.

National Research Council. (1989). *Everybody counts: A report to the nation on the future of mathematics education*. Washington, DC: National Academies Press.

National Research Council. (2001). *Adding it all up: Helping children learn mathematics*. Washington, DC: National Academy Press.

National Research Council. (2001a). *Eager to learn: Educating our preschoolers*. Washington, DC: National Academy Press.

National Research Council. (2002). *Scientific research in education*. Washington, DC: National Academy Press.

National Research Council and Institute of Medicine. (2000). *From neurons to neighborhoods: The science of early childhood development*. Washington, DC: National Academy Press.

National Scientific Council on the Developing Child. (2007). *New science provides compelling framework for early childhood investment: Scientists chart path to improving outcomes in learning, behavior, and health for vulnerable children*. Retrieved August 9, 2009, from http://www.developingchild. harvard.edu/ content/

NCES. (2003). *Young children's access to computers in the home and at school in 1999 and 2000*. Washington, DC: NCES. Retrieved from http://nces.ed.gov/pubs2003/2003036. pdf

NCREL. (2004). *An educator's guide to evaluating claims about educational software*. Retrieved from http://www.ncrel.org/ tech/claims/ index.html

Nelson, C. A., Monk, C. S., Lin, J., Carver, L. J., Thomas, K. M., & Truwit, C. L. (2000). Functional neuroanatomy of spatial working memory. *Developmental Psychology*, *36*(1), 109–116. doi:10.1037/0012-1649.36.1.109

Nelson, L., & Materson, J. (1999). Computer technology: Creative interfaces in service delivery. *Topics in Language Disorders*, *19*(3), 68–86. doi:10.1097/00011363-199905000-00007

NETC. (2005). *Northwest educational technology consortium*. Retrieved from http://www.netc.org/

Newcombe, N. (2002). The nativist-empiricist controversy in the context of recent research on spatial and quantitative development. *Psychological Science*, *13*(5), 394–401. doi:10.1111/1467-9280.00471

Newsweek. (1991, December 2). *The 10 best schools in the world and what we can learn from them*, (pp. 50-59).

Niess, M. L. (2005). Preparing teachers to teach science and mathematics with technology: Developing a technology pedagogical content knowledge. *Teaching and Teacher Education*, *21*, 509–523. doi:10.1016/j.tate.2005.03.006

Nikolopoulou, K. (2007). Early childhood educational software: Specific features and issues of localization. *Early Childhood Education Journal*, *35*(2), 173–179. doi:10.1007/s10643-007-0168-5

NSBF. (2000). *Safe and smart. Research and guidelines for children's use of the Internet*. Alexandria, VA: National Schools Boards Foundation.

O'Bannon, B., & Puckett, K. (2009). *Preparing to use technology: A practical guide to curriculum integration* (2nd ed.). Boston, MA: Allyn and Bacon.

Cognition and Technology Group at Vanderbilt. (2003). Connecting learning theory and instructional practice: Leveraging some powerful affordances of technology. In O'Neil, H., & Perez, R. (Eds.), *Technology applications in education: A learning view*. Mahwah, NJ: Lawrence Erlbaum Associates.

Oblinger, D., & Oblinger, J. (2005). Is it age or IT: First steps towards understanding the net generation. In D. Oblinger & J. Oblinger (Eds.). *Educating the Net Generation* (pp. 2.1-2.20). Boulder, CO: EDUCAUSE. Retrieved from http://www.educause.edu/ educatingthenetgen

OECD. (2006). *Starting strong II: Early childhood education and care.* ISBN 92-64-03545-1

Ojima, M. (2006). Concept mapping as a pre-task planning: A case study of three Japanese ESL writers. *System*, *34*, 566–585. doi:10.1016/j.system.2006.08.003

Olive, M. L., de la Cruz, B., Davis, T. N., Chan, J. M., Lang, R. B., O'Reilly, M. F., & Dickson, S. M. (2006). The effects of enhanced milieu teaching and a voice output communication aid on the requesting of three children with autism. *Journal of Autism and Developmental Disorders*, *37*(8), 1505–1513. doi:10.1007/s10803-006-0243-6

Oliver, K. (2009). An investigation of concept mapping to improve the reading comprehension of science texts. *Journal of Science Education and Technology*, *18*, 402–414. doi:10.1007/s10956-009-9157-3

Oller, J. W. Jr. (1979). *Language testing at school*. London, UK: Methuen.

Oravec, J. (2003, October). Blending by blogging: Weblogs in blended learning initiatives. *Journal of Educational Media*, *28*(2-3), 225–233.

Oritz, J., & Raine, A. (2004). Heart rate level and antisocial behavior in children and adolescents: A meta-analysis. *Journal of the American Academy of Child and Adolescent Psychiatry*, *43*(2), 154–162. doi:10.1097/00004583-200402000-00010

Ormrod, J. E. (2009). *Essentials of educational psychology* (2nd ed.). New Jersey: Merill, Pearson.

Osorno, D. E. (2010). *Nosotros somos los culpables*. Mexico, DF: Grijalbo Mondadori. ISBN 9786073100670

Paas, F. G. W. C., & van Merriënboer, J. J. G. (1993). The efficiency of instructional conditions: An approach to combine mental-effort and performance measures. *Human Factors*, *35*(4), 737–743.

Palestis, E. (1994). Lessons from Reggio Emilia. *Principal*, *73*(5), 16–18.

Papert, S. (1993). *The children's machine: Rethinking school in the age of the computer*. New York, NY: Basic Books.

Papert, S. (1991a). Perestroika and epistemological politics. In Harel, I., & Papert, S. (Eds.), *Constructionism* (pp. 13–28). New Jersey: Ablex Publishing.

Papert, S. (1991b). Situating constructionism. In Harel, I., & Papert, S. (Eds.), *Constructionism* (pp. 1–12). New Jersey: Ablex Publishing.

Papert, S. (2000). *From lunch boxes to laptops: The Governor King Initiative*. Retrieved from www.papert.org/articles/ laptops/laptops_master.html

Parent's Choice Awards. (2009). *Parents' choice award winners: Toys*. Retrieved from http://www.parents-choice.org

Parents, P. B. S. (2010). *Computers: Grade schoolers*. Retrieved from http://www.pbs.org/ parents/ childrenandmedia/ computers-grade.html

Parette, H. P., Boeckmann, N. M., & Hourcade, J. J. (2008). Use of Writing with Symbols 2000 software to facilitate emergent literacy development. *Early Childhood Education Journal*, *36*, 161–170. doi:10.1007/s10643-008-0270-3

Parette, H. P., Hourcade, J. J., Boeckmann, N. M., & Blum, C. (2008). Using Microsoft PowerPoint to support emergent literacy skill development for young children at-risk or who have disabilities. *Early Childhood Education Journal*, *36*, 233–239. doi:10.1007/s10643-008-0275-y

Parette, H. P., Hourcade, J. J., & Heiple, G. S. (2000). The importance of structured computer experiences for young children with and without disabilities. *Early Childhood Education Journal*, *27*(4), 243–250. doi:10.1023/B:ECEJ.0000003361.21759.48

Parette, H. P., & Murdick, N. L. (1998). Assistive technology and IEPs for young children with disabilities. *Early Childhood Education Journal*, *25*(3), 193–198. doi:10.1023/A:1025661329039

Parette, P., & McMahan, G. (2002). What should we expect of assistive technology? Being sensitive to family goals. *Teaching Exceptional Children*, *35*(1), 56–61.

Parsons, T. (1963). On the concept of political power. *Proceedings of the American Philosophical Society of the American Philosophical Society*, *107*, 232–258.

Partnership for 21st Century Skills. (2008). *21st century skills, education and competitiveness: A resource and policy guide.* Retrieved from http://www.21stcenturyskills.org/ documents/ 21st_century_skills_education_and_competitiveness_guide.pdf

Patterson, T. C. (2007). Google Earth as a (not just) geography education tool. *The Journal of Geography*, *106*(4), 145–152. doi:10.1080/00221340701678032

Pérez, B., & Torres-Guzmán, M. (1996). *Learning in two worlds* (2nd ed.). New York, NY: Longman.

Perez-Edgar, K., Schmidt, L. A., Henderson, H. A., Schulkin, J., & Fox, N. A. (2009). Salivary cortisol levels and infant temperament shape developmental trajectories in boys at risk for behavioral maladjustment. *Psychoneuroendocrinology*, *33*(7), 916–925. doi:10.1016/j.psyneuen.2008.03.018

Perkins, D. N. (1985). The fingertip effect: How information-processing technology shapesthinking. *Educational Researcher*, *14*, 11–17.

Petra, T. J. (2010). *Real world mathematics*. Retrieved on from http://www.realworldmathematics.org/ Real_World_Mathematics/ RealWorld Mathematics.org. html

Petrash, J. (2002). *Understanding Waldorf education: Teaching from the inside out*. New York, NY: Gryphon House.

Phillips, N. (1968). *Conversational English for the non-English speaking child.* New York, NY: Teacher College Press.

Piaget, J. (1952). *The origins of intelligence in children* (Cook, M., Trans.). New York, NY: New American Library. doi:10.1037/11494-000

Piaget, J. (1980). The psychogenesis of knowledge and its epistemological significance. In Piattelli-Palmarini, M. (Ed.), *Language and learning: The debate between Jean Piaget and Noam Chomsky* (pp. 23–34). Cambridge, MA: Harvard University Press.

Piaget, J. (1960). *The child conception of the world.* Totowa, NJ: Littlefield, Adams & Co. (Original published in 1926).

Pink, D. (2009). *Drive: The surprising truth about what motivates us*. New York, NY: Riverhead.

Plowman, L., & Stephen, C. (2003). A benign addition? Research on ICT and pre-school children. *Journal of Computer Assisted Learning*, *19*(2), 149–164. doi:10.1046/j.0266-4909.2003.00016.x

Plowman, L. (1998). Reading multimedia texts. *Language Matters, Spring,* 19-22.

Porges, S. W. (1996). Physiological regulation in high-risk infants: A model for assessment and potential intervention. *Development and Psychopathology*, *8*, 43–58. doi:10.1017/S0954579400006969

Porges, S. W., & Byrne, E. A. (1992). Research methods for measurement of heart rate and respiration. *Biological Psychology*, *34*, 93–130. doi:10.1016/0301-0511(92)90012-J

Porges, S. W., Doussard-Roosevelt, J., & Maita, A. K. (1994). Vagal tone and the physiological regulation of emotion. *Monographs of the Society for Research in Child Development*, *59*(2–3).

Porges, S. W., Doussard-Roosevelt, J., Portales, L., & Greenspan, S. I. (1996). Infant regulation of the vagal brake predicts child behavior problems: A psychobiological model of social behavior. *Developmental Psychobiology*, *29*, 697–712. doi:10.1002/(SICI)1098-2302(199612)29:8<697::AID-DEV5>3.0.CO;2-O

Porges, S. W. (1991). Vagal tone: An autonomic mediator of affect. In Garber, J. A., & Dodge, K. A. (Eds.), *The development of affect regulation and dysregulation* (pp. 111–128). New York, NY: Cambridge University Press. doi:10.1017/CBO9780511663963.007

Postman, N. (1994). *Disappearance of childhood.* New York, NY: Vintage Books.

Prensky, M. (2001). *Digital game-based learning*. New York, NY: McGraw-Hill.

President's Committee of Advisors on Science and Technology, Panel on Educational Technology. (1997). *Report to the President on the use of technology to strengthen K-12 education in the United States*.

Project, T. H. R. E. A. D. (2004). *Technology helping restructure educational access and delivery*. Retrieved from http://www.unlv.edu/ projects/THREAD /index.html

PT3. (2002). *Preparing tomorrow's teachers to use technology*. Retrieved from http://www.pt3.org/

Puma, M., Ghapin, D., & Pape, A. (2003). *E-Rate and the digital divide: A preliminary analysis from the integrated studies of educational technology*. Washington, DC: The Urban Institute.

Purcell, K. (2010). *Teens and the Internet: The future of digital diversity*. Presented at Fred Forward Conference. Pew Research Center's Internet & American Life Project.

Purpura, J. E. (2004). *Assessing grammar*. Cambridge, UK: Cambridge University Press. doi:10.1017/CBO9780511733086

Quellmalz, E. (1999). The role of technology in advancing performance standards in science and mathematics learning. In Comfort, K. (Ed.), *Advancing standards for science and mathematics learning: Views from the field*. Washington, DC: AAAS.

Racine, E., Br-Ilan, O., & Illes, J. (2005). fMRI in the public eye. *Nature Reviews. Neuroscience*, *6*(2), 159–164. doi:10.1038/nrn1609

Raine, A., Venables, P. H., & Mednick, S. A. (1997). Low resting heart rate at age 3 years predisposes to aggression at age 11 years: Findings from the Mauritius Joint Child Health Project. *Journal of the American Academy of Child and Adolescent Psychiatry*, *36*, 1457–1464. doi:10.1097/00004583-199710000-00029

Raine, A., Reynolds, C., Venables, P. H., & Mednick, S. A. (1997). Biosocial bases of aggressive behavior in childhood: Resting heart rate, skin conductance orienting, and physique. In Raine, A., Brennan, P. A., Farrington, D. P., & Mednick, S. A. (Eds.), *Biosocial bases of violence* (pp. 107–126). New York, NY: Plenum.

Raine, A., Venables, P. H., & Williams, M. (1995). High autonomic arousal and electrodermal orienting at age 15 years as protective factors against criminal behavior at age 29 years.

Rajah, M. N., & McIntosh, A. R. (2008). Age-related differences in brain activity during verbal recency memory. *Brain Research*, *1199*, 111–125. doi:10.1016/j.brainres.2007.12.051

Rand, E. (1995). *Barbie's queer accessories*. Durham, NC: Duke University Press.

Raphael, D., & Whalstrom, M. (1989). The influence of instructional aids on mathematics achievement. *Journal for Research in Mathematics Education*, *20*(2), 173–190. doi:10.2307/749281

Rathbun, A. H., West, J., & Hausken, E. G. (2003). *Young children's access to computers in the home and at school in 1999 and 2000*. (NCES-2003-036). Washington, DC: National Center for Education Statistics. Retrieved from http://nces.ed.gov/pubs2003/ 2003036.pdf

Ravitch, D. (2010). *The death and life of the great American school system: How testing and choice are undermining education*. New York, NY: Basic Books.

Reeves, T. C., & Oh, E. (2008). Generational differences. In Jonnasen, D. H. (Ed.), *Handbook of research on educational communications and technology* (pp. 295–305). New York, NY: Macmillan.

Reingold, H. (2006). *The pedagogy of civic participation*. In New Media Consortium Second Life Symposium on Impact of Digital Learning. Symposium conducted at the meeting of New Media Consortium, NMC Campus in Second Life. NMC (Producer). [Audio Podcast]. Retrieved from www.nmc.org/ podcast/ pedagogy-civic-participation

Resnick, M., & Ocko, S. (1991). LEGO/Logo: Learning through and about design. In Harel, I., & Papert, S. (Eds.), *Constructionism* (pp. 141–150). New Jersey: Ablex Publishing.

Rhodes, L., & Seiler, R. (2007). *Assistive technology for infants and toddlers with disabilities: A handbook for parents and caregivers*. Moscow, ID: Idaho Assistive Technology Project.

Richardson, W. (2005). Blog revolution: Expanding classroom horizons with web logs. *Technology and Learning*, *26*(3), 48.

Richardson, W. (2006). *Blogs, wikis, podcasts, and other powerful web tools for classrooms*. Thousand Oaks, CA: Corwin Press.

Richardson, D. C., & Spivey, M. J. (2004a). Eye tracking: Characteristics and methods. In Wnek, G., & Bowlin, G. (Eds.), *Encyclopedia of biomaterials and biomedical engineering* (pp. 568–572). Marcel Dekker, Inc.

Richardson, K. (2000). *Mathematics standards for pre-kindergarten through grade 2*. Clearinghouse on Elementary and Early Childhood Education. (ERIC document EDO-PS00-11).

Rideout, V. J., Foehr, U. G., & Roberts, D. F. (2010). *Generation M2: Media in the lives of 8- to 18 year-olds*. Menlo Park, CA: Kaiser Family Foundation.

Rideout, V. J., & Hamel, E. (2006). The media family: Electronic media in the lives of infants, toddlers, preschoolers, and their parents. *Kaiser Family Foundation. Retrieved from*http://www.kff.org/ entmedia/upload/ 7500.pdf

Rideout, V. J., Vandewater, E. A., & Wartella, E. A. (2003). Zero to six: Electronic media in the lives of infants, toddlers and preschoolers. *Kaiser Family Foundation. Retrieved from*http://www.kff.org/ entmedia/upload/ Zero-to-Six-Electronic-Media-in-the-Lives-of- Infants-Toddlers-and- Preschoolers-PDF.pdf

Ritchie, S., Maxwell, K. L., & Bredekamp, S. (2009). Rethinking early schooling: Using developmental science to transform children's early school experiences. In Barbarin, O. A., & Wasik, B. H. (Eds.), *Handbook of child development and early education: Research to practice* (pp. 14–37). New York, NY: Guilford.

Roberts, D. F., & Foehr, U. G. (2008). Trends in media use. *The Future of Children*, *18*(1), 11–37. doi:10.1353/foc.0.0000

Roberts, J., Jurgens, J., & Burchinal, M. (2005). The role of home literacy practices in preschool children's language and emergent literacy skills. *Journal of Speech, Language, and Hearing Research: JSLHR*, *48*, 345–359. doi:10.1044/1092-4388(2005/024)

Robinson, K. K., & Crenshaw, E. M. (2010). Reevaluating the global digital divide: Socio-demographic and conflict barriers to Internet revolution. *Sociological Inquiry*, *80*(1), 34–62. doi:10.1111/j.1475-682X.2009.00315.x

Roblyer, M. D., & Davis, L. (2008, Winter). Predicting success for virtual school students: Putting research-based models into practice. *Online Journal of Distance Learning Administration, 11*(4). University of West Georgia, Distance Education Center.

Rodríguez Martínez, G. (2002). *CENDI, report to OAS*. Retrieved from www.oas.org/udse/ readytolearn/quee.html

Rose, D. H., & Meyer, A. (2002). *Teaching every student in the digital age: Universal design for learning*. Alexandria, VA: ASCD.

Rose, D. H., Meyer, A., & Hitchcock, C. (2005). *The universally designed classroom: Accessible curriculum and digital technologies*. Cambridge, MA: Harvard Education Press.

Rosenthal, J. W. (1996). *Teaching science to language minority students*. Bristol, PA: Multilingual Matters Ltd.

Ross, J. (2009, Jun. 22). *Sacrificed on the altar of neoliberalism*. Pacific Free Press. Retrieved from www.pacificfreepress.com/ news/1/4307-abcs-for- mexicos-poor-kids-sacrificed- on-thealtar-of- neoliberalism.html

Roush, R. (1971). *Research using the videotape recorder in teacher education*. Alexandria, VA: Association for Supervision and Curriculum Development.

Rousseau, J. (1979). *Emile or on education*. New York, NY: Basic Books. (Original work published 1762)

Roy-Charland, A., Saint-Aubin, J., & Evans, M. A. (2007). Eye movements in shared book reading with children from kindergarten to grade four. *Reading and Writing*, *20*, 909–931. doi:10.1007/s11145-007-9059-9

Royer, R., & Royer, J. (2004). Comparing hand drawn and computer generated concept mapping. *Journal of Computers in Mathematics and Science Teaching*, *23*(1), 67–81.

Sammond, N. (2005). *Babes in tomorrowland: Walt Disney and the making of the American child 1930-1960*. Durham, NC: Duke University Press.

Sarama, J., & Clements, D. H. (2002). Building blocks for young children's mathematical development. *Journal of Educational Computing Research*, *27*(1&2), 93–110. doi:10.2190/F85E-QQXB-UAX4-BMBJ

Sarama, J., & Clements, D. H. (2003). Building blocks of early childhood mathematics. *Early Childhood Corner*, *9*, 480–485.

Sarama,J.(2004). Technology in early childhood mathematics: Building blocks as an innovative technology-based curriculum in engaging young children in mathematics: Standards for early childhood mathematics education.

Scarborough, H. S., & Dobrich, W. (1994). On the efficacy of reading to preschoolers. *Developmental Review*, *14*, 245–302. doi:10.1006/drev.1994.1010

Scarr, S. (1992). Developmental theories for the 1990s: Development and individual differences. *Child Development*, *63*(1), 1–19. doi:10.2307/1130897

Schepis, M. M., Reid, D. H., Behrmann, M. M., & Sutton, K. A. (1998). Increasing communicative interactions of young children with autism using a voice output communication aid and naturalistic teaching. *Journal of Applied Behavior Analysis*, *31*(4), 561–578. doi:10.1901/jaba.1998.31-561

Schlechty, P. (1990). *Schools for the twenty-first century: Leadership imperatives for educational reform*. San Francisco, CA: Jossey-Bass Publishers.

Schlechty, P. (2002). *Working on the work: An action plan for teacher, principals and superintendents*. San Francisco, CA: Jossey-Bass.

Schlechty, P. (2009). *Leading for learning: How to transform schools into learning organizations*. San Francisco, CA: Jossey-Bass Publishers.

Schmid, R. F., Miodrag, N., & Di Francesco, N. (2008). A human-computer partnership: The tutor/child/computer triangle promoting the acquisition of early literacy skills. *Journal of Research on Technology in Education*, *41*(1), 63–84.

Schrader, P. G., & McCreery, M. (2007). The acquisition of skill and expertise in massively multiplayer online games. *Educational Technology Research and Development*, *56*(5-6), 557–574. Retrieved from http://www.springerlink.com/ content/ n2496u376825u512/. doi:10.1007/s11423-007-9055-4

Schrock, K. (2010). *Kathy's Schrock guide for educators*. Retrieved from http://school.discoveryeducation.com/schrockguide/

Schwartz, E. B., Granger, D. A., Susman, E. J., Gunnar, M. R., & Laird, B. (1998). Assessing salivary cortisol in studies of child development. *Child Development*, *69*(6), 1503–1513.

Schwienhorst, K. (2002). Why virtual, why environments? Implementing virtual reality concepts in computer-assisted language learning. *Simulation & Gaming*, *33*(2), 196–209.

Scott, A. S., & Fong, E. (2004). *Body structures and functions*. Clifton Park, NY: Delamr Learning.

Seiter, E. (1991). *Remote control: Television, audiences, and cultural power*. New York, NY: Routledge.

Seiter, E. (1995). *Sold separately: Children and parents in consumer culture*. New Brunswick, NJ: Rutgers University Press.

Seiter, E. (1998). Children's desires/mother's dilemmas: The social contexts of consumption. In Jenkins, H. (Ed.), *The children's culture reader* (pp. 297–317). New York, NY: New York University.

Seiter, E. (1999). Power Rangers at preschool negotiating media in child care settings. In Kinder, M. (Ed.), *Kids media culture*. Durham, NC: Duke University Press.

SEP. (2003). *Fundamentos y características de una nueva propuesta curricular para la educación preescolar*. Retrieved from www.reformapreescolar.sep.gob.mx / actualizacion/programa/ fundamentos.pdf

SEP. (2004). *Programa de educación preescolar 2004*. ISBN 970-767-023-1

SEP. (2009). *La estructura del sistema educativo mexicano: Dirección general de acreditación, incorporación y revalidación, SEP, 2009*. Retrieved from www.sep.gob.mx/work/sites/ sep1/resources/LocalContent/ 127650/2/sistemaedumex09.pdf

Sharon, J., Puckett, K., & Burcu, C. (2004). Digital equity: New findings from the early childhood longitudinal study. *Journal of Research on Technology in Education*, *36*(4), 383–396.

Shaywitz, B. A., Shaywitz, S. E., Blachman, B. A., Pugh, K. R., Fulbright, R. K., & Skudlarski, P. (2004). Development of left occipitotemporal systems for skilled reading in children after a phonologically-based intervention. *Biological Psychiatry*, *55*(9), 926–933. doi:10.1016/j.biopsych.2003.12.019

Shaywitz, S. E., Shaywitz, B. A., Pugh, K. R., Fulbright, R. K., Constable, R. T., & Mencl, W. E. ...Gore, J. C. (1998). Functional disruption in the organization of the brain for reading in dyslexia. *Proceedings of the National Academy of Sciences of the United States of American*, *95*(5), 2636-2641.

Shilling, W. A. (1997). Young children using computers to make discoveries about written language. *Early Childhood Education Journal*, *24*(4), 253–259. doi:10.1007/BF02354842

Shin, E., & Alibrandi, M. (2007). Online interactive mapping: Using Google Earth. *Social Studies and the Young Learner*, *19*(3), 1–P4.

Shirtcliff, E., Granger, D. A., Booth, A., & Johnson, D. (2005). Low salivary cortisol levels and externalizing behavior problems: A latent state trait model in normally developing youth. *Development and Psychopathology*, *17*, 167–184.

Shonkoff, J., & Phillips, D. (2000). *From neurons to neighborhoods*. Washington, DC: National Academy Press.

Shulman, L. S. (1986). Those who understand: Knowledge growth in teaching. *Educational Researcher*, *15*(2), 4–14.

Siegle, D. (2007). Moving beyond a Google search: Google Earth, SketchUp, Spreadsheets, and more. *Gifted Child Today*, *30*(1), 24–28.

Sifteo. (2010). *Siftables*. Retrieved from http://sifteo.com

Sigelman, C. K., & Rider, E. A. (2008). *Life-span human development* (6th ed.). US: Thomson/Wadsworth.

Silk, E. M., Higashi, R., Shoop, R., & Schunn, C. D. (2009). Designing technology activities that teach mathematics. *Technology Teacher*, *69*(4), 21–27.

Simina, V., & Hamel, M. J. (2005). CASLA through a social constructivist perspective: WebQuest in project-driven language learning. *ReCALL*, *17*(2), 217–228. doi:10.1017/S0958344005000522

Sivin-Kachala, J., & Bialo, E. (2000). *2000 research report on the effectiveness of technology in schools* (7th ed.). Washington, DC: Software and Information Industry Association.

Skinner, B. F. (1957). *Verbal behavior*. Englewood Cliffs, NJ: Prentice-Hall. doi:10.1037/11256-000

Slattery, P. (1995). *Curriculum development in the post-modern era*. New York, NY: Garland.

Smaldino, S. E., Russell, J. D., Heinich, R., & Molenda, M. (2005). *Instructional technology and media for learning* (8th ed.). Upper Saddle River, NJ: Prentice Hall.

Smider, N. A., Essex, M. J., Kalin, N. H., Buss, K. A., Klein, M. H., Davidson, R. J., & Goldsmith, H. H. (2002). Salivary cortisol as a predictor of socioemotional adjustment during kindergarten: A prospective study. *Child Development*, *73*, 75–92. doi:10.1111/1467-8624.00393

Solomon, G. (2002). Digital equity: It's not just about access anymore. *Technology & Learning*, *22*(9), 18–26.

Son, J. Y., Smith, L. B., & Goldstone, R. L. (2008). Simplicity and generalization: Short-cutting abstraction in children's object categorizations. *Cognition*, *108*, 626–638. doi:10.1016/j.cognition.2008.05.002

Sowell, E. J. (1989). Effects of manipulative materials in mathematics instruction. *Journal for Research in Mathematics Education*, *20*(5), 498–505. doi:10.2307/749423

Spiegel-McGill, P., Zippiroli, S., & Mistrett, S. (1989). Microcomputers as social facilitators in integrated preschools. *Journal of Early Intervention*, *13*, 249–260. doi:10.1177/105381518901300306

Spindler, G. (2000). The four careers of George and Louise Spindler: 1948-2000. *Annual Review of Anthropology*, *29*, xv–xxxviii. doi:10.1146/annurev.anthro.29.1.00

Steen, K., Brooks, D., & Lyons, T. (2006). The impact of virtual manipulatives on first grade geometry instruction and learning. *Journal of Computers in Mathematics and Science Teaching*, *24*(4), 373–391.

Stiler, G. M., & Philleo, T. (2003). Blogging and blogspots: An alternative format for encouraging reflective practice among pre-service teachers. *Education*, *123*(4), 789–797.

Stokes, T. F., & Baer, D. M. (1977). An implicit technology of generalization. *Journal of Applied Behavior Analysis*, *10*, 349–367. doi:10.1901/jaba.1977.10-349

Stringer, M., Halloran, J., Hornecker, E., & Fitzpatrick, G. (2005). Situating ubiquitous computing in everyday life: Some useful strategies. Retrieved from http://www.informatics.sussex.ac.uk/ research/ groups/ interact/ papers/pdfs/ stringer_ ubicomp05. pdf

Subrahmanyam, K., Kraut, R., Greenfield, P., & Gross, E. (2000). The impact of home computer use on children's activities and development. *The Future of Children*, *10*, 123–1444. doi:10.2307/1602692

Suess, P. E., Porges, S. W., & Plude, D. J. (1994). Cardiac vagal tone and sustained attention in school-age children. *Psychophysiology*, *31*, 17–22. doi:10.1111/j.1469-8986.1994.tb01020.x

Suh, J., Moyer, P. S., & Heo, H. (2005). Examining technology uses in the classroom: Developing fraction sense using virtual manipulative concept tutorials. *Journal of Interactive Online Learning*, *3*(4), 1–21.

Sutherland, R., Facer, K., Furlong, R., & Furlong, J. (2000). A new environment for education? The computer in the home. *Computers & Education*, *34*, 195–212. doi:10.1016/S0360-1315(99)00045-7

Sutton-Smith, B. (1986). *Toys as culture*. New York, NY: Gardener Press.

Sutton-Smith, B. (1997). *The ambiguity of play*. Cambridge, MA: Harvard University Press.

Suydam, M. N., & Higgins, J. L. (1977). *Activity-based learning in elementary school mathematics: Recommendations from research*. Columbus, OH: ERIC Center for Science, Mathematics and Environment Education, College of Education, Ohio State University.

Sweller, J. (1988). Cognitive load during problem solving: Effects on learning. *Cognitive Science*, *12*(2), 257–285. doi:10.1207/s15516709cog1202_4

Sylvester, D. E., & McGlynn, A. J. (2010). The digital divide, political participation, and place. *Social Science Computer Review*, *28*(1), 64–74. doi:10.1177/0894439309335148

Tabors, P. (1997). *One child, two languages*. Baltimore, MD: Paul H. Brookes. (ERIC Document No. ED405987)

Tapscott, D., & Williams, A. D. (2006). *Wikinomics: How mass collaboration changes everything*. Portfolio Hardcover.

Tarpley, T. (2001). Children, the Internet, and other new technologies. In Singer, D. G., & Singer, J. L. (Eds.), *Handbook of children and the media* (pp. 547–566). Thousand Oaks, CA: Sage.

Technology Review. (2010). *Building blocks of a new interface*. Retrieved from http://www.technologyreview.com/ article/22801/

Technology. (2007). In *Merriam Webster's Dictionary* online. Retrieved from http://www.merriam-webster/dicionary.com/ technology

Thomas, A. (2006). MSN was the next big thing after Beanie Babies: Children's virtual experiences as an interface to their identities and their everyday lives. *E-learning*, *3*(2), 126–142. doi:10.2304/elea.2006.3.2.126

Thorne, B. (1993). *Gender play: Girls and boys at school*. New York, NY: Open University Press.

Tinker, R. F. (1991). Science for kids: The promise of technology. In K. Sheingold, L. Roberts & S. Malcom (Eds.), *Technology for teaching and learning. AAAS Forum Paper*. Washington, DC: American Association for the Advancement of Science (AAAS).

Tobin, J. (2000). *Good guys don't wear hats: Children's talk about the media*. New York, NY: Teacher's College Press.

Tobin, J. (2004). *Pikachu's global adventure: The rise and fall of Pokémon*. Durham, NC: Duke University Press.

Tobin, J., Hsueh, Y., & Karasawa, M. (2009). *Preschool in three cultures revisited: China, Japan, and the United States*. Chicago, IL: University of Chicago Press.

Tobin, J. (1992). A dialogical solution to the problem of field site typicality. *City and Society*, *6*(1), 46–57. doi:10.1525/city.1992.6.1.46

Tobin, J., Hsueh, Y., & Karasawa, M. (2010). *Preschool in three cultures revisited: China, Japan,& the United States*. Chicago, IL: The University of Chicago Press.

Tobin, J., Wu, D., & Davidson, D. (1989). *Preschool in three cultures: Japan, China & the United States*. New Haven, CT: Yale University Press.

Tobin, J., & Hsueh, Y. (2007). The poetics and pleasures of video ethnography of education. In Goldman, R. (Ed.), *Video research in the learning sciences* (pp. 77–92). New York, NY: Erlbaum.

Tobin, J. (2010, July). *The role of culture in early childhood education*. Keynote address at the Annual Conference of the Pacific Early Childhood Education Research Association, Hangzhou, China.

Tout, K., de Haan, M., Campbell, E. K., & Gunnar, M. R. (1998). Social behavior correlates of cortisol activity in child care: Gender differences and time-of-day effects. *Child Development*, *69*, 1247–1262. doi:10.2307/1132263

Tressel, G. W. (1994). Thirty years of improvement in precollege math and science education. *Journal of Science Education and Technology*, *3*(2), 77–88. doi:10.1007/BF01575187

Trueman, A. (2004). InterWrite SchoolPads take technology to a new level. *T.H.E. Journal*, *32*(1), 37.

Tsujii, T., Yamamoto, E., Takahashi, T., Masuda, S., & Watanabe, S. (2009). Longitudinal study of spatial working memory development in young children. *Neuroreport*, *20*(8), 759–763. doi:10.1097/WNR.0b013e32832aa975

Turkle, S. (1996). *Life on the screen: Identity in the age of the Internet*. London, England: Weidenfeld & Nicolson.

Turkle, S. (2005). *The second self: Computers and the human spirit*. Cambridge, MA: MIT Press.

Turkle, S. (1998). Cyborg babies and cy-dough-plasm: Ideas about self and life in the culture of simulation. In Davis-Floyd, R., & Dumit, J. (Eds.), *Cyborg babies: From techno-sex to techno-tots* (pp. 317–329). New York, NY: Routledge.

Turow, J., & Nir, L. (2000). *The Internet and the family 2000: The view from parents, the view from kids. APPC Reports, 33*. Philadelphia: University of Pennsylvania.

Twitchell, J. B. (2000). *Lead us into temptation: The triumph of American materialism*. New York, NY: Columbia University Press.

U. S. National Telecommunications and Information Administration (NTIA). (2010).

U.S. Department of Education. (2001). *Policy documents: Elementary & secondary education*. Retrieved from http://www2.ed.gov/ policy/elsec/ guid/states/index.html

U.S. Department of Education Office of Educational Technology. (March, 2010). *Draft: National educational technology plan. Transforming American Education: Learning powered by technology*. Retrieved from http://www.ed.gov/ technology/netp-2010

U.S. Office of Special Education Programs. (2007). *Individuals with Disabilities Education Act* (IDEA) data (Tables 1-14, 8-14). Washington, DC: Author. Retrieved from http://www.ideadata.org

Ueoka, R., & Hirose, M. (2008). Soundtag: Children's interactive play based upon RFID employed wearable computer. *Digital Creativity*, *19*(3), 162–173. doi:10.1080/14626260802312699

United States Department of Health and Human Services. (2006). *Administration for Children and Families: FFY 2006 CCDF data tables: 6-Percent of children served in all types of care*. Retrieved from http://www.acf.hhs.gov/ programs/ccb/ data/ccdf_data/ 06acf800/ table6.htm

United States Department of Education. (2009). *Elementary and Secondary Education Act*. Retrieved from http://www2.ed.gov/ policy/elsec/leg/ esea02/index.html

United States Department of Health and Human Services. (2009). *2009 Federal poverty guidelines*. Retrieved from http://aspe.hhs.gov/ poverty/ 09extension.shtml

Van Hiele, P. (1999). Developing geometric thinking through activities that begin with play. *Teaching Children Mathematics*, *5*, 301–317.

Van Manen, M., & Levering, B. (1996). *Childhood's secrets: Intimacy, privacy, and the self reconsidered*. New York, NY: Teachers College Press.

van Merriënboer, J. J. G., & Sweller, J. (2005). Cognitive load theory and complex learning: Recent developments and future directions. *Educational Psychology Review*, *17*(2), 147–177. doi:10.1007/s10648-005-3951-0

Vandewater, E. A., Rideout, V. J., Wartella, E. A., Xuan, H., Lee, J., & Shim, M. (2007). Digital childhood: Electronic media and technology use among infants, toddlers, and preschoolers. *Pediatrics*, *119*, e1006–e1015..doi:10.1542/peds.2006-1804

Vermer, H. J., & van IJzendoorn, M. H. (2006). Children's elevated cortisol levels at daycare: A review and meta-analysis. *Early Childhood Research Quarterly*, *21*, 390–401. doi:10.1016/j.ecresq.2006.07.004

Vygotsky, L. S. (1978). *Mind in society*. Cambridge, MA: Harvard University Press.

Vygotsky, L. S. (1986). *Thought and language*. Cambridge, MA: MIT Press.

Vygotsky, L. S. (1962). *Thought and language*. Cambridge, MA: M.I.T. Press. doi:10.1037/11193-000

Vygotsky, L. (1978). *Mind in society: The development of higher psychological processes* (Cole, M., John-Steiner, V., Scribner, S., & Souberman, E. (Trans. Eds.)). Cambridge, MA: Harvard University Press.

Wall, K., Higgins, S., & Smith, H. (2005). The visual helps me understand the complicated things: Pupil views of teaching and learning with interactive whiteboards. *British Journal of Educational Technology*, *36*(5), 851–867. doi:10.1111/j.1467-8535.2005.00508.x

Wang, Y., Stash, N., Sambeek, R., Schuurmans, Y., Aroyo, L., & Schreiber, G. (2009). Cultivating personalized museum tours online and on-site. *Interdisciplinary Science Reviews*, *34*(2/3), 139–153.. doi:10.1179/174327909X441072

Wartella, E. A., & Jennings, N. (2000). Children and computers: New technology. Old concerns. *The Future of Children*, *10*(2), 31–43. doi:10.2307/1602688

Watamura, S. E., Donzella, B., Alwin, J., & Gunnar, M. R. (2003). Morning to afternoon increases in cortisol concentrations for infants and toddlers at child care: Age differences and behavioral correlates. *Child Development*, *74*(4), 1006–1020. doi:10.1111/1467-8624.00583

Watson, J. B. (1930). *Behaviorism*. Chicago, IL: University of Chicago Press.

Weber, M. (1968). *Economy and society: An outline of interpretive sociology*. New York, NY: Bedminster.

Weigel, M., James, C., & Gardner, H. (2009). Learning: Peering backward and looking forward in the digital era. *International Journal of Learning and Media*, *1*(1), 1–18. doi:10.1162/ijlm.2009.0005

Weinberger, N., & Stein, K. (2008). Early competitive game playing in same- and mixed-gender peer groups. *Merrill-Palmer Quarterly*, *54*(4), 499–514. doi:10.1353/mpq.0.0006

Weir, S., Russell, S. J., & Valente, J. A. (1982). Logo: An approach to educating disabled children. *BYTE*, *7*, 342–360.

Weiser, M. (1991). *The computer for the 21st century*. Pervasive Computing. Retrieved from http://www.media.mit.edu/ resenv/classes/ MAS961/ readings/ weiser_reprint.pdf

Wells, L. (2006). Blog it: An innovative way to improve literacy. *Reading Today*, *24*(1), 40.

Wentworth, N. (2008). Future orientation. In Haidth, M. M., & Benson, J. B. (Eds.), *Encyclopedia of infant and early childhood development* (pp. 562–574). Academic Press. doi:10.1016/B978-012370877-9.00068-2

Wikipedia. (2010). *Ubiquitous computing*. In Wikipedia, the free encyclopedia. Retrieved from http://en.wikipedia.org/ wiki/ Ubiquitous_computing

Wilensky, U. (1991). Abstract meditations on the concrete and concrete implications for mathematics education. In Harel, I., & Papert, S. (Eds.), *Constructionism* (pp. 193–203). New Jersey: Ablex Publishing.

Wood, R., & Ashfield, J. (2008). The use of the interactive whiteboard for creative teaching and learning in literacy and mathematics: A case study. *British Journal of Educational Technology*, *39*(1), 84–96.

Wright, J. L., & Shade, D. D. (Eds.). (1994). *Young children: Active learners in a technological age*. Washington, DC: National Association for the Education of Young Children.

Yelland, N. (2005). The future is now: A review of the literature on the use of computers in early childhood education (1994-2004). *AACE Journal*, *13*(3), 201–232.

Yelland, N. (1994). The strategies and interactions of young children in Logo tasks. *Journal of Computer Assisted Learning*, *10*, 33–49. doi:10.1111/j.1365-2729.1994.tb00280.x

Yngve, V. H. (1996). *From grammar to science: New foundations for general linguistics*. Philadelphia, PA: John Benjamins Publishing Co.

Yoder, M. B. (2005, August). *Inquiry based learning using the Internet: Research, resources, WebQuests*. Paper presented at the 19th Annual Conference on Distance Learning and Teaching, Madison, WI.

Yoshikawa, H., et al. (2007). *Early childhood education in Mexico expansion, quality improvement, and curricular reform*. United Nations Children's Fund (UNICEF). ISSN: 1014-7837

Yukl, G. (2006). *Leadership in organizations* (6th ed.). Upper Saddle River, NJ: Pearson.

Zehr, M. A. (2007, April 12). Preschool attendance: More likely in Mexico than in the United States. *Education Week*. Retrieved from http://blogs.edweek.org/edweek / learning-the-language/2007/04/ preschool_attendance_more_like_1.html

Zelizer, V. (1985). *Pricing the priceless child: The changing social value of children*. Princeton, NJ: Princeton University Press.

Ziegler, N. E. (2007). *Task based assessment: Evaluating communication in the real world.* Master's thesis. Retrieved from http://etd.ohiolink.edu/ send-pdf.cgi/ Ziegler%20 Nathan %20E.pdf? acc_num=Toledo 1192757581

About the Contributors

Sally Blake is an Associate Professor in Early Childhood at the University of Memphis. Sally has been the PI on more than $600,000 dollars of Eisenhower funds and $700,000 of NASA funds for teacher training and professional development. Sally Blake was the Director and Co-PI of the NSF sponsored Partnership for Excellence in Teacher Education (PETE) and the Noyce Scholarship program at the University of Texas at El Paso. She was also a research fellow with the NSF Center for Research on Educational Reform,(MSP project) a teaching fellow with the NSF Center for Effective Teaching and Learning(MIE project), co-developer of the Research Pedagogical Labs and the MAT degree in the College of Science (MSP project), and Co-PI on the NSF GK-12 grant. She is the Faculty Research Director of the Barbara K. Lipman Early Childhood School and Research Institute.

Denise Winsor joined the academic community after working as a clinical psychologist. She piloted the Family Builders and Family Preservation grants in the 1980s. She has developed the *Dynamic Systems Framework for Personal Epistemology Development*, a systems model which aids the understanding of early childhood cognitive development. Her research interests include an emphasis on preschool-age children's knowledge and understanding, and how to more effectively educate preschool children using developmentally appropriate practices in early childhood classrooms. Currently, Dr. Winsor is working in collaboration with multiple research teams to develop a science curriculum for preschool using science inquiry methods and utilizing a systems approach (i.e., child, teacher, parent, and peer interactions) to better understand the epistemological development of very young children as they become school-ready. She is interested in teacher preparation methods, specifically metacognitive strategies that integrate theoretical, conceptual, and applied tasks that aid students in high-order thinking related to real world settings.

Lee Allen is an Associate Professor of Instructional Design and Technology and Information Science at the University of Memphis. Dr. Allen has previously served as an Assistant Superintendent for technology services in the Dallas, TX public school district, and as a teacher, school librarian, technology trainer, and director of instructional technology in Santa Fe, NM. Dr. Allen's primary research interests are technology as a vehicle for organizational/institutional change, online teaching and learning, electronic portfolio development, and situated learning in communities of practice. He is a Fulbright scholar, recently returned from the Ukraine.

* * *

Susan Hart Bell is a Professor of Psychology at the University of Toledo. She is winner of the Garvin Award for Outstanding Dissertation Research in the College of Education and Curry Award for Faculty Excellence and Kentucky Professor of the Year. Her focus is on consultation, psycho-educational assessment and intervention, behavior modification, and family intervention. She teaches General Psychology, Adolescence and Adulthood, Lifespan Development, Child Development, Developmental Psychopathology, School Psychology, Brain and Behavior, and Psychology of Religion. She has directed the Ohio Early Childhood Intervention Project, coordinated the work of early intervention consultants and research assistants in research funded by the Ohio Division of Early Childhood. She researches and investigates the use of the PASSKey model of intervention-based assessment to serve young children and families within eight counties of southwestern Ohio.

David Bicard is an independent consultant in Applied Behavior Analysis (ABA) with a focus in early childhood education. He earned his PhD at the University of Ohio and was a kindergarten teacher for several years, held academic positions in two universities and has a certification in ABA. He was PI on several grants and still publishes with his prior students.

Sara Bicard received her training and experience in behavior analysis at The Ohio State University. Prior to coming to the University of Memphis she was an Assistant Professor at Mercy College in New York. She was also an inclusion Teacher at Petal Middle School in Mississippi and a Behavior Analyst for Broward County Department of Children and Family Services in Florida. She has published in *Reading and Writing Quarterly* and *Journal of Direct Instruction*. Her research interests include reading instruction and active student responding. She is the Project Director of the West Tennessee Positive Behavior Support Initiative and RISE Project. She has been a BCBA since 2001.

Kathleen Cooter is a Professor of Early Childhood Special Education at Bellarmine University. Her research interests include improving language and literacy for children with disabilities, children who are at risk, or those have been traditionally under-educated. She has won numerous awards in the field of early childhood education for her work with communities, parents, and children.

Florian C. Feucht is an Assistant Professor for Educational Psychology in the Department of Educational Foundations and Leadership at the University of Toledo, Ohio. He received his Ph.D. in Educational Psychology from the University of Nevada, Las Vegas, USA, in 2008 and his Ph.D. in Curriculum and Instruction from the Carl von Ossietzky University, Germany, in 2006. Dr. Feucht's research interests involve the beliefs about knowledge and knowing of students and teachers and how they influence learning, instruction, and the use of technology. Among other courses, he teaches graduate course on "Cognition and Technology" and "Technology Applications in Qualitative Research." Dr. Feucht is a dynamic speaker and publishes his work in the context of the European Association for Research in Learning and Instruction (EARLI), the American Educational Research Association (AERA), and the American Psychological Association (APA).

Amy Gentry earned a Master of Science in Education with a major in Instruction and Curriculum Leadership with a concentration in Early Childhood Education, and will be starting her first year of teaching in the second grade this fall. Amy has worked with the PAWS and SPIRIT research teams studying the development of inquiry thinking across cultures in young children and the epistemology of teachers.

Andrew Gibbons has worked in a range of social and early childhood services, in London and Auckland and is currently teaching at AUT University in Auckland, New Zealand. He teaches in the Early Years, Bachelor of Education, Master of Educational Leadership and Graduate Diploma in Tertiary Teaching programs. Prior to these tertiary roles he worked as an early childhood teacher and a residential social worker. His book *The Matrix Ate My Baby* was published in 2007 by Sense Publishers. The book explores the intersections of discourses of play and technology within the contexts of the young child's learning. He has additionally published on a range of issues, from the politics of early childhood education in New Zealand, to the meaning and application of biculturalism. Andrew is Secretary of the Philosophy of Education Society of Australasia and Co-Editor of the online Encyclopedia of Philosophy of Education.

Brian Giza has a strong sense of inquiry and interest in learning. He is currently a researcher but has teaching certificates in Composite Science, Life/Earth Science, Art, Dance, Theatre Arts, and Geography and an endorsement in Gifted Education. He is a Professor of technology and science education at the University of Texas.

Kendall Hartley is an Associate Professor of Educational Technology at the University of Nevada, Las Vegas. Dr. Hartley conducts research in the area of effective instructional uses of technology. He has published articles related to hypermedia instruction in the *Journal of Educational Computing Research, Educational Researcher,* and *the Journal of Educational Multimedia and Hypermedia.* Before coming to UNLV, Dr. Hartley taught high school science in Bellevue, Nebraska.

Allison Sterling Henward is an Assistant Professor of Early Childhood Education in Department of Instruction, Curriculum, and Leadership at the University of Memphis. Her research focuses on the intersection of preschools, play, and popular/material culture.

Yeh Hsueh is an Associate Professor in Educational Psychology Research with a focus on child development. He earned his doctorate from Harvard University. His many honors include invited speaker - Shanghai Luwan District, International Conference on Early Childhood Education, invited speaker - Shanghai Municipal Education Commission, Shanghai Education Forum, Visiting Professor - East China Normal University, College of Preschool & Special Education, Visiting Research Professor - Department of Psychology, Central China Normal University, and a grant recipient from the Spencer Foundation. His current project is *Preschool in three cultures revisited: China, Japan and the United States* with J. Tobin & M. Karasawa. His focus is on cultural influences in early childhood environments.

Neha Kumar is a Senior at St. Mary's and has been an active member in educational psychology research groups on genetics and child development. She has presented at numerous professional conferences and is planning on entering the medical research field. Neha is a member of the digital generation and provides much insight into how technology is and has changed the new generation of students in the United States.

Lin Lin is an Assistant Professor of Learning Technologies at University of North Texas. Lin's research interest lies in the intersections of new media and technologies, information science, cognition, psychology, and education. In the past few years, she has conducted research in online learning environment, virtual gaming environment, exergaming, social networking, and media multitasking issues. Dr. Lin's research has been published in top-tier journals such as the *Proceedings of the National Academy of Sciences, Computers and Education*, *Computers in the Schools*, *Journal of Asynchronous Learning Network, Teachers College Record*, and *Teaching in Higher Education.* She has presented numerous research papers at major academic conferences. Dr. Lin received her Doctoral degree in Communication, Computing, and Technology in Education from Teachers College, Columbia University.

Jorge Lopez is the Chair of Physics at the University of Texas at El Paso and a native Mexican. He became involved with early childhood education through his work with the National Science Foundation. He has developed and piloted early childhood and primary physical science projects in El Paso and the Juarez, Mexico schools. Has written one book, one chapter in a book, edited two books, and written two articles included in books on nuclear physics. He has 63 articles published in 48 journal publications and in 15 conference proceedings, as well as 10 web and unpublished articles, and 83 abstracts. Has given 97 presentations in 40 national and international meetings, 11 regional meetings, and 46 seminars.

Julie McLeod currently studies and teaches Learning Technologies at the University of North Texas. She also teaches mathematics for Allen ISD where she and her students use many technologies during their learning. Julie's research interests include exploring children's curiosity, power, and motivation as they use technology to learn. She has also published book chapters and journal articles that discuss powerful ways to integrate technology by purposefully matching a proven learning strategy with the affordances of the technology to create a learning experience that maintains the integrity of the proven strategy while creating something not possible without the technology. Julie is currently working on her dissertation for her doctoral degree in Learning Technologies from the University of North Texas.

Andrea Peach has been teaching at Georgetown College since 1998. Her primary teaching and research interests include instructional technology, designing instructional multimedia (primarily including Web-based instruction), and assessment technologies. She is an Associate Professor of Education, the Director of the Instructional Technology Endorsement Program, and is the Assessment Director for the Education Department. Dr. Peach has an Ed.D. in Instruction and Administration (emphasis in Instructional Design and Technology) and a Master's and Bachelor's of Music in Bassoon Performance from the University of Kentucky. She has been married for over 20 years to Harold, and has a teenage son (Ryan). In her free time, Dr. Peach enjoys singing in her church choir and praise team, leading and playing in her church's handbell choir and playing the bassoon.

Shannon Audley-Piotrowski is a doctoral student in Educational Psychology. She was a former high school Science Teacher and Biologist. She has moved her focus to child development and works with the SPIRIT and PAWS research teams.

Amy Smith earned a Ph.D. in Educational Psychology and Research and has over 15 years of experience in early childhood education as a classroom teacher, college-level instructor, consultant, teacher trainer, and researcher. She is currently President of Pink Sky Education in Atlanta, Georgia.

Alexandru Spatariu is an Assistant Professor of Graduate Education. He earned his Ph.D. in Educational Psychology from the University of Nevada, Las Vegas. His research areas include online asynchronous discussions, epistemological beliefs, and Web-based causal diagramming.

Melanie Summer is a doctoral student in Counseling, Educational Psychology, and Research. She was a practitioner in the area of preschool for many years. Her research focus is child development.

Kevin Thomas is an Assistant Professor at Bellarmine University. His research interests include Web 2.0 applications and the mobile technology, specifically cell phones, in the K-12 classroom. He is presently researching the use of Kindle e-books with struggling readers.

Joseph Tobin is the N. M. Basha Professor in early childhood education in Curriculum & Instruction, Educational Leadership & Policy Studies at Arizona State University. He is the PI on the Preschool in Three Cultures study and currently working on another cultural project, Kindergartens for the Deaf in Three Countries: US, France, and Japan, funded through the Spencer Foundation. His area of study is cultural influences on young children.

Sheri Vasinda is in the Department of Curriculum and Instruction at Texas A&M University-Commerce. She is certified in Special Education and Early Childhood Education. Her areas of research are issues in curriculum development and assessment with a special focus on student voice, choice and power, Reggio Emilia, integrated curriculum, technology integration, and student motivation and success.

Nathan E. Ziegler is a doctoral student in Educational Psychology in the Department of Educational Foundations and Leadership at the University of Toledo, Ohio. He received his M.A. in English with a concentration in English as a second Language (ESL) from the University of Toledo in 2007. He has taught ESL in the United States and South Korea in elementary classrooms and at the collegiate level. Nathan Ziegler's primary research interests include second language development, instructional methods, and assessment, as well as critical thinking in second language learners.

Index

E

F

G

H

I

K

L

M

N

O

P

Q

R

S

T

U

V

W

Z

CPSIA information can be obtained at www.ICGtesting.com
Printed in the USA
268798BV00002B/3/P

9 781613 500590